Excerpts from some of the letters received after publication
of the recent book.

Never has a book like this been published—a book whose story gives hope of better health to millions! His life story is inspirational. —J.W.

Thank you so much for having this book published. The most important book I've read in the last 40 years and may save my daughter's life! —E.W.

I admire you very much for trying to help people. Jack Dreyfus will be remembered when others are forgotten. —P.A.

Jack Dreyfus is a true American hero. There seems to be so few of them left. —B.C.B.

Thank you for your persistence in this great effort. Bless you. —M.C.

When taking my 100mg of phenytoin I am in perfect health; when I stop symptoms occur. Thanking Jack Dreyfus and his foundation for many wonderful years of good health. —P.B.

I can't thank you enough for writing this book. Since I recently tried phenytoin I feel like a new person and I'm enjoying life again. —F.V.B.

Thank you for your research on phenytoin. It has helped me greatly. —D.I.C.

Needless to say, but I will, your book knocked my socks off. Thank you. —E.C.

Deep gratitude for the generous motivation which inspired Dreyfus' account. Dreyfus manages to keep a civil tone when most of us would lash out bitterly. —V.K.C.

I appreciate Jacks sense of humor as well as his commitment. —D.C.

The caring heart that lay behind this gigantic effort renews one's faith in humanity. It's nice to know that there's someone out there who cares for his fellow man . . . ! —S.L.E.

Your book has already benefited me more, than if I had earned 1000% on every stock fund I own!!

You are not a lion—you are a Tiger!! God bless you for all your work. You are truly the most wonderful person I have ever known. —R.D.

Thank God that Mr. Dreyfus had the means and the will to endure. What a marvelous tribute to tenacity. —G.H.

I commend Mr. Dreyfus for his perseverance. May God bless you for your efferts and bring the relief you found to others in need. —B.L.J.

I believe Jack Dreyfus is a truly great philanthropist and a creative individual. —F.S.M.

Surely you must know that your efforts combine humor, humility, honesty and hope in so many ways that I'm certain you will win a Pulitzer award and maybe even a Nobel citation. —C.M.

Thank you for sharing your life with us. The anecdotes, the humor, the wry reflections added to the powerful dimensions of the controlling motif—phenytoin and its being overlooked. —F.L.R.

What a life! What a book! Thanks for length of time and depth of subject. —M.R.

You cannot know how I feel—so grateful. Thank God Jack Dreyfus is on this planet. —R.S.

I am so exited about your book that I can't tell you how I feel— I think you are a most remarkable human being . . . I can't thank you enough for all your amazing efforts to bring this to the public. —H.M.W.

God bless Jack Dreyfus. Thank you. —M.L.H.

I consider this a great book and thank you for sharing your story. —D.C.

I was appalled to learn that phenytoin is still not available to millions of sufferers who might benefit from this medication. Professionally, I was impressed with the tremendous amount of research and scientific investigations that were noted in this book. —A.H.B.

I would have to say that, in the case of Jack Dreyfus, A Remarkable Man Has Been Overlooked—especially by the Nobel Prize Committee on Medical Research. —R.H.R.

I have just finished reading The Lion of Wall Street by Jack Dreyfus. Please convey to him my profound gratitude for his efforts on behalf of humanity. —D.B.B.

Jack Dreyfus deserves a lot of credit and is among the greatest men of our time. —D.M.

Thank you for all the sacrifices you have made to benefit humanity. —J.C.

Phenytoin has been a miracle in my life. I feel now that my ministry is to crusade for phenytoin. Tell Mr. Dreyfus I love him. —M.B.

Thank you for all the time, money and energy you devoted trying to help people. May God richly bless you for all you've done. You're truly a great man. —H.R.

What you have written is stunning, both from what you have to say about phenytoin and what I learned about the USA FDA. —M.K.

I just finished reading your book and I found it just as hard to put down as any Mark Twain or Zane Grey works. Quite a monument to the futility of trying to make sense out of politicians. —E.D.

Since I read your book I have felt the need to tell you how much I enjoyed your story. I really didn't want your book to end because it was so much fun—thanks for the pure pleasure. —S.R.B.

There just aren't any words for how grateful I am. I suffered from hypoglycemia, migraine headaches, terrible nausea, awful anxiety and many other symptoms. When my doctor gave me phenytoin—my life changed. I am enjoying life again. —M.B.

The most interesting book that I have ever read. When I think of how the FDA treated you, and your subject, I am reminded of Mark Twain, "When angry, count four, when very angry, swear." —C.B.G.

I have been on phenytoin myself for just one week and it has made a dramatic difference in my mood, energy level and focus. Thank you! —C.M.

You have done an invaluable service for others. God bless you for your dedication. —L.O.

Phenytoin has made an extraordinary difference in my life. What is so extraordinary is the clarity of mind which I'd thought I'd lost forever.
Thank you! —C.M.

I wanted to write to thank you. I've suffered from anxiety for 15 years, tried probably every medication that's indicated for this affliction, but never got the relief that I've gotten from PHT. —R.T.

I have just finished reading Lion with tears a plenty. Thank you for such a great contribution! —B.N.

Phenytoin has restored my joy, my vitality, my clarity and my balance. My life is just as stressful as ever but I can take a deep breath, focus and deal with it. I even feel joy again. —M.D.

Jack has a wonderful sense of humor. I was so sick I'd pray and ask God for wisdom and he let me find out about Jack and phenytoin! I've been given my life back. —M.B.

A
Remarkable Medicine
Has Been
Overlooked

including an autobiography—

and the clinical section

of *The Broad Range of*

Use of Phenytoin

Jack Dreyfus

Continuum • New York

1997
The Continuum Publishing Company
370 Lexington Avenue
New York, NY 10017

Printed in the United States of America
Designed by REM Studio, Inc.

Library of Congress Cataloging-in-Publication Data

Dreyfus, Jack, 1913-
    A remarkable medicine has been overlooked / Jack Dreyfus.
      p.   cm.
Rev. ed. of: The lion of Wall Street. © 1996.
Includes bibliographical references and index.
ISBN 0-8264-1069-3 (paperback : alk. paper)
      1. Dreyfus, Jack, 1913- . 2. Capitalists and financiers—
United States—Biography. 3. Dreyfus, Jack, 1913- —Health.
4. Depression, Mental—Patients—United States—Biography.
5. Phenytoin. I. Dreyfus, Jack, 1913- Lion of Wall Street.
II. Title.
HG172.D75D74   1997
332'.092—dc21   97-34597
[B]   CIP

This book is dedicated to
Mark Twain, to Helen Raudonat,
to Joan Personette, and to Johnny.

CONTENTS

AUTOBIOGRAPHY OF JACK DREYFUS

A REMARKABLE MEDICINE HAS BEEN OVERLOOKED

PRE-PREFACE

Pre-preface is a strange heading, but I didn't know what else to call this. A hardcover book *The Two Lives of The Lion of Wall Street* is being republished, with a different title, in this paperback edition. Important—in this book, is the addition of the clinical section of *The Broad Range of Use of Phenytoin*.

This book was written with only one purpose, to tell the public about the tragedy of a wonderful medicine being overlooked. About sixteen years ago Simon and Schuster published a book by me, titled, *A Remarkable Medicine Has Been Overlooked*. The present book contains that book in essence, preceded by my autobiography.

My life, remarkable as it has been, is not important. In it I was trained in probabilities and objectivity, and was given an unbelievable amount of money. Without these aptitudes and the money, I would not have been able to follow up on a piece of luck that took me out of a depression.

The truth about this medicine is spreading rapidly, internationally, much of this is due to the efforts of the Dreyfus Medical Foundation. The medicine is now being used in China, Russia, Ghana, India, and Mexico for over fifty symptoms and disorders (see pages 285–87). Although this drug was introduced in the United States fifty-eight years ago, it is still only listed with our FDA for one use. This is a great tragedy.

PREFACE

This is called Preface because of its location. It wasn't written until I had almost finished this book.

To write an autobiography one has to look back at one's life. I looked back at my life. Then I looked again—this time more closely—and was astounded. I've never known of any life, so diversified, with such a high degree of success. It's embarrassing to say something like that about one's own life, but it's the truth. It's a sure thing I didn't do all those things on my own.

Let me explain.

A few months ago I had thoroughly exhausted myself trying to get help from someone in the U.S. government. I was almost too tired to take a vacation. I selected a place where no one would know me, Blackberry Inn in the hills of Tennessee. I planned to do nothing and plenty of it.

When I arrived at the Inn I noted it was attractively furnished, and everybody there was extremely nice. There were 1,100 acres of wooded property and one could drive a golf cart around it. I'd brought two books with me: *In Search of the Miraculous* by P. D.

Ouspensky and *The Complete Essays of Mark Twain*. In the morning I would take the golf cart down to a beautiful little stream with a few chairs scattered near it. Each day I would sit in a different place and read.

I started with *In Search of the Miraculous*, which I'd read years ago. It's a story of Ouspensky's meetings with Georges Gurdjieff, a superbrilliant man, extraordinary in many ways. Some called him a mystic. The book is deep. I skipped around in reading it. On the third day I read (Mr. Gurdjieff talking to Mr. Ouspensky):

"Man is a machine. All his deeds, actions, words, thoughts, feelings, convictions, opinions, and habits are the results of external influences, external impressions. Out of himself a man cannot produce a single thought, a single action.... It all happens."

That stirred a memory of Mark Twain's "What Is Man?" which by coincidence, probably not by coincidence, was in the other book I had with me. In it, The Old Man talking to The Young Man says:

"Personally you did not create even the smallest microscopic fragment of the materials out of which your opinion is made; and personally you cannot claim even the slender merit of putting the borrowed materials together. That was done automatically—by your mental machinery, in strict accordance with the law of that machinery's construction."

Mr. Gurdjieff and Mark Twain don't need my concurrence, but they have it.

I'd like to go further. If something happens in an individual's life that can be of great importance to the rest of the creatures on this earth, it may not be that it "just happened." It is almost a sure thing that the life was influenced from above.

Most of my life I have been an agnostic. I'm not now.

AUTOBIOGRAPHY OF JACK DREYFUS

Ida Lewis Dreyfus
Section, Earth
Heaven

Dear Ida:

This is the year of your one-hundredth birthday. It is custom at this time for you to receive a report on the activities of your eldest child—in this case, your son Jack.

In 1939 your son was married to Joan Personette, a fine artist. They had a son, John. Although Joan and Jack have been divorced for forty-seven years, the love between them and John goes three ways.

A brief summary follows:

ATHLETICS

Golf—Before he was twenty, your son won the City Golf Championship of Montgomery, Alabama, twice. He has won eighteen club championships, at four different country clubs.

Jack qualified for the National Amateur Golf Championship on each of the three occasions he tried.

Tennis—When he was sixty-two, your son won the U.S. Open (Open means professionals and amateurs) Doubles Lawn Tennis Championship for 60s-and-over. Ten years later, in Australia, he won the World's Open Doubles Lawn Tennis Championship, for 70s-and-over.

CARD PLAYING

Jack qualified for the Masters Bridge Tournament when he was twenty-eight. When he was thirty he devised a scientific method of playing gin rummy and beat the best players.

For thirty years the *Encyclopedia of Bridge* said Jack was reputed to be the best gin rummy player in the United States.

HORSE RACING

Your son established Hobeau Farm, a thoroughbred breeding farm, in Ocala, Florida. The first horse he bred was a champion. Twice, Hobeau Farm won the New York Turf Writers' Award for Outstanding Breeder of the Year.

While Jack was head of the Horsemen's Benevolent and Protective Association, he received the Fitzsimmons Award, "One Who Contributed Most to Racing."

On two occasions your son was Chairman of the Board of Trustees of the New York Racing Association. He received the Eclipse Award, "Man Who Did Most for Racing."

BUSINESS

Your son became senior partner of a New York Stock Exchange firm when he was thirty-three.

Business was poor, and it was decided to advertise. The budget was so small that Jack, who had no experience in advertising, had to write the ads. His firm received the first Standard & Poor's Gold Trophy for Excellence in Wall Street Advertising.

Business improved, and a mutual fund was started. Your son was head of research for the Fund. For the twelve years he directed the research the Fund outperformed all other mutual funds by a large margin.

Your son wrote the prospectus and created the advertising for the Fund. He received an unusual award, one of the five best marketing persons of the 1960–1970 decade.

An article in *Life* magazine about your son was titled, "Maverick Wizard Behind the Wall Street Lion." In it was said, "He has been called an upstart, an interloper and a genius. Yet he is, without doubt, the most singular and effective personality to appear in Wall Street since the days of Joseph Kennedy and Bernard Baruch."

At the time he retired from Wall Street your son was one of the wealthiest men in the United States.

Your son received Honorary Doctor of Law Degrees from the University of Lehigh and from the University of Alabama, medical branch.

MEDICAL RESEARCH

In 1958 your son had a depression, called endogenous (coming from within). The intense part of the depression lasted for about a year, but it persisted for more than five years. He saw a neuropsychiatrist six days a week.

One weekend, he had thoughts about the effects of electricity in his body. As a result, he asked his physician to let him try a medicine not generally known to be useful for his symptoms. To the surprise of them both he promptly returned to good health. [*Note:* For a patient to be correct in selecting for himself one drug, from a pharmacopoeia of thousands, is believed to be without precedent.]

When your son saw six other persons, with symptoms similar to his own, have prompt recoveries with the medicine, he realized he had an obligation to investigate further. After unsuccessful attempts to get studies done by members of the medical profession, he established a charitable medical foundation and retired from business to work full time in it.

Your son participated in research studies. Then it was discovered that physicians around the world had published thousands of studies reporting the medicine useful for a broad range of disorders. The foundation painstakingly gathered this information and condensed it into bibliographies. On three occasions, bibliographies were sent to all the physicians in the United States.

Your son has spent many years trying to get officials in the U.S. Government to do something about this vital matter. But he found Government too busy with problems to have time for solutions.

Your son was not an author, and it took him six years to write a book, *A Remarkable Medicine Has Been Overlooked*. Written for the physician, the U.S. Government, and the public, all at the same time, it received excellent reviews.

The bibliographies and your son's book have been translated into many languages, and understanding of the medicine is increasing around the world. But the lack of understanding is still great, and much needless suffering exists. Your son must continue his efforts.

Ida, I have seen many reports. Permit me to observe that your son's is unlike any other I have seen.

With kindest regards,

The Reporting Angel

A self-addressed envelope is enclosed, if you care to use it.

Ida Lewis Dreyfus
Section, Earth
Heaven, June 14

The Reporting Angel
Department of Records
Heaven

Dear Reporting Angel:

Thank you for your kind letter and the spirit behind it.

I must tell you that a terrible mistake has been made—it's only fair to the mothers of the other boys whose records have been mixed in with my son's.

The part about golf and cards sounds like Jack. But you can see for yourself that for him to win National Tennis Championships doesn't make any sense at all.

One thing I can tell you, for my son to have become one of the wealthiest men in the United States is impossible—if I knew a stronger word I would use it. Before I left, Jack had had three different jobs, at fifteen dollars a week, and hadn't made a go of any of them. It was no secret in the family that he would have a hard time making a living. He was a nice boy, but lazy, and had no ambition at all. Once he told me, in confidence, if he ever made $100,000 he would retire and live on the income—but he knew he never would.

As far as the medical part you speak of, Jack knew nothing about medicine and had no interest in it. Apparently things got mixed up in the celestial computer. Could people from the U.S. Government be involved here?

Again, I'd like you to know how deeply I appreciate your thoughtfulness.

With warmest regards,

Ida Lewis Dreyfus

Office of the Reporting Angel
Department of Records
Heaven, June 18

Ida Lewis Dreyfus
Section, Earth
Heaven

Dear Ida:

My sending you a self-addressed envelope was unusual, in fact it required special permission. But I thought you might be dissatisfied with my letter—the opposite of its purpose.

Your comment that U.S. government people might be involved with my Computer requires no response.

As to your letter, I will explain.

The facts in my letter to you are correct. But you are also correct. It would not have been possible for your son to have done all those things, not on his own. He had to have a great amount of instruction, assistance, and direct aid from Departments up here.

Let me go back to 1908. At that time, the High Command, foreseeing the expanding use of electricity and radiation and the development of the nuclear bomb, decided it was necessary to give the human being a drug that would work against excessive anger and fear, by correcting inappropriate electrical activity in the body. In so doing, this drug would help against a host of symptoms and disorders, since almost all of the body's functions are electrically motivated. It would not affect normal function, sedate, or be habit-forming.

To achieve this our Pharmaceutical Department synthesized a medicine and our Messengers put it in the hands of Heinrich Biltz, a German chemist, who naturally thought he synthesized it himself. When our Messengers saw that Heinrich had sold the medicine to a drug company, they assumed that within a reasonable period of time the facts about the drug would become known. Then they left Earth. As you know, we are busy with more important places in the Cosmos.

Our Messengers checked back fifty years later and were astonished, no—nothing the human being does astonishes—they were dismayed to find that the medicine was almost exclusively thought of as an anticonvulsant. A miracle was not applicable here, but something had to be done. And it had to be done in a way that the human being would consider perfectly natural.

Your son was selected for a difficult assignment from among many candidates. One requirement was a good sense of probabilities, an aptitude that comes with the baby. Your son had that. And he had two other aptitudes—I should say disaptitudes—that made him an excellent candidate. His sense of direction was in backwards, and along with this came a faulty copying device. As you know, humans learn by copying and Jack can't learn that way. It is usually a disadvantage, but not for our purposes. Since he couldn't copy, he had to figure things out for himself. In addition, as you have said, he had no ambition. This was also an asset. We didn't have to struggle with any personal desires.

For our purposes it was necessary for your son to have a great deal of money. It was decided he should make it in Wall Street. While he was making the money there, we could accomplish other things. He could be trained in research, and his ability to communicate could be enhanced. These abilities would be needed later.

I am not at liberty to say more.

Be happy always,

The Reporting Angel

You will hear from me in a hundred years.

Mother

EARLIEST RECOLLECTION

My earliest recollection is of a debate I had with my mother. I was almost two years old and in my high chair.

Mother had brought me supper, which included a carefully mashed sweet potato. There was also an unpeeled sweet potato on the tray. I said I wanted that one. My mother said the mashed potato was for me. I said I wanted the whole one. Mother said I must eat the mashed potato. Then, appealing to my better instincts, she said the whole potato was for her, without it she wouldn't have any supper. My better instincts were small. I said I wanted the whole potato and got it.

That was about seventy-five years ago. I doubt if one remembers things that far back on a straight line. I thought of that potato every five or ten years, always with a sense of guilt. I was thirty-five or forty before I woke up and realized that Mother could have eaten my potato. Since then I've felt better.

Before going any further I should say that I think my mother was the sweetest person in the world. If she wasn't, at least she was tied for first place.

A story illustrates Mother's sweetness. She and her sister Bertha were driving from New York to Montgomery, Alabama. After about 150 miles they stopped at a roadside restaurant for lunch. Mother had to walk around the front of the car. As she passed the grille, she saw the usual gnats and moths to be expected there, and exclaimed, "My goodness, Bertha, can't you be more careful."

When Aunt Bertha told us this story we laughed at the idea of her driving down the highway dodging moths and other bugs. Years later it occurred to me that it showed how sweet my mother was. She even worried about little bugs.

Mother loved me, which wasn't always easy; I loved her, which was always easy.

AT THE BEGINNING

If you want to write an autobiography, you have to be born. I was, in St. Margaret's Hospital in Montgomery, Alabama, on August 28, 1913. This event was not attended by Halley's Comet, as was the case with Mark Twain.

After I had been sufficiently born I was brought to 307 Mildred Street, the home of my parents, in the Penick (pronounced Peenick) Apartments. The Penick Apartments were small brick houses, but called apartments because they were glued together by common walls. These walls must have been pretty thick because we never heard the neighbors.

There were four apartments on Mildred Street, and four, at right angles, on Mulberry Street. This semi-square was squared off in the backyard by a tall board fence. There were a couple of empty, optimistic garages if any of us got affluent. There were also eight large chicken coops—one for each apartment. Chickens were executed by our janitor, Reuben. When I was a little boy this didn't bother me. Now it would bother me a lot.

When I was four my father's business (he sold candy) was not good, and we moved to my mother's house in Newark, N.J., for a year or so. My mother's father had a large house on Shanley Avenue. He had established the I. Lewis Cigar Manufacturing Company, a successful business. I don't remember my grandfather well, but I liked him.

I have a few memories from Newark. I remember falling off the porch, and my Uncle Donald digging me out of four feet of snow. And I remember a Galapagos tortoise in the backyard. He was so big, and I was so small, I could sit on his back.

Across the street from our house was an empty lot. There I used to play marbles, for keeps, with a little kid from down the block. One day I bankrupted him—won all his marbles and ten cents besides. Apparently I was born with a gambling instinct. Fortunately, it came with a good sense of probabilities. My advice to the unborn is, don't be born with a gambling instinct unless you have a good sense of probabilities.

In the field where we played marbles, there were lots of weeds. That summer they got pretty high and dry. I considered what lighting a match to them would do. I tried it, and the effect was better than expected. It started a roaring fire. I departed the scene early, and before the fire was discovered was a couple of blocks away. I was suspected but had such an innocent look that nobody could be sure.

The fire was picturesque and also dangerous. It could have lapped over to the houses. Fortunately, it didn't. As the reader can see, I was rotten from the beginning. Later, my father's hairbrush didn't knock it all out of me.

■ ■ ■

When I was five we left Newark to return to the Penick Apartments in Montgomery. The one we returned to was 308 Mildred Street. It

On Mildred Street—my first horse

had two advantages over our previous apartment. It was an end apartment, with windows that gave us a side view. Also it had a small tree on the lawn. I loved to climb that tree.

At the corner of Mildred and Mulberry Streets, there was a big old house. On its lawn was a great magnolia tree with white blossoms, the shape of melons. They smelled wonderful. That was the nice part of the house. The other part of the house was two kids, six and seven years old, named Sam and Charlie Gordon. They were tough cookies.

I was six when Sam was six. One day I got in a fight with him, or rather Sam started a fight. Some of my friends were around so although I was scared to fight, I was more scared not to fight. So I fought. Apparently, it was a draw because Sam stopped. I was complimented by my friends, but I was not happy about the situation.

A few weeks later I found myself, fortunately, in front of my own house—at least I thought it was fortunate—in a debate with Charlie, who was a tougher cookie than Sam. We exchanged comments that could not be mistaken for flattery. The name of the game was to look tough. I saw my mother peeking out the window, and I thought, "Oh, thank goodness, she's going to get me out of this," but she had more wisdom than that. I was shaking in my boots, although barefoot, but somehow I bluffed my way through, and Charlie went away. I went inside and asked Mother why she hadn't helped me. She said that would have made things worse, he'd have caught me the next day.

Except for the fight with Sam Gordon I don't think I've ever had an actual fight. I used to wrestle in the fourth grade, at recess, with my friend Willie Winkenhopper, but that was for fun. And nobody ever won. I love the name Willie Winkenhopper. I'm not making it up.

When I was eleven or twelve, in the summer, a friend, Cooper Griel, and I used to get up early and go out to the Woodley Country Club. We'd play tennis when nobody was around until about noon, and we never seemed to get tired. We got up around seven o'clock in the morning—without waking our parents—with a toe-pull alarm I invented. It consisted of a string, tied around the big toe, and dropped out the window. Cooper and I would put the strings on before we went to bed. When Cooper pulled my string, I woke up—promptly. This alarm clock has two advantages. It's cheap—and it will wake up the dead. Cooper always woke up first, so I never had the pleasure.

When I got dressed, Cooper and I would walk up to Hull Street and take the streetcar which went out to the Woodley Club. There was a man on the streetcar who used to make change. I was very impressed with him. He had a little belt around his stomach, and he would press a button and eject nickels, dimes, and quarters. That's the job I wanted to have when I grew up. It was my only ambition. As fate would have it, streetcars were abolished so I never got to be what I wanted to be.

Cooper Griel was a nice boy and unusual in several ways. I've never heard of anybody else whose first name was Cooper. And he had a great Russian wolfhound named Zaree. And Cooper was a Griel. In Montgomery there was a small Jewish community. The leading family, the aristocracy so to speak, was named Weil. They were big in the cotton manufacturing business. The next best-known family was the Griels. There was an expression around Montgomery, "the Weils, the Griels, and the schlemiels." I never felt like I was one of the latter, but probably I was.

On the subject of religion, my parents were Jewish, by descent, but they never made any issue of it with me. Anyway, it never took. I'm neutral on the subject of which religion. As I see it, it's the question of whether or not there's a God. That's up to everybody. How He wants you to conduct yourself, as I see it, is between you and Him. I don't think anybody's got a lock on the right way, so to speak. So I've been neutral. The few times I think about it, it does seem that if people would deemphasize the religious thing and stop feeling they've got the only right way, we could spend more time being nice to each other. It really doesn't make much sense. There are a thousand religions, and everyone thinks theirs is the right one. This is probably not correct.

My father was born in Montgomery, and so were his brothers. He had an older brother, Morris, and three other brothers and a sister. I remember Grandpa Dreyfus. He lived to be eighty-seven and used to drink a quart of corn liquor every day. Grandpa and I used to play dominoes when I was about five. I beat him sometimes. He wasn't happy about that.

Grandpa Dreyfus was called "Major." I don't remember why. I think it was some sort of honorary title. I heard in the family that he was a cousin of Alfred Dreyfus of the famous Dreyfus case. My grandmother's name was Emma. I never saw much of her because she died when I was a few years old.

Apparently Grandpa hadn't been a businessman and my Uncle Morris had been the breadwinner for the family. When he was thirteen he had a little store, and from what I gather, that had supported the family. When he became older, Morris, with his brother Dave, started a company called The Dreyfus Brothers Candy Manufacturing Company, a very successful business. Their best seller was a huge peppermint cane that sold for a nickel.

Uncle Morris retired when he was forty-nine. Unlike some retired people it wasn't a drag on him—he found plenty of things to do. From a business point of view, he invested his money in mortgages with the people around town. I never heard of him foreclosing; I think he was lenient that way.

Uncle Morris had a little house which he bought for $10,000–in those days that was a lot of money. There was a bit of ground around the house and Uncle Morris became a gardener–planted all sorts of flowers. He loved to work in the garden. So between shopping and gardening and a little business activity, he was fully busy. He was a happy man and enjoyed his retirement. He lived with his wife, my Aunt Helen, and her mother. Living with your mother-in-law is not always a pleasure, but Uncle Morris took it in good spirits.

I'd never heard Uncle Morris say a cuss word. I sort of assumed he didn't know any, and I hadn't had any thought of teaching him.

Uncle Morris drove a middle-aged Buick and was an indifferent driver—that's a fancy word for lousy. One day, we were going up Hull Street, and he was driving. From the left a gentleman ignored the stop sign and flew right across Hull Street, while we were crossing the intersection. Uncle Morris deftly, for him or for anybody for that matter, pulled our car to the right. We went up on a sidewalk, up on a neighbor's lawn, around a neighbor's tree, down onto the sidewalk, past a telephone pole, and back onto Hull Street. No harm was done. However this released a new vocabulary from Uncle Morris. My surmise that he didn't know any cuss words had been wrong. He knew some. In fact, he knew some I'd never heard. Altogether it was a memorable experience.

I was told that my father went somewhere in Kentucky to bet on the horse races. He did well for a while but then went broke and wired Uncle Morris for money. Uncle Morris replied that he'd send him some, along with candy samples, so that Dad could work his way back, by visiting "jobbers," the name for candy wholesalers in the South. That's how my father became a candy salesman. Dad used to be away from home almost six months a year, visiting jobbers.

When I was twenty, Dad got the idea of not working with jobbers, but working with the large chain stores, of which there were about eight or ten, like Woolworth, Kress, and McCrory. A sale to one of them would be the equivalent of fifty sales to a jobber. It was a good idea, except it caused us to move to New York City.

I had two sisters, Lorraine and Joan. Lorraine was born about four years after I was. There was a great deal of fuss about Lorraine, and I didn't like it. I tried to swap her for a billygoat, but the transaction fell through. As we grew older I preferred Lorraine to a billygoat. Really, I loved her very much. Unfortunately, she died about ten years ago.

My sister Joan is still in good shape and bothering me regularly, and I love her very much. However, if someone would offer me two billygoats... Joan lives in Boston, the Hub—of the Universe I suppose.

Sunday mornings, Lorraine and Joan would come into my bed with me and I would read the funny papers. All week long we looked forward to Sunday. The funnies were so good that they were a section by themselves. I remember Maggie and Jiggs, Mutt and Jeff, Bringing Up Father, The Katzenjammer Kids, and Little Orphan Annie.

Lorraine had great faith in me. I had a BB gun when I was about seven years old. She would put a BB on her shoe and let me shoot it off, from two or three feet. I promised her I would give her a Kewpie doll for this. And I kept my word—on her fiftieth birthday I gave her one. This was a squarer deal than Mark Twain made with his brother, Henry. To secure favors, Mark promised to give Henry the first fifty-cent piece he found floating down the river on an anvil.

When I was six years old, I had to go to school.

GRAMMAR SCHOOL

I was six when I went to grammar school in Montgomery. I'd had the great fortune to miss kindergarten. One day, in the first grade, Mrs. Barclay, a sweet, blond, elderly woman of about thirty-eight, was playing the piano. The children were in back of her, singing, and she turned around and said, "Who is that singing like an angel?" I looked around for an angel and saw that all the children were pointing at me. That's the last time I have been confused with an angel.

After first grade comes second grade. Here I had another elderly teacher, Miss P., not nearly as sweet as Mrs. Barclay. In fact I think she was a witch. At that time, when we came to school, each class lined up in front of the school. There was to be an award for promptness among the different classes. One day I got there a few minutes late and Miss P. was not delighted. I had injured our chances, and she told me that, at recess the next day, she was going to have me "bumped." I didn't know what "bumped" meant but the way she said it made me think I wouldn't care for it.

Miss P. was mistaken about the next day because the next day I wasn't in school. I had a sore throat which my mother couldn't exactly put her finger on. Anyhow it persisted the following day. By the third day my mother thought my sore throat might do just as well in school, so I dragged myself back to second grade. Sure enough, Miss P. hadn't forgotten, and at recess she took me back to a fence and had four large boys—two holding my hands and two holding my feet—swing me back and forth and bump me against the fence. Well, it wasn't as bad as I had thought it might be, but, gosh, the anguish I went through before the bumping.

One day, before recess, I acquired, or obtained improperly—it's hard when you're talking about yourself to say stole—a ham sandwich from the lunch shelf. My parents didn't give me school lunches because they fed me pretty well and I was on the plump side. Anyhow, I did this deed, and the little girl who was the owner of the sandwich apprehended me in the backyard and brought Miss P. into the matter. I whipped out a lie, and said my parents had guests over for bridge the night before and had served baked ham. It was logical that I would have a ham sandwich. It was a close call, but perhaps Miss P., having had the pleasure of bumping me, thought, well, let him get away with this one. Now if you want to say that I was only seven and it was all right for me to steal and that I didn't know any better, you're wrong. I did know better. And this was an early lesson in the value of constructive lying. I'd gotten off to a good start.

When my father's business took a turn for the better he sent me to a private school called Barnes University School. I don't know what University had to do with it. I guess it just sounded good. It had a little over a hundred boys in it. We had to buy military uniforms which we wore on special occasions, not every day, thank goodness. It was a nice school. I remember a few things about it—playing touch football in a big back yard, and wrestling at recess.

Professor Barnes was a music buff, although I doubt if there was such a word in those days. He had a choir of eighteen boys. They sang for a half an hour every day. He also had a special, special choir of four boys, and I was in it. One day Professor Barnes said, "Dreyfus, could you sing like that by yourself?" I said, "Sure." So he asked everybody to hold it, and the piano started up. I couldn't open my mouth. Pure 100 percent stage fright. It's nice to remember that he had picked me as a soloist from the special, special choir. Right next to me was Frank Tennille. Frank became an outstanding pop singer.

One other memory from Barnes University School sticks in my mind. Many years later I read Mark Twain's "What Is Man?" In it he talks of the "flash of wit" and how it really is a flash. You don't have time to think.

It was such a flash that got me into trouble at Barnes. I was eight years old at the time. We were in Mr. Henderson's class, a kind man who wanted to do something nice for one of us—give us a little gift. Mr. Henderson asked Tommy Curtis to choose-up, to see who would get the present. In those days the custom was to say "eenie, meenie, minie, mo, catch a gentleman by the toe." It's gone out of style. Tommy started out in a way none of us had ever heard. He said, "eenie, meenie, dixie, deanie." And I said, "catch a doggie by his weenie," before he could finish. There was an uproar. Mr. Henderson admonished me on the spot and arranged a private meeting with Professor Barnes. After some stern comments from Professor Barnes I was let go, but I think I saw crinkles around his eyes.

I repeat this story because it's worth thinking about. Here's a little eight-year-old boy, minding his own business, and something like that pops out of his mouth. It sort of confirms Mark Twain's point.

*Mother, sisters Lorraine
and Joan, and me
in my Starke uniform*

I went from Barnes University School, which was nice, to Starke University School, which was, to say the least, rigorous. Starke's made a big deal about military issues. We had to wear uniforms daily, with a stiff two-inch collar. Some genius figured out if you have a stiff two-inch collar, you'll hold your head up right. I'd like to have gotten hold of his head.

We went through all the motions of a military school, including drilling with heavy guns. And we had guard duty, as a punishment. You'd get it in clumps of three hours, with a rifle that felt like a ton, and you'd have to walk back and forth for three hours. We drilled every day. I have a mixed-up sense of direction; when I pivoted on the wrong foot, Mr. Cochran who was drilling us would say, "Stick Dreyfus." Ouch, three hours guard duty.

Professor Starke was a bugger for the truth and had a little contraption called a hickory switch which he used on us when we were caught lying. I still remember the formal expression, "Hold out your hand, sir," and then the hickory.

Another pleasantry was called columns. One column was a word written fifteen times. Ten columns (150 words) was not too

tough if the word was cat or dog. But if it was interdenominationalisticism or paraminobenzoldiethyminoethynol, it was
suffering.

I remember getting ten columns of interdenominationalisticism
on a technicality. I used to kick my friend Hart Lyon in Mr.
Meyers' class. One day Mr. Meyers said, "Dreyfus, if you kick
Hart once more in class, I am going to give you ten columns of
interdenominationalisticism." I heeded. But when Hart went out
of the room, once he was over the doorstep, I kicked him and Mr.
Meyers said, "Okay, Dreyfus, ten columns." "But," I said, "Mr.
Meyers, Hart wasn't in class." I thought I had him on a
technicality. But it didn't work.

One day Bolling Starke, the son of Professor Starke, was asking
the students some questions. I don't remember what they were
about, but he gave me a compliment. He said, "Dreyfus, you're not
so dumb." I was amazed because I thought I was, or I wouldn't
have remembered it to this day.

Professor Starke was an unusual character. By the way, I never
knew what his first name was, we always called him Fessor
Starke. One day he told us how he'd made a mistake on his
income tax and shortchanged the United States government by
eighty cents. But he thought it unfair to send them a check for
eighty cents and put them to all that trouble. So he came up with
an idea he was proud of. He bought eighty cents worth of
postage stamps, and burned them. He told this to the class as an
example of integrity at its peak.

There was another time when Professor Starke, in a
grandiloquent mood, decided he was going to award three hours
guard duty, free, to the person who solved what he called a
riddle. He said there was a little boy and a few girls at a picnic.
The girls were chatting along. The little boy was shy but felt he
should contribute. Finally, he said, "Have you ever worked an
enema?" Professor Starke said the boy had misspoken and said,

"If you can guess what he meant to say, I'll give you three hours of guard duty, free." Please don't strain your brain. The boy had meant to say, "Have you ever worked an enigma?"

All the older boys took a shot at this, but nothing was right. As time was running out my friend Hart Lyon, feeling you shouldn't blow an opportunity like this without a try, held up his hand. Professor Starke said, "What did the little boy mean, Hart, when he said, 'Have you ever worked an enema?'"Hart said, "He meant to say, 'Has an enema ever worked you?'" I never heard such a spontaneous roar. Even the Fessor almost smiled.

I should mention part of the education at Starke's which was good, a course called Mental Arithmetic. It consisted of problems that we had to solve orally, standing up in class. I can still remember some of them.

Here's one. A man paid $35 for a bookcase. Three-sevenths of the cost of the bookcase was four-fifths of what he paid for a bureau, and three-fourths of the cost of the bureau was five-fourths of what he paid for a table. What did he pay for the bureau and for the table?

You stood up in class and said, "One-seventh of $35 is $5, and three times $5 are $15. Fifteen dollars is 4/5ths of what he paid for the bureau. One-fifth of what he paid for the bureau is 1/4th of $15.00 or 15/4ths of a dollar and..." I won't go further, you can't buy furniture that cheap nowadays.

Fessor Starke jumped on us if we said two times four is eight. Two times four are eight. I'll never forget that one times something carries an "is," and two or more carries an "are."

Now that I think about it, that was the best course I had in school. It got me to know fractions pretty well. To tell the truth, I wouldn't give you a nickel for percentages. I can understand them if I have to, but I hate those 0.1 things.

Play

I may have given the impression that during my grammar school days it was all work and no play. Not so, or I would be a duller boy. There was plenty of play—on weekends and those long wonderful days called summer vacation.

The first "play" I recall was when I was six years old. On weekends I would wake up at six, bounce out of bed, put on my overalls, and head for the bathroom. When duties were completed, I would glance at my toothbrush—I didn't have time to use it—and rush out to the backyard to play with my dog Scott. Usually my pal Rose Morris was there, and some of the other children, but that wasn't necessary. The juices of play were in me.

One morning I was in a hurry to get to the other side of the fence. I could have walked thirty yards and gone around it. Instead, I scrambled over the fence, and caught the top of my right foot on a protruding nail. The gash made a white mark on the top of my foot that lasted thirty years. It also settled a running argument with my mother, as to whether I should wear shoes.

About two blocks from my house there was a big lot. In the summer many children, fifty or sixty or more, came there every day. We ranged in age from six to fourteen and assorted ourselves accordingly. The older boys played softball, and at the end of the summer switched to touch football. The rest of us played anything—tag, hide-and-seek, mumbly-peg, and kitty-o-cat. For the uneducated—when four or more boys and a baseball and bat were present, someone would yell "first bat kitty-o-cat," and the others had a moral obligation to play. There was a pitcher, a batter, a catcher, and at least one fielder. The batter had to get to first base and back to home plate. Not too difficult due to the scarcity of fielders.

Those summer days were pure joy. I thought back to them about fifteen years ago when I was in Central Park, trying to write *A Remarkable Medicine Has Been Overlooked.* Each day around noon about a hundred children were let out of school. They came running into the park, yelling, jumping, skipping, and chasing each other. There was no semblance of a game. I said to myself, they have the juices of youth in them. Then I looked fifty yards away and saw the elderly sitting on the benches, quietly staring ahead, and thought, they have the juices of old age. This could be studied. There might be chemicals in the young that could be safely given to the aged, with benefit.

After I had gone to Starke University School for two years, my parents sent me to Sidney Lanier High, a public school. Maybe my father thought I'd learned how to tell the truth. More likely, my mother was tired of guard duty and the hickory stick. I was grateful for the change, but I must say that Starke's made a lasting impression.

HIGH SCHOOL

Sidney Lanier High School was not named after Napoleon Bonaparte. A piece of information that floated around the school was that Sidney Lanier (a renowned poet) had ordered the first shot to be fired at Fort Sumter that started the Civil War. We took pride in that. I don't know why.

Sidney Lanier was a great deal different from my previous four years of school. There wasn't that strict attitude—and there were lots of pretty girls. Barnes' and Starke's had been for boys only.

I don't remember much about high school, I was so absorbed with playing golf at that time. I played after school, weekends, and of course summer vacations. But I remember a few things.

My grades were average. The only course I remember was one I flunked. It was first-year Latin. I'd flunked it at Starke's, and I flunked it again at Lanier. The third time I took no chances. I studied hard—carried Miss Caldwell's tray at lunch—and passed.

Any possibility that I might have had a singing career came to an end at Lanier. I was singing in a large group. The teacher stopped us and said, "Dreyfus, you're off key." (My voice was changing and I didn't realize it.) Several of the students who knew my singing background said, "Mrs. Simpson, Jack's a wonderful singer." Mrs. Simpson was not impressed. She insisted I was doing the music no good. Since that put-down I've never sung, except to mumble "Happy Birthday." Mrs. Simpson may have cost us another Elvis, or even an Enrico.*

At school there was a big, quiet boy named Johnny Caine. He played on the football team, later went to the University of Alabama and made All American. He was extraordinary on kickoff, could consistently kick the ball out of the end zone. Wallace Wade, coach at Alabama, made a profit on this. He had Johnny line up on the right side of the field, and angle the ball to the opposite corner. Often the other team was stopped on the 5- or 10-yard line. I'm still proud of Johnny.

I was shy with the girls at school. I didn't realize how shy—you don't know how other people are. But I got objective evidence. In my senior year I sat across the aisle from a pretty girl named Jurelle. She sometimes sat with her dress a little above her rolled stockings. I noticed, but never when she was looking.

A few years later I met Jurelle. She told me that in our senior year she had bet three girls, twenty-five cents each, she could get me to look at her—and lost the bet. Imagine how shy I must have been for four girls to bet on the subject?

After high school comes college, for some people. As I've said, my grades were average, and colleges were not vying for my attendance.

Before going to college, let me talk about golf, an important factor in my life.

---

* Caruso, for recent arrivals.

GOLF—A PLEASURE

When Cooper Griel and I played tennis at the Woodley Country Club, we were only fifty yards from the golf course. I loved the look of that green expanse, and yearned to get on the course—there was a strong tug. But the Woodley Club had a rule you couldn't play until you were thirteen. On my thirteenth birthday I started, and didn't pick up a tennis racket for another thirty-five years.

My first rounds were with my mother and my Aunt Helen. They were not good, and bounced the ball along the ground about a hundred yards. I did the same. One day I made a spectacular shot—on a 170-yard par-three my drive trickled onto the green. Mother and Aunt Helen were ecstatic; I was a little puffed up myself. After a few more rounds with them I started playing alone.

Now the first thing you do when you play golf is grab hold of the club. This is called a grip. I had been taught a grip by Mr. Morris of the Penick Apartments, and it wasn't a good grip. It was what you would call a strong grip, with the right hand too much under and the left hand too far over. My powers of observation are impoverished so I didn't notice that other people's grips were different. I started with Mr. Morris' grip, and used it till I was twenty-one. The grip had a major disadvantage, it made you hook the ball. It never occurred to me to change the grip—when I started to hook, I changed something else. I brought the club back well on the inside, and then moved my body ahead fast, to get the blade open so that it would be square at impact. It was not easy but, with plenty of practice, I got to do it quite well. And it had one advantage. For my weight, less than 130 pounds, I hit the ball a long way, almost as far as Florian Straussberger and Dr. Blue Harris, the long hitters in Montgomery.

There was a place between the fifth green and the sixth tee, a little plateau of grass that I used to practice from. It was a spot where divots were not apt to bother anybody. I used to hit a bag of balls and my caddy, Perry, I'll tell you about him later, would bring them back and I'd hit them again, for hours.

In those days there was no such thing as a practice green at the Woodley Club. I pitched and putted for hours on the greens themselves. They were Bermuda greens, slow and tough, and nobody minded.

Pretty soon I was shooting in the high forties. One day I got a forty-three. That was my best score for a while. Then I had a thirty-nine—such a big drop that nobody in the clubhouse believed it. That was the beginning of my playing well.

By the time I was fifteen I got to the finals of the Woodley Country Club Championship, and almost won it. When I was sixteen I did win it, and won it the next three years.

There were two golf clubs in Montgomery, the Montgomery Country Club and the Woodley Country Club. The Montgomery Club was an eighteen-hole course and the Woodley a nine-hole course. Both were good golf courses. By coincidence, the Montgomery Country Club didn't have any Jewish members, and by coincidence the members of the

Woodley Country Club were all Jewish. That was just the way it was. I wasn't aware of prejudice in either direction.

Once a year the champion of the Montgomery Club and the champion of the Woodley Club would play a match, considered the City Championship, since there weren't any other golf courses. I won this twice, from Files Crenshaw at the Woodley Club, and from Dr. Blue Harris at the Montgomery Club. I felt at home at the Montgomery Country Club, and played there many times with my good friends Files Crenshaw, Dr. Blue Harris, Charlie Ball, and the fine pro, Bill Damon.

It was at the Montgomery Country Club that my name was changed. Charlie Ball noted that the barber put a saucer on my head and cut around it. He called me Saucer Head. It must have fit because everybody called me that. My close friends called me Saucer. For the next twenty years, in Montgomery, I was still Saucer Head.

Selma, Ala., is fifty miles from Montgomery. In Selma there were two brothers, Glen and Otis Crisman, both outstanding golfers. Glen won the Alabama State Championship. Later Otey became a pro, and a manufacturer of fine golf clubs. Otey used to drive over to Montgomery to play matches with me, for money. Each of us thought he had the best of it.

In our last match, my putting, or rather my putter, received an unusual compliment. I sank a long putt on the fifteenth hole, the third of the day, and Otey asked if he could see my putter. I handed him my old wooden putter. He examined it carefully— then broke it over his knee.

That was sixty years ago. I don't bear grudges. I forgave Otey last week.

■ ■ ■

Years after my match with Otey my putting got a more refined compliment. I was a member of Metropolis Country

Club in White Plains, N.Y. Paul Runyon, outstanding pro there, and I were playing at Century Country Club with a member and the Century pro. On the first tee Paul surprised me by telling the Century pro I was an excellent putter. In spite of that I putted well.

We had finished the sixteenth hole when the Century pro said, "Jack, would you come back and stroke a few putts while I watch?" I said, "Sure." After six or seven putts he said thanks, and we completed the round. The Century pro didn't adopt my putting style, but he became a good golfer. He was Ben Hogan.

∎ ∎ ∎

Before I leave Montgomery, let me tell you about my caddie, Perry Jones. Perry was my constant companion on the golf course in Montgomery. I didn't fully appreciate then what a wonderful relationship we had. We never talked about it, and I never thought about it—but it was there. Perry was a tall, lanky black man, in his thirties. He wasn't "black" in those days, he was "colored." If you called a man "black," it was an insult. "Colored" was the nice word, the polite word.

Perry was always there when I arrived at the country club. He didn't take other bags, he always waited for me. I wasn't a good tipper because I didn't have much money to tip with. So he must have liked me, and I liked him. Perry had good golf sense. The only arguments we ever had were about which club I should use. Sometimes I would drive to the Montgomery Country Club, and Perry would ride in the front seat. This was not considered proper. People called it to my attention, but that didn't bother me.

When I was fourteen, Perry helped me win the second flight of the City Championship, played at the Montgomery Country Club. On the last hole of the finals I had a 30-foot putt. Perry, who knew the course better than I, gave me the line. I stroked the ball too hard, but it hit the center of the cup, popped up about three inches, and fell in. On the way back to the clubhouse we overheard my opponent say to his caddie, "Luckiest little S.O.B. I ever saw." Perry reminded me of this from time to time.

When I think back, Perry Jones was one of the best friends I've ever had.

This is a tragic, unbelievable story. One spring I went to Century Country Club in White Plains, N.Y., and found that George Garvin, a young black man who had been assistant caddie master at the Montgomery Country Club, was now assistant caddie master at Century. George and I were happy to see each other. After we had exchanged remembrances, George said, "Did you hear what happened to Perry?" I said, "What happened?" His tone scared me. He said, "He was killed in a knife fight." My heart sank. That night I called my Uncle Morris and said, "Perry was killed in a knife fight, wasn't he?" Uncle Morris replied, "I don't think so, he caddied for me today." A tremendous relief.

Three months later Perry was killed in a knife fight. I can't explain this.

■ ■ ■

When I finished college, my father's business required that the family move to New York. I went along because I liked to eat. The thought was expressed by my parents that I should get a job. This didn't appeal to me, but I didn't say so. I was lazy and loved to play bridge for money. But my ears perked up when Dad suggested selling insurance—he thought my golf might be an asset.

I told Dad that with my grip, my golf game wouldn't hold up without a lot of practice. I talked him into letting me go back to Montgomery for six months, to work on my swing with Bill

Damon, the pro at the Montgomery Country Club. At the same time I could study the insurance business. It was partly a con job, but I don't think I fooled my father. I think he was being nice.

I moved back to Montgomery and lived with my Aunt Helen and Uncle Morris. Bill Damon corrected my grip and worked patiently on my game, daily. It took what seemed forever to break my bad habits. Near the end, to test my new swing, I played in the Valparaiso Invitational. My new swing held up, and I got to the finals. So back to New York.

The first tournament I played in, in New York, was the Metropolitan Amateur, at Metropolis Country Club, in White Plains. In the qualifying, I had a 78 on the first eighteen. In the afternoon I was one over par coming to the third hole, a dog-leg. I tried to shorten the hole by going over some trees. We weren't sure I was successful so I played a provisional ball. When we got around the bend, my first ball was in a good position.

A member of our threesome threw my provisional ball to me. I didn't see it coming. It hit me on the left temple and lowered me to the grass for a few seconds. Then I continued. I had a 68, the best score of the day. There was a theory that I was unconscious. A headline in the *Herald Tribune* said, "Beaned by Ball, Shoots Sensational Round."

Soon after that I became a member of Metropolis, later a member of Century Country Club also in White Plains, and then Mountain Ridge in Montclair, N.J., where my mother's relatives played. Altogether, I won fourteen club championships at these three clubs. I also qualified for the National Amateur each of the three times I tried. Since only sixty-four in the country qualified, that was good.

I made a great golf shot once. A great shot is more than a perfect shot. If you make a perfect shot and twenty enemies at the same time, that's a great shot.

There was a yearly two-ball tournament at Winged Foot Country Club, the Anderson Memorial Invitational Tournament. One year Howard Bergman and I were partners. We almost qualified. We were in a play-off for two positions, with ten other teams. We started out on the eleventh hole, twenty-two of us. When you think about it, that's five-and-a-half foursomes—quite a crowd.

On the eleventh hole all the teams got pars. The twelfth hole was a par-three. Howard shot first and hit his ball over the green, near a tree. With the chips down, I hit into the right-hand trap. Many of the players were on the green.

Howard's second shot didn't get on the green. We were in big trouble. When I found my ball, we were in bigger trouble. The trap was so deep that my caddy had to hold the flag up high for me to see it. What was worse, my ball was so close to the back ledge of the trap there was almost no room for a backswing.

Paul Runyan, pro at Metropolis, had a great short game. His method for playing trap shots was unique. Paul would lift his wedge almost straight up, bring it down so the flange landed in back of the ball, bring his arms forward and up, and the ball would rise, with plenty of backspin. Paul had shown this to me and I'd tried it a few times, but hadn't adopted it. Now I had no choice.

Howard was up on the green watching—with his fingers crossed. Seven or eight other players were with him—just waiting for me to get it over with. I took the club almost straight up and made the Runyan move. The ball bounced out towards the flag, with a nice feeling of backspin. I couldn't see what happened. All of a sudden Howard was jumping up and down. I thought I must be close to the flag. Then I looked at the other players. I've never gotten so many dirty looks—I can't blame them. My ball had landed a few feet past the hole and spun back in.

Howard and I won three matches and were beaten in a close match in the semifinals by Dick Chapman, amateur champion, and his partner.

■ ■ ■

A last story. I was again playing in the Anderson Memorial, scheduled to tee off at 10 A.M. Winged Foot is a forty-five minute drive from my house. My driver, Lee Robinson, wasn't exactly sure how to get there, so we left at 8:15. Even if it took an hour, I'd have time to change clothes and hit some practice shots.

At 9:30 we were still looking for Winged Foot, and I was in the back of the car, changing. We arrived at Winged Foot eight minutes past tee-off time. I grabbed my clubs and rushed to the first tee.

Two starters were on the tee. I apologized for being late and said, "I hope I'm not disqualified." One of them said, "Probably not, the tournament doesn't start till tomorrow."

Golf was a special part of my life.

TENNIS

I'm a little embarrassed to write about my tennis.

In my late forties I stopped playing golf and played a little tennis when I was on vacation at the Roney Plaza Hotel in Miami Beach. I played with the pros there, Marse Fink and Sol Goldman. I didn't play all year round, just two or three weeks a year. It was fun. Marse and Sol used to give me, and the bum they stuck me with, big handicaps and they beat us almost all the time. We played for "tickers," $50 (that was all Marse's heart could handle according to Sol). One day they paid me an unusual compliment. They said I was ranked third on the International Sucker List (behind a Frenchman in Monte Carlo and a Greek in Philadelphia). I didn't let this go to my head.

My game improved a bit. Of course, all my strokes were terrible because I couldn't copy what others did. My forehand is just a chop shot and my backhand is not believable. I turn my wrist around and use the opposite side of the racket—I wasn't trying to be different, I thought I was copying others.

I let Gardnar hold the cup

I was reasonably athletic and played sufficiently well to enjoy myself. One year Marse suggested that I play in New York when I got back, play all year round. I took his advice, and joined a club, and played about an hour a day. I met Tony Vincent who had been a great player, ranked in the first twenty in the world when he was young. Tony gave me the only good lesson I can remember. He told me, when at net, to move my left leg forward when the ball was coming to my forehand, and my right leg forward when the ball was coming to my backhand. That way I would get the ball sooner, and when it was higher over the net. This helped me become a fairly decent net player.

When I was fifty-six, I met Gardnar Mulloy in Miami. We had a match for money, as usual, against another pro and a bum like me. I don't remember who won the match, but I remember something else. There was a large black bug crawling on our court and Gardnar ran over to it and I yelled, "Don't step on it, Gar." Gar said, "I wasn't going to," and picked the bug up with his handkerchief and took it over to a grassy spot where the bug was happy. I was surprised, and gave Gardnar a good mark. Later I learned that he had a Pet Rescue Organization.

A few years later, when I was sixty-one, I bribed Gardnar, by contributing to the Pet Rescue Organization, to play with me in the National Doubles Lawn Tennis Championship, for 60s-and-over, at the Rockaway Hunt Club. To my surprise we got to the semifinals. When I was sixty-two, to my amazement, we won it.

Ten years later, Gardnar and his wife, Madeleine, and I went to Australia, and Gar and I won the World's Doubles Lawn Tennis Championship for 70s-and-over. I went into that event hoping to do well, my purpose being to show that Dilantin* was helpful with stamina and reflexes. I didn't expect to win the tournament.

■ ■ ■

When I tell friends that Dilantin won this tournament, they say, "But you can do anything you set your mind to." I have a stock answer. I say, "Next year I'm going to take up Sumo wrestling."

My good friend Eddie Dibbs, who was ranked in the first five in the world for five years, and was second to Jimmy Connors in the United States, said my winning the World's Double Tennis Championship for 70s-and-over shouldn't just be in Ripley's, it should be on the first page of Ripley's.

I hope it doesn't seem like bragging but I think I'm the worst tennis player ever to win a World's Championship—thank you, Gardnar.

* The subject of *A Remarkable Medicine Has Been Overlooked.*

MY PARENTS

I doubt if we are given a choice of parents. If we are, and I'd known what I know now about human beings, I'd probably have been an elephant. You say elephants are an endangered species, but believe me, human beings are an endangered species.

However, if I'd been given a choice of parents, and assigned to the human race, I'd have chosen Ida Lewis and Jonas Dreyfus. I might not have said that when my father's hairbrush was being applied to my bottom, when I was young. But looking at the whole record, he was the best.

My mother had a lovely face, and beautiful red hair, the sort called auburn. She let it grow long, but wore it in a bun in back of her head. Everybody commented on it. I've told you how sweet she was. My sisters Lorraine and Joan and I vied for her attention. And we all got an equal amount of love.

There was a fourth contender for Mother's attention. Her name was Trixy, a toy fox terrier, white with black spots. (There was a law in those days that all small female dogs be named Trixy.) Trixy liked my sisters and me, but she loved Mother. Whenever she had a choice, she was with her.

When Dad was out of town visiting candy jobbers, Trixy slept with Mother. Otherwise she alternated between my sisters' bed and mine. Even when Dad was in town, Trixy got use out of Mother's bed. As soon as Dad left for the candy factory, Trixy would be in the bed, a little lump under the covers. Mother didn't mind, she made the bed up later.

During school days my sisters came home for lunch between twelve and one. Mother would pick them up in our Buick—our family was sold on Buicks. Trixy made the trip—Mother wouldn't think of going anywhere without her. The first couple of times she had to wake up Trixy. From then on, just when Mother was ready to leave, Trixy would come out of the covers, in a rush.

Mother couldn't understand this. How did Trixy know just when to come out? Finally Mother caught on. Just before leaving, she would pick up the car key, on the key ring. There would be a tinkle—and Trixy.

■ ■ ■

When I was young my father was strict with me. I wouldn't say he was a disciplinarian, but of the school that said "children should be seen and not heard." His mother was German and Grandpa Dreyfus was from Alsace-Lorraine, German or French, depending on who won the last war. I was told that the Germans were stricter than most. Perhaps that influenced Dad's attitude although he was born in Montgomery.

As I have said, Dad went to Starke's University School and got the pernicious idea that lies were terrible. I quickly learned to avoid lies, unless absolutely necessary. For instance, sometimes you get into a spot where if you tell the truth you're going to get a licking—you have nothing to lose with a lie— occasionally it works.

Dad's procedure in giving me a licking was formal. We visited the bathroom together. He'd sit on the toilet seat and ask me to hand him the hair brush. Then I'd lie over his lap, and the brush would be applied to my behind. When I had received a certain amount of whacks, I would start to yell and my mother would rush into the bathroom and take the brush out of Dad's hand. He never argued with her—even when I wised up and started to yell before the first whack arrived.

Of course, that old "it hurts me more than it hurts you" was stated. The "but not in the same place" I kept to myself.

Dad used to correct me a lot, particularly at the dinner table. I began to think that good table manners were a sure way to Heaven. I like the song, "Mable, Mable, sweet and able, keep your elbows off the table." Elbows on the table were my biggest weakness. Sometimes my feelings would get hurt. I would cry, and leave the table without finishing dinner.

Recently I told this to my former wife, Joan, who didn't have corrective parents at all. In fact, I think she corrected them. She told me that sometimes her feelings got hurt at the table and she would leave, but she always took her plate with her.

Parents can love their children and bring them up differently. Mine, particularly Dad, were the corrective type. Joan's parents thought the best way was to let her figure it out for herself. I got a laugh out of her recently when I said, "If your parents saw you walking on the edge of the Grand Canyon, they would have said, 'Gee, I hope she doesn't slip.'"

■ ■ ■

I've always had a small ego. I am sure the psychologists would say that it was because of my father. But maybe my ego isn't small, just realistic, and is small by comparison with others that aren't realistic.

The main thing is that Dad loved me and was doing what he thought best. He did many things that gave me pleasure. I'll never forget when I was in my early twenties and had lost a lot of money gambling, I asked Dad if I could borrow $10,000. He lent it to me without even asking what it was for.

My mother died when she was forty-nine, of a stroke. It was a shock, and I didn't get over it for a long time. When Mother left she was convinced I'd never make a living.

Dad lived to be eighty-eight, and he was happy in his last ten years. We lived only a block apart in New York. I would visit him once or twice a week and spend an hour or two with him, and we both enjoyed it.

When Dreyfus & Co. started to be successful and our advertising campaign was going well, Dad eased up on "constructive criticism." When we did really well, my secretary, Helen, told me that every once in a while Dad would chuckle, and say, "We never thought Jack would amount to a hill of beans."

■ ■ ■

Recently I was listening to the beautiful music of Don McLean, in a plane 40,000 feet in the air. A thought came that brought tears to my eyes. President Nixon had just sent me his insightful book, *In the Arena*. It was autographed to "My favorite genius."

The thought that brought the tears was, "What if my mother and father could know that a President of the United States had written this to their little boy."

FAMILY LIFE

This book is not about my family life. That would be a book in itself. But a few words. . .

I was married to a beautiful girl, Joan Personette, in 1939. I didn't know it at the time but Joan had won a Joan Crawford look-alike contest. I think Joan Crawford got the better of it. In addition to being beautiful, Joan was a fine artist. I didn't realize how fine at the time.*

Joan and I were legally separated after four years. Not Joan's fault at all. I guess marriage was not for me because I never got married again or even considered it. After eighteen years of separation, Joan went to Reno for a divorce. She went with great reluctance—she associated Reno with divorce and gambling.

---

* Joan was a costume designer for the Roxy Theater for many years—she did magnificent costume sketches, exquisite in form and color, in my opinion the best ever done. Joan has become a wonderful painter. She's very modest, and never tried to sell her paintings. Recently her work came to the attention of The National Museum of Women in the Arts in Washington, D.C. This fine museum liked it so much that they recently held an exhibit of Joan's work in the important months of October, November and December—and it was extended for an extra month.

Once Joan got there, she found the country so beautiful she loved it, and decided to stay. There she met Bryce Rhodes, a fine gentlemen. Joan and Bryce have lived together for more than twenty years. Bryce and I are good friends.

Joan and I had a son, Johnny. When we became separated, Johnny was two years old and I didn't see him again until he was almost eight. Freud suggests that these young years are very important for a little boy's old man to be around. It's the greatest regret of my life that I wasn't. When Johnny was eight I visited him every Saturday and Sunday in Purchase, N.Y., and we'd play games. A stroke of luck, and a little help from me, brought Bill Damon, the fine golf teacher from Montgomery, to nearby Century Country Club as golf pro. Bill gave Johnny hundreds of golf lessons, while I watched. Soon Johnny became an excellent golfer, won the Club Championship a few times, had a 66 at Westchester Country Club, also qualified for the British Amateur. Johnny worked at Dreyfus & Co. until I retired. Since then he has done a great deal of volunteer hospital work, which he enjoys.

Six years ago Johnny went out to Reno to see why his mother liked it so much. He found out and bought a house on a street with a lovely name, Mark Twain Avenue, and has lived there ever since. We visit each other a few times a year, and talk on the phone several times a week. Sometimes we have arguments—we're both right, of course. A few years ago I told Johnny if my life were in peril and I was given the choice of one person to come to my rescue, I would pick him. He said I was right, but only after he'd had breakfast. I love Johnny very much. And I still love Joan.

Uncle Morris & Dad

Me and Hart Lyon

Joan in her Roxy Theater studio

Johnny and Nellie von Hoensheim

With Clemens and Ling Ling

Joan with Buffy

Three generations—taken when Dreyfus Corp. first traded on New York Stock Exchange

Stuart Little, me, and hibachi to keep warm, while writing "A Remarkable Medicine Has Been Overlooked"

Author's Note

This being my only autobiography, I'd assumed it could be written chronologically. Well, much of it can. But my life has been so diversified that some of it doesn't fit conveniently into the story. Take the chapter on golf. I played golf from the ages of thirteen to forty-five, but I couldn't interrupt the narrative every few pages with a golf story.

It's the same with card playing, horse racing, and a chapter titled "Experiences and Thoughts." They are separate chapters and I'll place them where I think they will interfere least with the chronology.

Following the chapter on "Wall Street," there will be a book I wrote about sixteen years ago, *A Remarkable Medicine Has Been Overlooked.* It's about the most important subject I know.

CARD PLAYING

I don't know how people learn to play bridge. Some take lessons I suppose, but most just pick it up.

When I was nine years old, my parents let me watch their bridge games with the neighbors. I sat behind Dad, by command. I was usually sent to bed before the conclusion. I don't know where my parents learned the game, but they were fair players and did well—except against the Gassenheimers, who were good players.

My father used to subscribe to some bridge pamphlet that he got weekly. There was always a double dummy hand by Emile Werk. Dad would Werk on it, pardon, for a while, and then tell me it was unsolvable. That would get my competitive juices going, and I would solve it. This would annoy Dad, and please him at the same time (he had such a smart son).

When I was twelve I started playing with other children in the neighborhood for a twentieth of a cent a point—two dollars if you were unlucky. I don't know where I got the money.

When I was about sixteen, I started playing against the best players in Montgomery, Julian and Hilda Slager—tournament players. They became close friends of mine. My partner against the Slagers was another friend, Perry Hewitt. These games were fun, and I have good memories. One memory isn't bridge.

Perry asked me to meet him at a restaurant one night. We could discuss bridge while he had dinner—then he would drive me to the Slagers. I got to the restaurant just as Perry's steak arrived. He started talking bridge. I said, "Perry, eat your steak while it's hot." He said he couldn't until he got his coffee. I said, "Oh," and talked bridge. Minutes later Perry's coffee arrived. He poured the whole cup of coffee over the steak, and started to eat. This was a first, and a last for me. It is not recommended as a health hint—but we beat the Slagers that night.

▪ ▪ ▪

As I said elsewhere, I deteriorated to New York City. There I played at a bridge club. There were plenty of games, and a reasonable card fee. At the club I met Morrie Elis, one of the best player of the cards there ever was (not just my opinion). Morrie was not a great bidder.

I should say that the game of bridge has changed since I was a boy. It had been Auction bridge, now it's Contract. In Contract bridge the bidding is of great importance. You only get credit, or grief, for what you bid. In Auction bridge you get credit for what you make, whether you bid it or not.

Contract bridge has the advantage of giving players more to yell about. They can call each other names for the bidding, as well as for the play. In some games the words "idiot" and "stupid" are heard as often as "diamonds" and "clubs."

I started playing in bridge tournaments with Morrie Elis, and we did well. In one tournament, playing with Morrie, one of the most important things in my life occurred. We had just finished two hands against P. Hal Sims, a great player, author of the Sims

System, and his partner Eddie van Vleck. We had gotten good
scores. As we were leaving, Hal was making some pointed
comments about Eddie's bidding. I noticed Eddie's neck getting
red with what seemed suffused anger. Morrie and I were at the
next table when there was a commotion. Eddie was on the floor
having an epileptic attack, as I was told. The convulsions looked
to me like a series of electrical shocks. Years later I remembered
this. If I hadn't seen it, *A Remarkable Medicine Has Been
Overlooked* wouldn't have been written.

At one of the tournaments I met Eddie Hymes, a member of
the Cavendish Club. Eddie suggested that I join the Cavendish.
He proposed me, and I became a member. At the Cavendish,
the smallest game was for a half a cent a point. I played in that,
and Eddie took half my game. A quarter of a cent was all I
could afford.

I hadn't been a member long before Eddie Hymes started
calling me "Baby Face." I supposed it was because of my looks.
I couldn't be sure because there was a famous outlaw named
"Baby Face" Nelson. Baby Face caught on, and I was called that
at the Cavendish for decades.

At the Cavendish Club there were great players. There was a
famous team, the Four Aces, which won more tournaments
than anyone in those days. Strangely, there were five Four Aces,
Oswald Jacoby, Howard Schenken, Jimmy Maier, David
Burnstine, and Michael Gottlieb. And there were Johnny
Crawford and Baron von Zedtwitz.

At another club nearby, Crockford's, Ely and Josephine
Culbertson were members. Ely had invented Contract bridge,
and deserves a lot of credit for it.

At the Cavendish, when I was playing with these outstanding
players, I was always trying to bid as I thought they wanted me
to bid. That's not a good way to play bridge. You've got to have
your own personality, your own style, and let your partner

cooperate with you on an equal basis. So I didn't do as well with those players as I should have.

When I was thirty I devised a scientific method of playing gin rummy, and used it against Oswald Jacoby and Johnny Crawford, the best players, and beat them regularly. Indirectly this helped my bridge. I got respect. Now I could bid my hand as I thought I should, rather than as I thought they thought I should.

Baron Waldemar von Zedtwitz—we called him Waldy—was an unusual person. In the first place, he was a multimillionaire. In the second place, he looked different from anyone I've ever seen. He was about six feet tall, very thin, almost nothing but bones.

Waldy was nice, but extremely serious. He liked to play with me as a partner because I bid psychics (bids meant to fool the opponents, but sometimes they fooled partner). Waldy was good at picking up psychics.

Waldy was renowned for guessing Queens. If a Queen could be finessed either way, he was great at guessing who had it. He told me he worked on vibes.

One afternoon the Baron and Harold Vanderbilt, the yachtsman, we called him Mike, were playing at Crockford's. They were playing Josephine and Ely Culbertson for large stakes—not to Mike or Waldy, but to me. I was the only kibitzer, behind Waldy.

There was a hand Waldy played in four hearts. To make his contract he had to guess which of the Culbertsons had the queen of hearts. The opening lead gave no indication. I was sitting in back of the Baron, enjoying the situation. I think he was aware of my thoughts.

Waldy played a couple of side suits. Then he went into his act. He brought his right arm up over his head, and started kneading his left earlobe with his finger tips. He did this for a while. Then he reversed the procedure, and kneaded his right earlobe with his left hand. Then he went all out. He put his cards on the table and put both arms over his head, and kneaded both ears.

The strain on the opponents had gotten intolerable. Ely had the queen, and was looking innocent. Josephine was looking slightly guilty. Ely, to be casual, decided to rearrange his cards. Something went wrong, a card popped out of his hand and arched slowly to the floor to the right of Waldy—face up. It was the queen of hearts. The Baron "guessed" it.

Oswald Jacoby, captain of the Four Aces, and a brilliant bridge player, was a good friend of mine. Ozzie had an aptitude for probabilities, an essential in a job he'd had as insurance actuary. He quit the job because he preferred to gamble for a living. He won money at bridge, poker, gin rummy, and would bet on anything. When I began to make money, he told me he was glad he wasn't rich, it would take the fun out of gambling—a profound thought.

Next to gambling Ozzie's favorite sport was eating. Frequently, after an afternoon session at the Cavendish, we would go to a nearby Longchamps restaurant. In the restaurant there was a large table with a variety of desserts. As we went in, Ozzie would pick up a strawberry tart or apple strudel and bring it to our table. He'd eat that as an appetizer. Then he'd have a shrimp cocktail, meal, and dessert.

I qualified for the Masters Bridge Championship when I was twenty-eight, and played in tournaments. But, as business got some of my attention, I gave up tournaments and just played rubber bridge. Later, when the Dreyfus Fund and Dreyfus & Co. occupied so much of my time, I gave the game up entirely, for about twenty-five years, and came back to it twenty years ago. I play at the Regency and the Cavendish now.

Bridge players are funny characters. When they're playing, the game is the only thing. They could have a view of Niagara Falls, but wouldn't care if the drapes were drawn. And don't try to tell a joke at a bridge table. You wouldn't be heard over the arguments about the last hand.

When I was sixty-two, I miraculously won the United States Open Doubles Lawn Tennis Championship for 60s-and-over, at the Rockaway Hunt Club, with Gardnar Mulloy. It was Sunday afternoon, and I went to the Cavendish Club to play bridge. I cut into a game with three of my friends, including Ace Greenberg, senior partner of Bear, Stearns.

Braggarts give me a pain, but this was too good to hold in. I said, "You fellows will be pleased to know you're playing with the U.S. National Lawn Tennis Doubles Champion." There was silence. While they were searching for compliments, I was thinking of modest responses. Fifteen seconds went by. Then Ace said, "Deal." I dealt.

Come to think of it, fifteen seconds of pure silence, from bridge players, is an accolade.

I've had some bridge hands written up in the *New York Times*, but I won't include any since this is not a bridge book.

■ ■ ■

Years ago I discovered an unusual way of playing gin rummy. I'll include a lesson in gin. If you're a gin player, this may be worth reading.

Lesson in Gin Rummy

The *Encyclopedia of Bridge* says I am "reputed to be the best American player of gin rummy." This compliment stemmed from a method of play that I discovered, by chance, many years ago.

I had finished playing bridge at the old Cavendish Club and sat down to watch George Rapee, a good friend, playing a hand of gin rummy. George's only prospect was in "filling" the five-three of diamonds. His opponent discarded the diamond four and I said to myself, "The lucky stiff, he got hit in the middle." Being "hit in the middle" at the time was thought of as the luckiest thing that could happen. I thought, "Only one card in the deck, and George got it." Somehow that started a train of thoughts and I realized that getting hit in the middle was no more difficult than drawing the jack of hearts to the king, queen—again only one card would do.

One thought led to another. I will skip detail. But it was apparent that a king can be used with four separate combinations: three combinations of kings—the king of spades can be used with the king of hearts, the king of diamonds, and the king of clubs—and in a run with the queen-jack. A jack down through a three can be used in six combinations. In addition to three of a kind, a jack can be used in a run with the king-queen, queen-ten, and ten-nine.

This was helpful because it made things exact, but most gin players have an idea of these probabilities.

One day the thought popped into my head that, at the beginning of a hand, a player rarely splits pairs. If, for example, my opponent discarded the nine of hearts, I could hypothetically eliminate the nine of spades from his hand. With the nine of spades eliminated, the eight of spades could be used only one way in a run, with the seven and six.

Also, since players don't split nine-eight combinations at the beginning of a hand, the play of the nine of hearts eliminates the eight of hearts. With the eight of hearts eliminated, the eight of spades could be used in only one combination of three of a kind, eight of diamonds and eight of clubs.

Therefore, when an opponent plays a card at the start of a hand, a touching card in a *different* suit becomes, hypothetically, a two-way player, twice as safe as a king, and three times as safe as a jack.

Example:

You've drawn and hold the following:

♠	♥	♦	♣
K	Q	J	8
6	3	3	3
	2	2	2

Your opponent's first discard was the seven of diamonds, and it's your play. The six of spades and the eight of clubs are by far the safest discards.

I won't go further. If you think about this, it will be a great help in making safe discards at the beginning of a hand, the most important part of the game.

Be lucky.

LEHIGH UNIVERSITY

Although my parents weren't wealthy, they decided to send me to college. The University of Alabama naturally came to mind. But a cousin, Monroe Lewis, was going to Lehigh University, and recommended it highly.

My father thought my getting out of the state might have a broadening effect on me (whatever that is). My grades were not up to Lehigh standards but I applied. Perhaps because I was from so far away they decided to take a chance. Lehigh was a nice university, and I wouldn't have wanted to go anywhere else.

■ ■ ■

I got to Lehigh, in Bethlehem, Pa., about a week before school started. It was like a new world. It was a time when freshmen were interviewed by fraternities, and fraternities were interviewed by freshmen. Some of the boys didn't want to join fraternities at all. My problem was simplified because my cousin Monroe was a member of Pi Lambda Phi. By mutual agreement, I joined.

The fraternity was in a large old house, a few blocks from the campus. It had about fifteen rooms, and we were paired up, two in a room. Being with so many boys was completely new, and we talked endlessly about nothing—that's called bull sessions.

There was a paper that published the names of all the freshmen. Mine was included. Instead of saying I was from Montgomery, it said I was from Montz, Ala. Nobody knew about Saucer Head, so for four years, at Lehigh, everybody called me Montz.

When you are a freshman they have a wonderful thing called hazing. You get your bottom slapped with a paddle, and there are other attractions. During hazing week you were constructively employed. As an example, I had to go out one night and come back with a live duck.

One task we all had was to go across the Bethlehem River to a cemetery, at night, find the grave of someone whose name we were given, and come back with the complete inscription. The night we were assigned to the grave hunt was very cold, about ten above zero. Eleven of us freshmen headed towards the Bethlehem River. There was a toll bridge across it that cost a penny. When we reached the river we found ourselves near a trestle that freight trains were supposed to use. We'd never seen a train on it and the other side of the trestle was near the cemetery—the toll bridge was half a mile away.

Si Miller made the sound suggestion that we walk across the trestle. The others agreed. I was the only one who was chicken. I said I would take the toll bridge and meet them there. Apparently there were other chickens in the group, so we headed for the toll bridge. We hadn't gone far when a freight train went over the trestle. We could imagine ourselves hanging from those icy rails, over the Bethlehem River. Cowardice has its uses.

▪ ▪ ▪

I tried to get good grades, but I didn't kill myself. I must be on the dumb side because I got straight Cs at Lehigh, with one exception. I got an A in Music Appreciation.

Professor Shields was playing César Franck's "Symphony in D Minor" in class. I was taking a light nap, hoping it would be mistaken for music appreciation. At one point Professor Shields stopped the music and said, "Dreyfus, what do you think of this music?" I woke up and said, "It's inexorable." I'd never used that word before or since, and I don't know where it came from. It probably wasn't in Professor Shields' immediate vocabulary either, because he gave me an A. Ever since then César Franck's Symphony in D Minor has been a favorite of mine. I recommend it for your listening.

Lehigh was an engineering school. I have a mechanical IQ of eight—some say seven. Taking an engineering course would have been ridiculous for me. I took a Bachelor of Arts course, majored in Latin, of all things, and then in Economics because it was an easy course. We didn't have to do anything except listen to Professor Caruthers, who was very interesting. I remember him saying an economist is a fellow who learns more and more about less and less. I don't remember the rest.

The only course in school that was useful to me was called Psychology. It was a "snap" course, and I took it for credits. I remember a paragraph on rationalization, the meaning of which I hadn't known. It explained that it was wish-thinking, that we see things from our own point of view, and we always give ourselves the best of it. When I got out into the real world—boy, was that true. There's a valuable thought in wish-thinking.

I took a course in Geology. All I remember is the word fault— I knew that already.

I think the main reason for going to college, unless you are going to be a specialist, is to say you are a college graduate, and for the feeling that you are educated. There are so many people that finish college and say, "Now I'm educated," and don't study anything else the rest of their lives that college may have been a hindrance.

My former wife, Joan Personette, knows she is ignorant. She didn't go to college and has been trying to catch up for the last fifty some odd years. Joan is better educated than almost anyone I know.

When I was graduated—you see if I hadn't gone to college I would have said "when I graduated"—I had a nightmare for over a year that they took my diploma back. Recently the Dreyfus Corp. ran an advertisement with my diploma in it—with Lehigh's permission. I feel they can't take it back anymore.

In college, I learned about girls. That is what they were called in those days. I have been a bachelor most of my life and have had adventures with the prettier sex, but that won't be part of this book. But don't despair. I may run for President, and the media will tell you everything.

Dates were usually double dates, and we usually visited bars. I didn't drink. A fellow named Joe Loeb, in Montgomery, had bet me five dollars I'd have a drink before I was twenty-one and I wasn't going to blow that money. I ate an awful lot of cracked ice.

There are some nice memories. There was a fellow in the fraternity house—I won't mention his name—who had a passion for Ravel's *Bolero*. He had it on records, numbered from one to eight, and played them all the time. At first I liked it a lot, then I liked it, then I felt I could do without it. The *Bolero* has a tiny bit of repetition in it. By the time my dreams were accompanied by the *Bolero*, I decided to make a move. In the dead of night I got hold of those records and scratched out the numbers. I think Ravel would have had a hard time re-numbering them. Anyhow, the music stopped and everybody in the fraternity house was grateful, except one. This has been a secret till now.

I'd been told so often by my father that I was lazy that I'd gotten to believe it. That's not fair to Dad, he just reminded me. I really was lazy. My only ambition, other than to be the man who makes change on a streetcar, was to be a hobo. Evidence for this was seen later when I named my horse farm Hobeau Farm, after my first stallion, Beau Gar, and my ambition.

The notion that I was lazy was so strong in me that I made an appointment with Professor Hughes of the Psychology Department. I asked Professor Hughes why I was lazy. He asked me if there was anything I liked to do. I said, "Yes, play golf." He asked me if I practiced. I said, "Sure, sometimes five hours at a time." Professor Hughes said I wasn't lazy, if the job was something that interested me. I didn't argue with him, although I thought golf was not a job, but he made me feel better.

At this late date, I'd like to thank Professor Hughes. Up There, I hope.

I was on the golf team at Lehigh, captain the last two years. Being captain doesn't mean anything, you just show up like the rest of the players. Saucon Valley Country Club was our home course. We alternated with schools in playing at home and away. The place that made the deepest impression was West Point, Army if you prefer. We had lunch with the cadets, and the uniforms reminded me of Starke's University School.

Fraternities are supposed to have heads. There must be a reason but I don't remember what it was. Anyhow, the head of our fraternity had the modest title of Rex. I preferred the English version, King. But Rex it was.

In my senior year I was nominated for Rex. On the opposite ticket was Si Miller. Si got twelve votes, and I had eleven. The one vote outstanding belonged to the fellow with the *Bolero* records. He disliked me, and he disliked Si, but he wasn't going to waste his vote. He disliked Brooklyn more than he disliked Montgomery, so he voted for me.

Twelve to twelve. We flipped a coin and it came up in my favor. I considered this a mandate.

Just as I was writing this, by coincidence or ESP, Si, whom I hadn't spoken to for thirty years, called me. He was laughing and said he just remembered the time he and I had balanced some shoes and books on top of Joel Rothenberg's door. They crashed down on Joel's head, and scared him half to death. We had nothing against Joel, except he was Rex and we were freshmen.

Si's call reminded me of something that happened after Lehigh. We'd been out of college for about fifteen years. Si was a member of the medical profession and I was a member of Century Country Club. One afternoon, we played a round of golf. A good friend, Leon Fletcher, walked around with us. After golf we drove to Roosevelt Raceway, to see the trotters. I was in the front car with Dr. Miller, Leon followed. When we got to the Bronx Whitestone Bridge, Leon was right in back of us. Si gave the toll attendant a dollar and told him to use the other fifty cents for the car behind us.

At the track we got seats and programs and had started handicapping, when Leon said, "Funny thing happened to me at the bridge. The man wouldn't let me pay." I keep a supply of lies handy and said, "We didn't pay either." Then I said, "I saw an article in the paper a couple of weeks ago about the bridge having amortized its cost down to forty-five cents a car. It was impractical to charge that, so for two hours a day, at random, they let people go through free." Leon looked at Dr. Miller for a second opinion, and got a nod.

A week later Leon came to the City Athletic Club to watch the gin game. Two friends of mine, Monroe Mayer and Ben Sokolow, had been primed. The four of us discussed the stock market for a few minutes when Monroe said, "A funny thing happened to me yesterday. I went over the Bronx Whitestone Bridge and they wouldn't let me pay." Ben said, "That's a lot of rubbish. What do you mean they wouldn't let you pay?" Leon came to Monroe's defense and said, "I had the same thing happen. The bridge has been amortized down to forty-five cents a trip. But it's impractical to charge that, so for two hours a day, at random, people are allowed to go through free." Sokolow said, "That is the worst bull I ever heard— ridiculous." Leon's reply took me by surprise. He said, "I read it in the newspaper." (There must be a moral in this—Leon was reasonably honest.) A heated argument followed, resulting in a $50 bet. Monroe, Ben, and I split the fifty bucks. I think we gave it back to Leon. If we didn't, I owe Dr. Miller $12.50, plus accrued interest.

■ ■ ■

In my senior year at Lehigh, my roommate was Matthew Suvalsky, possibly Polish. Matt was first-string guard on the football team. One night I came out of the bathroom with a toothbrush and toothpaste, and a tube of Barbasol, a brushless shave cream. Matt didn't see the toothpaste and said, "Do you brush your teeth with Barbasol?" I said, "Sure, everybody does." Matt said, "I think I'll try it." I gave him the Barbasol. A few minutes later Matt came out of the bathroom and I asked, "How was it?" He said, "It tastes good, but it makes my teeth feel awfully slippery."

In 1934 I was graduated from Lehigh—Summa Cum Ordinary. Now you're supposed to get a job.

GETTING A JOB

The purpose of getting a job, most of the time, is to make money. I didn't even know what money was for until I was ten. At that age the laws of Montgomery permitted me to go to the movies.

Saturday mornings my father would give me a dime and I'd go to the Strand Theatre to see a movie, preferably Tom Mix and his horse Tony, and Pathé news—sometimes twice. After the movies, if I had a surplus nickel given me by an uncle or my aunt, I would go to Franco's and get a hot dog, on a large roll with sauerkraut and red sauce. My mother told me these were poisonous, but that didn't stop me. Recently I've started to feel the effects.

The subject of making a living came up for the first time when I was fifteen. I was playing golf with a boy my age, Alan Rice. We stopped for a drink at the seventh hole water fountain. Alan told me that one day he was going to make $100,000 and retire on the income (invest it in sound mortgages that yielded $5,000 a year). I knew I'd never make that much money but, if I did, there would be two retirees.

■ ■ ■

When I left Montgomery the second time, with the sounder golf swing (as discussed earlier), I was in the insurance business. I played golf a dozen times with a wealthy gentleman who couldn't play at all. Finally, I got up the nerve to try to sell him an annuity. He didn't buy it. I went outside his office and cried real tears. That was the end of my insurance career.

My father thought I might be helpful to him in the candy business. I had little option, having no other suggestion. It was decided that I get my training in a candy factory that Dad was associated with, Edgar P. Lewis & Sons located in Malden, Massachusetts.

I liked making candy and for six months worked on the marmalade slab, making imitation orange slices, and struggling to lift 100-pound bags of sugar into a boiling cauldron. After work I'd go back to my boarding house and take a nap before dinner. Those were solid naps. When I woke up, I didn't know where I was, or who I was.

My salary at Edgar P. Lewis was $15 a week, and I had to live on it. Room and board was $10.50, lunch excluded. I had one luxury, an old Buick my father loaned me. Garage used up a buck a week. That left $2.50 for lunches and other frivolities. When I was on double dates with my old college friend Matt Suvalsky, Matt had to split the gas with me. A happy period in my life.

After six months my father felt that I had eaten enough candy, and was ready for sales training with him. My chore was to drive the car and carry the samples. I would listen while my father talked with the candy buyer. I remember the first meeting I attended. While candy was being discussed I toyed with a fountain pen on the buyer's desk. When we got to the street my hand went into my pocket and, to my surprise, came out with the fountain pen. My father was not elated.

We did this for a few months, but things don't always work out with father and son, and I guess selling wasn't my racket. Dad had always impressed on me how important the other man's time was, and I think he overdid it. So I retired from the candy business and still needed a job.

We hear about those people who, while still playing with their rattles, know exactly what they want to do in life. Well, I was twenty-two and didn't have any idea what I wanted to do. Naturally I got into the doldrums. My parents were patient and didn't push me. I lay around the apartment on West 88th Street, played bridge in the afternoon and evening, and fell asleep around 3 A.M. listening to Clyde McCoy playing *Sugar Blues* on the radio.

My father thought I should see a psychiatrist. And I did, twice a week. I used to lie on his couch. Whatever talking there was came from me.

An uncle got me a job with an industrial designer. Salary $18 a week—getting up there. The designer insisted I wear a hat, a Homburg, no less. That ate up my excess profits. I accompanied my employer to different stores, with the thought that I would catch on to the business. I wasn't a quick learner. However, before I could get fired, the designer offered to raise my salary to $50 a week if I stopped seeing the psychiatrist. He proposed we take a trip to Florida. I sensed an ulterior motive, and resigned.

Insurance, candy, and industrial design—two strikes and a foul tip. Back to bridge, and Clyde McCoy. My parents weren't surprised. My father always expected I'd have trouble making a living. I had no discernible useful aptitude, and Dad had a suspicion I was lazy. Privately, I agreed with him.

Around this time I had a creative idea. John D. Rockefeller was overloaded with money, but was too old to enjoy it. I thought I'd ask him to give me a million dollars. I could play golf, chase girls, travel around the world, and he could enjoy this, secondhand. I never got around to asking him. If I had, my whole life might have been changed. I'm sure he would have given me the million.

Anyhow, I didn't have a job. One night, at the bridge club, one of the players who knew I was indigent said I might like the brokerage business. Wall Street was the last place I'd thought of trying, and reluctantly kept an appointment he made. My father went with me to the garment district branch of Cohen, Simondson & Co., Members, New York Stock Exchange. I was interviewed by a registered representative, Mr. Roy. He needed an assistant to answer phones and keep his charts. I got the job, $25 a week. I thought I got it on my good looks. Years later, I learned that Dad had paid twenty weeks of my salary in advance.

This time I took an interest in a job. The fluctuating prices and the gamble of the stock market struck one of my aptitudes. And it wasn't hard to look at the pretty models in the garment district. In a week I felt so much better that I tendered my resignation to the psychiatrist.

The most important part of my first Wall Street job was posting weekly charts, on a daily basis. I could have gotten a hundred jobs that didn't have this requirement. It was pure luck because I developed an affinity for weekly charts, and put a large emphasis on them throughout my career.

After I had been at Cohen, Simondson for six months, I passed a stock exchange test, and became a junior customer's broker. Although I liked the business, I was not good at approaching people for commissions—it was selling again. But I got a modest amount of business from relatives.

■ ■ ■

After several years with Cohen, Simondson, I applied for a job as a full customer's broker at Bache & Co.—and got turned down. Then I went to E. A. Pierce & Co., later to become

Merrill Lynch, Pierce, Fenner & Bean. Jim Schwartz, in charge
of customer's brokers, looked me over carelessly, and gave me
a job at $75 a week, a fortune. I wasn't worth it, and didn't
earn it for a long time.

The E. A. Pierce office was spacious. There were tickers, an
order room, and about thirty customer's brokers. I was
assigned to a desk next to John Behrens, who later became a
partner of mine. Everybody in that office was nice, including
Mr. Pierce.

On the day I arrived, there was a memo on all our desks
from Lawrence Dennis, the firm's economist. It was titled "The
Third Great Boom." I'm sure Lawrence was right more times
than wrong, but not this time. That was the first day of the
bear market of 1938. My weekly charts kept me out of
trouble. In fact, my uncles made some money on the short side.

When the market got through going down, business dried
up. We had time on our behinds. When you have almost
nothing to do, you think of something.

John Behrens had a customer, Mollie Snyder. Occasionally
Mollie would come into the office to discuss investments with
John, for an hour or so. I didn't want her to get the impression
that she was John's only customer, which she was. From time
to time I would bring John, from the order room, an execution
of a fictitious order—Mr. Livingston bought 75 Coca Cola;
Mrs. Browning bought 200 U.S. Steel, etc. Mollie was
impressed. John started getting a little cocky himself.

I'd noticed that people have sending machines and receiving
machines. Many don't have their receiving machines turned on
very often. You'll have noticed it when you are trying to make a
point with someone. They're restless to tell their side of the story
and you know they're not listening. This observation helped me
win a bet. I bet a friend five dollars that I could say to Pop
Melcher, one of the customer's brokers, "My grandmother was

eaten by the cannibals," and not get a reaction. My friend wanted to bet more.

A few days later Pop buttonholed me, and started what seemed like a long story. I motioned my friend over. After a few moments Pop paused to take a breath and I said in a normal tone, "My grandmother was eaten by the cannibals." Pop nodded, and picked up his story where he'd left off.

There was a customer's broker, Ralph Kershaw, who used to trade in commodities. His customers followed Lawrence Dennis' recommendations. One week Lawrence recommended the purchase of corn, four days in a row. Each day it went down three or four cents and Ralph's customers were taking a beating. When a substantial loss had accumulated, I got a back office friend to make up a memo from Lawrence saying, "Would take profits in corn." When Ralph was out to lunch, I put the memo on his desk. Several of us were in on this.

Ralph returned from lunch, started to sit down, and saw the memo. Halfway down, he straightened up, and his face got red. Then, memo in hand, he marched stiffly to Mr. Pierce's office. We never heard what happened.

My Uncle Dave had sent me some stock certificates of bankrupt companies to see if they had any value. The certificates were impressive-looking but, as they say, not worth the paper they were printed on. One day I found a use for them.

Pop Melcher was to become a partner of the new firm, Merrill Lynch, Pierce, Fenner & Bean, to be headed by Charlie Merrill. One day Pop came in with an overnight bag and told us he was spending the night at the home of Mr. Merrill. I got my back office friend to make up an envelope, addressed to Robert Ruark, the firm's best customer, with "Insured for $250,000" stamped on it. We put Uncle Dave's certificates in the envelope, and made a hole so they would show through. I stuck it in Pop's overnight bag.

Later, Pop told us he talked with Charlie Merrill until about ten o'clock. Then he went to his room and took a shower. When he went for his pajamas he saw the envelope with the securities. This had to be reported. Pop brought the envelope to Mr. Merrill, who'd been sleeping soundly.

Now that I look back on it, I don't know how I got out of that office unscathed.

■ ■ ■

A few years after I'd joined the firm, the offices of Merrill Lynch, Pierce, Fenner & Bean were moved to 70 Pine Street. There were many different people in it, and a new manager, Victor Cook. Almar Shatford, eighty years old, and a partner, had an important effect on my life.

Coming from Montgomery, I felt frozen in the winter and wore heavy overcoats and gloves. I also got the flu, it was called *la grippe* in those days, at least twice a year. Mr. Shatford told me to stop that nonsense of heavy clothing and let my body get used to the climate, and I wouldn't have all those maladies.

The first year I tried it with just a topcoat, and got the flu only once. The next year I got rid of the topcoat and didn't get sick at all. And there was an extra benefit. I tried to get to the office at five minutes to ten. Sometimes I misgauged and was a little late. On those occasions, our office manager, Victor Cook, would give me an unkind glance, or a few words. Now, without a coat, Victor was stuck. He couldn't be sure if I was late, or just coming back from the men's room.

In those days the market opened at ten o'clock and closed at three. The hours were good for me. At 3:01 I was on my way to my real enjoyment, bridge at the Cavendish Club. I was never any good as a customer's broker, who is supposed to bring in commissions. At my peak, my salary was $12,000 a year. In market judgment I was above average. I kept my own weekly charts, and they were a big help.

Making $12,000 a year must have unsettled my brain. Although classified 4-F, I felt I should try to help win the war, and volunteered for the Coast Guard.

THE U.S. COAST GUARD

Naturally, with my college education, and my fine job on Wall Street, I was invited to take an exam for the Coast Guard Officers' Training School. My mechanical IQ enabled me to flunk it. I was awarded a job as apprentice seaman, equivalent to buck private in the Army. The Coast Guard base I was stationed at was called Manhattan Beach, located at Sheepshead Bay, N.Y.

Getting up for the opening ceremonies at 5 A.M. was not a pleasure to a fellow used to getting up at 9 A.M. "Hit the deck, Mate," is not one of my favorite expressions. But I got used to it, by going to bed at 9 P.M.

The first day, we were issued clothing—white suits, blue suits, and other stuff. A crowd of us were cramped together on the floor of a large room, and instructed to stencil our names on the clothing. I was given a stencil which spelled Jack Dreyfus, and a large bottle of ink.

The space each of us had was small, little more than a yard in diameter. We went to work. My hand and my brain are not too well connected. I spilled the bottle of ink three times (a record at the time). As you know, ink doesn't respect boundaries. After the second bottle was spilled there were growls from my neighbors. After the third, I got threats.

We had a contraption called a seabag. It was about four-and-a-half feet long and twelve inches in diameter. You were supposed to roll your clothing up and tie it

Apprentice seaman, U. S. Coast Guard

with pieces of rope so that, when packed, the circular seabag would have a squared appearance. Only a fiend could have thought of this. But that's not the worst of it. The only entrance to the seabag was from the top. Naturally, you put everything you wanted to be handy near the top. But sometimes you made a mistake. Then you had to empty the whole damned thing—excuse me, I had decided not to cuss in this book—to get the things at the bottom, and then repack the seabag. But perhaps I've been unfair. Maybe the seabag was designed by a genius, to keep us occupied.

The Coast Guard felt, with my college education, I would probably be competent to collect garbage. So I was assigned to a garbage truck. I was third in charge, although I had the highest position, on top of the truck. Garbage cans would be handed me by the second in charge, and I would empty them. At night I could tell how good business had been. When I took my clothes off there would be a brown line around my stomach or my chest, depending on the haul.

It was while I had this fine position that I learned the difference between garbage and slop. The difference is simple. Slop is slop. Garbage is slop—with coffee grounds added. You can't have garbage without the aroma of coffee grounds. This information should make you glad you bought this book.

Never leaving the base became an awful bore. I would have given anything just to walk through a grocery store. Some of the fellows were beginning to say dumb things, like they wished they could get into the fighting. But one day I got off the base. The three of us had a good load of garbage and were ordered to bring it to the Mineola garbage dump.

Not far from Mineola people started waving wildly at us. We thought, "How wonderful." We'd heard how much people appreciated the uniform, but had never experienced it. The people waved, and we waved back, and felt patriotic. We were enjoying this when a car, with the words Fire Chief on it, pulled alongside. The driver gesticulated for us to stop. We stopped—in the center of Mineola. Then we noticed we had a load of burning garbage. The chief ordered us to dump it, and we did. Firemen came, put out the fire, and shoveled the remains back into our truck, and we took it to the dumps. On the way back to the base nobody waved at us.

Going from garbage to psychology, we all have observed that we don't like to be caught without knowledge. There's no use admitting you don't know something, if you can get away with it. I have noticed this in the medical profession. Dr. Green will say to Dr. Brown, "As you know, Hempleworth and Snodgrass, in 1924, showed that eels have more cholesterol than sardines." Dr. Brown may never have heard of that paper, but he's not apt to let on. This is human. I saw it in the Coast Guard.

The canteen, where you bought everything from candy bars to clothing, was oblong and almost the size of a football field. At the entrance there were many telephone booths, so you could make phone calls. Then you went through a door into the canteen. Once you got into the canteen, you were not allowed to go back through that door.

One day it was raining hard. I was inside the canteen when I remembered a phone call I'd forgotten to make. I didn't want to go outside and make that long trip in the rain to get back to the phones. So I tried a maneuver—I don't know where I got the nerve. I approached the guard at the entrance door and started to go through. He said, "Where do you think you're going, Mate?" I said, "It's okay, I'm a furth burner." He said, "Oh," and I went through.

That was fun. I did it a few times when it wasn't raining, just to keep my spirits up. One day a guard was at the door who was less ashamed to show his ignorance. When I said, "It's okay, I'm a furth burner," he said, "What's a furth burner?" I said, "Where do you think they get the hydrocarbon in the canteen?" That was different, and I went through.

I had a temporary job teaching a course called "Captain of the Port." One of the subjects I was supposed to teach was the workings of the Chrysler Pump. I didn't even know how to plug it in. In class, I read my mates stories from *Reader's Digest*.

■ ■ ■

At Manhattan Beach the beds were double-deckers. I had an upper berth. There was a rule that all windows had to be cracked three inches from the top. It didn't matter if it was 45° or 6° above zero. After being in a steady draft of icy air for many nights, I developed back pains. I could sleep for an hour but then I would have to get up and walk around for half an hour, to loosen up my back. This continued for weeks, and I didn't get much sleep. Also I found, although I could drill all right, standing at attention for more than a few minutes was extremely painful.

I reported to the infirmary and they were skeptical. Back pains were high on the list for goldbricks. Fortunately, they took my sedimentation rate. It was 56. Normal is 0 to 15, I'm told. This confirmed that I did have a problem, and I was sent to the hospital at Sheepshead Bay.

My doctor was the most handsome man I'd ever seen, straight as a ramrod, six foot two, and a fine face. You would never guess what his name was. It was Twaddle. It was Dr. Twaddle who awarded me malaria (a mild case). There was a theory that the fever from malaria might cure my back. It didn't, but I can tell you about malaria. You start with a chill, I mean really a chill. You're so cold your teeth chatter, and the whole bed shakes. You are happy when the fever comes. Even a 104° fever is better than the chills.

After a couple of months, I was released from the hospital and found myself in what was called Convalescent Camp. In Convalescent Camp there isn't much to do but convalesce. To help me convalesce, I was given a long stick with a nail in the end of it. With this equipment I was supposed to pick up cigarette butts. I did this for a few days, but business was poor. I had a feeling that we could win the war without me and my stick.

There were some huge rocks, on an incline, that protected us from the bay. I climbed down them one day and made a wonderful discovery. There was a cave, just the right size for me. I spent February and March in that cave, accompanied by a book from the library, and a couple of candy bars from the canteen. When the sun was out, even if it was 10° above zero, I could take off all my clothes and get a suntan. I remember one day an ensign said to me, "What the hell's going on here, Dreyfus, you got a sun lamp on the base?"

Well, all good things have to come to an end. Because of my back, I was given a medical discharge. We won the war anyway.

HORSE RACING

There had been no horse races in Alabama. I was introduced to them in an unusual way.

P. Hal Sims, the famous bridge player, and T. Suffern Tailer (Tommy), and I played golf one day—I forget where. Hal was a good golfer, and a better bettor. Tommy had a one handicap. I don't remember the golf, but I remember what followed.

Hal and Tommy suggested we stop at Jamaica Race Track on the way home. I was outvoted, two-to-one. We got to Jamaica before the fifth race. There was a buzz around the track about a jockey named Alfred Robertson, who had won three of the first four races.

With my wealth of handicapping skills, I decided to bet on Robertson's horse in the fifth race. It won. I bet on his horse in the sixth race. It won. Robertson had tied the record of most races won in one day. In the seventh race Tommy gave me some sound advice, and told me Robertson's horse had almost no chance. I bet on him anyway, and he paid a big price.* There were only seven races, so I had to give up this good thing for the moment.

■ ■ ■

Well, I started to go to the races whenever I got a chance and used a system of betting given me by a friend. Later I read some books on handicapping and started figuring things out for myself.

Going to the races and betting became a great pleasure to me. Every day that I could get loose I went to the track. In my informal attire, I always visited the grandstands where I became friends with lots of the regulars.

There was a period when I was too busy with business to go to the afternoon races so I went to the trotters at night. They're called trotters although they're mostly pacers. I used to go at 6:30 and watch the early workouts. During the races I would mark my program as to which horses went wide. I must have been one of the best handicappers because I learned that when people gave the guard at the $50 window $5 for the "hot" horse he usually gave them my selection.

While watching the thoroughbreds, I observed a two-year-old filly named Bellesoeur and thought she was great. She was second to Bewitch in the Experimental Handicap that year. Bellesoeur didn't race at three and was bred to Count Fleet, who had just retired. Count Fleet was a great horse—not nearly as great as a stallion—but that wasn't known at the time. I wanted part of that first foal. At the time, I couldn't think of buying all of him.

A friend at the City Athletic Club was a friend of Laudy Lawrence, owner of Bellesoeur. He arranged for me to buy half of the foal, named Beau Gar, for $14,000. A friend of my father bought one-quarter. I could barely afford my $7,000 purchase.

* Robertson winning six races in the seven-race card is still a record.

Handicapping at Hialeah

Before Beau Gar's first race, let me tell a story. I was going with a girl whose roommate had been robbed and was in financial straits. I offered to give her roommate $50, but my friend said she wouldn't take it. I asked if she'd mind if I bet $10 on a horse that won, and gave her the money that way? My friend said, "What horse?" I said, "Beau Gar." She agreed, and I gave her $52, wanting it to look realistic. Three weeks later Beau Gar had his first race. He won and paid $10.40—exactly $52 for the $10 bet. Some handicapping.

Beau Gar raced under Laudy Lawrence's name and won a few more races. He had to be retired because of an injury to his back. I still had faith in him. A few years later, and a few bucks richer, I bought the other three-quarters of him, at the original price.

Bill Boland, Beau Purple
after winning the Man of War

Beau Gar had shown plenty of speed before his injury, and Maje Odom, his trainer, thought well of him. I loved his breeding and decided to take the long shot of trying to make him a successful stallion. Of course, no one else wanted to breed to Beau Gar and I didn't have any mares, or a lot of money.

If you have a mare and want a foal, you buy a service to a stallion. As you know I do things backwards. I had a stallion and wanted foals, so I leased mares, six of them for a year. I don't know if it's been done before or since, but it turned out well.

I bought one mare, Water Queen. Bred to Beau Gar, she produced Beau Purple, a great horse. Beau Purple won the Kentucky Derby Trial, but in it he fractured a bone in his leg and had to be retired for over a year. When he came back, he was sensational. He established five track records in a period of eight months, from seven-eighths of a mile, to a mile-and-a-half on the grass. Kelso was Horse of the Year five times in a row. Beau Purple beat him three times out of the six times they raced. He also beat Carry Back, Kentucky Derby winner, three times.

Beau Purple was the result of breeding my first horse, Beau Gar, to my first mare, Water Queen. In *Sports Illustrated,* I was quoted as having said, "It was 110% luck, the rest was skill."

■ ■ ■

For the first few years, Maje Odom was my trainer. Later, when my stable got larger, it wasn't convenient for him to handle it exclusively. I met up with Allen Jerkens, an exceptionally fine trainer, and to this day he trains for Hobeau Farm. Allen and I are the closest friends. He's a bit of a nut, quite like me, so we understand each other thoroughly.

Beau Gar initially stood at Henry White's Plum Lane Farm in Lexington, Kentucky. A few years later I got the impression that a higher percentage of good horses than would be expected, considering the quality of the breeding, were coming from Ocala, Florida. When I noticed Rosemere Farm was for sale, I went to Ocala and met Elmer Heubeck, who had been manager there for seventeen years.

Elmer and I liked each other from the beginning. He told me there was a cattle farm that he knew well, about fifteen miles outside of the city, that had plenty of limestone and beautiful oak trees. He thought it ideal for a horse farm, and it was for sale. Elmer recommended I buy it instead of Rosemere, and I did.

Elmer built the farm. We named it Hobeau Farm. Elmer and his wife, Harriet, built it with every thought from the horses' point of view. My former wife, Joan, made creative architectural suggestions, which were followed. And the fences are a lovely blue. Elmer built a first-class one-mile track. At that time, it was one of the few private one-mile tracks in the country. After a few years Elmer became a partner in Hobeau Farm. He and Harriet did a wonderful job, and I can't thank them enough.

■ ■ ■

For years I was a member of the Board of Trustees of the Horsemen's Benevolent and Protective Association (HBPA), a group of horse owners who defend the rights of the horse owners. On one occasion the President of the HBPA was absent for three months, and I found myself temporary President. It happened at a critical time. The owners were justifiably upset about the small end of the track profits they were getting. They were furnishing the entertainment, the horses, and felt they were not being paid properly.

The directors wanted to boycott the races, but accepted my suggestion to try discussion. I made arrangements to see Governor Nelson Rockefeller. He was gracious, listened to the story, and recognized that it was valid. The governor said he would make arrangements for us to get an extra half percent of the handle. The horse owners had wanted more, but they agreed.

About a week before we were supposed to get the half percent we found out that some members of the legislature had blocked the governor's proposal. At that point it was felt necessary to have the boycott. (For reasons best known to lawyers, we couldn't call it a strike.)

I found myself the equivalent of a labor leader of the HBPA. It was a lot of responsibility, and not a lot of fun. The New York Racing Association (NYRA) made it especially tough by saying that if only one horse was entered in a race, he'd get the purse. Somehow we held together for a week, and there weren't any races.

That was a tough week. I got two phone calls, with sinister overtones, from an alleged friend of one of the legislators. I pretended not to understand, but I did, and was worried. The weekend was particularly trying. I decided that on Monday I'd call Governor Rockefeller and get together with him again. When I got to my office I found the Governor had called me. It had been arranged for us to get the half percent. That was my first and last experience as a labor leader. The HBPA graciously presented me with its annual award, in memory of Sunny Jim Fitzsimmons, "One Who Contributed Most to the Best Interests of Racing."

This event brought me to the attention of James Brady, who had been, for six or seven years, head of the New York Racing Association. His little boy, Nicholas, recently was Secretary of the Treasury. Jim asked me if I would like to join the Board of the NYRA. I was surprised because I was from the grandstand side. But it was nice, and I accepted. Jim went a step further and said, "In a year or so I'm going to retire and maybe you'd like to take my job." That was flattering, but I took it with a grain of salt.

A year later, in 1970, Mr. Brady asked me if I would take the job as chairman, that he'd had it long enough, and would like a little rest. This happened at a particularly convenient time. The Dreyfus Medical Foundation had just sent a bibliography, *The Broad Range of Use of Phenytoin,* to all the physicians in the United States. With the world literature sent to the physicians and the government, I felt I'd done what I could, and others would take over. So I accepted Mr. Brady's proposal.

I thoroughly enjoyed the job. Everyone was wonderful to me. My secretary, Terry Troglio, helped me more than could be believed.

■ ■ ■

In those days, the backyard of Aqueduct was spacious, but occupied by cement and wire fences. My experience in the grandstand helped me understand the need for change. We had the backyard grassed over, and benches and chairs were added. They got so much use that a tote board was installed.

Races are run every half hour. Between races many of the less sophisticated handicappers are bored. We arranged for bands to play music at Aqueduct and Belmont. The public seemed to like this a great deal. My favorite band was one we got from New Orleans, the Preservation Hall Band.

After I had been chairman of the NYRA for a year I had to resign to spend full time in the medical field. Much new information had been published on phenytoin, and I had to assist in preparing a supplementary bibliography. This work was completed in 1975. By coincidence, I was again offered the position of chairman of the NYRA. I accepted again.

The second time I became chairman, I did it with the reservation that I might not be able to keep the position long, and suggested we have an assistant chairman. Dinsmore (Dinny) Phipps took the job. It was a pleasure working with him and we have been the best of friends ever since. When, a year later, I felt obliged to spend more time in the medical field, Dinny became chairman and did a splendid job.

The second time I was chairman I had some fun stirring up the advertising for the track. A series of ads was done on the race horse as the fastest animal in the world. He is not as fast as the cheetah for a hundred yards, but for a mile, he's the fastest animal (I think). Other ads were done on taking a half-day vacation from the city by going to the track. There was a noticeable improvement in attendance following these ads.

■ ■ ■

Hobeau Farm won the Turf Writers' Award for best breeder, twice. This was a tribute to Allen Jerkens' training. One year we won nineteen races at Saratoga, a twenty-four-day meet—a record at the time.

In 1977 I received the Eclipse Award, Man Who Did the Most for Racing, which I deeply appreciated. The award was given in Los Angeles.

On the way to Los Angeles a nice thing happened. I had my own plane but it couldn't go that far in one hop, so we stopped in Phoenix, Arizona. President Nixon had told me he thought the

Arizona Biltmore was the finest hotel in the world. I figured his opinion would be pretty good, he'd been around a little. So I stopped at the Biltmore, getting there around eleven o'clock in the morning. It was too early for lunch and too late for breakfast, but I was hungry.

There was a large menu in my room. On it was continental breakfast. I don't go for formality. If I wanted that, I'd ask for coffee, rolls, and jelly. But what the heck, in Rome do as the Romans do. So I dialed the number. A nice female voice said, "How may I help you?" I said, "This is Room 346. Could I have a continental breakfast, please?" The nice voice said, "Which continent would you like it from? This is the overseas operator." What a wonderful put-down.

I'm still on the Board of the New York Racing Association. I miss a few of the meetings because of medical research. Every once in a while I make a speech about how crazy it is for the state to charge the bettors 17 percent per race. It's ruined the business. Anybody but government would change it to 10 percent. Now I've said it in writing, and gotten it off my chest—again.

I'd like to finish this chapter with a story for my friend Gloria Steinem, of Women's Lib renown.

Robyn Smith was one of the earliest female jockeys. My trainer Allen recognized her talent and was one of the first to give her mounts. Much later Robyn was married to Fred Astaire.

One day I got to Aqueduct too late to make a bet on the first race. It was winter, the grandstand was enclosed with glass, and I hurried to the front window to see the race. There were a lot of people in back of me. Robyn was riding a seven-to-two shot. As the race started, I heard a distinctive voice yell, "Come on, Robyn." Robyn's horse broke second to the favorite. As it pursued the favorite up the back stretch, the voice urged, "Come on, Robyn. Come on, Robyn." When the horses came into the stretch, Robyn's horse started gaining on the leader. The voice became more intimate and said, "Come on, Honey. Come on, Honey." As Robyn's horse went over the finish line, the winner, the voice lowered and said, "Okay, bitch."

Now that wasn't nice.

Before leaving this chapter I should say I've thoroughly enjoyed my association with the members of the Board of the NYRA. As a group, and as individuals, they have been a pleasure to be with.

EXPERIENCES AND THOUGHTS

In this chapter I'll discuss aptitudes, my personality, Mark Twain, and a suggestion for Congress.

Aptitudes

In the chapter on Probabilities in *A Remarkable Medicine Has Been Overlooked,* which follows, I discuss aptitudes at some length, so I'll be brief here.

Some of my aptitudes or disaptitudes, you might call them, I got from my father.

Aptitudes as I see it are gadgets in the brain that come with the baby. I can't prove it by pictures of the brain. But think of the homing pigeon and his perfect sense of direction, and the bird dog and his aptitude for smelling.

One aptitude we all have, a strong one, is an aptitude not to die. If we didn't have that aptitude our manufacturer would be wasting His time. Another aptitude that most of us have is what we call a conscience. It's really a judge in the brain. When He decides we've done something good, He makes us feel better with a little happy juice. When He decides we've done something bad, He punishes us with a little unhappy juice. The neurotic has a tough judge.

I lack many aptitudes. My sense of direction is in backwards. My copying device is faulty. My ability to remember names is so bad it's embarrassing. And I have a mechanical I.Q. of about seven. One good aptitude I was born with is a sense of probabilities.

My aptitudes to forget names and get lost I inherited directly from my father. Let me illustrate Dad's ability to forget names:

Dad and my wife Joan and I were taking a train to Ocala, Florida. Hobeau Farm was being built by my farm manager and friend, Elmer Heubeck, and his lovely wife Harriet. On the train we drilled Dad. Every couple of hours we'd have him repeat Elmer and Harriet, Elmer and Harriet. We arrived at Hobeau Farm and went to a trailer to have lunch. Dad walked in and said, "Hello, Elmer. Hello, Harriet." And Joan and I were proud.

Harriet has a pet name for Elmer. She calls him Abbie. During lunch she would say, "Abbie, may I have some coffee." "Abbie, please pass the butter." Abbie this, Abbie that. Dad couldn't stand it any longer. He said, "I know this is Elmer. I know this is Harriet. But why does she keep calling him Chuck?"

I could give you illustrations of my father's ability to get lost, but why pick on Dad. I'll tell you a story that demonstrates my own talent:

One day I was at the races at Aqueduct and didn't have my car. An apprentice jockey, Terry Drawdy, had just come to New York and had won the last race on a horse of mine. I was wondering how I could get a ride home when my trainer, Allen, said Terry would drive me, if I would show him the way. That was no problem, I'd been to Aqueduct at least 2000 times.

We had the bad luck to leave on the wrong road, and the first thing I knew we were on Atlantic Avenue, heading for

Brooklyn. I was unperturbed and asked a gas station attendant how to get to New York. He said, "No problem. Just follow this road till you come to the Manhattan Bridge, take that and you'll be there." We followed instructions and went over the bridge. Now we were supposed to be in Manhattan, but I knew Manhattan was loaded with street numbers, 10, 11, 12 and so forth, and we couldn't find any. We drove around and around, looking for street numbers. I thought, this is peculiar. Finally we came to a familiar sign, Holland Tunnel. Now I knew where we were. Years earlier at Lehigh, Monroe Lewis used to drive me to New York and we always went through the Holland Tunnel.

So we went through the Holland Tunnel—and came out in New Jersey. I'd overlooked the possibility that the Holland Tunnel went both ways. No problem, we went up the Jersey side to the Lincoln Tunnel, through that, and up to 75th and Madison, where I live. It took us three hours and twenty minutes to make a forty-minute trip. I've been told this is the only time anybody went from Aqueduct to 75th Street by way of New Jersey.

I could tell endless stories about my getting lost but it'll seem like I'm bragging, because in *A Tramp Abroad,* my friend Mark Twain said, "For me, East is West, and West is East."

Personality

I prefer not to be called Mr. Dreyfus, and try to get everybody to call me Jack. A few won't, they say it doesn't show proper respect. But believe me, you can disrespect a person and still call him Mister.

They say, clothes make the man. I don't think that's all of it. I wear good clothes but not a tie and coat, if I can get away with it. Take Donald Trump for instance. People wouldn't mistake Mr. Trump for an unsuccessful person, without a tie and coat. Donald has a presence. Apparently I have an absence.

A few illustrative experiences follow, most with ladies. That's what I call them, being raised in Alabama. I'd have to be reincarnated before I'd call them guys.

After watching the horses train at Hialeah, Maje Odom and I went to a diner for breakfast. On the way to our table there was a lady with a tiny baby. To be friendly, I said, "They're making them awful small these days." Her response was, "I'll have a coke, please."

While I was in my bathing suit on the beach at the Roney Plaza Hotel in Miami, a lady strode up to me and said, indignantly, "I'd like to report that the toilet in the ladies' room isn't working." I said I was sorry and passed the word along.

I was sitting on a bench in Miami Beach, waiting to be picked up. A lady came up to me and asked, "What time does the bus leave?" An empty bus was about fifty yards to the left. I said, "I don't know, Ma'am." She said, "You don't know? Aren't you the bus driver?" I demurred.

■　■　■

Now to the height of my career.

For several years I ate lunch at a small restaurant on 62nd Street, called Truffles. It had two window tables, a small one in the corner and a narrow one parallel to the window. One day I sat at the small table, facing the interior of the restaurant.

I'd ordered my usual sandwich, cheese and tomato on a toasted roll, when two young ladies came in and sat at the other table. They hadn't been there long when the one whose back was close to me turned around and started searching the floor. I said, "Did you lose something, Miss?" She said, "Yes, my wallet." I looked around on the floor and said, "I don't see anything." She turned back to her companion and a moment later they had a heated discussion.

My sandwich had arrived when the young lady turned around and glared at me. At first I didn't get it, but when she continued to glare, I said, "My goodness, Miss, I don't have your wallet." She said, "You're the only one who could. It was in my bag on the back of my chair."

At that point the ladies got up and started to leave. I got up too and my new acquaintance said, in a loud voice, "I don't mind the money but please leave my wallet, it has papers in it I need."

I went back into the restaurant and sat at my table, facing all the other guests. The lady nearest me seemed to shrink together with all her possessions. Everyone was staring at me. Understandable. It's not often you can enjoy lunch, and look at a pickpocket at the same time.

I counseled myself, "Now, cool it, don't get upset. You haven't done anything to be upset about. Don't let this bother you. Eat your sandwich. Chew well," and similar thoughts.

After about ten minutes my friend came back. I stood up and she said, "I'm awfully sorry, I found my wallet in my car." I could have given her a blast. But I said, "You've got a lot of guts to come back, and I appreciate it."

■ ■ ■

Let me conclude with a nice story.

I have been to Milan, Italy, twice—both times for medical conferences. The second time, I was staying at a lovely hotel, Principe di Savoia. I was to be picked up at 8:45 A.M. I had breakfast and went out front a little early. In the seven days I was in Milan, I saw the sun only once, but the air was always nice, compatible with my body's electricity.

When I got outside, I saw a little pussycat. It wasn't that it was so little, it was so skinny it looked little. I hurried back to the breakfast room and bought some ham and turkey. When I came out the kitty was still there and I gave him the food. He didn't eat it, he just inhaled it. I've never seen food disappear so quickly, and I realized I hadn't given him enough.

Now I had a problem. I had a few hundred dollar bills, but no small change. So I went to the desk to get change. The desk had a piece of plastic on top of the nice wood that made it difficult to talk over. I waved to the young man who had shown me to my room. He spoke a fair amount of English. He came over, and I handed him a hundred dollar bill over the plastic and said, "Could I get change for this, please?" He said, "Oh, thank you *so* much, Mr. Dreyfus, this is so nice. I really appreciate this. You don't know how much this means to me!" Well I remembered what Jesus said, "It's better to give than to receive," but this was a borderline case. I decided that I would go along with the thought, and smiled at him. I think I smiled—it felt more like a wince. Then I went back into the restaurant, negotiated a loan, and got more ham and turkey for the pussycat. This time it was eaten rapidly, but not inhaled, so I felt it was enough for the time being.

I was picked up and taken to the meeting, and came back around 3:45. I was tired and went to my room, washed up a bit, and went out to enjoy the nice Milan air.

Across the street from the hotel was a tiny park, the shape of an ellipse. As I got to the park I saw two elderly people sitting on a bench. Their clothes looked more elderly than they. I was about to offer them some money, but decided against it—their feelings might have been hurt. I went to the other side of the park, sat on a bench, and enjoyed the air. It was so relaxing I lay down. Pretty soon I was asleep.

I was wakened by a tap on my shoulder. I sat up and there was a well-dressed serious-looking lady holding out a ten-lire note. I couldn't take the money, of course. But remembering my thought from the other side of the park, I took the note from the lady and thanked her very much. As she left there was a little smile on her face, proving that Jesus was right. And I had a feeling that in taking the note I'd given something myself, and felt happier too. It was a nice day.

Mark Twain

Of all the people I know, leaving the Bible out of this, I think Mark Twain was the greatest. His sense of humor was so extraordinary that many think of him as a humorist. That was just part of him. And his ability to write was beautiful. That was just part of him. The greatest part of him was his insight into members of the human race. Stories by him, "The War Prayer," "My First Lie and How I Got Out of It," "What Is Man?" and others, have great depth and importance—and I recommend them to you.

There was a time when some black people thought that Mark Twain was prejudiced against them, and suggested barring his books. I'm glad this is in the past because he was anything but prejudiced against black people. In fact he was an outstanding supporter. A quote from "My First Lie" makes that clear:

> "It would not be possible for a humane and intelligent person to invent a rational excuse for slavery."

∎ ∎ ∎

Suggestion for Congress and the American People

Many years ago, when I read that Mark Twain said, "Government is organized imbecility," I thought he was being humorous. I'm not so sure now. For twenty-five years I've been trying to give the United States Government a great present.* But I've found that there's no place in government to receive presents. There are plenty of places to receive problems. However, I don't think we should pick on the politicians about this. I think we should pick on ourselves.

Congress and the President are supposed to have the most important jobs in the United States—they run our country. And we should pay them top salaries, but we don't even come close. Our Senators get $135,000, plus perks. Let's call it $150,000. The same for Congressmen. Our President gets $200,000, plus perks. For easy figuring, let's call it $300,000.

During the recent baseball strike you read that the average major league baseball player (there are 700 of them) received $1.2 million a year. In other words, the average baseball player earns eight times as much as a Member of Congress, and four times as much as our Chief Executive Officer, the President of the United States.

Here are some annual earnings of recent date:

Top CEOs (in millions): $25.9, 23.8, 16.6, 15.8, 14.7, 14.6, 13.7, 12.4, 12.3, 12.1　—*Business Week*

Top Athletes (in millions): $30.0, 16.7, 14.8, 13.6, 13.5, 13.5, 12.1, 12.0, 11.4, 11.3　—*Forbes*

I won't give you any more figures, you'll find them in the sports pages every day.

Suggestion—Let's pay our Senators $4 million, Members of the House $3 million, the President $7.5 million. If you say they're not worth it, that may be so. But that's just the point. If we pay outstanding salaries in government maybe we'll get outstanding people.

* Explained in *A Remarkable Medicine Has Been Overlooked.*

WALL STREET

When I was discharged from the Coast Guard, the law of gravity required I return to my job as a customer's broker at Merrill Lynch. I found that my best customer, who had been handled by a partner while I was away, did not want to change back to a customer's broker. It wasn't the partner's fault, but it didn't make me happy.

I had been in civilian life a few months when Chester Gaines, a specialist on the floor of the New York Stock Exchange, who played gin rummy with me at the City Athletic Club, told me that judging by my gin game, I would do well trading on the floor of the Exchange. I'd never thought of such a thing. Besides, it needed the purchase of a stock exchange seat. My capital for such a purchase was about 97 percent short.

In those days I used to play golf with a friend, Jerry Ohrbach, at Metropolis Country Club. One day, when we were in the same foursome, I got a seven on the first hole, an easy par-five. I was steaming, and asked Jerry what odds he would give against my getting a 33 on that nine. Par was 35, so that meant I would have to be four under for the next eight holes. Jerry said 1,000-to-1. I said I'll take a hundred dollars worth of that if you like, and he said okay. He could afford the hundred thousand and I could afford the hundred dollars. Jerry had the best of the odds and I had a shot at my Alan Rice fortune. I made him sweat to the last hole. I needed a birdie there for the thirty-three, but didn't come close.

When Chester Gaines made the suggestion of the stock exchange seat, I spoke to Jerry about it. He told me that the golf bet had scared him so much he would like to be partners with me. By borrowing from my father, one of my uncles, my wife, and adding my own few dollars, I got up 25 percent of the necessary capital. Jerry and his father, Nathan, put up the rest and became limited partners in the small firm, Dreyfus & Co., members of the New York Stock Exchange. And we lived happily ever after. Well, not quite.

We cleared through Bache & Co., the firm that had turned me down for a job as a customer's broker. John Behrens became a partner and handled business in the office.

I was on the floor of the Exchange. I executed orders for Bache, and traded for the firm's account, with a small amount of capital. The first year, we made $14,000 trading. Jerry and his father, Nathan, didn't realize how good that was. It was a bear market, the sort of market in which they say, "not even the liars made money."

Nathan Orbach had wandered into a brokerage firm in 1929 and had gotten the indestructible notion that you couldn't make money trading in the market, and wanted us to get into the brokerage business. One day Jerry introduced me to a partner of Lewisohn & Sons, a stock exchange firm that cleared its own transactions. The story was that the partners of Lewisohn were getting old and wanted to get out of the business. Another reason, which we didn't know at the time, was that the business was in bad shape.

Jerry thought we should take over the firm. I wasn't keen about this, knowing nothing about managing a brokerage firm, but went along with it because three of the partners were going to stay on. To shorten this story, after a year or so those partners were gone and I had to leave the floor, where I was reasonably competent, and start managing a brokerage firm, where I had no experience at all.

Business was bad. I cut my salary to zero, and the Ohrbachs didn't draw interest on their money. We couldn't even go out of business without considerable loss. In this pickle, we decided to try advertising. In those days New York Stock Exchange ads were proper—and dull. But if we wanted to advertise, the natural thing was to go to the agency that handled all the Wall Street advertising. The first and only ad they did for us, I wrote.

In those days the margin requirement for stocks was a ridiculously high 75 percent. I wanted to comment on that and wrote an ad titled "On Returning from the Moon." In the ad it was said, you have just returned from a five-year trip to the moon. Having made a fortune selling Blue Moon Cheese to the natives, you are anxious to invest some of this money. You haven't seen a stock table for five years and you ask your broker for vital statistics on five of your favorite stocks. After getting the statistics, you thought the stocks were reasonably priced and told your broker to buy 100 shares of each. Then the ad went on to say that all the statistics were correct, but the price of the stocks was one-half of what you'd been told. And it was suggested that the stocks were that cheap because of the ridiculously high margins.

Whether the ad had an effect or not, three weeks later the margin requirements were reduced to 50 percent.

It didn't take long for me to learn that the agency that did the Wall Street advertising was set in its ways. I went to a new, imaginative agency, Doyle, Dane & Bernbach. The first ad they wrote for us was different from Wall Street advertising, in appearance and in content. It said you don't have to be old-fashioned to be conservative. I wasn't crazy about that because it suggested that other firms were old-fashioned. When I was told that the agency planned to run this ad quite a few times (our budget, $20,000, was so small they couldn't afford to spend much time on new copy), I decided to try to write the ads myself.

This struck an unexpected aptitude in me. At that time I didn't realize that my copying device was faulty. This can be a hindrance, but in this case it was an advantage. I tried to do ads that would get attention and be enjoyable.

Freddy Dossenbach, our account executive, and I lunched at Schwartz's on Broad Street. Freddy would bring old prints and cartoons. Inspired by liverwurst, Swiss cheese, and iced tea, I would dream up copy to fit them. Our firm had little to brag about, so I just tried to give general advice hoping it would reflect favorably on us. Apparently it did. To my astonishment we won the first Standard & Poor's Gold Trophy for excellence in advertising. Some of the ads follow on the opposite page.

As a result of the ads some customer's brokers who had decided to leave their firms for one reason or another applied for jobs. When a customer's broker came with us, no matter how small his business, we ran a good-sized ad announcing that Joe Doaks had joined Dreyfus & Co. This ad was expensive, but valuable. Some of Joe Doaks' customers might have been thinking of leaving him, but seeing his name in the business section of the *Times* made a good impression. So it helped him with his customers, and it also helped him with potential customers. There was another benefit that I'm not sure I recognized at first. When customer's brokers considered leaving their firm, and that was always happening in the Street, they

"PETS" CAN BE EXPENSIVE

Too often, investors become sentimentally attached to stocks which have done well for them in the past. These "pets" can be expensive if they are allowed to prejudice sound judgment. Be sure that you use unsentimental, clear-headed analysis so that every stock in your portfolio today is there because of present merit.

Dreyfus & Co.

TODAY'S METHODS FOR TODAY'S MARKETS

EVERYBODY MISSES OCCASIONALLY

The successful investor recognizes that he will be wrong a certain percentage of the time – that everybody misses occasionally. Don't allow stubbornness or pride to keep you from admitting and correcting errors as quickly as possible. The times you are right will then work to your best advantage.

Dreyfus & Co.

TODAY'S METHODS FOR TODAY'S MARKETS

"WISHING WELL" WON'T WORK

There is no room for wishful thinking in your investment program. Keep in mind the security markets are not concerned with your desires. If you think clearly and unemotionally you are much more likely to get the best results.

Dreyfus & Co.

TODAY'S METHODS FOR TODAY'S MARKETS

NEEDLESS RISKS

Sometimes an investor acts like a man pulling a lion's tail – he takes risks with little or nothing to gain. When you speculate, or even when you invest, there is always some risk. But be sure that the possible gain more than offsets the risk you run. Expert advice can help you.

Dreyfus & Co.

TODAY'S METHODS FOR TODAY'S MARKETS

considered coming to Dreyfus & Co. because they knew they would see their names in the paper. So the firm grew steadily.

Sizable producers came with us. Some with so much business they insisted on partnerships. At that stage it seemed desirable to take on partners, if they were the right sort. Soon we had enough partners to always have a quorum for an argument.*

■ ■ ■

At the age of thirty-three, without experience, I found myself managing partner of the firm. Most of the customer's brokers were older than I. My only method was to try to work with people as friends. I could never boss people around. Once in a while somebody would call me "boss" and I would jump a foot. I don't like that word.

What I learned at Lehigh about wish-thinking and rationalization was solid. Almost all of the customer brokers felt they weren't being paid enough. Even when they knew they were being paid enough, they worried that a neighbor might be being paid more. (There were two brothers, not with us long, who were the worst. I used to say the Blank brothers were 100 percent honest, Max 60 percent and Arnold 40 percent.) I solved the problem for all by putting the customer's brokers on a sliding scale, the larger the production, the larger the percentage of commission.

I won't bore you, or myself, with the details of the growing of a brokerage firm. Just one illustration of my managerial skill.

One of our customer's brokers, a small producer, was making more errors than he brought us in commissions. English was not his native language. Finally I called Dan into my office, talked

---

* Over the years I've enjoyed partnerships with John Behrens, Samuel Pearson, Samuel Strasbourger, Robert Tulcin, John Cranley, Raymond Schibowski, Thomas Bligh and Duncan Cameron.

firmly to him, and told him he had to be more careful. He listened, and left. I was wondering if I'd done any good when the door opened a little. Dan's face came in, beaming. He said, "Don't worry, Jack, from now on I'll be at my wits' end." Success.

The firm continued to grow. The time came when our nice offices at 50 Broadway were too small, and we had to move. A new building was being built at 2 Broadway and, before it was finished, we took the top two floors. While they were being built, my former wife, Joan, made the wonderful suggestion that the window levels be lowered so that we could have a beautiful view of the harbor. It cost us $40,000 but it was well worth it.

When we moved into these offices with the wonderful view, I felt good about them and wanted the public to know about them. But my small ego wouldn't allow me to say it in a straight-forward fashion. Finally, after much thinking, we decided on a television ad.

I'd seen some wonderful cartoons on TV. I forget who did them. In them there were a couple of ping-pong players—elderly gentlemen who spoke with a British accent. The table they played on was small. They hit the ball back and forth in the air—it never touched the table.

Our agency designed an ad. A camera takes you through the entrance of a posh club and into a room where two old English gentlemen are playing ping-pong. After a few bats of the ball, one of them says, "Who's your broker, old chap?" The other says, "Broker?" The first one says "Yes, stocks and bonds, that sort of thing." The other says, "Oh, Dreyfus—Dreyfus & Company." The first says, "Why old chap?" Here you expect "a great research department" or something like that. But the response is, "Magnificent view of the harbor, boats and all that."

The ad was a lot of fun, and it got the idea across in the best way. It was popular and we ran it often. I remember when some

Germans came over to look at Wall Street advertising they selected our lion (I'll tell about him later) and the ping-pong players for reproduction in German. These old English gentlemen, talking in German, were a sight to hear.

■ ■ ■

One day John Nesbett, a fine gentleman, applied for a position as a customer's broker. John was the president of a small mutual fund, the Nesbett Fund, which he had been trying to develop for three years. The fund had only reached $500,000. With 1/2 percent management fee, John couldn't make a living.

When I had been a customer's broker with E. A. Pierce & Co. I had suggested to Mr. Pierce that a mutual fund would be a good idea, but nothing had happened. I still liked the idea. Unsophisticated investors would have their money handled by professionals, who spend their time studying the market. Also, as a customer's broker I'd noticed that if I had ten customers, seven might do well and three poorly. Not necessarily my fault, the three had an instinct for picking my worst recommendations. But I worried about those three. In a mutual fund, the investments would be the same for all.

An arrangement was made with John for the name of the Nesbett Fund to be changed to the Dreyfus Fund. He and I managed it jointly until he left, two or three years later. It took us nearly five years to get the size of the Dreyfus Fund up to a million dollars (mostly by stock appreciation). During this time, Dreyfus & Co. lost a lot of money on the Fund, and my partners started giving me strange looks. Fortunately the five-year performance of the Fund was so good that it became easier to sell.

Managers of a mutual fund have two chief responsibilities. First, and most important, is the management of the money in the fund. Second, for management to make money, advertising and promotion are necessary. Let me discuss the latter briefly, then the management of the Fund.

When the Fund was still very small, Frank Sweetser, who was with Value Line, suggested we needed a sales department, which we certainly did. Frank offered his services and they were accepted. After Frank had been with us a short while he suggested that our logo be changed from DF to a stylized lion, and we did this. A few years later Frank left us for greener fields, but I thank him for the lion.

One day Freddy Dossenbach and I were having lunch at Schwartz's. Over the Swiss cheese and liverwurst, I broached the subject of a TV advertisement for the Fund, with a live lion. Fred liked the idea and his firm went to work on producing it.

They did a splendid job. The commercial had a majestic lion coming up out of a Wall Street subway, walking casually past a news dealer, into our lobby at 2 Broadway, jumping up on a block of wood, and freezing into the Dreyfus Fund logo. This one-minute commercial was accompanied by the wonderful lion music of Saint-Saens' "Carnival of the Animals." During the lion's walk, an announcer, in a quiet voice, said, "The Dreyfus Fund is a mutual fund in which management hopes to make your money grow, and takes what it considers sensible risks in that direction."

The advertisement was a great success. Nobody got tired of the lion, or the music. That was fortunate because we had to run the same ad thousands of times—shortly after it was approved the SEC put restrictions on TV commercials.

My inability to copy was valuable in the Dreyfus Fund prospectus. Other prospectuses were written by lawyers. Not knowing any better, I wrote the nontechnical part of our prospectus.

I was surprised and delighted when *Barron's National Business and Financial Weekly* made the nice comment: "Dreyfus Fund's latest prospectus is like none we have ever seen. Instead of the usual forbidding makeup with its weighty and legalistic prose, Dreyfus has substituted color and supplied the facts in an attractive manner...Dreyfus is the first fund to acknowledge, in its prospectus, that the average small investor is not a financial lawyer. And this is quite a step forward."

One day Freddy Dossenbach and I were lunching at Schwartz's with a representative from the *New York Times* who made the suggestion that we put the balance sheet of our prospectus in a Sunday *Times* supplement. I enlarged on the idea, and we put the entire prospectus in the Sunday *Times*, as a supplement. It was excellent advertising, and we used the supplement as our official prospectus—a bargain, the *Times* sold us copies for three cents apiece.

■ ■ ■

As to the management of the Fund. I'm keenly aware that today's markets are vastly different from the markets of those days. Today there are options, puts and calls, indexes, and other things. Today 400 million shares a day are ordinary. In those days, the average volume was three to four million shares. But I think certain fundamentals still exist.

The management fee of $2,500 (1/2 percent of $500,000) was so small when we started the Fund that we couldn't afford a research staff. A young man, Alex Rudnicki, and I ran the Fund. Alex was a nice boy, extremely shy—even more shy than I. We were so shy that neither of us had the courage to call an officer of a company and ask how the company was doing. Maybe this was an asset. According to the Arthur Wiesenberger report, during the twelve years Alex and I made the decisions the Dreyfus Fund outperformed all other mutual funds, by a large margin.

Alex was never found without a Standard & Poor's or Moody's booklet in his pocket. Alex was strong on the fundamentals. He had been a student at the Graham Dodd School of Investing. Graham Dodd believed that if a stock had $12 in cash, it was all right to pay $8 for it. I'm exaggerating a little, but the principles were that you had to be very sound. My method, of course, was different. I didn't object to soundness, but I was interested in market timing.

I had used weekly bar charts, posted daily, from my beginning in Wall Street. I found these the best for me. Daily charts gave too many opinions, monthly charts didn't give enough. So weekly charts, posted daily, and *looked at daily*, were what we used. We had six hundred of them made up, on a large scale. I didn't try to squeeze opinions out of the charts. Perhaps 5 percent of the time a chart position formed which, based on my experience, indicated the stock a probable buy or sale (in those days funds were not permitted to sell short). Then we acted. Even then we made enough mistakes to satisfy ourselves. When the stock didn't act as we expected, we took our loss. We didn't want to become what was called "involuntary investors."

In our commercials we said, "We're trying to make your money grow and management takes what it considers sensible risks in that direction." But how did we think of that money? Well, I struck on an idea which we used. We thought of it as our mother's money. The emphasis was on *our*. If it was someone else's mother's money we would be inhibited by what her accountant or her lawyer would think. This was our mother's money. At the same time it was a mother's money, so we were not going to take wild risks.

We always had in mind that the dollar bill was just a piece of paper. It would seem that if you wanted to be careful, you'd just keep the paper. But there were signs of inflation, and keeping the paper wouldn't necessarily keep the purchasing power. You just couldn't buy bonds and be safe, you couldn't buy stocks and be safe. You had to keep thinking.

One of our general rules was to follow the major trend. Markets in those days—not as much now—had major trends. The markets tended to go up as a unit, or down as a unit. If you've got an escalator that's going up, you're better off betting on an individual on that escalator than on an individual on an escalator that's going down. The whole market was like an escalator. In other words, if a company did poorly, a bull market escalator would usually keep it from going down. The opposite was so in a bear market. Of course there were exceptions.

Although it was our mother's money, we had our minimum limits. We didn't often buy "cats and dogs" (that was an expression in those days)—they call them secondary stocks now. Occasionally we did, but I was careful about it. That's where Alex and his Moody's handbook helped.

A fundamental fact of the market was explained, I think by Jeb Stuart or Stonewall Jackson (not General Schwarzkopf), who said, "Get there fustus with the mostus." That meant that you can win a battle, even if you've got a smaller number of people, if you get there first. In the days that I'm talking about, margin accounts swung the whole market. They were a small part of the total investment holdings, but margin traders worked in concert—the investors worked individually. When an investor sold his house, he might invest the proceeds in the stock market. If he wanted to buy a house, or spend money, he would sell stock to do it. But that wasn't in concert with other investors. And the investment accounts managed by the banks and investment funds were not too flexible. In those days there was a little bit of "buy a good stock, put it away, and forget about it."

But the margin accounts were very flexible. They were in constant touch with their brokers. When a piece of news occurred, they responded. Obviously, they had varying opinions.

The only time they worked in concert, unfortunately, was when they were overextended. When too many of them were fully margined and the market went down, the brokers had to call the weakest accounts for more money. Many of these accounts didn't have more money and the only way of getting it was by selling stock. This would cause the market to break and then the next group of accounts would come under pressure. This continued until those who were on the most conservative margins had to sell. There had been a domino effect (I hate the expression). When the margin accounts had been cleaned out there was usually a good deal of pessimism, and the market was usually a buy.

We must keep in mind that being bullish doesn't put the market up. Having purchasing power is what puts the market up. Being bearish doesn't put the market down. Having selling power, being long of stock, can put it down. So, comparatively speaking, a small segment of the investment public, the margin trader, had a lot to do with market swings.

The short interest was an important gauge. It was like a Gallup poll of market sentiment with the margin traders. Most people didn't sell short, but you knew that when the short interest was high, a large percentage of the other margin accounts would be in cash. When the short interest was low, you knew the margin traders were mostly long of stock. That was the most reliable way of knowing what the margin players were doing.

In the management of the Fund, we had certain principles. One of these was to not pound the table when we had an idea. The reason for that was simple. Once you pound the table, you take away some of your flexibility (it's harder to admit you were wrong). And admitting that we were wrong was something that we put high on the list, because taking losses early is a valuable thing when you're speculating in the market. So we never pounded the table.

As I said earlier we tried to follow the major trends. We thought of the money as our mother's money. We tried to be flexible. But the only rule we had, that was an absolute rule, was to keep thinking.

■ ■ ■

There was one stock that was an exception to our flexibility rule. We bought it for long-term investment. The stock was Polaroid. It was by accident that I knew about Polaroid. My brother-in-law, Dr. Elkan Blout, was head of research at the company and told me about the 3-D glasses they were making. Some of you will recall that for a while movies were being made in three-dimensions. It required special glasses to see them.

Taken with a Polaroid camera— enjoyed sixty seconds later.

Once I got interested in Polaroid, because of the glasses, my upside-downness saw the value of the camera. I thought if that had been the first camera invented, you would have had a devil of a time selling an Eastman Kodak camera, even with its larger picture and negative.

The Dreyfus Fund took a large position in Polaroid. Dreyfus & Co., of which I owned about 51 percent, did also. Polaroid was an outstanding growth company.

Dr. Blout introduced me to Hal Booth, Vice President in charge of advertising at Polaroid. I designed a few ads, which Hal ran. I include one here, with a picture of my son Johnny, and my bulldog Henry.

■ ■ ■

When I found it necessary to retire from the management of the Fund, for reasons of medical research, I had an important decision to make. Who should take my job as head of the Dreyfus Fund? A fine firm called Head Hunters introduced me to four candidates, one at a time. After each introduction, Howard Stein, in our own organization, began to look better and better. I offered Howard the position and he accepted. One of the best decisions of my life. When Howard took over the management of the Fund it was less than $1 billion. With his creative management the Dreyfus Corporation now manages over $70 billion. Howard is one of my best friends.

To shift to today's markets for a moment. The indexes are not a large part of the investments, but they have a powerful effect. You can buy an interest in hundreds of stocks in an index on less than 10 percent margin. But if you want to buy General Motors or Dupont, you have to put up 50 percent. This is one of the strangest things I have ever seen. It happened when I was looking the other way—not that I care one way or the other. But you have in those indexes a tail that can wag the dog.

It's just possible the market of 1987 was an index market. You don't have bear markets that quickly. While people were looking for the second leg of the bear market to go down, the whole bear market had happened, not just one leg, but a leg, an ankle and a foot.

I don't want the reader to get the impression that markets of today can be approached with the methods of twenty-five years ago. Let me say flatly they can't. Today's markets are no longer dominated by margin traders. The investor's money is largely in the hands of professionals, mutual funds, and other funds. Many of these investors are not on margin. Although these managers are flexible, they don't act in concert.

I'd like to be able to give you a suggestion as to how to manage money now, but I'm not competent to do so. However, I think some general advice is as good now as it was then.

About fifty years ago, Tobias Stone, an excellent bridge player and friend, and I were dining sumptuously at Horn & Hardart's Automat (35 cents apiece). Stoney asked me a hypothetical question, what would I do if I had a million dollars. I asked him what he would do if he found himself on the moon. But his question stimulated a thought. I asked him, if he had a million dollars, would he bet it if someone offered him ten-to-one on the toss of a coin? He said, "Of course. I'd be getting so much the best of the odds." I told him he was nuts. His first million was worth a lot more than the next ten million, so he'd be getting the worst of the odds. That brings us to the general subject of investments.

A young person with $30,000 and a good salary should not be unwilling to put that money in a speculative account. If it's lost, it's not a disaster since most of his capital is his earning power. On the other hand, an older person with a substantial amount of money and not much earning ability, I believe, should put 25-40 percent of his money in very conservative holdings and the rest in the hands of someone who would try to make the money grow. No longer can one keep one's money in dollar bills because of inflation. There's no sure way to be safe and one should split the difference.

One other thing. Unless you have made a study of the market and have time to continue to study it, and have confidence in your judgment, it's well worth a half a percent or one percent to put your money in the hands of professionals. Good professionals will keep up to date on current events and study the many factors that are involved in this complicated market, and earn their money. Of course some professionals are better than others. If one wants, one can diversify by putting his or her money in the hands of more than one professional.

Let us leave Wall Street now.

The last thirty-five years of my life have been occupied with medical research. It's a different field, but in it objectivity and sense of probabilities are the same.

A Remarkable Medicine Has Been Overlooked, which follows, was written sixteen years ago, before my autobiography was even thought of. For that reason there will be a slight amount of repetition. Please forgive it. This is an urgent matter. Besides, there may be many who read *A Remarkable Medicine* without reading the autobiography.

At the end of *A Remarkable Medicine* there will be a new chapter. Following that there will be the Clinical Section and a summary of the "Basic Mechanisms of Action" from *The Broad Range of Clinical Use of Phenytoin*.

A REMARKABLE MEDICINE HAS BEEN OVERLOOKED

When *A Remarkable Medicine* was published by Pocket Books in 1982, quotations from the lay and medical press were included. Some are reprinted here.

"'Jack Dreyfus, Maverick Wizard Behind the Wall Street Lion' was the title of a long article in *Life* back in 1966... His book is sure to become a classic."

—HARRY SCHWARTZ
Fortune

"The Foundation's efforts to examine PHT in such extraordinary detail represents the first time in medical history that a single substance has been so thoroughly investigated as a potential remedy for such a variety of aches and ills."

—ALBERT ROSENFELD
Science 81

"How Jack Dreyfus became acquainted with this remarkable medication is a story that's exciting and full of human drama. It should be a best-seller."

—*The Berkshire Eagle*

"As a rule, I'm not much for battle stories. But *A Remarkable Medicine Has Been Overlooked* is an exception. Dreyfus deserves our admiration for his truly heroic efforts."

—RUTH B. SCHWARTZ
The American Council on Science andHealth

"Dreyfus, a winning competitor in whatever he attempts...the book contains an exhaustive bibliography and abstracts from 2,140 published references to PHT research."

—*Medical World News*

"A man who cannot be overlooked... Dreyfus tells the story of his experiences with simplicity and humor...."
—*MD Magazine*

"I believe this book is a labor of love by a man who has chosen to take on the established mode of looking at things that often precludes fresh thinking."
—SUSANNE HARVEY
Pharmaceutical Executive

"This successful author is the founder of the Dreyfus Mutual Fund, a power on Wall Street. How he got out of his Wall Street business to establish and work in a charitable medical foundation is a story in itself... a service to physicians."
—BETH HARRIS
Desert Sun

"This remarkable man has sketched in simple and beautiful prose the story of his life..."
—RAY KERRISON
New York Post

"Nobody doubts that Dreyfus has a good deal more than a lick of sense... His message is simple: PHT, best known as the antiepilepsy drug Dilantin, has been shown rigorously to be useful for the treatment of more ailments than any other compound known to medical science."
—WILLIAM HINES
Chicago Sun-Times

"A book with a dramatic and often spellbinding quality—on the side of the angels."
—PETER SCHWED
Turning the Pages

The drug that is the subject of this book is known by two generic names, diphenylhydantoin and phenytoin. Phenytoin (PHT) is used in this book.

PHT is a prescription medicine, which means it should be obtained through a physician.

CONTENTS

TO THE READER

In 1963 a great piece of luck led me to ask my physician for a medicine that was not supposed to be useful for the symptoms I had. It took me out of a miserable condition. When I saw six others have similar benefits, I felt I had the responsibility of getting the facts to the medical profession. This was not as easy to do as I thought. I had to retire from two successful Wall Street businesses. A medical foundation was established. Soon it became apparent that the medicine had been overlooked for the widest variety of disorders.

This book begins with a letter to President Reagan in which this matter is outlined and his help was sought.

For eight years, from 1966 through 1973, I did all I could to awaken the federal government to its obvious responsibilities in this matter with little success. By 1975, the Foundation had sent two extensive bibliographies on PHT to all the physicians in the U.S.* When the second bibliography had been sent to physicians, it seemed that all a private foundation could do had been done. And there was progress, but it was slow. Something was wrong.

It's a national pastime to look for culprits. I looked for culprits but I didn't find individual ones. It took me a long time to realize that the culprit was a flaw in our system of bringing prescription medicines to the public.

The only option left was for me to write about my experiences and explain the flaw in our system for the public, the physician, and health officials, all at the same time. That might get something done.

Nowadays, when you start to read a book, a hand reaches out of the TV set and takes it off your lap. Since this book is about health, you might consider cracking the hand across the knuckles and keep on reading.

Good luck,
JACK DREYFUS

Note: The following letter to former President Reagan was written in 1981. It was an introduction to the original book. It is retained here because it gives a good outline of the matter.

---

* Since this letter was written: In 1988, a third bibliography, containing 3,100 medical references, was sent to all the physicians in the U.S., along with a copy of *A Remarkable Medicine Has Been Overlooked.*

DREYFUS MEDICAL FOUNDATION
NEW YORK, NEW YORK

August 5, 1981

The President
The White House
Washington, D.C.

DEAR PRESIDENT REAGAN:

I write you about a matter of such urgency and importance that it requires the attention of your office.

The properties of a remarkable and versatile medicine are being overlooked because of a flaw in our system of bringing medicines to the public. This is to the great detriment of the health of the American public, and many millions of people suffer because of it. This tragic condition can be remedied.

This letter is meant as a briefing, Mr. President. Material outlined in it will be expanded on elsewhere.

The medicine is a prescription medicine. Its best known trade name is Dilantin; generic, phenytoin (PHT). The first disorder for which it was found useful was epilepsy. This was in 1938. In those days it was customary to think of a single drug for a single disorder, and PHT promptly got the tag "anticonvulsant."

Since this early discovery, many thousand medical studies have demonstrated PHT to be one of the most widely useful drugs in our pharmacopoeia. Yet today, forty-one years later, PHT's only listed indication-of-use with the Food and Drug Administration is as an anticonvulsant. This description is accurate but tragically misleading and plays a major role in the misunderstanding of PHT by the medical profession.

If you will look at the Table of Contents (pp. 305–10), it will give you an idea of the breadth of use of PHT. It's been reported useful for over 50 symptoms and disorders, in over 250 medical journals throughout the world.*

When we see the number of symptoms and disorders for which PHT has been found therapeutic, our credulity is strained. Nothing could be that good, we say. But then we look closer, and we reevaluate. In number the studies are overwhelming. Not having been sponsored by a drug company they were spontaneous and independent, the authors' only motivation being scientific interest and a desire to help others.

A brief discussion of the basic mechanisms of action of phenytoin will be helpful. A general property of PHT is that it corrects inappropriate electrical activity in the body, even at the level of the single cell. When we consider that most of our bodily functions are electrically regulated, our messages of pain are electrically referred, and our thinking processes are electrically conducted, it makes it easy to understand PHT's breadth of use.

Although PHT corrects inappropriate electrical activity, in therapeutic amounts it does not affect normal function. Thus it can calm without sedation and effect a return of energy without artificial stimulation. PHT is not habit-forming, and its parameters of safety have been established over a forty-year period.**

You may ask, Mr. President, why I haven't brought this matter to the Department of Health or the Food and Drug Administration. Well, that was the first thing I thought of years ago. And for eight years I spent an eternity with officials in government, being shuffled back and forth from one to another with encouragement and even compliments. During this period I saw three Secretaries of HEW, two Assistant Secretaries of HEW,

---

* That was in 1981. Today the figures would be over 70 symptoms and disorders, in over 350 medical journals.
** Sixteen more years since this paragraph was written.

two Commissioners of the FDA, members of the staff of the FDA, a Surgeon General, and other officials.

It took me a long time to realize this was the wrong approach. Although everyone agreed that something should be done, no official seemed to think he had the authority or responsibility to get it done. (See "Travels with the Government," p. 200.)

About the flaw in our system for bringing prescription medicines to the public:

Years ago doctors concocted their own remedies, but that's in the past. Today the origination of new drugs is left to the drug companies motivated by that reliable incentive, the desire to make profits. Between the public and the drug company is the FDA.

The FDA was set up to do for many individuals what they could not do for themselves. Although its broad purpose was to improve the health of our citizens, it was set up as a defensive agency, to protect against ineffective drugs and those more dangerous than therapeutic, and was not equipped to reach out for an overlooked drug.

Since 1938 drug companies have been required to seek approval from the FDA as to the safety of new drugs and, since 1962, approval of both safety and effectiveness. When an FDA listing is granted it entitles a company to promote a drug for the purposes for which it has been approved. If the drug sells well the company has a good thing. Patent protection gives up to seventeen years of exclusive use. During this period profit margins are high. When patents expire, the financial incentive to look for a new drug is far greater than it is to study new uses of an old drug.

The process patents on PHT expired in 1963 and much of the incentive to do research on the drug expired at the same time. It should be noted that Parke-Davis, the company that had the patents on PHT, did not synthesize the drug, and physicians outside the company discovered it to be therapeutic. There is reason to believe that Parke-Davis never understood its own product. In addition to no patent incentive, this could be a reason it has not applied to the FDA for new uses.*

The public's access to a prescription medicine is through the physician. Physicians get their information about prescription medicines from the drug companies, through advertisements and salesmen, and from the *Physicians' Desk Reference*, which carries only those uses for a drug that are listed with the FDA.

One can see how an FDA listing may carry more weight than is intended. In fact some people think of the lack of FDA approval as the equivalent of FDA disapproval. This is clearly wrong. How could the FDA disapprove a use for a drug if it hasn't even had an application for it?**

Let's look at the overall picture. Doctors were taught that PHT is an anticonvulsant. The usual sources that the doctors rely on for prescription medicines only indicate that PHT is an anticonvulsant. Is it any wonder that doctors have PHT out of perspective, and that as far as the public is concerned most of the benefits of PHT might as well not exist?

It is apparent that no drug company is going to apply for new uses of PHT. The clock has run down on that probability. Perhaps the FDA does not have a specific means to reach out for this medicine. But since the FDA's broad purpose is to protect the health of the American public, the neglect of a remarkable drug should be in its province, and a means should be found.

A simple solution would be to put the matter in the hands of those qualified—the 450,000† physicians in this country. The FDA could address itself to the basic mechanisms of action of PHT and list it as a substance effective in the stabilization of bioelectrical activity, and refer the physicians to the literature of

*   One exception, see A Flaw in the System.
**   The FDA has made this clear in their 1982 Bulletin. (See Appendix, p. 424.)
†   Now over 510,000.

their colleagues. There are other solutions. The fact is any official nod from the FDA to the physician would let the light shine from under the bushel, and PHT would find its own level, pragmatically, by its use vis-à-vis other medicines.

Mr. President, this letter is a public one because it is also meant for government officials in health as well as for physicians and the public. The information in this book, for all to see at the same time, should be helpful if you decide to use the influence of your office in this matter. I hope you will. I think you will.

Respectfully,

Jack Dreyfus

Dreyfus Medical Foundation

FROM INSIDE A DEPRESSION

Until I was in my forties, I never really thought about my nerves—a sure symptom of a person with good nerves. I was President of the Dreyfus Fund and a partner in Dreyfus & Co., with responsibilities in research, in sales, and in management. People would ask, "How do you do all the things you do?" "How do you stand the strain?" I hardly understood the question because at the time I felt no strain.

Sometime in my forty-fifth year I became aware of a change in myself. At partners' meetings, which I'd used to enjoy, I began to notice that my patience was shorter and I was anxious for the meetings to end. Occasionally I felt a trembling inside me that I didn't understand. On weekend trips to the country it had been my habit to read or take a nap in the car. These trips had been relaxing, but they weren't anymore. My mind would become occupied with pessimistic and aggravating thoughts, thoughts I couldn't turn off.

In 1958 I had spent a few trying weeks with a problem in the stock market. It was resolved successfully, but I had been under a good deal of pressure and needed a vacation. I went to Miami and stayed at the Roney Plaza, a nice old-fashioned hotel that I had visited many times before. Usually after a day or two, with the sun and salt water, I would unwind and relax. But this time I didn't relax.

Some premonition made me invite a good friend, Howard Stein, to come down and join me. Howard accepted, and the next day he was at the Roney. Two days later my depression started.

■ ■ ■

I awoke at six o'clock in the morning in a state bordering on terror. The early sun was shining, and the birds were singing. In my room at the Roney I was in the safest of surroundings. Yet I was overwhelmed with fear. The fear couldn't have been greater if a tiger had been clawing at the door. I knew there wasn't any tiger, and common sense told me I was safe. But common sense wasn't in charge—fear was. The fear was so great I was afraid to be alone. I called Howard, at that early hour, and asked if he would come to my room. When he got there I told him I knew it didn't make any sense but I was afraid to be alone.

Howard arranged for me to see a doctor, and a few hours later we were in his office. The doctor said, "Miami is the right place for you. Get some sun, go swimming, play a little golf or tennis, and relax." Normally this would have sounded great. But now this advice didn't seem right, and at two o'clock that afternoon I was on a plane back to New York. Although it was a Saturday and I wouldn't see my doctor until Monday, I hoped more familiar surroundings would make me feel better.

I still remember that trip. The plane was half-filled and I had a seat in a row by myself. Even with a dozen or more people in the plane I felt alone, and was afraid. I wanted to ask one of the stewardesses to sit next to me and keep me company, but I didn't because I thought it would be misunderstood. I couldn't tell a stewardess that I was afraid to sit by myself.

My former wife, Joan Personette, one of my closest friends, met me at the plane, and I spent the weekend at her home in Harrison, New York. It was difficult to explain to Joan how frightened I was. My brain was filled with fearful thoughts I couldn't turn off. Saturday night I slept little. Sunday we went out in the cold weather and roasted hot dogs over a fire— something I'd always enjoyed. But this didn't help. The intense fear never left me.

On Monday morning I saw Alfred Steiner, my family physician. He sent me to a neuropsychiatrist, Dr. Maximilian Silbermann. The first question I asked was, "Have I gone crazy?" I'd never had an experience like this intense fear without apparent cause. And my mood was so pessimistic that the worst seemed plausible. Dr. Silbermann assured me that I was sane but said he thought I was depressed. I remember that he said, "When people are insane, they may think others are a little off, but they rarely question their own sanity."

That first day Dr. Silbermann asked me what I liked to do, what I really enjoyed. I told him that going to the racetrack was something I enjoyed a lot. He said, "Well, why don't you go to the races tomorrow? Don't worry about business." He also suggested that I not be alone and have someone spend the night with me in my apartment.

The next day I intended to go to the races. But I didn't. They had no appeal for me, and even seemed a problem. That day, when I saw him for the second time, Dr. Silbermann diagnosed my condition as an endogenous depression. He explained that endogenous meant "coming from within," and he differentiated it from a reactive depression, one with an outside cause. He assured me that this condition was temporary and that I would come out of the depression. He said he didn't know how long it would take; it could be gradual or it could happen suddenly. Being told this was important to me intellectually, but emotionally I had a hard time believing it.

That was the beginning of a long and close relationship with Dr. Silbermann. For the next few years I was to see him five or six times a week. From the start Dr. Silbermann told me that good sleep was important for my condition and prescribed sleeping medication. With the help of this medicine I slept soundly, and the benefits of sleep carried over. In the morning I was at my best. As the day wore on my mind became busier and busier with worries and fears, and occasional angry thoughts. Frequently around dusk a little depressive cloud would descend upon me; I would tremble and my hands and feet would get cold.

Seeing Dr. Silbermann almost every day was important to me. In his warm office, with his friendliness and willingness to listen, I would unburden my brain of the thoughts that were tormenting me. But intense fear persisted for almost a year. During that period I was afraid to be alone, and I arranged for my housekeeper to spend the night at my apartment.

Of course I had my business responsibilities, and I asked Dr. Silbermann what to do about them. He told me that people misunderstood depressions, and it might be best not to tell anyone about it. He suggested that I leave it vague and say I would be away from the office for a period of time. But this was in conflict with my sense of responsibility, and I didn't feel right about it. Mark Twain advised, "When in doubt, tell the truth." So I told the truth to my partners and asked them to run things without me for a while. Although I was not aware of feeling better, a realistic source of worry was removed.

Dr. Silbermann advised me to try to get out of the house and keep myself occupied, as long as I could do things that were not abrasive to me. I visited museums. One of my main haunts was the Museum of Modern Art and I had many lunches in the cafeteria there. I became friends with the paintings and with the sculptures in the backyard. The attention I gave these pleasing objects was helpful in taking attention off myself. I had similar benefits from the Central Park Zoo where I spent time with the seals, polar bears, and other nice creatures.

I tried to avoid things that would upset me. I found that my mind would magnify the slightest unpleasantness by some large multiple. Newscasts were anathema to me and I couldn't listen to them. If a busload of children overturned in Nevada the news would be dragged fresh and gory to our attention in New York. I quickly learned that the news, with its disaster *du jour*, made things worse. One piece of news I couldn't avoid was the dog in the Sputnik space capsule. I couldn't get it out of my mind, and I suffered with thoughts of that dog for many weeks.

I gave up watching movies on television. There'd be some sad theme or violent incident that would upset me, and the image of it would stick in my head. I had a similar problem with most books. One author I could always read was Mark Twain. I'm sure I missed many of his subtleties but he never dragged me through unpleasantness.

When I'd been in the depression for about six months Dr. Silbermann asked me if I thought it might make me feel better to be in a hospital. I said I didn't know but I was willing to try it. So he got me a room at the Harkness Pavilion of Presbyterian Hospital. In the room I noticed that the windows were discreetly barred, and I asked the nurse about this. She explained that sometimes deeply depressed persons had to be protected from themselves.

Fortunately I was not classified as deeply depressed. I had outpatient privileges and walked in the neighborhood a few hours each day. It was cold and I would have a bowl of hot soup in a nice little corner restaurant. During the walks I had plenty of time to think. The conversation with the nurse reminded me that Dr. Silbermann had once tactfully brought up the subject of suicide. Now I gave it honest thought and realized I'd never considered it. Not that life seemed that desirable. At that time everyone was talking about the next rocket to the moon, the first to carry men. In my mood I thought chances for success were almost nil. But I remember thinking if a high authority told me it was for the good of the country I might be willing to make the trip.

After three days in the hospital, not feeling better or worse, I returned home. Each day Dr. Silbermann and I talked over my, mostly imagined, problems. Part of me knew that some of the worries were not logical, but the rest of me couldn't feel it. Max cautioned me not to make any major business decisions while I was depressed because my perspective would be out of kilter. This was good advice. The Dreyfus Fund was not large at that time, but quite successful, and the only problems it had were the healthy ones connected with growth. Yet on more than one occasion I wished I could give the Fund away.

My apartment was just a few blocks from Dr. Silbermann's office. Often I would leave for my appointment as much as an hour early and kill time by walking. I usually felt cold, and would seek the sunny side of the street. After the appointment, if it was daylight, I would walk in Central Park. I would still try to stay in the sun. As the shadows moved across the park I would walk faster to keep ahead of them.

During these walks I used to think about my condition. I was aware of daily headaches, frequent stomach irregularity, chronic neck pain, and lack of energy. But my dominant symptom was a turned-on mind that never gave me rest and was always occupied with negative thoughts related to anger and fear. And the fear was the worst.

When you have fear in you, you'll find something to be afraid of or to worry about, even if you have to make it up. This happened to me all the time. I'll give two illustrations.

One Sunday, on Madison Avenue, I saw a woman looking at a dress in a small shop. She seemed to be looking at it longingly, as though she wanted it but couldn't afford it. I felt unhappy for her. The dress looked so old-fashioned and unattractive it made me feel even sadder. Now this woman was a complete stranger. For all I knew she might have been able to buy that block of Madison Avenue. But my mood made me decide she couldn't afford the dress. This unhappy picture stuck in my brain and bothered me for days.

Another incident occurred at a cocktail party. One of the guests, a young girl of seventeen, was introduced as the daughter of a famous movie actress. She mentioned that she would have to leave in a little while because she was taking dancing lessons. The girl seemed plain-looking and I felt sad for her. I knew she didn't have a chance to be successful, and was trying to follow in her mother's footsteps because it was the thing to do. When she left, she kissed us all good-bye. She'd even adopted Hollywood ways, and this made me feel even sadder. I worried about this poor girl for many days. It wasn't really necessary—the "poor girl" was Liza Minnelli.

It is almost impossible to convey to a person who has not had a depression what one is like. It's not obvious like a broken arm, or a fever, or a cough; it's beneath the surface. A depressed person suffers a type of anguish which in its own way can be as painful as anything that can happen to a human being. He has varying degrees of fear throughout the day, and a brain that permits him no rest and races with agitated and frightening thoughts. His mood is low, he has little energy, and he can hardly remember what pleasure means. He's in another country, using a different language. When he uses words such as "worry" and "afraid" he may be expressing deep distress. But these words seem mild to the person whose mood is all right.

■ ■ ■

The deepest part of my depression lasted for about a year. Then it lessened gradually and there were periods of improvement. These better periods alternated with periods of mild depression for the next few years. "Mild" depression is plenty unpleasant, but I use the term to distinguish it from severe depression.

It began to look as if chronic depressive periods might be with me for life. Then I had an incredible piece of luck.

AN INCREDIBLE PIECE OF LUCK

Dr. Silbermann and I had numerous discussions about why I was depressed, without reaching any conclusions. There was a theory, proffered by relatives of mine in Boston, that I was neurotic and needed to be psychoanalyzed. Dr. Silbermann didn't agree that psychoanalysis was what I needed, and as a practical matter felt that it would be too arduous while I was depressed.

On my own, as objectively as I could, I considered my relatives' suggestion. I didn't question that I was neurotic. But I didn't see how that could be the answer. Presumably I'd been neurotic before the depression, yet my nerves had been fine.

I began to notice that changes in my mood frequently occurred without apparent environmental or psychological cause. And the same stimulus didn't always evoke the same response. Sometimes, while driving in the country, I would see a dead woodchuck on the side of the road. The sight would hit me like a blow and I couldn't get it out of my mind. But on other occasions I'd see a dead woodchuck and react in what seemed a normal way. The difference in reactions couldn't be caused by my being neurotic; my childhood from one to five hadn't changed. It seemed plausible that these disparate reactions were due to changes in my body.

I discussed this with Dr. Silbermann, and he was inclined to go along with the idea that there might be something wrong in my body "chemistry." But Max said that he didn't really know, and emphasized that when he said "chemistry," he was using the word in quotes.

■ ■ ■

One night, a seemingly insignificant incident started a chain of events that changed my life. A young woman took my hand and massaged my fingers. I was full of tension at the time. As she pressed my fingertips I felt the tension slip away, and I had the feeling that electricity was going out of my body. This didn't make sense to me. I'd never heard of electricity in the body—but the impression was strong. The next day, a Sunday, the impression of electricity was still with me.

It's a misconception, I believe, that we originate ideas. I used to think we did, but I don't anymore. Too often I find my brain does what it wants—it's on automatic pilot most of the time. That was the case this particular Sunday because, without instruction from me, my brain went into its files and came up with three experiences I'd had with electricity. The first went back almost forty years.

One. When I was a little boy I saw a brass plate with a hole in it, in the baseboard. It aroused my curiosity. I stuck my finger in the hole and my curiosity was satisfied. The electric shock I got, and the sudden, intense fear that came with it, were indelibly impressed on my memory. I remember that after the shock I had a flat, metallic taste in my mouth.

Two. I had gone into a garage with my former wife to get the car. I picked up an old vacuum cleaner, to get it out of the way, and received an electrical jolt. I said to Joan, "This damn thing shocked me."

"It always does that," she said quietly.

At this calm appraisal I exploded. "What do you mean, 'It always does that!'" and I took Joan by the shoulders and shook her. This was so unlike me that I felt my explosion of anger had been caused by the electricity.

Three. On two successive nights I'd had the same frightening dream, or was it a dream? Each of these nights, before going to sleep, I had intense feelings of fear. The "dreams" occurred early in the morning. I felt that I was awake and couldn't open my eyes. I tried to reach for the table light but couldn't move—in the dream I felt I was frozen with electricity.

Each of these experiences with electricity was associated with a symptom of my depression. As I reviewed them, side by side so to speak, they seemed to be related. Numbers one and three made a connection between electricity and fear. Number two connected electricity with anger. And number one also made a connection with the metallic taste in my mouth which I associated with fear.

The logic of these connections was not clear then. But the pieces held together well enough for me to say to myself, When I see Max on Monday I am going to bring up the subject of electricity.

That Monday my appointment with Dr. Silbermann was after dinner, around ten o'clock. I had some "problems" that I wanted to talk out. It wasn't until late in the hour that I brought up the subject of electricity. I said to Max, "You know, I think my problem is electricity, and electricity causes some people to get depressed, others to bump themselves off, and others to go crazy." I said this as though I meant it, but actually I had little conviction.

At that moment my brain jumped back twenty years to a bridge tournament. My partner and I had got the best of two hands, and one of our opponents, a famous player, P. Hal

Sims, made some pointed remarks to his partner. I noticed the partner's neck getting red. As we moved to the next table there was a commotion, and I turned and saw the man on the floor, having convulsions. Someone said he was having an epileptic attack. Now, as I thought back to the attack, the convulsions looked like they had been caused by a series of electrical shocks.

I continued with my hypothesis and said, "And some people have an electrical explosion which we call epilepsy." Max said, "It's curious that you mention epilepsy. We know from brain wave tests that the epileptic has a problem with his body electricity." This was the first time I'd heard that there was such a thing as body electricity. Also, connecting the epileptic to an electrical problem was a direct hit. When I'd started the discussion I'd thought the odds were 10,000-to-1 against me. But now the odds dropped sharply, and they were realistic enough to make the subject worth pursuing.

I knew a girl who'd had an epileptic attack when she was six. She was now fifteen and seemed to be leading a normal and happy life. She had been given a medicine for her epilepsy and I asked Dr. Silbermann what it was. He told me it was Dilantin.

"Well, why don't I try that?" I asked.

I didn't realize then how crucial Max's answer would be for me. He could easily have said no—and that might have been the end of it. But he said, "You can try it if you like. I don't think it will do you any good, but it won't do you any harm."

That night Max gave me a prescription for Dilantin and told me of an all-night drugstore where I could fill it. He suggested that I take 100 mg before going to bed and skip my sleeping pill. He thought the Dilantin might put me to sleep.

I followed instructions. Around midnight I took 100 mg of Dilantin, and no sleeping pill. Apparently I was dependent on the sleeping medication because when I went to bed I promptly fell awake. Before I finally got to sleep, at four in the morning, I thought, this medicine is a flop. Not until years later did it occur to me that I would not have lain quietly in bed for four hours if I'd had my usual fears. I'd have gotten up and taken the sleeping medicine.

I awoke at eight the next morning and, as Dr. Silbermann had instructed me, took another 100 mg of Dilantin. I had missed half a night's sleep. Sleep was so important that when I saw Max that afternoon, I started to tell him the Dilantin didn't work. But Max said, "You look better than you did yesterday." Then I looked at myself and realized that in spite of the loss of sleep I felt much better. We agreed that I should continue the Dilantin.

The following morning, according to routine, I called Dr. Silbermann. I couldn't make an appointment to see him because I was going to be too busy that day. The next day I was too busy again. The third day, when I was going to make the same excuse, I realized that I wasn't too busy. I was ducking the appointment. It was the first time in five years that I didn't feel a need to see Max.

I saw Dr. Silbermann only three more times in his office. My need for psychotherapy was gone, and we just talked as friends. Max told me he had never heard of Dilantin being used for the purpose I was using it. And he was a close friend of Dr. Houston Merritt, of Putnam and Merritt, who, twenty years earlier, had discovered the first clinical use for Dilantin. So for a while we were waiting for the phenomenon to go away. At least I'm pretty sure Max was. Intellectually I was too. But my feelings told me things were all right.

On my last visit Max gave me a renewable prescription for Dilantin. I haven't seen him as a patient since. We've stayed the closest of friends, and frequently have dinner together to swap lies and trade psychotherapy.

From the day I took Dilantin my major symptoms of distress disappeared. I noticed fundamental differences. My brain, which had been overactive and filled with negative thoughts, was calmer and functioned as it had before the depression. The headaches, the stomach distress, the neck pain all disappeared. And my patience returned. I enjoyed partners' meetings again and could sit back and observe someone else getting impatient, which was a switch.

Before taking Dilantin I'd been so tired and worn out I just dragged myself around. Although Dilantin had a calming effect on me, to my surprise it didn't slow me down. On the contrary my energy returned full force. It was as though the energy that had been wasted in my overactive brain was made available for healthier purposes.

I didn't realize it right away, but my good health had returned. I was neither tranquil nor ecstatic. I was just all right. For the first time in my life I realized how good you feel when you feel "all right."

NEW EVIDENCE AND
A BROADENING PERSPECTIVE

What had happened to me doesn't happen in real life. You just don't ask your doctor to let you try one drug, out of a pharmacopoeia of many thousands, and find that it works. But this did happen. And it happened so casually, in such a matter-of-fact way, that the vast improbability of it didn't occur to me at the time.

Being of the human race, I naturally returned to routine. Much of my new energy went back into the Dreyfus Fund and Dreyfus & Co., as though I were trying to make up for lost time. Still, much of my thinking was on Dilantin and the intriguing puzzle it presented. There were many questions to be answered.

The first question was whether Dilantin had been the cause of my return to health. My body might have been due for a recovery and a coincidence could have occurred. But this question was soon answered in the affirmative because I was able to observe benefits from Dilantin an hour after taking it. A second question, about the safety of the medicine, was answered by Dr. Silbermann. He told me it had side effects but they were rarely serious, and it had been tested by time, millions of people having taken it daily for many years. A question that could not be answered right away was whether the benefits of Dilantin would last. But as months went by, and I continued to feel well, I gained confidence they would last.

The most important question was a broader question. Could Dilantin help others as it had helped me? It seemed highly improbable. How could important uses for a medicine have been overlooked for twenty years? It didn't make sense, it seemed almost impossible. But if it were so, I clearly had an obligation to do something about it. I needed more facts.

In the course of the next year I was to get more facts. During this period I saw six people, in succession, benefit from Dilantin. I wasn't looking for these cases. They just happened in front of my eyes, so to speak. Each of the six cases was impressive. But the first two, because they were the first two, had the most significance and will be described in some detail.

■ ■ ■

The first person I saw benefit from Dilantin was my housekeeper Kathleen Fenyvessy. A month after I had started taking Dilantin I noticed that Kathleen was not her usual self and seemed depressed. Normally she was energetic but now she seemed worn out. Kathleen, who had recently come from Hungary, spoke imperfect English, and I was in the habit of talking slowly to her. Now she would interrupt before I could finish a sentence, saying, "I understand, I understand" and most of the time she didn't. Obviously she was extremely impatient.

I asked her what was wrong. She told me her mind was busy with miserable thoughts and she couldn't stop them. She'd seen several physicians and they'd told her she was having a nervous breakdown. She'd tried a variety of medicines that hadn't helped.

I thought of Dilantin. There seemed little to be lost, and much to be gained, by her trying it if Dr. Silbermann agreed. At my suggestion Kathleen visited him. After considering her condition he prescribed 100 mg a day for her.

Since I saw Kathleen at least a few hours every day, I was in a good position to observe the effects of Dilantin. Within a day or two it was apparent that her good disposition had returned. And she was full of energy again. As for patience, she no longer interrupted me in mid-sentence. I could even tell her the same thing twice.

Kathleen found her recovery hard to believe. In a letter to her sister describing it, she said, "It was due to a medicine used for an entirely different disorder. If someone else had told me they'd had an experience like this I would not have believed it."

About a month after Kathleen had started taking Dilantin, she and I participated in an unplanned experiment. Without consulting each other, we both stopped taking Dilantin for three days. We had gone to Hobeau Farm in Ocala, Florida, a thoroughbred breeding farm managed by Elmer Heubeck, my good friend and partner in the farm. It was pure vacation for Kathleen. Except for the horse business it was vacation for me too.

At that time I thought Dilantin only helped me with stress and problems. By problems I really meant areas of interest. They were not always problems; when they went well they could be pleasures. But the negative mood that I had been in made me think of them as problems. I had five such interests, some of a business nature, some personal. I went over them; they were all in good shape. So it seemed to me that in the nice relaxed atmosphere of the farm, I wouldn't need Dilantin. I stopped taking it.

The third day off Dilantin I felt a certain tingling in my nerves. I remember a funny expression entering my mind, that I had "worry gnats." I thought maybe I'd feel better if I went to

Miami, played some tennis and swam in the salt water. So I made arrangements to take a plane to Miami at eleven o'clock that night.

That afternoon I said something to Kathleen. It might not have been as tactful as it should have been, but it couldn't possibly have called for the response that it got. Kathleen burst out crying. I was astonished. Then something occurred to me, and I asked, "Kathleen, have you stopped taking Dilantin?" She said she had; she'd thought it would be so nice on the farm she hadn't brought any. "Why didn't you take some of mine?" I asked. She said she hadn't because she'd noticed I had only a few capsules left. Before I left for Miami, Elmer told me he would arrange for Kathleen to get Dilantin.

At 11 P.M. I got on the plane to Miami. Now I was quite conscious of the "worry gnats," and I thought of Dilantin. I figured it wouldn't help since I didn't have any stress or problems. But something inside me said, Well, you're research-minded. Why don't you take some anyway and see if anything happens. My bags were accessible on the plane and I went forward and got a capsule of Dilantin. I took it and looked at my watch. In a little while I thought I felt better, but I wasn't sure. I checked the time; it was twenty-eight minutes since I'd taken the medicine. When the plane arrived in Miami it was an hour since I'd taken the Dilantin. The "worry gnats" were gone. As I walked through the airport I had the nicest feeling that peace had descended on me.

The next morning I called Kathleen. Even before I could ask how she felt, her cheerful voice gave the answer.

Kathleen's experience and my own, in stopping Dilantin and recontinuing it, confirmed our need for the medicine, and seemed to indicate this need was not based on realistic problems, but on something in our nervous systems at the time.

Now I was in Miami again. I had gone there for the last few years on doctor's orders. These trips were meant to be vacations, but there had been no fun in them. When a vacation is not in you, you don't have one. But now I was on vacation and in a frame of mind to enjoy it. I still stayed at the lovely, dilapidated old Roney Plaza. Everything was beautiful—the air, the sea, just walking to breakfast. I was happy. And I know why. As Mark Twain said in "Captain Stormfield's Visit to Heaven," "Happiness ain't a thing in itself—it's only a *contrast* with something that ain't pleasant." I had the contrast.

Tennis was a pleasure again. I had taken up tennis about eight years earlier, mostly for the exercise. Golf had been my game since childhood and I'd loved it. I'd been almost a fine golfer, won lots of club championships, and at my best had a one handicap. But in recent years golf had started to bore me. Maybe it was my perfectionism. More likely it was the long walks between shots when all that was going on was the windmills of my mind.

I had started playing tennis with the local pros at the Roney Plaza. At this time Marse Fink was pro of record. Sol Goldman was pro emeritus. I didn't play with the pros to get lessons. I'd had barrels of lessons in golf and I looked forward to doing everything wrong in tennis.

We got up all sorts of games and bet on them all. They gave me large handicaps. Sometimes Marse and Sol played doubles against me and some bum they got as my partner. Sol and Marse were good friends, but if the match got close, they were not loath to comment on each other's play. They called each other names their mothers hadn't taught them. I'd get so interested in their descriptions of each other that I would lose my concentration—and they'd usually win. On the rare occasions they lost, Marse would go to his desk in the tennis shop and mutter to himself, so we could all hear, "I'll never play with that son-of-a-bitch [Sol] again." And he never did until three o'clock the next afternoon.

Sol, a remarkable character (the world's leading authority on everything), was the second person I saw benefit from Dilantin. In his youth Sol had been a great athlete, acknowledged to be the best one-wall handball player in the world. When he was thirty he took up tennis and became an outstanding player. In a different field, Sol had ambitions to be an opera singer. He had a fine singing voice and might have made it to the Met if he hadn't damaged a vocal cord.

One morning Sol and I had breakfast at Wolfie's on Collins Avenue. The waitress brought mushroom omelettes and Sol ignored his. He seemed in a fog and was staring into the distance. I'd heard that you could pass your hand in front of someone's face and they wouldn't notice, but I'd never believed this. I passed my hand a few inches in front of Sol's face and didn't get any reaction at all.

I asked Sol what was bothering him. He said that a couple of weeks ago a wealthy friend of his, whom I knew well, had bought six pairs of tennis shoes from Marse. Sol thought it terrible that Marse had charged his friend retail prices for the shoes. This was of such monumental inconsequence that I had a hard time believing the thought was stuck in Sol's brain. But after listening to him I realized that it was almost an obsession. Then it occurred to me that Sol's tennis game had been off, and he'd been uncharacteristically quiet on the court.

I asked Sol how he'd been feeling. He told me he had constant headaches, that he slept badly and was having nightmares. His worst complaint was that he would wake up at four o'clock in the morning hearing himself shouting. His only relief was to get in his car and drive around for an hour or so. He told me he'd seen a doctor. But the medicines he'd been given hadn't helped and made him feel dopey. It seemed that Dilantin might be worth trying. I telephoned Dr. Silbermann about it, and he arranged for Sol to get a prescription.

The next day we were at Wolfie's again. Sol had eaten earlier and was keeping me company at breakfast. He had his Dilantin with him and took the first 100 mg at that time. I had found Dilantin effective in myself within an hour, and this was a chance to observe its effects in someone else. I wanted an objective reading but didn't know how to go about it. By chance I asked Sol, "What about Fink and Russell this afternoon?" We had a doubles game with them for fifty dollars a team. Sol said, "They're awful tough." This answer startled me—it was so unlike Sol, a fierce competitor. I thought, "Fink and Russell" will be a good test question. I looked at my watch.

We left Wolfie's and walked to the beach at the Roney Plaza, a couple of blocks away, and I went in swimming. When I came back it was thirty-five minutes since Sol had taken his Dilantin. I said, "Sol, do you think we've got a chance with Fink and Russell this afternoon?" Sol said, "We've *always* got a chance." With emphasis on the always. That was more like him.

Twenty-five minutes later, an hour after Sol had taken the Dilantin, I asked again, "What about Fink and Russell?" Sol said, "We'll knock the crap out of them." Sol was back to normal.

That night Sol slept soundly and straight through. He started taking Dilantin daily and continued to sleep well—no more waking up at four in the morning. His daily headaches disappeared. The monumental matter of the retail shoes shrunk back to size. And once again Sol became his usual objectionable self on the tennis court.

■ ■ ■

In that first year I saw four more people benefit from Dilantin. Each was depressed and each had symptoms of an overbusy brain occupied with emotions related to fear and anger.

Each additional case had a parlaying effect on the probability factor. A year earlier it had seemed almost impossible that important uses for Dilantin could have been overlooked. Now it seemed highly probable that they had been overlooked.

Which brings up the subject of probabilities.

THE SUBJECT OF PROBABILITIES

As I look back, I realize that it was a good instinct for probabilities that pulled me through that early period of my pursuit of Dilantin. Without this instinct I could never have survived the negative inferences drawn from the fact that the medicine had been around for over twenty-five years. I used to think that everyone had a pretty good sense of probabilities. But I don't now, and I've heard some strange comments about probabilities in the medical field.

Probabilities are an important underlying theme of this book and, partly to qualify myself on the subject, I will depart from the narrative and discuss them.

In some fields a sense of probabilities is much more important than in others. An insurance actuary would feel naked without a sense of probabilities. A painter, on the other hand, might swap his sense of probabilities for a two percent improvement in color sense. In medicine a sense of probabilities is more important than generally realized. Sometimes weighing the probabilities—the use of a potentially dangerous procedure against the dangerous condition a patient is in—is the whole medical question. In the FDA the weighing of risk vs. gain looms large in the question of whether a drug should be approved for listing.

I've always had a good sense of probabilities—born with it I believe—and I used to think of it as a form of intelligence. But as I began to assess some of my other "forms of intelligence" and found them lacking, I decided I'd better think of them all as aptitudes.

The word aptitude itself suggests wide variances. It seems that aptitudes come with the baby. We're not all born with a good sense of direction, and a good sense of probabilities is not standard equipment either. On the way to the subject of probabilities, let's discuss aptitudes. If the reader doesn't have a good sense of probability this should make him feel better.

Some of the genetic blanks I drew when aptitudes were being handed out were in mechanics, in remembering names, and in sense of direction.

Things mechanical are a mystery to me. In World War II, I took an exam to qualify for Officers Training School in the U.S. Coast Guard. My aptitude for mechanics helped me get a grade of 29 out of a possible 100. After looking at this score the Coast Guard decided it had enough officers, and awarded me the post of apprentice seaman.

I can't remember people's names no matter how hard I try. I seem to have a scrambling device in my head. If two strangers come into the office, my secretary discreetly writes their names on the side of a paper coffee cup and I have to refer to it constantly.

My most conspicuous aptitude—in absentia—is my sense of direction. For that reason, and because there is evidence of genetic origin, I will discuss it more fully.

My sense of direction is fine—but it's in backwards. This is not easy to explain to a person with a good sense of direction. I believe such a person has a tug he's not conscious of that pulls him in the right direction. I have such a tug, but it pulls me in the wrong direction. For example, when I leave a washroom in a strange airport, without hesitation I turn the wrong way.

Apparently my aptitude for going the wrong way is not only lateral but vertical. For fifteen years my office was on the twenty-ninth floor of 2 Broadway and our boardroom was on the thirtieth. When I was in a hurry to get to the thirtieth floor I would invariably walk down to the twenty-eighth.

I don't have to climb the family tree very high to see where I got my sense of direction. It was bequeathed me by my father. His sense of direction was in backwards too—and was even stronger than mine. He got lost all the time but it never occurred to him to blame his sense of direction, he just thought it was bad luck. It's a good thing Dad didn't have to make his living as a wagon scout in the old days. He'd have set out for California with his train of covered wagons and, if things had gone well, in a few months he'd have discovered Plymouth Rock.

It's not surprising that the family hero is the homing pigeon. You can put this rascal in a dark bag, take him 500 miles from home, and without consulting a road map or following the railroad tracks he will fly directly to his coop. Scientists may say he takes radar soundings or something. But what of it? Could Shakespeare do it, could Beethoven? The pigeon has quite an aptitude.

Without realizing it, we gravitate in the direction of our aptitudes. We bounce from one field to another, being repelled or attracted, and if we're lucky we come to rest where our aptitudes are at a premium. When I got out of college, I bounced around for a few years and wound up as assistant to a customer's broker in the stock exchange. The stock market appealed to my sense of probabilities and to another aptitude, gambling (speculation as it's called in the market).

An aptitude for gambling by itself is a dubious asset; it's fortunate for me that this aptitude came in a package with my sense of probability. This steered me into games of skill and away from casino games, such as dice and roulette, where the odds against you are slight but inexorable.

My first gambling game was marbles for keeps. I remember bankrupting a kid from down the block when I was six. When I gave up marbles, I took up other games—contract bridge, gin rummy, and handicapping the races. In these games a good sense of probabilities is an asset.

There are two kinds of probabilities. There is the mathematical kind that can be arrived at precisely. As a simple example, the chance of calling the toss of a coin correctly (provided it's not weighted) is exactly one in two. The chance of calling it correctly twice in a row is one-half of one-half of a chance, or one in four, and so forth. If you wish to determine the exact probability that a coin tossed a hundred times will come up heads thirty-one times, there's a formula for it. I don't know it.

Another kind of probability cannot be arrived at by mathematical formula. It's an estimate—exact figures can't be placed on it. Let's call it free-form probability. We use it all the time, some of us more consciously than others. For example, when I make a phone call I start to assess the probability that the person I'm calling is at home. With adjustments for the individual, I might figure it's three-to-one against his or her being home after the third ring, eight-to-one after the fourth ring, etc. After the fifth ring I usually hang up. (When I call my former wife, if the phone is answered before the fourth ring, I know I've got the wrong number.)

One who makes a living by the application of free-form probabilities is the racetrack handicapper. After studying the many variables, he comes up with the probable odds for each horse in a particular race—the morning line. Over a period of time the handicapper's "line" should be close to the odds made by the betting public, or as my friend Dingy Weiss says, "He can tell his story walking."

Free-form probability also deals with odds of a larger magnitude. Some examples. The odds against five horses, in a ten-horse race, finishing in a dead heat. The odds against finding a lion in your backyard in Manhattan. The odds against the next person you meet having a wooden leg and offering you a banana. Or, for a pertinent example, the odds against thousands of physicians, working independently, finding a drug useful for over fifty symptoms and disorders, and that drug being useful for only a single disorder.

When the odds are this large, it's easy to be approximately right. Whether you estimate one chance in a million or one chance in a billion, the estimates are almost the same—the difference between these figures is less than one in a million. (If the reader's sense of probability is like my sense of direction, his feelers will tell him this is wrong.)

A feel for probabilities is essential in two of the card games I've played, bridge and gin rummy. Although I haven't played gin in fifteen years, the *Encyclopedia of Bridge* is still kind enough to say, "Dreyfus...is reputed to be the best American player of gin rummy." This compliment, no longer deserved, is based on a system of play I discovered many years ago that relies heavily on probabilities.

Gin rummy deals mostly with exact probabilities. Another game I've played, the stock market, deals largely with inexact probabilities.

■ ■ ■

October. This is one of the peculiarly dangerous months to speculate in stocks. The others are July, January, September, April, November, May, March, June, December, August, and February.
—MARK TWAIN, *Pudd'nhead Wilson.*

With this cautionary note the reader will be given instructions on how to buy a stock.

Take the five-year earnings record of a company, its current earnings and your estimate for the near future, its book value, its net quick assets, the prospect for new products, the competitive position of the company in its own industry, the merits of the industry relative to other industries, your opinion of management, your opinion of the stock market as a whole, and the chart position of the individual stock. Put all this where you think your brains are, circulate it through your sense of probabilities, and arrive at your conclusion. Be prepared to take a quick loss; your conclusion may be wrong even though you approached it the right way.

My introduction to Wall Street was in 1941. I got a job as an assistant to a customer's broker in the garment district branch of Cohen, Simondson & Company, at a salary of $25 a week. One of my duties in this job was the posting of hundreds of weekly charts. This early experience with charts influenced my Wall Street career.

Skipping the intervening travail—fascinating as it would be to nobody—I found myself, in the early fifties, responsible for the management of a small mutual fund, The Dreyfus Fund. The fund was so small that the management fees were only $2,500 a year. Perforce, the fund could not afford a large research staff. Actually our staff consisted of a fine young man, Alex Rudnicki, and myself. Alex was a fundamentalist, a student of the Graham Dodd school. I was a student of charts and market technique. We were at the opposite extremes of investment approach, but we worked together as friends.

Alex had a wonderful memory for the earnings of companies and other statistical information; my contribution was six hundred large-scale, weekly line charts. From my experience, monthly charts were too "slow" to be of much use, and daily charts were too volatile to be reliable. I split the difference with weekly charts, posted daily. I developed my own theories about the charts, and read no books on the subject. It seemed best to make my own mistakes—at least then I'd know whom to blame.

In those early days, our statistical information was no more up-to-date than the latest quarterly reports. Alex and I were too chicken to call a company and ask a vice-president how things were going. Of necessity we put more emphasis on the technical side of the market than did most funds.

When you study the technical side of the stock market you deal with two components. One component is major market trends—bull or bear market. The other is the timing of the purchase or sale of individual securities.

In those days, more than now, the market tended to move as a whole—being right about the major trend was more than half the game. We focused a good deal of our attention on this. With three- and four-million-share days, the trading of the speculator was a key factor in market moves. Speculators tended to move in concert. Excessive optimism, with the parlayed purchasing power of their margin accounts, caused the market to get out of hand on the upside; forced selling in these same margin accounts caused the market to get out of hand on the downside.

The more money a speculator had, the healthier the technical side of the market—he had purchasing power. The more stock the speculator had, the weaker the technical side—he had selling power. Human nature being what it is, when a speculator owned stock he talked bullish. When he had cash, or was short of stock, he talked bearish. In estimating whether we were in a major uptrend or downtrend, the speculator's chatter was taken into consideration, along with changes in the short interest and the condition of the margin accounts. And of course our charts were helpful.

Objectivity—difficult to come by—is important in any field. It didn't take us long to learn that stubbornness, ego, and wishful thinking could mess up the best of market techniques; so we tried to keep our emotions separate from our decision-making. When we bought a security we didn't pound the table to emphasize how sure we were that we were right. Instead, we tried to prepare ourselves for the possibility that we might be wrong so that when the unexpected happened, which it frequently did, we were psychologically in a position to take a loss.

Our sense of probabilities was always in play. We wouldn't buy a high-risk stock, one that could go down 50 to 60 percent, unless we felt we had a chance of at least doubling our money. If we bought a conservative stock, one not likely to go down more than 20 percent, a 30 percent profit was worth shooting for.

Since our methods differed from those of most other funds, it was likely that our performance would vary considerably from the average. Fortunately for our stockholders this variance was in the right direction—it could have been the other way. At the time of my retirement, our ten-year performance was the best of any mutual fund—nearly 100 percentage points better than the second-best fund.*

That was a long time ago. Recently, my good friend Bill Rogers, of two-Cabinet-post renown, said, "Jack, I guess you're doing well in the market as usual." I said, "No, Bill, to tell the truth recently I've been in a stupid streak." It's nice to see a friend have a good laugh.

■ ■ ■

Back to medical probabilities. Including my own case, I had seen seven consecutive persons benefit from Dilantin. If each case had been the flip of a coin, 50-50, the odds against seven in a row would have been 127-to-1. But the response to Dilantin had been so prompt and the symptoms that responded so similar, that each case deserved a weight far exceeding 50-50.

---

* 326 percent to 232 percent, Arthur Wiesenberger, Inc.

Of course my objectivity could be questioned. But that didn't bother me; it's only other people's objectivity that bothers me. Even at that early date I placed a high probability figure on the chance that Dilantin was more than an anticonvulsant.

■ ■ ■

During the first year of my experience with Dilantin I had gathered some helpful information on the subject of electricity in the body. This will be discussed in the next chapter.

BODY ELECTRICITY

For the first few months that I took Dilantin (PHT) I gave little thought to how the medicine worked. How it worked was a lot less important to me than that it did work. But one day I noticed that the flat, metallic taste in my mouth, which I'd associated with electricity, was gone. As I thought back about it, I realized that it had been gone since I'd started taking PHT.

A hypothesis about electricity had led me to ask for PHT. Was this a coincidence? It seemed unlikely. When a hypothesis precedes and leads to a finding, the hypothesis is apt to be correct. My thinking went back to electricity in the body.

Recently I found some notes to myself, made in 1963. These notes help me remember what my thoughts were at that time.

[From my notes] "I noticed figures of speech that described human emotions in electrical terms. Before then I'd thought of these terms as imaginative inventions of writers. But perhaps they weren't. Maybe sensitive people had used them instinctively because they were near the truth. There are enough of these electrical expressions to make a parlor game. Some follow:

state of tension	shocking experience
room charged with tension	state of shock
get a charge out of something	it gave me a jolt
electrifying experience	blow your fuse
the touchdown electrified the crowd	blow your top
	sparks flew
dynamic personality	explosive temper
magnetic personality	explode with anger
galvanized into action	

"This list, with its references to anger and fear, led to other thoughts. I knew that an electric goad was used in rodeos to frighten animals into rambunctious performances, and that batteries had been used to make race horses run faster. I'd read that an electric jolt causes the hair to stand on end.

"Could electricity be the mechanism that makes the fur on a dog rise when he is angry or when he is frightened? Could it account for the spectacular bristling of a cat in the act of welcoming a dog? How about our own fur? When we're scared the hair on the nape of our neck rises and we have 'hair-raising' experiences. And don't we bristle with anger? Didn't these things seem to connect anger and fear with electricity in the body?" [End of the notes]

I had gone as far as I could as an amateur. I needed a professional to tell me whether my ideas about electricity in the body made sense. But where could I find such a person?

Whenever I'm stumped as to how to find someone or locate something, I have a simple method. I ask Howard Stein. I don't know how he does it but he never lets me down. I asked Howard, "Do you know how I can meet with somebody who's an expert on electricity in the body?" Howard said he thought so. He went to Yura Arkus-Duntov, head of the Dreyfus Fund's science research. Within a week Yura had made arrangements for me to meet with Dr. Peter Suckling, a neurobiophysicist from Downstate Medical Center.

Dr. Suckling, with his nice Australian accent, had good vibes for me (a modern electrical term?). He was an expert on bioelectrical activity and had been an associate of Sir John Eccles, an authority in the field and a Nobel Prize winner.

Dr. Suckling and I had three long meetings in my office at 2 Broadway. It was a nice office, facing New York Harbor, and Peter liked it. He said he thought the moving scenery of boats helped with thinking. I hoped so.

The first question I asked Peter was, "Can you weigh the electricity in a cat?" I thought cats had an extra share of electricity, because of their hair-raising act. Peter disappointed me by saying electricity can't be measured that way. It's inside the body, but the whole animal itself is grounded. I didn't know what that meant but I took his word for it.

For the first time, I heard about the excitatory nervous system, the inhibitory nervous system, membranes, axons, synapses, negative potentials, sodium and potassium, and how a disproportionate amount of chemicals inside and outside the cell made for the electrical potential across the membrane.

Peter labored hard to explain the working of bioelectrical activity to me. By using simple illustrations, he got into me, shoehorn fashion, a rudimentary idea of how electricity works in the body. I won't burden the reader with the whole discussion, but I will summarize some of what Peter said.

The cell is a complicated entity in which thousands of activities take place. Peter said most of them were not relevant to our discussion. What was relevant was the electrical potential of the cell. He explained that the body of a cell is enclosed by a membrane, and in a nerve cell the electrical potential is minus 90 millivolts, relative to the outside of the cell. Peter said the reason there is this negative potential is because of a disproportionate amount of substances inside the cell relative to outside the cell—particularly sodium and potassium. Peter spoke of the membrane with obvious admiration: "This very thin membrane can sustain an electrical tension better than most insulators. The insulation strength is high. It has to be strong; it's so very thin." Then, in considerable detail, he explained the electrochemical mechanisms involved in the discharge of electrical activity. I won't go into that here.

Peter said that there are about 10 billion* cells in the brain—each with an electrical potential. He said that even a slight imbalance in individual cells, because of the proliferative possibilities, could cause a problem in a large area of the brain. He told me that cells vary in length in the human. In nerve cells the speed of impulse transmission varies from one hundred meters a second to three meters a second.

All the cells in the human body, although they do not have the same amount of electrical potential, work on the same principle. Peter said this was true in other animals and, for that matter, all living things. Apparently when the Lord came up with a good thing like the cell he used it over and over again.

At the beginning I didn't tell Peter what my interest was. I didn't want to influence him one way or the other. I realized later that this had been a needless precaution because we were dealing with a pretty exact science. In the meantime, Peter had been trying to figure out why the president of a mutual fund and partner of a brokerage firm was asking all these questions. He'd assumed my interest was in business. On the third day, when I told him about PHT, Peter astonished me by saying, "Oh, my goodness, I thought you were considering giving testosterone to the customer's

---

* This figure was imprecise. The latest census has it considerably higher.

brokers to make them produce better." Perhaps like making hens lay eggs faster (Merrill Lynch—consider).

Then I explained to Peter what my experiences with PHT had been. Apologizing for the unscientific sound of it, and speaking allegorically, I said I felt that the brain of a person who needed PHT was like a bunch of dry twigs. It seemed that a thought of fear or anger would light the dry twigs, the fire would spread out of control, and the thoughts couldn't be turned off. PHT seemed to act like a gentle rain on the twigs, and the fire (and thoughts) could be kept under control.

I asked Peter if these impressions made sense. Peter said he had not done specific work with PHT, but my impressions were not inconsistent with the known fact that PHT prevented the spread of excessive electrical discharge. That was good news.

■ ■ ■

A few weeks after our last meeting, Peter performed an invaluable service. He sent me a copy of Goodman & Gilman's *Pharmacological Basis of Therapeutics,* considered to be the bible of pharmaceuticals by the medical profession, and said he thought I would find it useful.

I hadn't known there was such a book. In the section on PHT I found this:

> Coincident with the decrease in seizures there occurs improvement in intellectual performance. Salutary effects of the drug PHT on personality, memory, mood, cooperativeness, emotional stability, amenability to discipline, etc., are also observed, sometimes independently of seizure control.

I read and reread this paragraph. I could hardly believe it. Salutary effects in mood, emotional stability, etc. Here it was—in a medical book of high repute. Yet none of the doctors I'd met had ever heard of these uses. How could this be?

A SOFT VOICE IN A DEAF EAR

The time had come to tell the story to the medical profession. I had seen seven persons benefit from PHT, the electrical thoughts had been checked out and were not implausible, and there was the medical support of the Goodman & Gilman excerpt.

Now that the time had come, I didn't know how to proceed. I had always assumed that if I had enough evidence I would just "turn it over to the medical profession." That would be no problem, I thought. Now, faced with turning it over, I realized there was no "receiving department" in the medical profession—and I didn't know where to go. Dr. Silbermann and I discussed this problem at length and finally came up with what seemed a sensible plan.

Max, an associate professor at Columbia Presbyterian, was a personal friend of Dean H. Houston Merritt. This was the Merritt of Putnam and Merritt who had discovered that PHT was useful for epilepsy. What could be more logical than to bring the story to Dr. Merritt and Presbyterian Hospital?

At Max's suggestion we invited Dr. Merritt to have dinner at my home. Dr. Merritt accepted and brought with him Dr. Lawrence C. Kolb, chief of Psychiatric Research at Presbyterian.

Since this was the first opportunity I'd had to present the PHT story in some detail, I was anxious to have other physicians present, and I invited my family physician, Dr. Alfred Steiner, and Dr. Ernest Klarch, a psychiatrist, whom Max had consulted in one of the seven cases. Also at dinner was my friend Sol. He had come from Miami so that the physicians could hear about PHT from a person other than myself.

Sol and I related our experiences with PHT. Then I told the physicians about the other five cases, and reported my observations of the medicine's effects on anger, fear, and the turned-on mind. They didn't express skepticism, but I think that the story, coming from a layman, was hard for them to believe. I was glad I could conclude with the quote from the respected medical source, Goodman & Gilman. To repeat:

> Salutary effects of PHT on personality, memory, mood, coopera-
> tiveness, emotional stability, amenability to discipline, etc., are also
> observed, sometimes independently of seizure control.

Dr. Merritt appeared surprised by this excerpt from Goodman & Gilman. He said he hadn't heard of it but hoped it was true. Then he suggested that maybe Presbyterian could do a study. Dr. Kolb agreed and said it could be arranged.

I couldn't let Dr. Merritt get away without asking him about possible side effects of PHT. He said that PHT had been in use for about twenty years, and a good record of safety had been established. There were side effects but they were rarely serious. He said PHT was nonhabit-forming, and unlike many other substances it was not sedative in therapeutic doses. This was good news and I thanked Dr. Merritt. At the end of the meeting Dr. Kolb said he would be in touch with me.

Postscript to the dinner. When I'd invited Dr. Steiner and Dr. Klarch, appreciating their time was valuable, I said they could bill me for it. Dr. Steiner didn't send a bill. Dr. Klarch (fictitious name) sent a bill for $500. This seemed high. His only contribution to the meeting had been "Please pass the butter."

A few days after the meeting, Dr. Kolb phoned and told me he had arranged for Dr. Sidney Malitz to conduct the study. Dr. Malitz and I had dinner, and I repeated the PHT story. He said he was surprised to hear such a plausible story from a layman; he hadn't expected it. Apparently Dr. Kolb hadn't told him much about our discussion.

Dr. Malitz told me that he would set up two studies and I could fund them for $5,000 each. I said the matter was so urgent that I'd prefer to give $10,000 for each study, and this was agreed upon. I told Dr. Malitz I would appreciate it if he would keep me in close touch with how things were going. I didn't ask how the studies would be conducted; it didn't seem proper. But I had the feeling that much of my responsibility to PHT was now in the hands of professionals.

Alas. Week after week went by without my hearing from Dr. Malitz and a head of steam built up in me. When I finally called him after three months, I regret that I said, "Why the hell haven't I heard from you? You know how important this is." I don't think Sidney liked this opening remark and I can't say I blame him. He explained that the patients he had selected for the study were used to getting medicine three times a day, and since I'd only suggested 100 mg of Dilantin (one capsule) he was wondering if Parke-Davis could make it in smaller dosages, so it could be given three times a day. This excuse was so lame it needed crutches. Apparently Sidney had so little faith in PHT that he didn't think it could help unless the patients were psychologically influenced, and he hadn't even tried it. Further, if he'd looked into it, he would have found that Parke-Davis already made it in smaller dosages—a breakable 50 mg Infatab, a 30 mg capsule, and a liquid. After explaining to Dr. Malitz the different forms Dilantin came in, I expressed the hope that the study would now move forward.

Four more long months went by. I called Dr. Malitz again and this time, in the quietest way, asked him how things were going. He told me the study hadn't gotten started yet because he hadn't been able to get a placebo from Parke-Davis. I thanked him politely, and hung up with a heavy heart. Maybe Dr. Malitz couldn't get a placebo from Parke-Davis in seven months, but in those days most drugstores could supply a placebo in forty-eight hours.

In a last futile attempt I met with Dr. Kolb. He defended Dr. Malitz and said it was better to proceed slowly and carefully than the other way around. I didn't even argue with this platitude—it was such nonsense. Seven months had been wasted and I was discouraged. I'd taken what I thought was my best shot and hadn't got any results at all—not even negative.

Occasionally it may seem to the reader that I'm being critical of others. This is the opposite of my intention; I have too many motes in my own eye. But sometimes things have to be spelled out—otherwise this story would be too hard to believe. Looking back, it's easy to understand the position Dr. Malitz was in. He had been taught to think of PHT as an anticonvulsant. The idea that it had other uses came from an implausible source, a layman, and that didn't make it any easier for him. He undoubtedly had other research projects to which he gave priority—and PHT got on a back burner.

On other fronts things had not stood still. I had continued to send friends and acquaintances to doctors for trials with PHT. The effects were prompt and similar to those of the earlier cases. The numbers were mounting up. By now there were about twenty-five cases. In addition, I had a new source of information.

Dr. A. Lester Stepner, of Miami, had treated one of the first six people I'd seen take PHT. He had been so impressed with the results that he tried PHT with other patients. In a letter of April 1965, he summarized the cases of twelve patients he'd treated with PHT. In eleven of the twelve (he was unable to follow up the twelfth) he found PHT effective in treating anxiety, depression, anger, impulsiveness, temper outbursts, and incoherent thinking.

Coming at this time, Dr. Stepner's observations were a big psychological help to me, but they didn't seem to mean much to Dr. Silbermann and others I spoke to. I was beginning to understand the French phrase *ideé fixe*.

The evidence was growing, but my confidence that I could convey it to others was shrinking. For months I had been buttonholing any doctor I ran into and informally talking about PHT. I must have spoken to a dozen of them during this period. None of them had heard of PHT being used for anything other than epilepsy. They were all (with one exception) polite, even kind, but they didn't give me any encouragement. That one doctor looked at me the way a Great Dane looks at a cricket and explained: "Medicine is a complicated matter, and I'd advise you to stick to Wall Street." Bless his heart.

I called a council of peace with my friends who knew of my interest in PHT. These friends were Dr. Max Silbermann, Dr. Peter Suckling, Yura Arkus-Duntov, and Howard Stein. We met in my office in early 1965 to decide the best way to get our information to the medical profession. For the first half of the meeting, we went over many cases in detail. By this time both Howard and Yura had each seen persons benefit from PHT, and we discussed how consistent our observations were with those reported in Goodman & Gilman.

We tape-recorded the meeting. Reading the transcript brings back those days in a lively way—I can still feel the warmth of my frustrations. There wasn't a suggestion I would make that Peter,

Max, or Yura couldn't find an objection to. Toward the end I must have worn through my daily supply of PHT because I was hopping up and down with frustration.

The transcript of the meeting remembers better than I do. Here are a few excerpts:

JACK: The problem before us is to awaken the doctors in the country to the potential of Dilantin. We're not in this for financial reasons, and we're not in it for glory. It's almost a crime not to try to get this information to the doctors....We've got a lot of cases and we could do a thorough job of writing them up. If Dr. Silbermann would be willing...

DR. MAX S: Jack, that would not be accepted by any medical journal. You could publish that at your own expense, there's no law against it.

JACK: Why wouldn't this be accepted by a medical journal?

DR. MAX S: Because. You know the old story. There is no blind control, and no medical journal would accept any drug study unless...

DR. PETER S: Unless you have had a computer in on it.

JACK: Max, are you serious? This can't be so.

YURA and DR. MAX S: Oh, yes this is so.

JACK: Yura, we are talking about research, right? Please listen before you say no. None of these people who took PHT knew each other. As far as they were concerned the study was blind. I asked them to write me letters that included details of their experiences. The same results from PHT are reported over and over again. This reinforces the evidence.

DR. PETER S: It is not accepted as proof and there's a devastating word that is applied to it, called anecdotal evidence. It doesn't go.

YURA: It's indirect proof.

JACK: Sorry fellows. Nobody in the room is thinking. These individuals wouldn't know which way to lie if they wanted to. They didn't know each other.

DR. PETER S: No, no. It's not that. This is the way...

JACK: Please. Let's not move the medical people all the way down to diapers. At least keep them in rompers, okay? I'm saying that if we added the Goodman & Gilman to Dr. Stepner's observations and the evidence of our twenty-five cases, write it up carefully, it's got to be received. We won't say we discovered America or anything like that. You, Dr. Silbermann, have got to make the effort.

DR. MAX S: Well, if we write it up and I publish it under my name and I send it in, no medical journal will accept it.

JACK: All right, Max, then no medical journal will accept it. At least we can send the information to the heads of the hospitals and say, "It would be a sin if we didn't tell you what we've found. Evaluate it on the basis of your own experience and do what you want." Once we've told the heads of fifty hospitals, at least part of it should be off our conscience. Let the non-use of it rest on other people's consciences...

I don't care if machines are not involved. I can get machines that will lie like anybody else. Will that help? [I wouldn't have done that—in those days I was over 80 percent honest.]

YURA: No, Jack. We are talking about the best means to achieve this.

This discussion seems funny now, but it was very real then. I was too near my own suffering and I was impatient to get PHT to others. This impatience stayed with me, but after bumping into enough brick walls and closed minds, I realized it got in the way, and tabled it—with the help of PHT. Without PHT I'd have had an implosion.

For several weeks after the meeting, I thought about what was said. I had argued with my friends at the top of my lungs. But I knew they had my best interests at heart, and I had to pay attention to them because they had experience where I had none.

In the course of business I saw Howard Stein almost every day. Every once in a while Howard would say, "If you want to get anything done, you've got to do it yourself." I didn't even respond to this remark at first. But about the fourth time I heard it, I said, "Why are you persecuting me with that cliché?" He said, "I'm not using it as a cliché; I mean it." "How can I do this myself?" I asked. "I don't have any medical background, and besides I have other dishes to wash, like the Dreyfus Fund and Dreyfus & Co."

But Howard said, "You'll see."

ESTABLISHING
A MEDICAL FOUNDATION

---

and the Story of My Life (the Best Parts Left Out)

When I started to do well in business, I established a small foundation, the Dreyfus Charitable Foundation, for the purpose of giving money to what seemed good causes. It was my hope to be generally helpful, and the foundation gave money to numerous organizations and contributed equally to Protestant, Catholic, and Jewish charities. The responsibility of how to spend the money was left to these organizations.

But now I wanted to take over the responsibility of spending this money—I felt it should be spent on PHT research. PHT would need all the money I had been contributing and more, so I had to discontinue my usual contributions. And I could do this with a clear conscience—if the work on PHT was successful there would be many sources of charitable inquiry that would be helped by it. Consistent with this thinking, in 1965 the Dreyfus Charitable Foundation was changed to the Dreyfus Medical Foundation.

A medical foundation needs a medical director—but such a person can be difficult to obtain. Good physicians are fully occupied with their own matters and not easily sidetracked by what might seem a will-o'-the-wisp. After several months of search, Dr. Suckling introduced me to Dr. William J. Turner, a neuropsychiatrist at Central Islip Hospital on Long Island.

At the first meeting with Dr. Turner I got a fine impression of him, and it's never changed. He said he had been anxious to meet with me because he had seen a number of persons, with disorders other than epilepsy, respond to Dilantin. We had several long discussions. After thinking about it for a few weeks Dr. Turner decided to join the Foundation as Medical Director.

At that time I thought that the Foundation would be able to achieve its goals within two or three years. It seemed unwise for Dr. Turner to break his connections with Central Islip Hospital and move to New York City, so he joined us as Director on a part-time basis. Bill took a small office near his home in Huntington, Long Island, hired a secretary and medical assistant, and we were in business. (Jumping ahead a few years—when it became apparent that my timetable was optimistic, I was fortunate in being able to persuade Dr. Samuel Bogoch, a professor at the Boston University School of Medicine and Chairman of the International Institute for the Brain Sciences, to join the Foundation on a full-time basis as General Director; Dr. Turner continued as Director.)

At the outset, Dr. Turner and I had the objective of proving—or disproving—that PHT was more than an anticonvulsant. We were as open to negative possibilities as to positive ones. I had my ideas as to what we would find: but if they were wrong, I didn't want to spend my time trying to prove something that wasn't so—there are pleasanter ways of making a fool of oneself.

Our plan was simple. The Foundation would sponsor a few studies at medical institutions. My guess was that this might take $150,000 to $200,000 a year for the next two or three years. If these studies were successful, the facts about PHT would then be in the hands of professionals. Once this happened I thought the word would spread like wildfire throughout the medical profession, and the job would be done. If I had been told, then, that in the next fifteen years the Foundation was going to spend over $15 million* (and the job not completed), I wouldn't have believed it. One reason is that $15 million was three times as much money as I had at that time.

Talking about money in connection with this work is awkward for me. I don't want to sound like I think I'm a Boy Scout. But there is a point to be made here. If I hadn't been lucky enough to have the money, I wouldn't have gotten to first base.

When I think back to my first job, at $15 a week, I realize what an implausible person I was to have a lot of money. Implausible is too weak a word. I'll tell how it happened. If you believe in fate, or whatever, you're entitled to believe the money was given to me to spend on PHT.

When I was a boy my parents were not poor, nor were they rich. Once, my father, who sold candy wholesale, was out of a job and down to his last two weeks of spending money for the family. But that was his low point, and I wasn't even aware of it at the time.

When I was ten years old, I learned what money was for. The laws of Montgomery, Alabama, permitted me to go to the movies by myself at that age. My parents would give me a dime on Saturday mornings, and the Strand Theater was assured of an early customer. I would see the Pathé News, the "To Be Continued Next Saturday" serial, and a movie—sometimes twice.

When I was sixteen, my father had enough money to send me to college, Lehigh University. I studied the minimum and got a C average—my only A was in Music Appreciation, and my only distinction was that I was captain of the golf team. At college my brain didn't come to grips with the problem of how I would earn

---

* By now, 1997, over $80 million.

a living; it didn't occur to me to study something practical. It's just as well. Lehigh is a fine engineering school; if I'd fooled with that, I would have flunked out.

When I got out of college I didn't know what I wanted to do. Well really, I guess I did, but I didn't discuss it with my father. What I wanted to do was to not work. Sometimes I had this nice fantasy. I thought if I had the courage (I wasn't even close) I'd ask John D. Rockefeller for $1 million. My reason was that he was too old to thoroughly enjoy his money, and I wasn't too old to thoroughly enjoy his money. I could play golf, travel, and be happy in every way, and he could enjoy this—secondhand.

If the reader has gotten the impression that I lacked enthusiasm for work he is on the right track. However, I had to get a job. I tried selling insurance and couldn't stand it. Everybody I said hello to was a prospect. I worked on my first potential customer for two months and must have played golf with him a dozen times (he couldn't hit the ball out of his own shadow) and finally got up enough courage to try to sell him an annuity. He turned me down. I went out to the street and cried—and retired from the insurance business. Money earned in insurance: zero.

My next effort was in the candy business. My father thought that maybe I could help him in sales. By then we had moved to New York. He was concentrating on selling candy to just a few large customers, the chain stores—Woolworth's, Kress, McCrory, and others. To help me learn the business, he got me a job in a candy factory, Edgar P. Lewis, of Malden, Massachusetts. I liked making candy, and for six months worked on the marmalade slab, making imitation orange slices, and barely lifting 100-pound bags of sugar into a boiling cauldron. In the late afternoon I'd go back to my boarding house and take a nap before dinner. Those were solid naps. When I woke up I didn't know where I was or what I was.

My salary at Edgar P. Lewis was $15 a week—and I lived on it. No hardship, but not luxurious either. Room and board was

$10.50 (lunch excluded). Both breakfast and dinner had the advantage of baked beans. I had one luxury (a necessity in getting to work), an old Buick my father had given me. Garage used up a buck a week. That didn't leave much out of the $15. When I was on double dates with Matt Suvalsky, an old college friend, Matt was encouraged to split the gas with me. A happy period in my life.

After six months my father felt that I had eaten enough candy and I was ready for sales training with him. My specific chores were to drive the car and carry the samples; and I would listen while my father talked to the candy buyers.

Well, we struggled along for a few months, but you know how it is with father and son, they don't always work well together. Besides, I guess selling wasn't my racket. My father had always impressed on me how important the other man's time was, and I think he overdid it. So I retired from the candy business and still needed a job.

We hear about those people who, while still playing with their rattles, know exactly what they want to do in life. Well, I was twenty-two and I'd never had any idea what I wanted to do. Naturally I got in the doldrums. My parents were patient and didn't push me. I lay around the apartment on West 88th Street, played bridge in the afternoon and evening, and fell asleep around 3 A.M. listening to Clyde McCoy playing *Sugar Blues*. My father thought I should see a psychiatrist. And I did, twice a week.

During this period an uncle got me a job with an industrial designer. Salary, $18 a week. The designer insisted I wear a hat, a Homburg no less; this purchase ate up my excess profits. I accompanied my employer to different stores he represented, with the thought that sooner or later I would catch on to the business. But I wasn't a quick learner. However, before I could get fired the designer offered to raise my salary from $18 a week to $50 a week, if I stopped seeing the psychiatrist, and he proposed we take a trip to Florida together. I was just bright enough to sense an ulterior motive, and resigned.

Insurance, candy, and industrial design—three strikes. Back to bridge, Clyde McCoy, and the psychiatrist. My parents were discouraged but they weren't surprised. My father always expected I'd have trouble making a living. I had no discernible useful aptitude, and my father had a suspicion that I was lazy (which suspicion he didn't keep from me).

Anyway, lazy or not, I didn't have a job. One night at the bridge club one of the players, who knew I was indigent, said I might like the brokerage business. Wall Street was the last place I'd have thought of trying, and with reluctance kept an appointment he made. My father went with me to the garment district branch of Cohen, Simondson & Co., members of the New York Stock Exchange. I was interviewed by a customer's broker who needed an assistant to answer his phones and keep his charts. I got the job, $25 a week. Years later I learned that my father had paid the customer's broker twenty weeks' salary in advance.

This time I took an interest in a job. The fluctuating prices and the gamble of the stock market struck one of my aptitudes. And it wasn't hard looking at the pretty models in the garment district. In a week I felt so much better that I tendered my resignation to the psychiatrist. Six months later I passed a stock exchange test, and became a junior customer's broker.

Although I liked the stock market, I was no threat to make a fortune; part of the job was approaching people for business and I didn't like that, it was selling again. After several years with Cohen, Simondson, I applied for a job as a full customer's broker at Bache & Co., and got turned down. Then E. A. Pierce & Co., later Merrill Lynch, Pierce, Fenner & Bean, took a chance and gave me a job at $75 a week—which I didn't quite earn.

I wasn't what you'd call a hard worker. There was usually an hour for lunch at Wilfred's across the street, and when the market closed at three o'clock I was on my way to my real enjoyment, bridge at the Cavendish Club. At my peak I was no more than a mediocre customer's broker. In market judgment I was probably above average—my charts were a big help here—but in commissions for the firm I was a dud. My career high was a salary of $1,000 a month.

Making a thousand a month must have unsettled my brain because, although classified 4-F, I volunteered for the Coast Guard. At Sheepshead Bay I worked my way steadily up through the ranks, to Seaman 2nd Class. The Coast Guard sifted through my talents, and put me in a high position on top of a garbage wagon where I was third in charge. But enough of my wartime exploits.

From the Coast Guard I returned to Merrill Lynch and my job as a customer's broker. One afternoon, after playing gin at the City Athletic Club, Chester Gaines, a specialist on the floor of the New York Stock Exchange, said that judging by the way I played gin I'd do well trading on the floor, and should buy a seat. It was a good idea but the funds I had were a little short of the purchase price—about 97 percent short.

In those days I used to play golf with a friend, Jerry Ohrbach, at Metropolis Country Club (let me brag and say I won the club championship seven years in a row). One day, when we were in the same foursome, I got a seven on the first hole, an easy par-five. I was steaming, and asked Jerry what odds he would give against my getting a thirty-three on that nine. Par was thirty-five, so that meant I would have to be four under for the next eight holes. Jerry said 1,000-to-1. I said I'll take a hundred dollars worth of that if you like, and he said okay. He could afford the hundred thousand and I could afford the hundred dollars. Jerry had the best of the odds and I had a shot at a fortune. I made him sweat to the last hole. I needed a birdie there for the thirty-three, but didn't come close.

When Chester Gaines suggested the stock exchange seat, I spoke to Jerry about it. He told me that the golf bet had scared him so much he would like to be partners with me. By borrowing from my father, one of my uncles, my wife, and adding my own few dollars, I got up 25 percent of the necessary capital. Jerry and his father, Nathan, put up the rest and became limited partners in the small firm, Dreyfus & Co., members of the New York Stock Exchange. And we lived happily ever after. Well, not quite.

Our back-office work was done by Bache & Co., the firm that had turned me down as a customer's broker. A friend of mine, John Behrens, handled my accounts in the office, and I went to the floor of the Exchange where I did two-dollar brokerage and traded for the firm's account. I liked the floor. It was a lot of walking—with a little thinking thrown in—and the hours of ten to three fitted well with my lazy bones.

In the first year, 1946, with capital of $100,000, we made $14,000 trading. Not as bad as you'd think—1946 was a bear market. A floor joke describes it, "The market was so bad that not even the liars made money." I don't think Nathan Ohrbach realized how well we did not to have lost our shirts. Nathan, who had the misfortune to walk into a brokerage office for the first time in 1929, had the indestructible opinion that you couldn't beat the market and was restless for Dreyfus & Co. to become a commission firm.

One day Jerry introduced me to one of the partners of the firm of Lewisohn & Sons. The capital partners wanted to retire, and Jerry and Nathan thought we should take over this old firm, stop clearing through Bache, and do our own back-office work. I mildly resisted—it didn't look like that good a deal, and besides it sounded like work. But I was told that three of the Lewisohn partners would remain and run the business, and I could stay on the floor. So I agreed.

Well, we bought this turkey, with trimmings. The Ohrbachs and I got the trimmings.

Without going into the reasons, it wasn't long before I had to leave the floor, where I was reasonably competent, and take on managing a brokerage firm, where I wasn't competent at all. Nathan Ohrbach soon found there were more ways of losing money on Wall Street than trading in the market. Our capital went down rapidly—mine vanished. We couldn't even go out of business easily, and decided to try to stick it out. The Ohrbachs were good about it and drew no interest on their money. I cut my salary to zero, and we struggled along.

After a while business got so good we broke even. The Ohrbachs and I thought we should advertise, and we set aside $20,000 of hard (unearned) money for the purpose. In those days one agency handled all the Wall Street advertising, and it was dreary. I thought we should try another agency.

At that time the firm of Doyle, Dane, and Bernbach was in swaddling clothes. The partners were friends of the Ohrbachs and agreed to handle our account. But for our budget they couldn't afford to write the copy. So I had to. To my great surprise I loved it; it was an aptitude that had been hidden from me. Our account executive, Freddie Dossenbach, and I used to have lunch at a corner table next to a window at Schwartz's on Broad Street. Inspired by Swiss cheese and liverwurst, with iced tea, I'd write copy to fit Freddie's cartoons. The ads were so different from what was being done on Wall Street that we got a lot of attention for the money being spent. Business got better and the firm started to grow. Soon we had enough partners to always have a quorum for an argument.

One day the Dreyfus Fund walked through the front door and we didn't know it. A fine gentleman, John Nesbett, applied for a position. John was the sole proprietor of a $500,000 mutual fund, the Nesbett Fund. He had struggled with it for several years, but with a management fee of $2,500 a year it had become impractical for him to continue. When John joined Dreyfus & Co. the name of his fund was changed to the Dreyfus Fund, and we took over the struggle. In the next five years Dreyfus & Co. lost about a million and a half dollars of its earnings on the Fund. During that period I got looks from some of my partners that at best could be called askance. But one day the Fund started to break even. From then on it became a winner.

I made money in the stock market, a great deal of it in Polaroid stock. Did I carefully screen the list to select this stock? No. I wouldn't even have known there was such a company if I hadn't had a brother-in-law who worked there. I bought the stock initially for the wrong reason—Polaroid's 3-D glasses—and made money because of the camera.

It would appear I had some luck. The Ohrbachs pushed me into the commission business, the Dreyfus Fund walked into the office, and I bought the right stock for the wrong reason. As I said earlier I was an implausible person to have made a lot of money.

In the late 1960s I retired from my businesses. Since then I have worked full time with the Dreyfus Medical Foundation.

▪ ▪ ▪

The newly established Dreyfus Medical Foundation funded its first study in 1966—with hope, and $57,000. It was a dud. It could be called a waste of time and money. But that wouldn't be quite right—it was part of education. I was learning how difficult it was to develop anyone's interest in PHT. As to the study, I'll make it brief. And I'll skip names. As explained earlier, complaining is not one of the purposes of this book.

Dr. Turner introduced me to members of the staff of a large hospital in the metropolitan area. They said they were interested in PHT and had a good patient population for conducting a study. I explained what had happened in the previous study—I didn't want to make that sort of mistake again—and said I'd like to be present in the early stages of the work. My experience, unsophisticated as it was, might be useful. They agreed to this and asked for $57,000 for the study.

I'd been given the impression that the study would start without delay, but it wasn't for several months that I was invited to attend the first interview with patients, conducted by Dr. Blank.

Four patients were interviewed in my presence. To my dismay, I was not allowed to say a word to these patients, although I sat just a few feet from them. If I wanted to ask a question, I had to write it on a slip of paper and hand it to Dr. Blank. Using "local mail" didn't improve my ability to communicate with these patients. One case is worth mentioning, a man who said he jackknifed in bed at night. Dr. Blank didn't ask for particulars, but I did—by note—and learned that several times each night, before he fell asleep, the patient's legs would jerk up almost to his head. I was surprised that PHT had not already been tried with him—these involuntary movements seemed a form of convulsion. After the session I expressed the opinion to Dr. Blank that three of the four patients were good candidates for PHT. I was never told whether they were given it—there was an air of mystery about everything—but I don't think they were.

The upshot of this study was that, two years later, the physician in charge of the study made the vapid statement at a medical meeting that "more work was needed in this field." Well, you couldn't argue with that.

It's hard to realize how frustrating this was. Here I was, eager to give money for studies on an established medicine, and I couldn't find the right people to give it to.

▪ ▪ ▪

One fine day, in 1966, Dr. Turner asked me if I'd like to participate in conducting a study. I told him I'd like to, but I didn't know it was possible. Bill said he thought it could be arranged. A few weeks later Bill made arrangements through a friend of his, Dr. Oscar Resnick of the Worcester Foundation, for that foundation and ours to conduct a joint study at the Worcester County Jail.

Bill and I visited Dr. Resnick at his home in Worcester, Massachusetts, the following Sunday. On both sides of a nice lunch we discussed the proposed study. Until Bill had brought up the subject, I'd never thought about a study in a prison. After all a prison is not a hospital and doesn't necessarily have sick people. But now that I thought about it, it seemed that nervous conditions could be a contributing cause in many criminal acts, particularly those of anger and violence. I discussed this with Dr. Resnick, who had done many studies at this jail. He agreed and said he thought we'd find an ample number of people who had problems with their nerves.

When we discussed how the interview with the prisoners should be conducted, Oscar won a lifelong friendship with me when he said, "Look, Jack, you know what you're looking for. It'll be a lot easier if you ask the questions. I'll chime in when I think it's necessary."

This jail study was to be an unusual experience for me—in some ways the most fruitful of my life.

ELEVEN ANGRY MEN

In 1966 Dr. Resnick and I conducted a study on the effects of PHT with prisoners at the Worcester County Jail in Massachusetts. It was done on a double-blind crossover basis. Helping us with the study was Ms. Barbara Homan, medical assistant to Dr. Turner.

The Worcester County Jail was a "short-term" jail. Although some of the inmates had committed serious crimes, no one sentenced to more than eighteen months was sent there.

From the outside the jail looked like an ordinary building. On the inside, except in the cell area, it resembled an old high school. For our work we were assigned a small room with a nice window on the second floor. This room was plainly furnished but comfortable, with a long table and some chairs. Liaison with the prisoners was handled by Lt. William D'Orsay, a kind and well-liked man.

Drug studies were not uncommon at the jail.* It was the custom for these studies to be done with volunteers, paid a dollar a day. We followed custom. Ms. Homan did preliminary

---

* Clearance for the study was given by the warden, Sheriff Joseph Smith, and Dr. Cyrus Paskevitch, the prison physician.

screening of forty-two volunteers, and eliminated twenty of the least likely candidates. This left twenty-two volunteers for Dr. Resnick and me to interview.

These twenty-two volunteers were interviewed carefully. This was a study of individuals, not prisoners; we had no intention of giving PHT to anyone just because he was in prison. We were looking for individuals who had symptoms we thought would respond to PHT. Among the most important of these symptoms were: excessive anger, excessive fear, and an overbusy mind that was difficult to turn off.

After two days of interviews, eleven prisoners were selected. Most of them had participated in other drug studies and didn't expect to get a medicine that would actually help them. They thought we were doing the study for our own purposes and they had volunteered mainly to ease their boredom. When we told them that we wanted only the truth about what the medicine did, they expressed skepticism that it would do anything. This attitude was good—it minimized the possibility of their being psychologically influenced.

In the initial interviews I was glad I was not alone in the room with a few of the prisoners. There was an animalistic bristle about them you could feel. One man had eyes with a yellowish glow that reminded me of an ocelot I'd seen. After a few interviews, whether because of PHT or getting to know them better, I felt comfortable with all the prisoners.

Dr. Resnick left most of the questioning of the prisoners to me. I tried to keep the interviews comfortable and friendly. This seemed to help the subjects relax, and they spoke freely. Some of them were more expressive than others, but communication was good with all of them.

Procedure. The eleven prisoners chosen for the study were interviewed for a second time, this time intensively. As specifically as we could, we got an inventory of their symptoms and complaints. Then they were placed on PHT (100 mg in the morning and 50 mg in the afternoon) and were not told what to expect of the medicine. They were interviewed several hours after the initial dose, the next day, and again at the end of a week.

Remarkable improvement in symptoms was observed. To see if similar results would be obtained under the most objective circumstances, we decided to do a double-blind, crossover to single-blind, study.

To do such a study it was desirable to approximate the original conditions. We thought this could be achieved by taking the prisoners off PHT for a week. However, when they were interviewed at the end of the week, their general condition was better than when we had first met them. It was as though the week on PHT had been a vacation from their nerves and the benefits had carried forward. We had to wait a second week before the original conditions were approximated.

Before starting the double-blind study we explained the procedure to the prisoners. Some of them would receive PHT, others an inert substance called a placebo. The capsules would be identical in appearance—the prisoners wouldn't know what they contained and we wouldn't know, thus "double-blind." Then they would be interviewed as before: a few hours after the first pill, after a night's sleep, and a week later. At that time we would make our decision as to which of them had received PHT, and which placebo.

What we did not tell the prisoners was that when this decision had been made, those subjects we thought had been on placebo would be placed on "single-blind." They would be given PHT without being told it was PHT. In that way, further nonsubjective evidence would be obtained.

Summary

We were correct in our assessment of ten of the prisoners on the double-blind. We were incorrect in one. The unusual circumstances in this case explain why.* In the study it was observed that the eleven prisoners had many symptoms in common that responded to PHT. Among these symptoms in common were restlessness, irritability, fear, anger, inability to concentrate, poor mood, lack of energy, sleeping problems, and an overactive brain.

Symptoms not common to all prisoners, such as headache, stomach distress, chest pain, muscular pain, skin rash, and dizziness, disappeared while the subjects were on PHT and reappeared when it was withdrawn.

This study was recorded on tape with the prisoners' permission. Transcribed, there are 605 pages covering 130 interviews.

The results were exceptional. Brief summaries of five cases are included here. The other six cases were just as successful. In the earlier edition of this book, summaries of the other cases were included in the Appendix. It is not practical to do that here.**

JAMES L.

Before PHT:

I feel miserable, a bunch of nerves.

I have a grudge on me I can't get rid of...I take it out on everyone. It's so bad that sometimes I have myself locked in so I won't cause any trouble.

---

* In the early part of the study, Danny R.'s response to PHT was like that of the other prisoners. During the control part of the study, Danny R. got news that made him think his daughter was going blind. He didn't tell us, and we misassessed his realistic nervousness and decided he was on placebo. It wasn't until a few years later I learned that while PHT relieves unrealistic problems, it doesn't remove realistic problems—a desirable feature.

** For those interested in the welfare of prisoners, an 80-page condensation is available through the Dreyfus Medical Foundation, Lenox Hill Station, P.O. Box 965, New York, N.Y. 10021-0029. The 605-page transcript is on file at the Foundation.

I can't work or nothing. When you're down-and-out there isn't much you can do.

I can't digest my food right...I don't feel like eating nothing.

My thinking is bad, there are quite a few thoughts in my mind, I can't concentrate at all. It takes me a day-and-a-half to write one letter.

I get them phantom limb pains [he had a wooden leg] quite a bit, at least three times a week. The pain, I can just take so much of it. I can't sleep and I can't sit still or nothing.

Sometimes I have them headaches in the afternoon and at night I get them right back again.

With PHT (Non-Blind):

I feel a lot better. All the guys down there say I ain't the same guy...because I let them all out of their cells. [James L. was a trusty.] I didn't lock nobody up.

Now I'm eating like a fool, before I couldn't eat.

I get them headaches once in a while but not too often. That's why I stopped taking those aspirins.

After Being Off PHT (Two Weeks):

I never get to sleep...I sleep about an hour, that's all.

I get weak but I can't seem to hold my weight. The guys put me on the bed and I come out of it after a while.

I get them headaches quite often now. I'm getting phantom limb pains again...I had it again yesterday. I couldn't even lay down on the bed. I kept twisting and turning.

I'll read a story and, as a matter of fact, I won't even know what I read.

With Placebo (Double-Blind):

I'm down and out right now. My mind's all bunched up now. I passed out Wednesday. I get headaches.

Anger, about the same as it was before the pills.

I had those phantom limb pains Wednesday.

With PHT (Single-Blind):

I feel good right now...I feel altogether different...I feel much better since I got them pills.

I've been kidding around with everybody...For the last two days the fellows have been saying I'm not the same guy. No headaches. No phantom limb pains.

DAVID H.

Before PHT:

I have a temper that shouldn't be...I shake when I'm angry and can't stop. I have stomach trouble...I think it's from nerves.

If something happens, I twist and turn it in my mind until I've made a problem out of nothing...I can't turn my mind off. I can't go to sleep.

Quite often I'll get depressed and start worrying about home and what's going on outside these lovely walls. I lose all hope and energy.

With PHT (Non-Blind):

Well, I feel I'm a lot calmer... I can sit still, without jumping up.

For the past five or six days I've been sure of myself in the things I say and what I do. I get angry just as fast but I can control it...it doesn't keep poppin' back into my mind.

I used to read three or four chapters without knowing what I read. Now I can lie there and remember what I've read.

I've been eating my meals and enjoying them.

After Being Off PHT (Two Weeks):

I feel very tired, irritable and grouchy. I'm not getting along well...People are getting on my nerves to the extent where I'm ready to assassinate them.

I don't eat hardly anything...I'm not sleeping very well...I feel just terrible.

I got a few problems and I just can't get them out of my mind. I'm worrying about them all the time...I've tried my case a thousand times.

With PHT (Double-Blind):

I think I'm on the Dilantin right now. I'm not nervous...I'm not tense or ready to jump at anyone.

I'm not grouchy...I seem to still have a temper, but I go into a situation with a little more confidence. I don't just jump off the handle.

I seem able to push my thoughts aside...read a couple of stories and know what I read.

I feel fine as far as my stomach goes...My appetite has picked up...I been sleeping better...able to go right to sleep.

CLIFFORD S.

Before PHT:

I'm very high-strung...I let everything build up inside...Then I just explode. I do a lot of thinking.

I get these wicked headaches...I'll take six or seven aspirin...and the headache won't go away. I'll have it all day.

I don't sleep well. Between twelve and two in the morning I usually get these nightmares...scare a guy right out of his head.

With PHT (Non-Blind):

I just feel wonderful...You know how I can feel my nerves are relaxed? I've done four paintings; I don't paint when I'm nervous because I can't concentrate...If I can sit down and do a painting a day it makes me happy.

I'm in a good mood. I don't feel angry at anybody...I've only really got mad once since the last time I seen you. It went right away.

I've been sleeping a lot. I ain't jumpy all the time. I ain't looking behind me anymore.

After Being Off PHT (Two Weeks):

I'm tense inside, I can't stay in one place too long, I get up and move around...I just pick a book up, look at it and throw it back down.

I feel that anger...Whenever I get in a fight I can't control myself.

I wake up about five or six times during the night.

With Placebo (Double-Blind):

My nerves are jittery inside...I can't sit in one place too long.

This week when I was lifting, I got dizzy three or four times and I was only working out with light weights.

I know my mind's always been going on. Actually, I don't feel these pills have done anything for me.

With PHT (Single-Blind):

I just feel good. I am completely relaxed...I ain't nervous, tense or nothing.

There's no anger at all.

Sleep better...ain't tired...all kinds of energy; washing windows, floors. I can concentrate better.

PHILIP B.

Before PHT:

I am quite nervous now. I've been more or less nervous all my life. And shake a lot, you just feel it, that you're shaking.

If I get nervous my hands break out in a little rash. I get tightness in my chest quite often. It's a pain, it takes your breath away sometimes.

I think a lot, there is too much on my mind. I try to put it out of my mind and it just stays there. The mind wanders and it doesn't focus on what I'm doing. Sometimes it's 3:00 o'clock in the morning before I get to sleep.

With PHT (Non-Blind):

I feel good all over now. I seem to relax a lot more. Since I've been taking the pills I haven't been walking around, pacing back and forth so much. These past few nights I've been going right to sleep.

I haven't been so depressed. I've been eating better. And I haven't had those pains in my chest. And I can concentrate better on my work. And I'm not making as many mistakes.

After Being Off PHT (Two Weeks):

Well, I feel I'm right back where I was before I started taking the pills. I don't sleep well. I walk around all the time. Nervous all the time—agitated, quick-tempered, get shook up.

I'm always thinking—wandering away—always thinking of different things. I've been very depressed.

With PHT (Double-Blind):

I feel good, very good, feel a lot better, honestly. And I haven't had those chest pains this week at all. The rash it cleared right up. I'm more relaxed.

I can just forget about things now. I've been able to do my work better. The last few days I've been goin' to sleep right off. I feel much better than I have for the last three years.

JOHN G.

Before PHT:

I'm nervous, irritable, and I brood a lot over things that are already over and done with. I make more of them inside which keeps me in quite a state of nervousness, anger, tension, what have you.

I magnify everything to the extent where I make myself uncomfortable...I'm never relaxed enough to take time to try to figure out what makes me move—I can't control myself and I just don't seem to give a damn one way or the other.

With PHT (Non-Blind):

I'm quite relaxed. I feel good.

I slept real good...I'm not as worked up so I stay awake...When it's bedtime, I'm ready to go.

I'm more easygoing...I'm not as short with the fellas as I usually am...I've only blown my top once...It just lasted a few seconds...I didn't brood about it afterwards.

After Being Off PHT (Two Weeks):

Before I took the medicine, I felt the same way as I do now...More or less quick to jump. In fact, a lot of times I might jump before I think it over.

I've had two good arguments since I've been off the medication.

I've had a few headaches in the morning...A lot of times I have a headache during the day when I get worked up over something.

I'm not sleeping. I wouldn't say I'm sleeping sound at all...I'm having some dreams...they are very unpleasant...and uncomfortable, tiring.

With PHT (Double-Blind):

I think I'm improved all over...An hour after I took the pill I could have told you it wasn't sugar...You could feel the engine just slowing right down.

I'm very relaxed and I'm not uncomfortable in any way...I can sort of think ahead.

I been sleeping soundly, no trouble, no lying awake thinking about things. That's more or less what kept me awake; the brain was overactive...but now I just drop right off.

I still have anger but I don't blow up...Quite a bit of restraint which I never had...The anger doesn't hang on like it did before.

■ ■ ■

Suggestions from the Prisoners for the Use of PHT in Prisons

When the study was over we met with the inmates as a group for the first time. Each of the prisoners had told us he wanted to continue taking PHT. But I learned this was not going to be permitted, and there was nothing I could do about that. But I could tell the prisoners what I knew about the medicine—it might be useful to them later on.

We had a long, friendly discussion. As we were saying goodbye, John G. volunteered:

JOHN G: If this pill was ever put on the market it would be a godsend to both Walpole and Concord prisons. Judging by this group here, it'd work miracles up there. You have men doing ten, fifteen, twenty, and life. And that's where I'd like to see them back up a whole truckload of the stuff and—

JACK D: You mean Dilantin?

JOHN G: Dilantin is right. Those guys are walkin' on edge all the time. There's where the trouble starts, more so than here. These fellows are all going fairly short. Up there you got a bunch of fellows that got nothing to lose and, well, they're all packed in together.

JACK D: You think that in those prisons...

JOHN G: I think they need it even worse than the fellows do here. You can ask Jim and Spike.

JACK D: Do you agree with that, Spike?

Victor M: Oh, yes, I agree with that very much.
JACK D: What would you say, Jim?

JAMES L: The same thing. I was there for a while myself and I know. It would help a lot of them guys. You walk around there and if you say the wrong thing, you're liable to go bouncing off the wall.

JOHN G: Those guys are so on edge they gotta take yellow jackets and bennies once in a while to relieve that. What if they didn't have this tension built up? They wouldn't have the trouble they do now.

JACK D: Well, John, thank you for the thought.

The prisoners' suggestion that the use of PHT, on a voluntary basis, be permitted inside a prison should be considered. Some prisoners are in jail because of problems in their nervous systems, and these problems are exacerbated by their confinement. With too much time to think and brood, it's no wonder that some prisoners live in a sort of hell and can't help imposing it on those around them.

Allowing PHT to be taken on a voluntary basis could make an important difference to those individuals who need it—and to others who are endangered by their potential for violence. When one realizes that PHT is not habit-forming, withholding it from prisoners is the opposite of protection of their rights.

■ ■ ■

As stated earlier, this study was not of prisoners as such but a study of individuals with problems of their nervous sytems. The objective was to see if, in a double-blind study, the effects of PHT that had been observed on an uncontrolled basis would be confirmed. They were, and additional effects of PHT were observed.*

I felt the time had come to go to the federal government.

---

* I participated in two further studies in institutions, one with Dr. Resnick at the Lyman Reformatory for Boys in Lyman, Massachusetts, the other at the Patuxent Institution in Maryland, with Dr. Joel Elkes, head of psychiatry at Johns Hopkins, and Dr. Joseph Stephens and Dr. Lino S. Covi, also of Hopkins. Although not controlled studies, the results were similar to those of the Worcester study. (See the Appendix, p. 423.) Since this was published three other studies were done at correctional institutions outside the United States.

TRAVELS WITH THE GOVERNMENT

Few of us have a clear picture of the federal government and how it operates. With millions of people in it, government has to be run by regulations. This leads to routine. Where there's routine, innovation doesn't thrive. I'm not being critical, government means well. But I'll tell you this, if you want the government to do something outside of routine—and expect to see it happen in your lifetime—you'd better arrange for reincarnation.

I didn't know this in 1966, and with the optimism of a Boy Scout I approached the federal government. I would have gone to the government sooner but had felt the evidence was too informal. Now, with the jail study done, the time was right. I had two thoughts in mind. The first was that the government might take the matter off my hands. I hoped for this, but wasn't counting on it. My second thought was that I didn't want to do anything contrary to government policy. Their objectives and mine were the same. If I was to proceed on my own, I needed official advice.

There were two logical places to go: the Department of Health, Education and Welfare, and the Food and Drug

Administration. Since I was a layman, the Department of Health seemed the appropriate place. At that time John W. Gardner was Secretary of HEW. It took me about a month to get an appointment with the Secretary. That seemed like a long time. When I got to know the government better I realized that a month was instantaneous.

I met with Secretary Gardner in Washington in May 1966. We talked for fifty minutes. That is, I talked for the first forty minutes and he talked for the last ten. In those forty minutes I summarized my experience with Dilantin and my observations of its benefits in others. I told him of my disappointment in the two hospital studies I'd sponsored, of setting up the Dreyfus Medical Foundation, and of the double-blind study at the Worcester County Jail.

Secretary Gardner listened. From the experience I'd had it wouldn't have surprised me if he had been skeptical. But he wasn't. The Secretary seemed to sense that I was on the right track. Although he didn't suggest that the government take a hand, he gave me three helpful suggestions.

The first suggestion had to do with my unmedical terminology. The Secretary laughed when I made my "dry twigs" analogy. He said he liked it but thought more sophisticated language would stand me in good stead in talking with physicians. Of course he was right, and now I talk of "post-tetanic potentiation" and "post-tetanic afterdischarge" as if they were old friends. His second suggestion was that I should tell Parke-Davis about my findings. I followed this suggestion, too, as will be explained later.

The third suggestion came as a surprise, but I welcomed it. The Secretary said I should seek national publicity for the story. He understood my disappointment with the lack of results from the two hospitals. However, he was sure that somewhere in the United States there were hospitals and physicians who would be interested in the story.

I told Secretary Gardner I could try *Life* magazine. A few months earlier *Life* had done a kind article about me by Marshall Smith with the understated title, "Maverick Wizard Behind the Wall Street Lion." Marshall and I had become good friends, and I thought he might introduce me to *Life's* science department. The Secretary said that *Life* would be an excellent place for this story, if they would do it.

The meeting with Secretary Gardner was most helpful. His suggestions were good and I followed them all.

■ ■ ■

It wasn't easy to get *Life* magazine to do a medical article recommended by a layman. Albert Rosenfeld, *Life's* science editor, was understandably cautious. He had several sessions with me in which he listened carefully to the evidence. Then Al said he would like to do the story, but *Life* would require a medical event as a peg. He said a medical meeting would serve the purpose. Before making a firm commitment, however, Al wanted to get the reactions of a good friend, Dr. Joel Elkes, director of psychiatry at Johns Hopkins.

Before I met Dr. Elkes I thought of him as a hurdle. But after a discussion with him, I found I had a friend. Dr. Elkes said the subject was of particular interest since ten years earlier he had planned to do research on PHT with other physicians. But just at that time an exciting new medicine, thorazine, had appeared, and their interest had been sidetracked. Dr. Elkes was helpful in setting up the meeting that *Life* required, and in 1966 a symposium on PHT was held at the annual meeting of the American College of Neuropsychopharmacology.

In September 1967 *Life* published an article by Albert Rosenfeld—"10,000-to-1 Payoff." The article was a turning point. The response to it, and to the *Reader's Digest* condensation of it printed in thirteen languages, forced us to increase our small staff to keep up with phone calls and to answer letters. Many physicians wrote that they were using PHT for a variety of purposes.

We received thousands of letters from the public. The best side of human nature showed up. The writers expressed deep appreciation for benefits they got from PHT as a result of the articles. Many described their experiences in detail in the hope that by so doing they might help others. We selected a hundred of these letters and made a booklet for physicians. But readership was poor; doctors consider letters "anecdotal."

The *Life* and *Reader's Digest* articles opened things up. Now there were institutions and individual physicians with genuine interest in doing work on PHT. Soon the Foundation was sponsoring over a dozen studies. We got as far from home base as Chichester, England. There, Dr. Lionel Haward, in a series of double-blind studies with normal volunteers, demonstrated that PHT improved cognitive function. In the United States, perhaps the most significant of these early studies was by Stephens and Shaffer at Johns Hopkins. In a double-blind crossover study, they found PHT to be markedly effective in reducing symptoms related to fear and anger.

During this period Dr. Turner was searching the medical literature to see if previous work had been done on PHT. To my surprise he and his staff found hundreds of studies, published over the previous twenty years. These studies, in addition to confirming our observations in thought and mood, reported PHT to be useful for a variety of other disorders. Among them were cardiac disorders, trigeminal neuralgia, migraine, diabetes, pruritis ani, ulcers, and asthma.

■ ■ ■

Three years after I had met with Secretary Gardner, I was ready to go back to the government. When I had seen the Secretary I didn't have a lot of evidence. But now I was loaded for bear. This was a mistake. I should have brought an elephant gun. Republicans were in.

In the sequence of events we come to President Richard M. Nixon. By chance I had known Mr. Nixon before he became president. I'd seen his interview on the David Susskind Show, and as a result, without being asked, had contributed to his presidential campaign. When Mr. Nixon was defeated I got to know him. When he lost the race for Governor of California I knew he had no chance to become President. If you can't win your own state, you can't win the United States.

That's what I thought, but Mr. Nixon was nominated for President in 1968. Again I contributed to his campaign; I also contributed to the campaign of Senator Hubert Humphrey. And I did what I suppose was an unusual thing—I told each I was contributing to the campaign of the other. In this matter of public health, it was important for me to be known by whichever one became President. I was able to talk to both before the election. With Mr. Nixon, I had a long conversation about PHT at Key Biscayne.

My discussion with Senator Humphrey about PHT took place at his headquarters in New York. When we finished he said, "Listen, son [that nearly got my vote], whether I win or lose, I want you to get back to me on this." I couldn't have hoped for anything nicer than that. After the election I was anxious to get back to the Senator but it took three months to get an appointment. We had coffee in his suite at the Waldorf-Astoria. He showed up from a bedroom in shirt sleeves, and I had the feeling we were going to get down to work. I started off enthusiastically. Then I noticed there was no response in his face, and his gaze was fixed on a picture on the wall in back of me. In about fifteen minutes my enthusiasm started to run down. When I left soon after, I had the feeling that Senator Humphrey was relieved. I was too, but deeply disappointed.

■ ■ ■

After Mr. Nixon became President I waited a few months for him to settle into position, so to speak, and then called Rose Mary Woods, his nice and well-known secretary. I spoke to her for quite a while, explaining what an urgent medical matter this was, and told her I would send her some written information. I asked her to please not talk to the President about it, just give it some thought and advise me on the best way to approach him on the matter. I'm really dumber than the law allows. Of course Rose Mary, as any good secretary would, told President Nixon about it. A few days later she called to tell me the material had been sent to Secretary of Health Finch and I would hear from him shortly. I had hoped to see the President himself, but this was fine. I waited to hear from Secretary Finch.

Days went by without my hearing from the Secretary and I started to get restless. By the time three months had elapsed I was beside myself (not easy). I didn't have sense enough, or guts enough, to pick up the phone and call Secretary Finch, so I spoke to a friend who had a friend who knew the Secretary. This worked. Apparently the material Miss Woods had sent three months earlier hadn't reached Secretary Finch on the conveyor belt that carries things to the desk of a Secretary of Health. I got a call from Secretary Finch's secretary and an appointment was made.

Dr. Bogoch and I met with Secretary Finch in his office in December 1969. The Secretary didn't say whether he had discussed the matter with President Nixon, but he'd had a chance to look at the material I had sent the President, the *Life* and *Reader's Digest* articles, excerpts from letters from physicians, and a condensed version of the Worcester Jail Study. I hadn't wanted to burden the President with medical studies. But for the Secretary of Health I brought, in a bulging briefcase, hundreds of medical studies on the use of PHT for a variety of disorders. The Secretary was impressed.

After we'd been with Secretary Finch a short while, he asked Dr. Jesse L. Steinfeld, who had been appointed Surgeon General the previous day, to join us. Then, with both present, Dr. Bogoch and I briefly summarized the clinical evidence and basic mechanisms of action of PHT.

When we finished I told Secretary Finch about my meeting with Secretary Gardner three years earlier, and the advice he'd given me. Since that time so much new information had come into the possession of the Dreyfus Medical Foundation, facts not generally known, there was no question that this was now a matter for the government. To convey the information to the government, Dr. Bogoch and I proposed that we have a two-day conference with a broadly representative group of government physicians including members of the FDA. At such a conference we would present the medical information, and the government would be able to take it from there.

After we had made our proposal, Secretary Finch turned to the Surgeon General and said, "Let's get moving on this. How long will it take you to get a group together to meet with the Dreyfus Medical Foundation? How soon can you get a conference set up?"

"Probably in a couple of weeks," Dr. Steinfeld said.

"Well, do it faster if you can, but do it within two weeks," Secretary Finch told him. Apparently my sense of urgency had been picked up by the Secretary. We thanked him, and after exchanging telephone numbers with Dr. Steinfeld, Dr. Bogoch and I left with the feeling that the government would soon play its part.

When we got back to New York, Dr. Bogoch and I started the hard work of getting the data organized for the conference in two weeks. Four days went by before it occurred to me that we hadn't heard from the Surgeon General. Although Secretary Finch had given him explicit instructions to hold this meeting without delay, I thought it possible Dr. Steinfeld might be waiting for a call from me. I phoned him. His secretary said he was in conference and would call back. He didn't call back and I called again the next day. He was still in conference. This was the beginning of my awareness that phoning the Surgeon General and getting to speak to him were not exactly the same thing.

Several days later the Surgeon General called to say that he had been thinking about the conference; he thought we should have a meeting to discuss it and would like to have Dr. Bert Brown, head of the National Institute of Mental Health, with him. We were prepared to meet without delay, but he said he would be tied up for a week and suggested that the four of us meet in Washington on January 14. I could see that things were not going as smoothly as I'd hoped; the meeting to discuss the meeting that was supposed to have taken place in two weeks wouldn't take place for three weeks.

On the fourteenth Dr. Bogoch and I arrived in Washington to have dinner with Dr. Steinfeld and Bert Brown. Dr. Brown was not present. The Surgeon General explained that his secretary had forgotten to invite him. Without Dr. Brown the Surgeon General felt we didn't have a "quorum" and would have to have another meeting. We were taken aback. Still, we felt the time could be put to good use if we enlarged on Dr. Steinfeld's sketchy background on PHT. We did our best, but we didn't seem to have the Surgeon General's full attention because he would frequently interject, "I don't know how my secretary forgot to call Dr. Brown."

Before we left Washington we discussed our next meeting with Dr. Steinfeld. Where we should meet seemed a problem to him. He said maybe we should meet in a motel. I didn't know what that meant, but to get things moving I would have met in the men's room. We left Washington with no definite date. I began to have the feeling that I was looking at the "Finch medical conference" through the wrong end of a telescope.

I was not born with an oversupply of patience. Even with Dilantin I am short of perfection. This is to explain to the reader that the next six months were about as frustrating and exasperating a period of time as one could hope not to enjoy. It was that long before we had another meeting with the Surgeon General, this time with Dr. Brown. Both before and after this meeting, with a skill unequaled in my experience, Jesse Steinfeld ducked and dodged, retreated and sidestepped, and left me so off balance that I felt something was going to happen any day. Each time I managed to catch the Surgeon General on the telephone, a new subject would come up for consideration, such as, what physicians we should bring with us, where the meeting should take place, how many people should attend, what medical disciplines should be represented, and who should chair the meeting. (It was finally decided that Jesse should chair it.) It could have been chaired by Little Orphan Annie because the meeting never took place.

We kept contact with the Surgeon General, and this mirage of a meeting, for well over a year. His superb talent for keeping our interest alive, without doing anything other than that, explains why we did not think of going back to Secretary Finch until it was too late. (He left office six months after we met.)

The end came in the following way. We had gotten the Surgeon General pinned down to a meeting, the date made well in advance and its importance emphasized. Dr. Bogoch and I were going to review the medical data at length, feeling that this would motivate Dr. Steinfeld to set up the conference without further delay. And I was determined at this meeting to lay it on the line—either get results, or not.

A few days before the scheduled meeting I got a telephone call from Dr. Steinfeld's secretary saying she was sorry but we'd have to cancel the meeting for the coming Monday. I said, "But we had things all arranged for a full presentation. Why can't he make it?"

"He has to go out West on Monday to investigate the earthquake," she said. (An earthquake had occurred in California a week earlier.) If Jesse had been going to California to prevent the earthquake, well, good luck. But to cancel a medical meeting of this importance to visit an earthquake that had already happened, and not even propose a new date for the meeting, was too much. I said to myself, the heck with it, and Jesse didn't have any more of my phone calls to dodge.

I never did find out what a Surgeon General was supposed to do. He didn't do surgery, and he didn't command troops. Maybe the government couldn't find out either because when Dr. Steinfeld left, the office was retired.*

At the time Dr. Steinfeld left government, the *New York Times* reported him to have said that federal health affairs were in a "kind of chaos." He was "frustrated seeing how much good I might have achieved and how much was actually accomplished."

In a nutshell.

■ ■ ■

I had placed a lot of hope on the government's taking over PHT. I admit that part of this was because I wanted to be relieved of the responsibility and the work. But there was a more important reason. With its medical institutions, and its enormous resources and authority, the government could do a far better job than a single foundation. However, it wasn't long after the Finch conference that I began to get the idea that government lacked enthusiasm about taking over its responsibilities.

* The Office of Surgeon General has been resurrected. We wish the new Surgeon General the best of luck.

Maybe I should sum up my thoughts during this period. At the outset, when I became convinced that PHT had been overlooked, I knew that medical studies would be necessary to persuade others. After the initial unsuccessful attempts, the Foundation had sponsored numerous successful studies on PHT and was continuing in this effort. But by far the most important source of evidence was already in the medical literature. This evidence had been there for the picking, like good apples under a tree.

I don't know exactly when we passed the equator of ample evidence, but at some point our goal changed, and we decided that communicating already existing evidence was more important than finding new evidence. You know that old philosophical question about the tree falling in the forest—if nobody hears it, was there a sound? I'm not sure about that, but here was a practical question. If a great amount of evidence exists for the usefulness of a medicine, and the physician doesn't know about it, does it do any good? The answer is obvious. So communication became our number one objective.

Something other than trying to tell the story to the government had to be done. By this time we had collected so many published studies on PHT they would have filled a barrel. I would like to have Xeroxed the studies and sent each physician a barrelful saying, "You'll find this useful." But it wasn't practical. We had to attack the barrel ourselves, organize the studies, and condense them for the physicians. And that is what we did.

When we finished we had a bibliography and review of PHT, the clinical section arranged chronologically, the contents fairly evenly divided between clinical and basic mechanism of action studies. It was exhausting work for our group, and just the writing of it took over a year and a half. To keep our spirits up we worked on the theory that if a doctor matched a thousand hours of our effort with ten minutes of his own (aye, there's the rub) we'd show a profit—with 350,000 doctors in the U.S.A.

The bibliography, *The Broad Range of Use of Phenytoin,* was the first of two that the Foundation published. About 400,000 copies were sent to physicians and basic scientists in the United States in 1970. The response was excellent, and we had letters of thanks from nearly a thousand physicians. Still, the facts about PHT did not spread as fast as I had hoped.

■ ■ ■

One Sunday morning in July 1971, my brain was playing with the communication problem. The Foundation was sponsoring studies of PHT, mostly in new fields, but we had no other immediate plans. The thought that government had the key responsibility for PHT was always in my mind. But I had taken my best shot with the government—President, Secretary of Health, and Surgeon General. Something else had to be done; I couldn't figure out what, and it bugged me.

It's funny how we remember unimportant things if they are associated with something important. That Sunday, my housekeeper Ida Thomas, whom I love and who has a feeling for me, sensed my mood and said, "Let me fix you something for breakfast instead of those old eggs and tomatoes you eat every day." I thanked her, and went back to thinking about the government. Interesting smells started coming out of the kitchen. Soon a delicious-looking pancake arrived, with powdered sugar and hot blueberry sauce. The first bite was on my fork when the phone rang.

A voice said, "This is Walter Tkach at the White House. I'm President Nixon's doctor, and I was just telling the President and Mrs. Nixon what a wonderful piece of work I thought you'd done." If an ancestor had called I couldn't have been more surprised. Just when I was wondering how to get back to the government, here was a spontaneous recommendation to the

President, from his own doctor. I steadied my voice and thanked Dr. Tkach. Dr. Tkach went on to say, "The President suggested that I invite you to visit me in Washington and I hope you can make it soon." I said I could. We made a date for the following Tuesday. Then I ate Ida's pancake and two more.

Tuesday I took a sensible morning plane to Washington that got me there at 9:45. Dr. Tkach met me and drove me to the White House in his car. During the drive he told me that after a personal loss he had benefited from PHT, and had the *Life* article to thank for it. I was glad he had first-hand experience with PHT; there's nothing like it to get an understanding of the medicine.

When we got to the White House, Dr. Tkach walked me past the gendarmes, and for a moment I had the feeling I was infiltrating the place. But when we got to his office Walter made me feel like a dignitary. He put me in a comfortable chair, got me a jug of coffee, and became a voluntary and patient listener for several hours. In that sympathetic atmosphere I did a good job of summarizing the PHT story.

At about 12:30 Dr. Tkach suggested lunch would be appropriate. He didn't have to drag me—I've always noticed that mental effort uses more calories than physical effort—and we went to the White House cafeteria. Walter hadn't told me we would have company for lunch, but he had invited Kenneth R. Cole, Jr., and James H. Cavanaugh, two members of the President's staff, to join us. I didn't get to eat as well as I'd hoped because I had to give a forty-five-minute summary of PHT. I emphasized the government's responsibility. Ken and Jim ate well and listened well.

When lunch was over Ken Cole, who outranked Jim Cavanaugh on the President's staff, said they would both try to be helpful in getting the story to the FDA. He said I could call him whenever necessary, but Jim would work with me on a regular basis. In the past I had been treated with courtesy by the government, but I'd felt a little like a salesman, carrying samples in his briefcase. Now I was being offered help without soliciting it and it put me in a different posture. When lunch was over I thanked them all.

Dr. Tkach drove me back to the airport. He said there wasn't any question that the government should do something about the PHT matter. But he cautioned me against being too optimistic. He said the problem wouldn't be with people I would meet but with the nature of bureaucracy. It was so big, and so besieged on all sides by people clamoring for its attention, that it was distracted from important matters—even if it could figure out which they were. A few years earlier I would have argued with Walter. Now I just kept my fingers crossed.

That same week Jim Cavanaugh came to New York and spent a day with Dr. Bogoch and me. It was one of those calorie-consuming days. I spent at least four hours going over clinical evidence, and Sam spent nearly half that time on the basic mechanisms. When he left, Jim had a good grasp of the facts. He said the next move would be for us to talk to Dr. Charles Edwards, Commissioner of the FDA.

Jim Cavanaugh made the appointment with Commissioner Edwards, and Dr. Bogoch and I spent a morning in the offices of the FDA. After a long talk with the Commissioner, he said he'd like us to explain this matter to senior members of his staff. I don't remember their names, I saw them only once, but they were sympathetic and tried to be helpful. After we outlined the story, they told us that the Foundation itself might be able to apply for new listings of PHT. They suggested that Dr. Herbert Ley, the previous Commissioner of the FDA, would be a good person to consult about procedure.* I didn't understand why the

---

* We got in touch with Dr. Herbert Ley. Dr. Ley said he would like to review the summaries of the PHT studies in our bibliography; they seemed almost too good to be true. After spot-checking the summaries for a day and a half, he was satisfied. Subsequently, Dr. Ley became a member of the Foundation's Advisory Board.

Foundation should apply to the FDA in a matter of health for the American public when that health was a direct responsibility of the FDA itself.

Still, I would have considered following the suggestion except for two reasons. One was that PHT appeared to be useful for so many disorders that to get them through the FDA in the routine way, single-file so to speak, would have taken forever. The second reason was that if the Foundation did make applications for new uses of PHT, we might be required to be silent on the subject while applications were pending. We couldn't risk that.

Dr. Edwards visited the Foundation a few weeks later. When he had spent most of a day absorbing the medical information, he agreed that a conference with medical officials would be appropriate and said he would help set up such a conference.

Dr. Edwards made the arrangements and a two-day conference was held in our offices in February 1972. Since Dr. Edwards had already spent a day with us on PHT, he attended only the first day of the meeting. Others in attendance were Dr. Theodore Cooper (Director, the National Heart and Lung Institute), Dr. John Jennings, Dr. James Pittman, Dr. Samuel Kaim, James Cavanaugh, Dr. Samuel Bogoch, and myself.

This conference was hard work. There were four two-hour sessions in the two days. Dr. Bogoch and I conducted them and, except during the discussion periods, we did all the talking. I assure you I looked forward to lunch and coffee breaks (see Agenda, pp. 216-217).

By the time we got to the last discussion period, on the afternoon of the second day, the clinical effects of PHT and its basic mechanisms of action had been outlined, and we got down to cases—what the government could do. But none of our visitors could think of a handle for the FDA to grab PHT by; nothing like this had happened before. The only suggestion I remember was that perhaps the government could give the

Foundation a grant. I appreciated this, but I didn't want us to lose any freedom of action.

As the meeting was breaking up, Dr. Kaim said to me, "Well, the ball is in your court." This struck my unfunny bone. "In my court?" I said. "Where the devil do you think it's been all these years and when should it get in your court?" As many of us do, I make the mistake of thinking that an individual in the government is the government itself. Dr. Kaim meant no harm by his comment, but I repeat it because it is typical of a thousand I've heard from people in a position to do something about PHT themselves. They seem to clear their consciences by giving me advice as to what I should do. I've got enough of this advice. It's saved up in a hermetically sealed tank and I plan to sell to a utility—when fuel prices rise a bit more.

Although nothing specific came of the meeting, at least some members of the government had a better understanding of PHT. Jim Cavanaugh kept in touch with me regularly. Jim had a way of saying, "I'll get back to you next week." And he always did. I appreciated his efforts so much that I never pressed him as to when he would call. It was usually about 4:45—on Friday.

Occasionally I was able to get Commissioner Edwards on the phone. Charlie, who told me he was trying to work out something with members of the department, finally came up with a suggestion. He said that if we could get a political figure to write a letter of inquiry about PHT to Secretary of Health Richardson, the reply—which would be an official statement and could be made public—might shed light on the matter. By that time I was so worn out I would have settled for an old shoe. But Dr. Edwards' idea seemed constructive.

Since the Foundation was located in New York, I asked Dr. Edwards if a letter from Governor Rockefeller would serve the purpose. He said it would. When I asked Governor Rockefeller,

DREYFUS MEDICAL FOUNDATION
CONFERENCE ON PHT WITH FDA

February 22 and 23, 1972

Tuesday, February 22

10:00 A.M.   Background
               Early evidence
               Institutional studies (with reference to both
                       crime and problems within the institutions):
                   Worcester County Jail Study (double-blind)
                   Lyman School for Boys (juvenile delinquents)
                   Patuxent Institution

1:00 P.M.   Lunch

2:00 P.M.   Basic mechanisms of action of PHT:
               Effect on hyperexcitable nerve cell
               Suppression of post-tetanic potentiation
               Stabilization of membrane
               Regulatory effect on sodium and potassium
               Resistance to anoxia
               Increase of energy compounds in brain
                       (glucose, ATP, and creatine phosphate)
               Stabilizing effects on labile diabetes
               Cerebral and coronary vessel dilatation
               Protection against digitalis toxicity
               Protection against cortisone toxicity
               Other antitoxic effects of interest: DDT,
                       cyanide, alloxan, radiation, etc.

3:15 P.M.   Coffee and Discussion

3:30 P.M   "The Broad Range of Use of PHT"
               Review of thought, mood, and behavior disorders
                       (1938-1971)
               Discussion

5:00 P.M.   Recess

7:30 P.M.   Dinner

Wednesday, February 23

9:00 A.M.	Review of "The Broad Range of Use of PHT"
	Symptoms and disorders for which PHT effectiveness has been reported
	Discussion of cardiac uses
	Brief review of other somatic disorders
	Alcoholism and drug addiction
	Safety and toxicology
10:15 A.M.	Coffee
10:30 A.M.	The effects of PHT on overthinking, anger, fear, and related emotions
	The One-Hour test
11:30 A.M.	Recent work reporting therapeutic benefits of PHT in glaucoma, steroid myopathy, hostility in chronic psychotics, violence, radiation, hock lung, asthma, digitalis toxicity, and hypertension
12:30 P.M.	Lunch
1:30 P.M.	PHT's value is based on the combination of many factors:
	Broad range of effectiveness
	Rapidity of action
	Beneficial "side effects"
	Not addictive
	Not a sedative at therapeutic doses
	Safety established by long period of use
	How PHT has been overlooked
	Discussion
4:00 P.M.	Conference ends

to whom I had spoken previously about PHT, he said he would write such a letter. And he did.

Secretary Richardson's response* meant more to me than it would to someone unfamiliar with the background. It showed that the Foundation's efforts had had some effect. The Secretary's comment: "Conversations with health officials in the Department..." indicated the letter had FDA approval.

■ ■ ■

I invaded the U.S. government only once more. About two months into President Nixon's second term, I made one more try. I called Rose Mary Woods and told her the PHT matter was just too important to hang in limbo any longer. I had done the best I could with government for the last four years and now I needed presidential advice. Rose Mary understood, and a few days later called back to say a date had been set up for lunch with the President—I should come at 11:30 so we would have more time to talk about PHT. Perfect.

I couldn't be late for such an appointment and planned to go to Washington the day before. But when I found the chance for rain approached zero, I made a reservation for a flight scheduled

---

* From Secretary Richardson's letter:

"Conversations with health officials within the Department have revealed that phenytoin (PHT) was introduced in 1938 as the first essentially nonsedating anticonvulsant drug...

"A review of the literature reveals that phenytoin has been reported to be useful in a wide range of disorders. Among its reported therapeutic actions are its stabilizing effect on the nervous system, its antiarrhythmic effect on certain cardiac disorders, and its therapeutic effect on emotional disorders.

"The fact that such broad therapeutic effects have been reported by many independent scientists and physicians over a long period of time would seem to indicate that the therapeutic effects of phenytoin are more than that of an anticonvulsant.

"The FDA encourages the submission of formal applications...."

(For the full text, see Appendix, p. 424.)

In the Oval Room — thirty-five minutes late

to get to Washington at 9:15, which gave me almost two hours leeway. That darn plane ("Doing What We Do Best") managed to be two-and-a-half hours late, and I was thirty-five minutes late for my appointment. If that wasn't embarrassing. But no one other than I appeared ruffled. The President set me at ease and listened closely to my experiences with the government. I told him the situation was incredible. Everyone had tried to be helpful, but they were so busy with problems they didn't have time for a solution. I said I couldn't get it out of my head that if someone with authority had the facts he'd see to it that something got done in this matter so urgent to public health.

The PHT story was not new to the President, having heard it from me on three occasions. He agreed that something should be done and asked for my suggestion. I had anticipated the possibility that he might ask. I told him that political jokes for at least a century suggested that Vice Presidents of the United States were not overworked. I said that if this applied to Vice President Agnew, he might be able to help. This suggestion got a prompt presidential veto (I lacked the two-thirds majority to overrule).

The President said he thought Secretary of Health Caspar Weinberger would be the man for me to see. I told him I had already seen two Secretaries of HEW and found them pretty busy; on average I'd spent an hour apiece with them. This time I had to have enough time to tell the whole story. He asked how long this would take. I said at least two days, at a quiet place away from the telephone. I thought this was shooting for the moon, but the President saw the sense in it. He said he'd make arrangements, that at the moment the Secretary was up to his elbows in some matter, but I would hear from him within thirty days. I thanked the President and took a plane back to New York. Of course it got there two minutes early.

Back home I waited for Secretary Weinberger's call. After four weeks had gone by I began to have Finch flashbacks. But, on the twenty-ninth day, Secretary Weinberger called and made a date to spend the following weekend at Hobeau Farm. Mrs. Weinberger came to the farm with the Secretary and Dr. Bogoch was with me. Over the two days we had four long sessions, during which Dr. Bogoch and I poured information about PHT into the Secretary. Mrs. Weinberger was an interested listener.

Late Sunday we went our separate ways, the Weinbergers to Washington, Dr. Bogoch and I to New York. Caspar said he wanted to cogitate on the matter and would get in touch with me soon. Time went by, more than I'd expected, and I was afraid I had struck a black hole (a semi-anachronism—they were around in those days but who knew). But after two months Secretary Weinberger called and invited me to come to Washington to meet the newly appointed Commissioner of the FDA, Dr. Alexander Mackay Schmidt.

Our meeting was in the office of our friend, Charlie Edwards, who had become assistant head of HEW. Secretary Weinberger was present, but I got the feeling that, not being a physician, he was reluctant to make suggestions of a medical nature to the FDA, and he had asked Dr. Edwards, who knew the subject well, to introduce Dr. Bogoch and me to Dr. Schmidt.

After the introductions we all chatted for a few minutes in Dr. Edwards' office about nothing I can remember. Then Dr. Schmidt and Dr. Bogoch and I went off to another room to have a talk. I assumed, of course, that Dr. Edwards or the Secretary had given Dr. Schmidt the bibliography of the Dreyfus Medical Foundation and a thorough briefing on the nature of our interest in PHT. I was totally unprepared for Dr. Schmidt's opening words, "My number one objective in my new position is to see that the FDA is run in an honest and honorable fashion."

Son-of-a-gun!

After all the years of work with the government it was apparent Dr. Schmidt hadn't even been briefed. I was back at the starting line, with a new Commissioner of the FDA, and the baton hadn't even been passed on.

I considered getting up and going home. But I wasn't delighted with the implications of Dr. Schmidt's opening remark, and I wanted to get that straightened out. I told Dr. Schmidt we were a charitable medical foundation, had no private interest of any sort, but a damned important public one, and that trying to be helpful with our government was getting to be a tiresome job.

Dr. Schmidt's response was a lot nicer than I expected. He said, "Take your time and tell me about it." For the umpteenth time I started telling the story of PHT.

After about an hour Dr. Schmidt said he had an appointment that he couldn't get out of, but he saw how important this was and he intended to pursue it personally. He said of course he knew PHT was more than an anticonvulsant. In fact he had been teaching its use in cardiac arrhythmias since 1969. I said that's just one example of what I'm talking about. "As you know, PHT does not have a listed indication-of-use for arrhythmias." Dr. Schmidt said, "You're mistaken. I'm sure PHT has such a listing." I didn't argue, this not being an opinion but a fact that could be checked. But I said I thought I was right.*

Just before we left, Dr. Schmidt mentioned that he was a specialist in communication. I said, "I've come to believe that communication is just a word in the dictionary, but if there is such a thing, you sure have a good spot to use your specialty."

Well, it turned out that Commissioner Schmidt was a gentleman of the old school (an endangered species). Even with the pressures of his new office he kept his promise to look into PHT himself and visited the Foundation twice in the following month. The second time, he spent a full day getting the facts about PHT from Dr. Bogoch and me and even stayed into the evening so we could finish our discussion at dinner. By that time I had a feeling of empathy with Mack, and with the help of a glass of wine, I emptied myself of my feelings on the subject of the great sin of neglect of PHT. Dr. Schmidt understood. Then he said something I'd been hoping to hear from a government official but had given up on. "You've done what you can. Now the ball is in our court."

Well, that was it; there was no more to do. I had been trying to turn the responsibility for PHT over to the U.S. government for ten years. Finally a Commissioner of the FDA had accepted it.

---

* A week later Dr. Schmidt called to say that it was hard to believe, but PHT did not have a listed indication-of-use for arrhythmias. The head of the Heart and Lung Institute, Dr. Theodore Cooper, had made the same mistake. At our medical conference, he had said, "There is no question of the usefulness of PHT as an antiarrhythmic, and this is an approved indication-of-use in the package insert."

■ ■ ■

Epilogue: Of course I should have figured that a man as sensitive as Mack Schmidt wouldn't last long in government. Five months later he was back at the University of Illinois, and there was a new Commissioner of the FDA.

I have not visited the government since and have no ambition to. That's one reason this book is written. It's for members of the staff and government officials in health, all at the same time. I hope it will make it easier for them to do whatever they think is right.

TRAVELS ABROAD

(England—Italy—Russia)

It's said that the further you get from where they know you the more respect you get. And so it seems.

Before discussing the "flaw in the system," in the next chapter, I would like to tell you of some experiences I've had with PHT abroad, and of an unusual relationship that developed between the Dreyfus Medical Foundation and the Institute for Experimental Medicine in Leningrad.

England

My first trip abroad, on the subject of PHT, was to England in 1965. Soon after Dr. Turner joined the Foundation, he and I went to Chichester, England, to visit a friend of his, Dr. Lionel Haward. At the Graylingwell Hospital in Chichester, Dr. Haward introduced us to a group of his colleagues. We all sat at a large round table and for an hour I described my experiences with PHT. When I finished, to my surprise, they applauded. I know it was just English good manners but it gave me a nice feeling.

As a result of our trip, Dr. Haward did a series of five controlled studies on PHT.* They were excellent studies, three of them unusual in that they were influenced by his background as a pilot. In simulated air control tests, he demonstrated with students and experienced pilots that PHT was significantly effective in delaying fatigue and accompanying errors. Haward made the point that it's an unusual substance that can calm without sedation and also effect a return of energy and improvement in concentration.

Italy

Dr. Rodolfo Paoletti, scientific director of the Institute of Pharmacology at the University of Milan, a friend of Dr. Bogoch's, frequently visited our office when in New York. On several occasions I talked to him about PHT. During one of the times Dr. Paoletti said, "Why don't you come over to Milan and talk about PHT at a meeting of the Giovanni Lorenzini Foundation?" He suggested a date four months in the future and I accepted.

A week before the meeting I found out what I had let myself in for. I was not to be one of many speakers, but the only speaker, before a large group of physicians. I had talked at formal medical meetings before, but only as one of the speakers. This was different.

At the meeting in Milan there were about 120 physicians. Dr. Paoletti gave me a kind introduction, put me on the podium with a microphone attached to me, and told me to speak in my normal way—a UN-type device would see that it came out in Italian. I was close to stage fright, but after I got started it was all right. I talked for an hour and twenty minutes, and apparently it went well because I got a letter from Dr. Paoletti saying, "From the comments I heard afterward you certainly caught everyone's attention," and he invited me to come back the next year.

* See *The Broad Range of Clinical Use of PHT.*

After the meeting a number of physicians came up to say hello, and I learned that PHT was already being used for purposes other than epilepsy. One physician, G. A. Bozza, who seemed an especially kind man, talked to me about his use of PHT with retarded children, a use I was not familiar with. A few months later he sent me his paper, "Normalization of intellectual development in the slightly brain-damaged, retarded child."*

Russia

One day in October 1972, Dr. Bogoch phoned and said he was coming to the office with a Russian doctor he thought I'd like to meet, and that we might have lunch. The doctor was in New York for an International Brain Sciences Conference, of which Dr. Bogoch was chairman. At eleven o'clock that morning Dr. Bogoch arrived in the office with Dr. Natasha Bechtereva. Sam had not overdescribed Dr. Bechtereva when he referred to her as a Russian doctor. Dr. Bechtereva had the most impressive credentials of anyone I've met in the medical profession.

At that time Dr. Bechtereva was chairman of the Commission on Public Health of the USSR. She was also Director of the Institute for Experimental Medicine, formerly the Pavlov Institute, a group of seven large hospitals in Leningrad. Dr. Bechtereva was the first woman to become Director of the Institute and she was Chief of its neurophysiological branch.

I remember our meeting clearly. Dr. Bechtereva, Dr. Bogoch, and I sat in chairs at a window overlooking New York Harbor. I had intended to talk about PHT for half an hour or so and, if Dr. Bechtereva showed interest, give her a copy of *The Broad Range of Use of Phenytoin*. When lunch arrived at one o'clock I was surprised to find that I'd been talking for two hours. Dr.

* Presented at the Italian National Conference of Child Neuropsychology, 1971.

Bechtereva hadn't said a thing, but the patience with which she had listened and something in her remarkable eyes had kept me going.

When I had finished Dr. Bechtereva spoke for the first time. She said, "What you say seems too good to be true but it's not illogical, and I can find out to my own satisfaction. In our Institute we have sensitive electrical equipment that can test PHT. Would you be kind enough to send us a supply of your brand of phenytoin? If our tests should disagree with what you say I wouldn't want you to think it's because our brand is different from yours." That made sense, and I said we would send the Dilantin.

After many difficulties, the Dilantin arrived in Leningrad. Several months later I received a letter from Dr. Bechtereva (mail in those days took about a month—now it's not so rapid). Dr. Bechtereva's electrical instruments had not been disappointed. From the letter:

> Thank you very much for the prospect of Dilantin and the Dilantin itself. The Dilantin—really a most peculiar medicine.
>
> I am advising it to more and more people. I simply can't resist doing it—you know how one feels. And so, step by step, Dilantin is used for nonepileptic purposes, not only in Leningrad but in Moscow and Kiev as well.

Dr. Bechtereva has a refreshing way of putting things. In a later letter she said, "People use Dilantin much more, though it met the normal prejudice determined by the engram fixed in each doctor's memory: Dilantin → epilepsy." Apparently we don't have a monopoly on this engram.

A few months after Dr. Bechtereva started work with PHT, she invited Dr. Bogoch and me to visit the Institute in Leningrad, at our convenience. We accepted. Having heard too much about the Russian winters we selected June for the visit. Four of us made the trip—Dr. Bogoch and his wife Dr. Elenore Bogoch, and Joan Personette, my former wife, and I.

We stayed in Leningrad for a week at the Hotel Astoria, a very old hotel, like the Ritz in Paris, but otherwise dissimilar. But the people were nice, which is the most important thing. When we had time we saw the sights, the beautiful cathedrals and the extraordinary Hermitage, and we walked around Leningrad as we pleased. The days were long. We were near the land of the midnight sun, and it got dark at 11 P.M. and light at 2 A.M. It seemed strange reading by daylight at 10 P.M. in a park across from the Astoria.

Dr. Bechtereva's hospitality was reminiscent of our best Southern hospitality. We had a delicious dinner at her home with her family, were taken out to dinner by her, and thoughtfully left to ourselves. The food in the restaurants was good, if you like garlic, which I don't. On one occasion, out to dinner with Dr. Bechtereva, I was trying to finesse my way around the meat and Natasha said, "My dear Jack, you suffer so much." A keen observer.

The first day we were in Leningrad, Dr. Bechtereva took the Drs. Bogoch and me to one of the seven hospitals and introduced us to key members of her staff. Later we went through other hospitals, getting to meet many doctors. I was surprised that so many of the doctors were women until I was told that 70 percent of physicians in Russia are women.

The second day we were there, Dr. Bechtereva introduced us to three patients who'd had dramatic benefits from PHT. Each had a different disorder. The patient I remember best was a woman who'd had severe headaches for many years and had to be hospitalized periodically. This time she had taken Dilantin for a few days and was on her way home. She explained, through an interpreter, that the pain in her head would get so bad she'd sit absolutely still and if anyone came near her it would make her furious. While she was explaining this in Russian, she was smiling happily, as though she were talking about someone else.

The next day Dr. Bechtereva called a meeting and Dr. Bogoch and I had the opportunity to talk about PHT to eighty physicians. I talked for about two hours. That was like talking one hour because translation was not simultaneous. Then Dr. Bogoch discussed the basic mechanisms of action. Several of the Institute's physicians also addressed the group. I was told that they had given favorable reports on PHT.

The day before we left, Dr. Bechtereva and I were alone for a few moments and I brought up what I considered a delicate subject. I told her that I was most impressed with the work the Institute had done. I said our Foundation had funded numerous studies on PHT, some outside the U.S.A., and, if proper, we would be happy to do it here. Natasha set me at ease. She said she appreciated my asking but that her Institute was well financed by the government. However, we might consider a "joint cooperative effort." She said such a possibility was provided for in the recent meeting between President Nixon and Premier Brezhnev.

I thought this a fine idea and asked how we should proceed. Dr. Bechtereva said since we had introduced the PHT idea it would be best if we initiated the matter through our Department of Health to their Ministry of Health. We discussed it. Our thought was that we'd exchange ideas and information by mail, and would periodically visit each other. It was agreed that when I got back to New York I would introduce the matter to our Department of Health.

I won't bore you with details. The mills of government grind slowly all over the world. But in 1976, a formal approval was given for a "joint cooperative effort" between the Institute for Experimental Medicine and the Dreyfus Medical Foundation. I have been told that this is the only venture of its sort between a Russian and an American institution.

Before closing I'd like to say that Natasha Bechtereva is one of the most remarkable persons I've ever met, and I thank her for her help.

A FLAW IN THE SYSTEM

Parke-Davis—the Physician—the FDA

A medicine can get overlooked for a million years if no one discovers it. But can the benefits of a discovered medicine get overlooked for decades when thousands of studies have demonstrated its usefulness? The answer is it can.

We have a flaw in our system of bringing prescription medicines to the public. That there's a flaw is no surprise. We're human and all our systems have flaws. But this particular flaw should be explained. It has acted like a barrier between the American public and a great medicine.

■ ■ ■

From drug company, through FDA, to physician—that's the route a prescription medicine takes to get to the public. That's our system. It was not set up by anyone, it just evolved. But we're used to it; it has become custom. And as Mark Twain said, custom is like iron.

Years ago doctors concocted their own medicines—and leeches outsold aspirins. But for the last century the business of pharmaceuticals has been in the hands of the drug companies. Drug companies, formed for the purpose of making money for shareholders, are not charged with a responsibility to the public that is not consistent with making money. That is not to suggest that drug companies are not interested in public welfare but they are not charged with a responsibility for it.

In 1938 the FDA was empowered to protect us against medical substances more dangerous than therapeutic. Since that time drug companies have been required to get approval as to safety of a new chemical entity and, since 1962, approval as to its effectiveness. Although the neglect of a great drug can be far more deadly than the use of a bad one, correcting such neglect does not appear to be a function of the FDA.

When a drug company synthesizes a compound which it believes to be therapeutic, it's brought to the FDA. If the drug satisfies that agency's requirements, the company is awarded a "listed indication-of-use," which permits it to market the drug. Getting FDA approval is time-consuming and expensive; it has been estimated, on average, to take seven years and to cost $11 million. (Today, the cost is far greater.)

Drug companies patent their new compounds. Patents give the company exclusive rights for seventeen years. If the FDA approves a drug and it becomes popular, the drug company has a winner since the drug will sell at a high price for the life of the patent.* However, when the patent expires, competition enters the picture and the price of the drug drops dramatically. At that point there is more financial incentive for the drug company to look for a new drug to patent than to look for new uses of an old drug.

FDA approval is the second of the three steps in our system. The third step is to introduce the drug to the physician. This is

---

* This is reasonable; a drug that is a winner has to pay for the research that went into it, the expense of getting FDA approval, and for money spent on the many drugs that are not successful.

a function of the drug company and is done through advertisements in trade journals and by visits of their salesmen to physicians.

That is the system—and physicians have come to depend on it. If a doctor doesn't hear from a drug company about new uses for an old medicine, the doctor infers there aren't such uses. This is a reasonable inference. But in the case of PHT it's wrong.

So this is the flaw in the system. When a drug company doesn't do what is expected of it, and the FDA can't or doesn't do anything about it, the physician doesn't get vital information. And, as in this case, a great drug can get overlooked.

Parke-Davis

Parke-Davis's research did not discover PHT. The company bought the compound from a chemist in 1909. For twenty-nine years this remarkable drug sat on the shelf doing nobody any good. Then Putnam and Merritt, two physicians outside the company, discovered its first therapeutic use. Parke-Davis paid almost nothing in money for PHT. They paid less in brains for PHT.

Still, were it not for Parke-Davis we might not have PHT today. Someone in the company did buy the compound, and someone else in the company did give it to Putnam and Merritt for trial. It should also be said, to its credit, that Parke-Davis has been consistent in manufacturing a good product.

■ ■ ■

It is not easy to understand how a drug company can overlook its own product. An outline of my own experience with Parke-Davis may help.

In 1966, as Secretary Gardner had recommended, I made contact with Parke-Davis. I phoned the company and spoke to the President, Mr. H. W. Burrows. I told him of Secretary Gardner's recommendation that I speak to Parke-Davis, and supposed that would arouse his interest. But as I talked I didn't hear the noises one expects from an interested listener. To get his attention I said, "Look, I've spent $400,000 on your medicine and I don't want anything for myself, I just want to tell Parke-Davis about it." That got Mr. Burrows' attention. He said, "I wouldn't know anything about this, I'm just a bookkeeper."

That startling statement was my introduction to Parke-Davis. President Burrows said he would have someone get in touch with me. Two months later I got a call from Dr. Leon Sweet of Parke-Davis's research department. He was calling at Mr. Burrows' suggestion and made a date to meet with me in New York.

We met at my home. Dr. Sweet brought Dr. E. C. Vonder Heide with him. Dr. Turner was with me. Dr. Sweet said that Parke-Davis's recent head of research, Dr. Alain Sanseigne, had left the company a few months earlier to go to Squibb, and Dr. Vonder Heide, a former head of research now retired, had come along to be helpful.

Dr. Turner and I talked at length about the overlooked uses of PHT. Dr. Vonder Heide said it didn't surprise him that PHT was more than an anticonvulsant. In fact Parke-Davis had had numerous reports that Dilantin helped with alcohol and drug addiction. He said that he had tried to get doctors to conduct studies in this field without success. He was rather critical of the doctors. I remember thinking, What's going on here? The doctors depend on Parke-Davis to do something, and Parke-Davis depends on the doctors to do something. This is an interesting game of tag, and the public is "it."

I didn't realize till years later what a poor excuse Dr. Vonder Heide had given. Many research-minded doctors had already done a great deal, and at that time, 1966, Parke-Davis's files were stocked with a variety of clinical studies on PHT. Yet apparently neither Dr. Vonder Heide nor Dr. Sweet had heard of them. It seemed Parke-Davis's research department and its filing department were not acquainted with each other.

Our next contact with Parke-Davis came a few weeks later when we had a visit from a friendly gentleman, Dr. Charles F. Weiss. Dr. Weiss explained that he was a pediatrician and didn't know anything about PHT, but had come to see us because he'd been asked to. He offered the opinion that Parke-Davis was a little disorganized. He said he wished some company would take them over. Well, he got his wish—but not for six years. Today the company is a subsidiary of Warner Lambert.

When Warner Lambert took over in 1971, Mr. J. D. Williams became President of the Parke-Davis division. I felt I should bring the matter of PHT to the attention of the new management, and had several discussions on the telephone with Mr. Williams. The talks were friendly but not useful in furthering the PHT cause. On one occasion Mr. Williams expressed a thought I'd heard from Parke-Davis before, that since we were working on their product, it might be better if we stayed apart—some notion that the FDA might like it better. I couldn't understand this—I was sure the FDA would want a drug company to know all it could about its own product.

But such is life. An item in the *Arizona Republic* (at the time I retired from Wall Street in 1970) will give the picture. The paper reported Dr. Joseph Sadusk, Vice President for Medical and Scientific Research of Parke-Davis, to have said that the Dreyfus Medical Foundation is doing "an excellent job" in investigating PHT. As a result he said Parke-Davis has made only "a minimal effort" in this area of research. "Results from an unbiased third party like Dreyfus," he said, "would mean more to the Food and Drug Administration."

I appreciate compliments. But the division of labor seemed uneven. The Dreyfus Medical Foundation should do the research, influence the FDA—and Parke-Davis should make the profits.

There appears to have been only one person who, while passing through Parke-Davis, got a good grasp of PHT. That was Dr. Alain Sanseigne, head of research before Dr. Sweet. Dr. Turner brought PHT to Dr. Sanseigne's attention. Dr. Sanseigne graciously acknowledged this in a letter to Dr. Turner in which he said, "Your very thorough knowledge of Dilantin put me to shame."

Once his attention had been directed to PHT, Dr. Sanseigne, in 1965, reviewed its pharmacology, site of activity, and therapeutic activity.* It's an impressive review, and it refers only to information on PHT available over twenty years ago. There are no signs that this review stirred Parke-Davis.

When Dr. Joseph Sadusk said Parke-Davis's efforts had been "minimal" he selected the right word. I know this from firsthand experience. A few years ago Mr. Williams changed his mind about Parke-Davis staying apart from our Foundation

---

* From Dr. Sanseigne's review:

The Parke-Davis Medical Brochure includes as indications of Dilantin the following:

Epilepsy	Migraine
Chorea	Trigeminal neuralgia
Parkinson syndrome	Psychosis

The following indications...have been studied and seem to show considerable therapeutic response to treatment with PHT:

Cardiac arrhythmias	Wound-healing acceleration
Neurosis	Polyneuritis of pregnancy
Asthma	Tabetic lancinating pain
Myotonia	Pruritus ani
Diabetes insipidus	Adolescent behavioral disorders

The following are indications on which the possibility of favorable response to PHT should be investigated:

Prophylaxis and treatment of cerebral anoxia (carbon monoxide poisoning and other asphyxiation, precardiac and pulmonary surgery)	Wilson's disease
	Poorly controlled diabetes
	Cicatrization of oral surgery
	Osteogenesis imperfecta
	Conditions related to hypothalamic disorders

and graciously arranged for three members of the research staff to meet with us on the subject of Parke-Davis's Dilantin package insert. (This package insert will be discussed later.)

At this meeting, I met the senior research officer of Parke-Davis. When we finished our discussion he mentioned that the FDA had not approved Parke-Davis's application for the use of PHT in cardiac arrhythmias. The reason, he said, was that the company did not supply cardiograms requested by an individual in the FDA. The research officer said, "We could get them for $100,000 but why spend the money, all the cardiologists are using PHT anyway." I won't take sides in this hassle between the FDA and Parke-Davis. There was foolishness to spare.* But you'd think Parke-Davis would have considered it a privilege to spend the $100,000.

A few weeks after this, a physician applied to our Foundation for a modest grant ($6,000). He had done interesting preliminary work on the use of PHT as a protection against brain damage after cardiac arrest. We intended to make the grant, but it occurred to me that the new Parke-Davis management might appreciate the opportunity. I called my new acquaintance, the research officer, and asked him about it. It didn't surprise me that I was told no. It did surprise me how quickly I got the answer, on the phone, without consideration of the matter. The senior officer explained that Parke-Davis was spending its research moneys on a new medicine the company hoped to patent. I thought there will be snow on the Devil's roof before they came up with as good a medicine as Dilantin. But I got the point—patents on Dilantin had expired.

Well, to sum up, Parke-Davis got Dilantin by luck. They didn't understand their own product, have done little to try to

---

* PHT is so widely used for cardiac arrythmias that AMA Drug Evaluations has it in the category of antiarrhythmic agents.

understand it, and haven't spent a bean in furthering its understanding. This has contributed to the overlooking of PHT.

But let's see Parke-Davis in perspective. There's no Mr. Parke, no Mr. Davis—just an entity with those names. Since Parke-Davis did not get PHT by the sweat of its research there was none of the interest in the drug that would be found in a company that had developed its own product. As a result, new uses for PHT was a job never assigned to anyone and no one took it upon himself. It has been easy to cuss Parke-Davis, the entity, but not the people. In fact I've never met anyone at the company I didn't like.

▪ ▪ ▪

About Parke-Davis's Dilantin package insert.

I was weaned on the Securities Exchange Commission. The SEC is a fiend for full disclosure—the positive as well as the negative. If Parke-Davis operated under SEC regulations the SEC would have the company in court for the rest of the century because of the great amount of positive data that's not disclosed in its package insert.

But Parke-Davis operates under FDA regulations. Apparently full disclosure is required on the negative side, but no disclosure is permitted when the evidence is positive, unless it has an FDA listed indication-of-use. No matter how flimsy the evidence for the negative, it must be disclosed. No matter how solid the positive evidence, it may not be mentioned. It seems a poor way to run a railroad.

An example of inexplicable illogic. For some years prior to 1972, Parke-Davis's package insert made reference to a number of the uses of PHT other than epilepsy. In 1971 the insert stated: "Dilantin is also useful in the treatment of conditions such as chorea and Parkinson's syndrome and is employed in the treatment of migraine, trigeminal neuralgia and certain psychoses." In 1972 reference to these uses was deleted, although the evidence for their use had been substantially increased.

Unfathomable. I don't know whether this was the fault of Parke-Davis or the FDA. But an innocent public has suffered.

The Physician

I had taken PHT for about a year when I started talking to doctors about it. These were informal talks and occurred when chance brought me together with physicians, as at a dinner or in a locker room. I must have spoken to more than twenty doctors during that early period. None of them had heard of PHT being used for anything other than epilepsy. The discussions were friendly, but it was almost impossible to get a physician interested in the subject of PHT. I thought this was because, as a Wall Street man, I was an improbable source of medical fact.

But my lack of credentials was the smallest part of the communication problem. In the physicians' minds there was the fixed notion that PHT was just an anticonvulsant. They had been taught this in school, the "knowledge" had been in their heads for a long time, and had calcified. Don't pick on the physician. Calcification of ideas is a human trait not special to him.

There was an even bigger obstacle—the sure knowledge the physician had that if Dilantin had as many uses as I said it had, they would have heard about them from Parke-Davis. After all, Dilantin was their product, wasn't it? And they wanted to make money, didn't they? This "irrefutable logic" always defeated me. If I tried to explain, time would run out before we could get back to PHT.

There's been a recent trend to knock the doctor. I think it's a reaction to the pedestal position we had him in a decade ago. We learned from "Dr. Kildare" and "Marcus Welby, M.D." that there are two physicians to every patient. In real life this isn't so. Doctors rarely make house calls anymore. They can see three patients in the office for one in the home—and still it's hard to get an appointment. Don't blame the doctor. It's the ecologists' fault—they've allowed the spread of *Homo sapiens* to get out of hand.

When you are giving a member of the medical profession a hard time (in your head of course—who would dare do it in person), consider that the doctor's day never ends. Sick people don't care what time it is, and the doctor has to go around with a beeper attached to him or be in constant touch with his telephone service. This means twenty-four hours' tension. We complain about what the doctor doesn't do. But do we appreciate the things he does that we wouldn't do?

■ ■ ■

We come to an important subject: medical literature. Medical studies are called literature (Shakespeare might demur) when they're published in a medical journal or as part of the record of a medical conference.

There is a great deal of this literature. You could wallpaper the world with it and have enough left over to do your kitchen. The notion that physicians know what's contained in the literature is bizarre. But some of them sound like they half believe they do. If you ask a physician a question he can't answer, don't be surprised if he responds, "Nobody knows." Which seems to suggest he has read all the literature and has total recall.

It's estimated that there are 3,300 medical journals in the world. A poll in seventeen counties of upstate New York (not exactly the boondocks) showed that the average physician subscribed to 4.1 of these journals. Double this figure if you like. Even if he read the 8.2 journals cover to cover, he would still be 3,291.8 journals short. You can see it's impossible to expect the physician to read the medical literature to determine which drugs he should use. That's why, in this day of specialization, this is left to the drug companies and the FDA.

However, when a physician gets a new idea about an approved drug, he may apply it.* But the opportunity doesn't come up often. Usually new uses of a drug are well explored by the drug company that introduced it. PHT has been a marked exception, and a rare opportunity was presented to the physicians.

The medical profession did not fail us. The work of thousands of physicians has given us a rich literature on PHT. This literature, international in scope, covers a wide variety of medical disciplines. Published in many languages over a period of years, it is spread far and wide. But intermingled with millions of other studies, this literature is almost lost unless someone seeks it out.

The science fiction writer Robert Heinlein calls it the Crisis of the Librarian:

> The greatest crisis facing us is not Russia, not the Atom Bomb...It is a crisis in the organization and accessibility of human knowledge. We own an enormous "encyclopedia" which isn't even arranged alphabetically. Our "file cards" are spilled on the floor, nor were they ever in order. The answers we want may be buried somewhere in the heap....

Let me give you an example of how difficult it would be, even in a single field, for a physician to be acquainted with the literature on PHT. Disorders in the field have many names. A general description of the field is uncontrolled muscle movement, or continuous muscle fiber activity.

---

* Former FDA Commissioner Charles C. Edwards states: "Once the new drug is in a local pharmacy, the physician may, as part of the practice of medicine...vary the conditions of use from those approved in the package insert, without obtaining approval of the FDA." *The Federal Register*, Vol. 37, No. 158, Aug. 15, 1972. This was clearly restated in the April, 1982, FDA *Drug Bulletin*. (See p. 424.)

To illustrate the point, we made up a table of twenty-one published studies on this subject in 1975.* These studies show dramatic recovery in intractable patients when given PHT. In many of the cases myogram readings (electrical muscle recordings) confirmed the clinical observations. The difficulty an individual physician would have in becoming acquainted with this work is shown by the following:

The studies were published in eight different countries, in sixteen different journals—*Journal of Neurology, Neurosurgery and Psychiatry, Lancet, The Practitioner, South African Medical Journal, Klinische Wochenschrift, Arquivos de Neuro-Psiquiatria, Acta Neurologica, Proceedings of the Australian Association of Neurologists, Ceskolovenska Neurologie, Connecticut Medicine, Neurology, Archives of Neurology, New York State Journal of Medicine, California Medicine,* and *New England Journal of Medicine.*

In only two of the twenty-one studies was the word phenytoin used in the title. The other studies were published under such dissimilar titles that Scotland Yard couldn't have found them, without the key word phenytoin.

Some members of the medical profession have prescribed PHT for a variety of purposes for many years. The breadth of its use has been more than might be imagined. IMS America Ltd. surveys the use of thousands of drugs. For their estimate of the many clinical conditions for which physicians are using PHT, see Appendix, p. 427.

One might draw the conclusion from the IMS America survey that the medical profession knows all about PHT. But this is not the case. Many physicians know of one or several uses of PHT. Few have an overall picture of the drug. Thus we have a strange

---

* Since then many more studies have been published. See *The Broad Range of Clinical Use of PHT.*

situation. Dr. Jones prescribes PHT for depression. Dr. Smith uses it for migraine. Dr. Hemplewaith for trigeminal neuralgia. But, if a patient asks Dr. Snodgrass if he could try PHT for any of these purposes, he may get ushered from the office with the admonishment that PHT is only for epilepsy.

The right of a physician to prescribe whatever drug he wants is fundamental. But in making his decision he should have a reasonable amount of evidence on which to base his judgment. A reasonable amount of information has not been available to the physician, at least not from the expected source, the drug company. The information has been there, but it's been hidden in millions of medical papers, like trees in a forest.

When physicians know more about PHT they will realize they have been imposed on by the system and deprived of a remarkable therapeutic tool.

The FDA

This is not going to be a treatise on the Food and Drug Administration. I haven't the facts or the desire to write such a treatise. The FDA is in this book because of its relation to PHT.

The FDA was established, in the best tradition of good government, to help American citizens in matters of health, in ways they can't help themselves. But it was conceived as a defensive unit. If it were a football team it would have six tackles and five guards, and no one to carry the ball. All that was expected of the FDA was defense—to protect us from dangerous substances and unwarranted claims of effectiveness.

Understandably the founding fathers of the FDA presumed that the drug companies, with their profit incentives, would furnish the offense. It could hardly have entered their minds that a drug company would leave a great medicine "lying around." Nor would they have been able to figure out how to equip the FDA against such an eventuality unless the FDA were put into the drug business, which is a far cry from the original premise—and is not being recommended here.

The FDA has done nothing about PHT. That is to be expected when a drug company doesn't play its role. Unfortunately this does not leave the FDA in a neutral position. Through no fault of the FDA's, PHT's narrow listing has a negative effect. Absence of FDA approval is thought of by many as FDA disapproval—or at the least that something is lacking. The system of drug company through FDA to physician has become such a routine that the physician, with other things on his mind, waits for the system to bring him PHT. It's been a long wait.

The real purpose in establishing the FDA was to improve the health and well-being of the citizens of the United States. The neglect of a great drug certainly falls into that category. If a man were drowning and a doctor was prepared to throw him a life preserver that had more lead than cork, the FDA would say, "Hold it! That thing might hit him and kill him, and even if it doesn't it can't help him." Nice work, FDA. But suppose the FDA knew there was a good life preserver under a tree, which the doctor didn't see. Shouldn't they say, "Try that one, Doc." Of course they should.

It is not suggested that the FDA go into the drug business. It is more than suggested, in this extraordinary case, where thousands of physicians have furnished us with many times the evidence required to get approval of a new drug (keep in mind this drug has been approved for comparative safety and has stood the test of over forty years of use), that the FDA should no longer take a hands-off policy. It's a sure thing our public shouldn't suffer any longer because Parke-Davis stayed in bed after Rip Van Winkle got up.

Let us understand the magnitude of what we're talking about. The non-use of PHT has been a catastrophe. We are not accustomed to thinking of the non-use of a medicine as a catastrophe. We think of a catastrophe as a flood, a famine, or an earthquake. Something tangible, overt, something in the positive tense. But something passive, such as the non-use of a great medicine that can prevent suffering and prolong lives, is also a catastrophe.

Something must be done. How it is done is for the government to decide. But here is a suggestion. It would seem a waste of time, and thus to the disadvantage of the American public, for the FDA to attempt to approve the many clinical uses of PHT separately. That could take forever. It would be far simpler for the FDA to address itself to the basic mechanisms of action and give PHT a listed indication-of-use as a stabilizer of bioelectrical activity, or as a membrane stabilizer. Certainly the published evidence for this is overwhelming. Such a listing would stimulate the physician to think of clinical applications of PHT and to refer to the existing medical literature.

Even a nod from the FDA to the physician would help. It could take the form of a letter to the physician, calling attention to the literature of his colleagues, and reminding him that since PHT has been approved for safety he is permitted to use it for whatever purposes his judgment suggests. Certainly the FDA would never try to tell the doctor how he should use PHT. That's always the doctor's decision. But such a letter would lift the cloud of negativism, and the physician would get an unobstructed view of PHT and the work of his colleagues.

I'm sure the problem-agriculturists will say that if the FDA takes any action in this matter it will set a precedent. Fine. Good. If this happens again, if another established drug is found useful for fifty or more disorders by thousands of physicians, then the FDA should take this as a precedent.

Every once in a while, routine or no routine, a little common sense should be permitted. This is an extraordinary matter, vital to our health. If the FDA was set up to help the American public, here's a chance to do something great for them—with no one's feelings hurt except routine's.

EVIDENCE

*Over the years frustration has caused me
to write a few stories about evidence.
Put together they are pertinent.*

The Placebo

When one is trying to determine if a medicine is effective, the use of a placebo is sensible. If a doctor gives a patient a medication with the expectation of helping the patient, the patient may pick up on that expectation and rationalize that it's going to help him. Psychologically this might actually help for a while. If a medication is useful, comparing it to a placebo will demonstrate that it was not expectation that made the patient feel better, but the medication itself.

A placebo is not needed with a drug that is effective in a clear-cut fashion. But initially that might not be known, so starting with a placebo makes sense.

The Negative Placebo

Suppose a patient has a disorder and the doctor gives him a drug with the hope it will help him. Suppose the patient rationalizes that it's going to help and gets a psychological lift, which wears off after a while. Then the doctor prescribes a second drug to the patient. This time the patient is less optimistic, but a little bit of wishful thinking may be left. This drug doesn't work and the doctor gives a third one. This time the patient's wish-thinking device is depleted and he's not expecting any results. You could say he's placebo-proof. Let's say that drug doesn't work either, and a fourth drug is given. By now, there's a negative expectation by the patient. He expects the drug not to work because, if the first three didn't, why should the fourth?

There are thousands of studies on PHT in which a variety of drugs had been tried. These are well-controlled studies—the drugs that had been used had the effect of a placebo. In many, they might have been better than placebo studies—there might have been a negative placebo effect.

Substantial Evidence

In the Federal Food, Drug and Cosmetic Act the FDA is required to have "substantial evidence of effectiveness." The word substantial, in this context, cannot mean quantity. A study of 10,000 cases could be inconclusive. The evidence from a few cases can be "substantial." Let's take one example of how the evidence from just eight cases could be substantial.

For the purpose of this example, we eliminate the possibility of collusion or hoax.

Suppose there is a government station in North Carolina that is set up to receive reports of UFOs. On average they receive one call a day. Suppose that one night, between 3:00 and 3:10, eight calls come into this station all reporting similar observations, to wit, that a huge ball of fire was seen slowly floating a few hundred yards overhead, and that suddenly at tremendous speed it went upward, and disappeared from sight. Remembering our premise that collusion is eliminated, what are the probabilities that this really happened?

Since one call a day, at random times, is the average, the first call at 3:00 AM means no more than any other call received by the station. The second call could have been a coincidence. However, because it was within a ten-minute span of the first, this coincidence would occur, on average, once in 144 days (there are 144 ten-minute spans in 24 hours). The third call would be one heck of a coincidence, one hundred forty-four times one hundred forty-fourths of a chance. By the eighth call, the odds that there had been an unusual occurrence around 3 AM would be:

$$1/144 \times 1/144 \times 1/144 \times 1/144 \times 1/144 \times 1/144 \times 1/144,$$

$$\text{or } 1{,}283{,}918{,}464{,}548{,}864\text{-to-}1.$$

This is "substantial evidence."

Now, in the UFO example, we took a premise that we couldn't take in real life, that collusion or hoax were impossible. The fact is that collusion would seem far more likely than anything else, and the investigators of this matter would spend a lot of time proving or disproving this.

We now come to the real life proposition, the evidence that PHT is a widely versatile medicine. Here the probability of collusion is ruled out by applying common sense to the facts.

Let's look at the facts before we apply the common sense. Physicians in at least 48 countries have reported PHT to be useful for more than 70 symptoms and disorders, in over 350 medical journals, written in twenty different languages. Since the average physician receives seven or eight medical journals (less than 1/4 of 1% of the world literature) it's obvious that the reporting physicians could not know of the work of more than a few of their colleagues. Common sense rules out collusion. Thus, the probability that PHT is a widely versatile drug is of the same order of magnitude as in the UFO example.

The Rules of Evidence

The Rules of Evidence have something in common with the Law of Gravity. Neither can be amended by Congress nor by any branch of Government. The Rules of Evidence are simple. They are the application of common sense to probability.

Let us apply the Rules to the question of whether or not phenytoin is useful for thought, mood and behavior disorders. The material on which this exercise is based is found in the Thought, Mood and Behavior section of *The Broad Range of Clinical Use of Phenytoin*.

There are many kinds of evidence: Studies with placebo. Studies in which a drug is effective after other drugs have failed. Trials in which a drug is found effective—is withdrawn and symptoms return, reinstituted and symptoms disappear. Clinical studies in which improvements are confirmed by laboratory means. All of these methods have been used in establishing PHT's effectiveness.

Before arriving at a probability figure for thought, mood and behavior disorders, we will define them, for these purposes, to be problems of excessive anger and related symptoms such as impatience, irritability, impulsivity, hostility and violence; excessive fear and related symptoms such as worry, anxiety, apprehension, depression; also uncontrolled thinking, occupied by negative thoughts and interfering with concentration.

In four papers PHT was not found "significantly" effective (not necessarily ineffective). For these purposes we allowed the four papers to eliminate ten positive papers that we have assessed the chance of being correct of 1 in 2.

To arrive at an overall probability figure of PHT's usefulness for thought, mood and behavior, we assess individual probability figures to each of the studies. This is done by estimate, but since most of the authors assess the chance of their own work being correct in excess of 19-to-1 or 99-to-1, the following estimates are conservative.

	Probability that PHT is effective
	1 in 2
	1 in 2
For each of the first seven reports, controlled	1 in 2
by phenobarbital and/or bromides, we assess	1 in 2
the probability of being correct of	1 in 2
1 chance in 2.	1 in 2
	1 in 2
Lindsley and Henry, the first paper in	
non-epileptics, in problem children	1 in 2
Brown and Solomon, in delinquent boys	1 in 2
Silverman, in a jail study, 64 prisoners, double-	
blind crossover, placebo—also other drugs	5 in 6
Bodkin, observations of 102 nervous patients	3 in 4
Goodwin, 20 patients out of 20 nervous patients	2 in 3
Walker and Kirkpatrick, 10 behavioral problem	
children out of 10, all improved	2 in 3
Zimmerman, 200 children with severe behavior	
disorders, 70% of cases improved	3 in 4
Chao, Sexton and Davis, 296 children, response	
rapid, often striking	4 in 5
Jonas, in his book, *Ictal and Subictal Neurosis*	
162 patients - over 12 years	3 in 4
Lynk and Amidon, 125 delinquents	3 in 4
Dreyfus, 80 patients	1 in 2
Rossi, behavioral problem children	1 in 2
Turner, 46 of 56 adult neurotic patients	2 in 3
Tec, 15 years' experience	2 in 3

Boelhouwer, et al., 78 patients, double-blind
    crossover and placebo   4 in 5
Baldwin, 109 children with behavior problems   3 in 4
Stephens and Shaffer, double-blind, 30 adult
    outpatients   4 in 5
Goldberg and Kurland, double-blind, 47 retardates,
    ages 9 to 14   3 in 4
Daniel, aged patients   1 in 2
Bozza, 21 slightly brain damaged retarded children   1 in 2
Alvarez, in a book covering 25 years' experience   5 in 6
Stephens and Shaffer, second double-blind with
    10 patients   3 in 4
Maletsky, episodic dyscontrol, 22 adults—other
    drugs had failed.   3 in 4
Maletsky and Klotter, episodic dyscontrol,
    24 adults, double-blind with placebo   4 in 5
Solomon and Kleeman, 2 cases episodic dyscontrol   1 in 2
Bach-Y-Rita, et al., 130 adults with assaultive
    and destructive behavior   3 in 4
Kalinowsky and Putnam, 60 psychotic patients,
    improvement in over half   1 in 2
Freyhan, 40 psychiatric patients, behaviorial
    problems   2 in 3
Kubanek and Rowell, double-blind, 73 psychotic
    patients unresponsive to other drugs.   4 in 5
Haward, double-blind, 20 psychotic patients   3 in 4
Haward, three double-blind studies: 3 in 4
    concentration—last study, 59 pilots   3 in 4
Smith and Lowrey, 20 adult volunteers, double-
    blind—cognitive function   3 in 4
Smith and Lowrey, 10 aged adults, double-blind
    crossover—cognitive function   2 in 3
Stambaugh, hypoglycemia, unresponsive to dietary
    management—including 6 hour glucose test   3 in 4

Wermuth, et al., double-blind crossover, 19
   "binge eaters"   2 in 3

Based on the foregoing, the chance that PHT is useful for thought, mood and behavior disorders is:

$$8,453,784,125,030,400,000\text{-to-}1.$$

PHT's parameters of safety have been established over a 58-year period, by millions of people taking it daily, for long periods of time. It has properties which, viewed together, set it apart from other drugs. It acts promptly, calms without sedation, energizes without artificial stimulation, and has beneficial side effects. PHT is not habit-forming.

Conclusion—Having PHT listed in the Physicians' Desk Reference (PDR) only as an anticonvulsant is a grave injustice to the American public.

The Tuna Fish Story

Once upon a time some people were shipwrecked on a desert island. Their only food was tiny fish they caught daily. To get the most from the fish they constructed a machine that ground them up, including the heads and tails.

A year went by and all the food the people ate went through the machine. Five years went by, ten years, and still their food went through the machine.

One day a man caught a tuna. "Now we will all have plenty to eat," he said.

"Put it through the machine," the people told him. "It's too big," he said, "it won't fit." "Then we can't eat it," they said.

The phenytoin story is too big. It won't fit in the FDA machine.

OBSERVATIONS ON PHT

It used to be that the word drug had a solid respectable meaning. But in recent years drug and abuse have been put together in the same sentence so often, without discrimination, that the word drug has come into disrepute. It's confusing, and a shame. Today people brag, just before they ascend, "I never took a drug in my life." As if St. Peter cared.

Good drugs are a cheerful feature of our society. We should stop tarring them with the same brush we use on the bad ones and be grateful for them. With this general comment off my chest I would like to make some observations about PHT.

■ ■ ■

PHT would appear to be the most broadly useful drug in our pharmacopoeia (unless another is hidden in the literature). Paradoxically, this valuable feature, this versatility, has interfered with our understanding of the drug. The idea that one substance can have as many uses as PHT has been difficult to accept. And this is understandable. Not too long ago the thinking was a single drug for a single disorder.

A discussion of the basic mechanisms of action of PHT will help us understand how one drug can have so many uses.

A basic mechanism of action study was the first study to demonstrate that PHT might be a therapeutic substance. In 1938 Putnam and Merritt tested PHT on cats in which convulsions were induced by electricity. Of a large group of substances, including the best-known anticonvulsants, it was the most effective in controlling the convulsions. Putnam and Merritt said, Eureka! We have a superior antiepileptic drug.

They did. And not only was PHT the most effective anticonvulsant but it was found to have another remarkable property. Unlike previously used substances it achieved its therapy without sedation.

Let's go back to Putnam and Merritt's original study and apply hindsight. Suppose, instead of inferring that PHT would help the epileptic, Putnam and Merritt had drawn a broader inference from their data. Suppose they had inferred that PHT worked against inappropriate electrical activity. That also would have been a correct inference—but with far broader implications. And the properties of PHT would not have been obscured by the label "anticonvulsant." Today basic mechanism scientists use broad terminology for PHT. They refer to it as a membrane stabilizer.

From the early basic mechanisms study of Toman, in 1949, PHT has been found to correct inappropriate electrical activity in groups of cells, and in individual cells. This includes nerve cells, brain cells, muscle cells—in fact, all types of cells that exhibit marked electrical activity. Whether a cell is made hyperexcitable by electrical impulse, calcium withdrawal, oxygen withdrawal, or by poisons, PHT has been shown to counteract this excitability. Further, it has been demonstrated that, in amounts that correct abnormal cell function, PHT does not affect normal function.*

When we understand that PHT is a substance that stabilizes the hyperactive cell, without affecting normal cell function, we see its therapeutic potential in the human body, a machine that runs on electrical impulse. It is estimated that there are a trillion cells in the body, tens of billions in the brain alone. Thinking is an electrical process, the rhythms of the heart are electrically regulated, the rhythms of the gut are electrically regulated, muscle movement is electrically regulated, messages of pain are electrically referred, and more.

It's important to know that after a cell has been stimulated to fire a few times it becomes potentiated, easier to fire than a normal cell. This is called post-tetanic potentiation. If the stimulation is continued, the cell starts to fire on its own, and continues to fire until its energy is depleted—post-tetanic afterdischarge. PHT has a modifying effect on post-tetanic potentiation and a correcting effect on post-tetanic afterdischarge. This may account for PHT's therapeutic effect on persistent and repetitive thinking and on unnecessary repetitive messages of pain.

■ ■ ■

PHT has a number of properties that set it apart from most substances. For ten distinctive characteristics see *The Broad Range of Clinical Use of PHT,* p. 312. For purposes here we should consider several of these properties.

PHT is a nonhabit-forming substance.** The desirability of a nonhabit-forming drug that can calm and also relieve pain is

---

* See *The Broad Range of Clinical Use of PHT*—Basic Mechanisms of Action.
** This is *not* to be confused with the well-known fact that a person with epilepsy should *not* abruptly discontinue PHT.

apparent—it may be particularly useful during withdrawal from habit-forming substances.

PHT, in therapeutic amounts, has a calming effect without being a sedative. This characteristic is unusual, and clinical observations, supported by basic mechanisms studies, show that PHT does not affect normal function. Not only does PHT not sedate but it has been shown to improve concentration and effect a return of energy. This can be attributed, at least in part, to the fact that an overactive brain (hyperexcitable cells) wastes energy compounds.* One can conjecture that when thoughts with negative emotions are diminished, the effect of these "down" emotions is eliminated, and "psychic" energy may return.

Now that preventive medicine is being given more and more consideration, PHT may be of special interest because of its general properties and its versatility.

PHT, as do other drugs, has side effects. Safety and Toxicology of PHT is reviewed in *The Broad Range of Clinical Use of PHT*. A replication of Parke-Davis's package insert is included in the *Physicians' Desk Reference*. It should be noted that PHT is not on the government's list of Controlled Drugs.

PHT can be used on a regular basis or on an occasional basis by the nonepileptic—depending on need. In the nonepileptic, effective doses tend to be lower than those used for epilepsy. The reader is reminded that PHT is a prescription drug and should be obtained from a physician.

■ ■ ■

When the Dreyfus Medical Foundation was preparing *The Broad Range of Use of Phenytoin*, in 1970, there were many published

* PHT has been shown to increase energy compounds in the brain. See *The Broad Range of Clinical Use of PHT*—Basic Mechanisms of Action.

studies to draw on—1,900 by the time of publication. Seven hundred and fifty references were selected and over 300 of them were summarized. These summaries were presented chronologically in order to show in sequence how the information about PHT developed.

Five years later when *PHT, 1975* was published, there were more than twice the number of studies to review, and the interrelationship between the clinical effects and basic mechanisms of action of PHT was in better perspective. In this bibliography the medical material was arranged according to subject matter for the convenience of the reader. Examples of this are found under such headings as Stabilization of Bioelectrical Activity, Anti-anoxic Effects, Antitoxic Effects, Treatment of Pain, and others.

As an instance, under Anti-anoxic Effects of PHT, ten studies are grouped.* They were published in nine different journals, over a span of twenty years. Each of them is interesting but, by itself, would not carry much weight. But when these studies are reviewed together, the evidence that PHT has an offsetting effect against oxygen lack in animals is highly significant.

These basic studies furnish rationale for the clinical findings first made by Shulman in 1942, *New England Journal of Medicine,* that PHT is effective in asthma—and other studies in asthma, by Sayer and Polvan, *Lancet* (1968), and Shah, Vora, Karkhanis, and Talwalkar, *Indian Journal of Chest Diseases* (1970).** They also furnish rationale for exploration of new uses.

■ ■ ■

* This was in 1975. In the present Bibliography, there are forty-one studies.
** The latter authors give an additional rationale, PHT's potential usefulness against the paroxysmal outbursts of asthma by its ability to stop repetitive afterdischarge.

Exploration of Possible New Uses

Since Putnam and Merritt's discoveries in 1938 that phenytoin was a therapeutic substance, a steadily increasing number of uses for it have been found. The probabilities are high that there are more to come. Evidence from existing clinical and basic mechanisms of action studies furnishes clues for further exploration.

PHT has been reported effective in a wide variety of severely painful conditions. Its usefulness as a nonhabit-forming analgesic in many forms of pain has been established.*

The antianoxic effects of PHT point to its possible usefulness in stroke, emphysema, shock, and, in fact, in any condition where oxygen lack is a problem.

There are a number of references in the literature to beneficial effects of PHT on hypertension. Recently, in a study of mildly hypertensive patients, treatment with PHT was reported effective.* Further study of PHT in hypertension, both by itself and in combination with hypertensive drugs, seems indicated.

A use of PHT that has received little attention, and that may have great potential, is its use topically, for the treatment of pain and for the promotion of healing.

Systemic PHT has been reported useful in healing in a variety of disorders—in leg ulcers, stomach ulcers, scleroderma, pruritus ani, and epidermolysis bullosa.*

The foregoing was written sixteen years ago. Since then there has been substantial evidence from at least six countries that, used topically, PHT is rapidly effective against the pain of burns, ulcers, wounds and other surface conditions, and that it speeds healing time. In recent years, its effectiveness against intractable ulcers of leprosy has been established.

* See *The Broad Range of Clinical Use of Phyenytoin.*

THE ONE-HOUR TEST

When the *Life* and *Reader's Digest* articles were published in 1967, there began a steady flow of people to the Dreyfus Medical Foundation. Many were struck by the similarity of the symptoms they had to symptoms I'd had, as described in the articles, and wanted to talk to me about it. After they'd gotten a prescription I had the opportunity to talk with many of these people before they took their first PHT. These talks were beneficial to both of us—informative for them and educational for me.

I haven't kept exact count—no study as such was being done—but over the years I've talked with over a thousand persons before and after they've taken PHT. As a result of these talks, a test evolved. The test is in two parts. The first part deals with somatic conditions and is outlined at the end of this chapter. The second part deals with the effects of PHT on thoughts and emotions—in an explicit way. Because it differs from other tests, I will discuss it in some detail.

■ ■ ■

While I was in the depression, described earlier in this book, my brain was busy with thoughts I wanted to turn off but couldn't. These thoughts were invariably unhappy ones, mostly associated with fear, sometimes with anger. My brain worked on its own. It paid little attention to the landlord, I hesitate to use the word owner. When I took PHT this symptom disappeared, and I had an insight (in the literal sense) into the effects of PHT on thoughts and emotions. In those days I thought of this symptom as the "turned-on mind." It still seems an appropriate description.

The turned-on mind is a symptom that most of us will identify with. Let me describe what I mean by it. We're told that we're always thinking about something. But "always thinking" can be misleading. There's a great difference between normal cerebration and abnormal. For example: You sit in the park relaxed, listening to the birds, enjoying the trees, and smelling the grass. Beautiful, and healthy. Or, you sit in the park and your mind is so busy you're not even aware of the birds or the trees or the grass. This might be because you have a real problem. But if you don't have a real problem, then it's the turned-on mind.

My first opportunity to observe this closely was in the Worcester Jail study. Its effects were clear. The brains of the prisoners were so overactive that concentration was impaired. This interfered with reading. The subjects would see the words, but thoughts would intrude and they couldn't absorb what they read. They couldn't even remember what they'd seen on TV. The prisoners made it clear that their turned-on minds were busy with thoughts connected with the emotions of anger and fear. Obviously, with these emotions predominant, their mood was poor.

Subsequent experience showed that the turned-on mind is a common complaint with most of the people who need PHT. For years my only way of ascertaining this was by the straightforward question, "Do you have any thoughts now, other than what we are talking about, that you can't turn off?" Answers were usually in the affirmative. I got replies such as "I can't stop thinking for a minute," "My mind is like a five-ring circus," "My brain is going around and around." And similar comments. An hour after 100 mg of PHT, the same question got a different response. It was apparent that the overthinking had quieted and the mood had improved. But the change couldn't be measured. I would have liked to have had a more objective test.

One day I was talking to a young woman before she took her first 100 mg of PHT, and asked the standard question, "Is your brain busy with thoughts you can't turn off?" She said, "Oh yes, a lot of them." Something in the way she answered made me ask, "How many?" She said about fourteen. "Fourteen?" I said, and challengingly asked if she could write them down. I gave her pencil and pad and almost without pause she wrote down twelve thoughts. I was astonished that she could locate these thoughts and write them down. It didn't occur to me to ask her questions about the thoughts.

An hour after PHT I again asked if she could write down her thoughts. She said she could—this time there were just two. One of them was, "I am angry with my mother." Earlier, she had written, "I am very, very angry with my mother." With PHT her mother was two very's better off.

The following day I met with a man I'd known for several years. Jim was thirty-five and had a lot going for him. But he said he was depressed. PHT had been prescribed and he wanted to talk with me before taking it.

These were Jim's circumstances as he related them. He was doing so well in his work that he was leaving a firm he'd been with for years to go into business for himself. The firm had been good to him and he felt badly about leaving. Also, there was a change in his private life. He had fallen in love with another woman and was leaving his wife and two children to get married again. It was a mixed bag. There were things to be happy about, and there were realistic concerns.

As with the young woman the day before, I asked Jim if he could write down the thoughts he couldn't turn off. He considered for a moment and then wrote steadily. When he finished, he said there were nine thoughts. (See column on the left, below.)

At that point I asked a question I'd never asked before. I asked Jim to think of the first thought on his list, and if any emotions came with it to write them down. He thought, and then wrote. I asked him to repeat the procedure with the second thought, and so on.

The preceding was the list of Jim's thoughts and the emotions attached to them. When he handed it to me he volunteered, "'Unfocus' is the worst problem in my life."

With his thoughts and emotions in writing, Jim took 100 mg of PHT. Not wanting my presence to have a possible effect, I left him to his own devices for an hour. When I rejoined him I gave him a fresh piece of paper and asked the same questions. This time he wrote:

Job
Girl
Money
wife }

- Success · Guilt
- Love -
- ?
- Sadness

When he finished Jim looked at what he'd written and had a belly laugh. He said, isn't that a typical American boy's story— JOB, GIRL, MONEY, WIFE. I report the laugh because there weren't any laughs in Jim an hour earlier.

This was the first complete one-hour test for thoughts and emotions. It is a good test for illustration purposes; it demonstrates three points:

One. A striking diminution of extraneous and unnecessary thoughts is seen within an hour after PHT. These thoughts are usually accompanied by emotions related to anger and fear.* When the thoughts disappear, the negative emotions disappear with them.

Two. The PHT needer has poor concentration and is unlikely to remember what his condition was before he took PHT. That is why it is necessary to get things down in writing. Before taking PHT, Jim said that "unfocus" was his worst problem. An hour later I asked, "What is your worst problem?" Jim couldn't remember "unfocus."

Three. PHT does not cause realistic concerns to go away. Jim had two real problems. They were still there but in better perspective. After PHT he still felt guilt in leaving his firm, but now "guilt" was coupled with "success" (he was starting his own business). He still had realistic concern about his family, but instead of *children (guilt, remorse)* this was moderated to *wife (sadness).***

---

* Note that on Jim's first list, with the exception of love, all the emotions are related to anger and fear.
** This was the first of many hundreds of such tests. These tests were not "controlled" by placebo or other drugs. The persons were taking PHT for therapeutic reasons and that was out of the question. However, there was an

Let me re-emphasize that the test should be done in writing. People who need PHT are poor observers and are almost sure to forget how they were an hour before.

■ ■ ■

Everybody's talking at me
I don't hear a word they're saying
Only the echoes of my mind.
—"Everybody's Talking,"
Midnight Cowboy

"Only the echoes of my mind." What a beautiful and perceptive line. To a lesser or greater degree it describes the PHT needer.

Until this test evolved it wouldn't have occurred to me that a person could identify the thoughts alive in his brain, think of them singly, and write down the emotions that came with them. I'd always thought of "echoes of my mind" as being unconscious or subconscious. I still think they are—most of the time. But when a specific question is asked, the echoes become conscious and can be identified. Thus the same questions, asked before and after PHT, enable one to compare quantitative changes in thoughts and qualitative changes in emotions.

A majority of PHT needers have persistent thoughts they can't turn off. A small minority do not have persistent thoughts, but a jumble of thoughts flashing in and out. Both conditions are corrected or improved within an hour. The effects of PHT are so consistent that it helps to remember that, in the

_____

interesting element of control. Initially, I wasn't sure how long it took for PHT to become effective and I experimented with repeating the questions at different time intervals, including five and ten minutes after PHT. In these two time periods I never saw positive results. On the other hand, beneficial effects of PHT were always seen between forty-five minutes and one hour.

laboratory, PHT always corrects repetitive afterdischarge. It makes no exceptions, regardless of the type of nerve or the cause of excitation.

The turned-on mind is not just a daytime phenomenon. It continues at night and can make it difficult to fall asleep. It can also be the cause of light sleep filled with unpleasant dreams and frequent nightmares. That is why PHT's effectiveness against the turned-on mind is helpful with sleeping problems.

Only two more tests will be discussed here. One test was with a woman who used to be seen frequently on television. You could call her an intellectual, in a nice way. Before she took PHT I asked if she had any thoughts, other than what we were talking about, alive in her head. "Oh, I always do," she said. "Doesn't everyone?" Then she wrote down seven thoughts she couldn't turn off. All of them were connected with worries and concerns. When she finished she said, "I always have music playing in my head. It's like a jukebox and I can tell you what record is on."

An hour after taking PHT, before I could ask any questions, this woman volunteered that she was trying to be objective but she didn't think PHT had any effect. Again, I asked if there were any thoughts that she couldn't turn off. She said no—in the most matter-of-fact way. I said, "What is playing in your jukebox now?" She said, "Nothing." That woke her up, and she exclaimed, "My goodness, I feel like a weight is off my chest."*

One other test. It was with a physician who was doing research on PHT. He mentioned that he had been sleeping badly and that he was a little depressed. I suggested it might be useful for him to try PHT, both for personal reasons and also for research purposes. He agreed.

---

* This sort of comment is not uncommon. When negative emotions are relieved, people tend to become more lighthearted and have a return of energy.

After I asked him the standard questions* he started writing down the thoughts "alive" in his brain. He wrote and wrote. When he had written twenty-six, he paused for a moment and looked up. I said, "That's enough, Fred, you've already set a record. Now go back to the first thought, think of it for a moment, and write the emotion or emotions that come with it."

For our purposes, and to save space, I'll leave out the thoughts and just show the last twelve emotions.

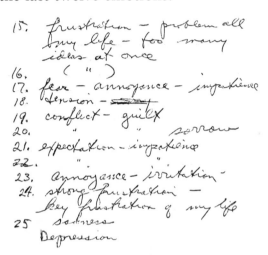

Fred took 100 mg of PHT. An hour later I asked the same questions. He wrote:

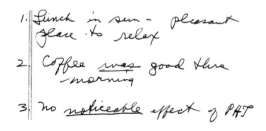

* It is helpful to start with the question, "Do you remember what you had for breakfast?" When the subject tells you, you explain, "You weren't thinking of that until I asked. You got it out of your memory. That is not the type of thought we're interested in. What we want to know is, are there any thoughts alive in your head that you can't turn off?"

When I read No. 3, "No noticeable effect of PHT," I thought he was putting me on. But I saw he was serious. I said, "Fred, get out the list you wrote an hour ago." He looked at the list—and it all came back to him. He wrote:

The turned-on mind is usually occupied with the same thoughts, repeated over and over again. This last test illustrates a less frequent condition—a confusion of thoughts flashing in and out. As Fred described it, "frustration—problem all my life—too many ideas at once."

■ ■ ■

By now the Foundation has done more than a thousand One-Hour Tests with consistent success.

This test works as well in Chinese as it does in English. Six years ago, Dr. Smith and I had the privilege of meeting for two weeks with fifty-three Chinese physicians from different parts of China. After discussing phenytoin with them for eight days, we were invited to go to a reform school.

Based on interviews with five of the children, three were selected for the one-hour test. The results were so good that six Chinese physicians asked to have the test. The nine tests follow.

ONE-HOUR TESTS IN CHINA

	Somatics (scale of 1 to 10)		Before PHT—Thoughts that couldn't be turned off	Emotions	1 Hr. after PHT[1]
	Before 100 mg PHT	1 Hr. after PHT			
Three Juvenile Delinquents					
Pain in knee	2	0	3	fear	all
Hands Sweaty	6	0		fear	thoughts
Trembling inside	3	0		fear	gone
Headache	2	0	4	cry	all
Pain in eyes	6	4		anxiety	thoughts
Pain in back	7	0		unhappy	gone
Headache	3.5	0	5	worry	all
Pain in shoulders	3.5	0		guilty	thoughts
Knots in stomach	2	0		fear	gone
				depression	
				depression	
Six Chinese Physicians					
Headache	5	0	4	worry	all
Shortness of breath	4	0		anxious	thoughts
Butterflies in stomach	4	0		anxious	gone
Chronic pain in back	7	2		anxious	
Energy	-4	0			
Headache	7	1	3	worry	all
Cold hands and feet	2	0		worry	thoughts
Stomach distress	5	1		worry	gone
Energy	-5	0			
			5		
Stomach distress	4	0		worry	all
Pain in abdomen	5-6	0		worry	thoughts
Energy	-3 to -4	0		worry	gone
				worry	
				angry	

	Before 100 mg PHT	1 Hr. after PHT	Before PHT— Thoughts that couldn't be turned off	Emotions	1 Hr. after PHT[1]
Six Chinese Physicians (cont.)					
Headache	6	0	4	anxious	all
Pain in back	3	0		homesick	thoughts
Cold hands and feet	8	4		depressed	gone
Trembling inside	5	0		fear	
Throb in chest	6	0			
Heart Palpitations	5	0			
Energy	-4	0			
Pain in neck	3	0	3	anxious	less anxious*
Pain in chest	2	0		little depressed	gone
Pain in base of thumb	3	0		fear	gone
Cold hands and feet	2	0			
Throb in chest	2	0			
Dizziness	5	0			
Energy	-2	0			
Knots and butterflies in stomach—nervous	4	0	9	anxiety	all
Pain in both calves	5	0		worry	thoughts
Energy	-3	0		worry	gone
				worry	
				anxiety	
				worry	
				fear	
				worry	
				fear	

[1] When the thoughts are gone, the emotions that come with the thoughts are also gone.

*realistic problem

In Chengdu, China, with 53 Chinese physicians

As you can see, there were forty negative thoughts in the nine people. An hour after PHT only one thought remained. We asked the physician if it was a realistic thought and he said it was. That is as it should be, phenytoin doesn't remove realistic thoughts.

Note the marked improvement in the somatic conditions of these nine people. I did not ask the question about energy of the three children, but I did with the physicians. All had minus energy before PHT. An hour later all returned to normal.

Consider this, negative thoughts are associated with being down-hearted—with low energy. When the negative thoughts are removed, one becomes lighter-hearted and has more energy.

■ ■ ■

The one-hour test is in two parts. As to the somatic part of the test: No person has all of the listed symptoms, but three, four, or more are not uncommon. An hour after PHT, moderation or elimination of symptoms is almost always observed.

It's essential to grade the symptoms on a scale. We use 1–10. The average phenytoin needer has many thoughts going on, interfering with concentration, and his memory is poor. A person may have a severe headache, which might be rated "8." An hour later, the headache might be mild (a "2"), but the person might say, "I still have a headache."

As to the second part of the test: Unnecessary thoughts usually disappear in one hour and the negative emotions that come with them are eliminated. This is a more objective method of assessing changes in mood than asking, "How do you feel?" before PHT and again an hour later.

(Outline of the one hour test follows.)

THE ONE-HOUR TEST

PART I—SOMATIC CONDITIONS

These questions pertain to how you feel now. If you answer yes to any question, grade your symptom, on a scale of 1–10 (1, minimal; 10, most severe).

	Before PHT	After PHT
Do you have a headache?	_____	_____
Any pain or blurring in the eyes?	_____	_____
Any ache or pain in the neck?	_____	_____
In the shoulders, the back, or chest?	_____	_____
Shortness of breath?	_____	_____
Aches or pains in arms or hands?	_____	_____
Aches or pains in legs or feet?	_____	_____
Are your hands or feet hot or cold?	_____	_____
Any tingling sensations?	_____	_____
Any "knots" or "butterflies" in stomach?	_____	_____
Are you trembling now? Hold out hands and observe.	_____	_____
Do you feel any trembling inside?	_____	_____
Do you feel a pulse, or beat, or throb inside you?	_____	_____
Do you have any pain or discomfort not asked about?	_____	_____
How is your energy now? (use 0 for normal, and + or - figures)	_____	_____

PART II—THOUGHTS AND EMOTIONS

You could begin by asking the patient what he had for breakfast. When he tells you, remind him that he got that out of his memory, it wasn't alive in his brain. Tell him what you want are thoughts that are going on now, that are difficult to turn off.

If there are such thoughts, ask the patient to write them on the left side of a piece of paper (you don't need to see them, they might be personal). Then ask the patient to think each thought, separately, and write opposite it the emotion or feeling that comes with it.

An hour after 100 mg of PHT, ask the same questions.

Before PHT

THOUGHTS   EMOTIONS

_____   _____

_____   _____

_____   _____

_____   _____

_____   _____

_____   _____

After PHT

_____   _____

_____   _____

_____   _____

_____   _____

_____   _____

CONCLUSION AND
PERSONAL NOTE

―――――――――

"Truth is a precious thing and should be used sparingly."—
Mark Twain. I have squandered a good deal of this precious
commodity in writing this book—my supply is low—and it is
time to conclude.

With the completion of this book I will have done what I can
to communicate the facts about PHT. The Dreyfus Medical
Foundation is going out of the communications business. It is
not that we have lost interest, but to continue to argue the case
for PHT could be counterproductive. This is a matter for others
now.

Duplicates of the Foundation's extensive files on PHT are
herewith offered to the federal government. Access to these files
will continue to be available to physicians. The Foundation
intends to stay in the field of PHT and hopes, selectively, to
sponsor research in new areas.

Thank you if you have read some of this book. And the best
of everything to you. As for me, I am going to get in a rowboat
and float upstream.

Foundation Changes

In 1976, with mutual understanding our Scientific Director, Dr. Samuel Bogoch retired and returned to his personal interests in the field of scientific research. I thanked him for his fine assistance and his invaluable help with our bibliographies. And I thank him again.

An ever-increasing amount of medical studies were being published around the world. Our excellent librarian, Vivian McDermott, and her assistants continued to collect this literature. Soon it was obvious that another bibliography was necessary.

In 1984, Dr. Barry Smith, an outstanding neurosurgeon, joined the Foundation as Scientific Director. The PHT story appealed to Barry's heart and he's been an extremely hard worker. With his help a third bibliography, *The Broad Range of Clinical Use of Phenytoin*, was written—3,100 medical references. It was sent to all the physicians in the U.S. (508,000) along with *A Remarkable Medicine Has Been Overlooked.*

SIXTEEN YEARS LATER

"Conclusion and Personal Note" was written sixteen years ago. I'll try to summarize what has happened since then.

Complaining is not my game. But sometimes telling the facts is essential—and may sound like complaining. Please read the bibliography Table of Contents (pp. 305–10). Then consider. Phenytoin, a drug introduced in the U.S. 55 years ago, has been reported useful for over 70 symptoms and disorders by thousands of independent physicians from 48 countries, yet it is still listed with our FDA only as an anticonvulsant. This is such a detriment to the health of the American people that it is the cause of a great catastrophe.

We are used to the word catastrophe being applied to volcanoes, hurricanes and earthquakes, where hundreds or more people are killed. We can count them, they're before our eyes. These are overt catastrophes. The labeling of PHT exclusively as an anticonvulsant by our FDA is the cause of a covert catastrophe. Millions of people suffer and die because of it. We just can't count them.

■ ■ ■

This has been discussed before, so I'll be brief.

In 1938 Drs. Putnam and Merritt, looking for a better anticonvulsant drug, jolted cats with electricity until the cats had convulsions. PHT was the most effective medicine tried in preventing these convulsions. And it was approved as an anticonvulsant by the FDA.

Shortly after PHT was used in epileptic patients, physicians published studies saying that those who'd received it had improvements in personality, mood, memory, concentration, and amenability to discipline. That was the beginning of physicians around the world starting to report, in medical journals, PHT's use for an ever-increasing number of symptoms and disorders.

There are almost thirty-four hundred medical journals. The average physician receives seven or eight. Thus he has less than 1/4 of 1% of the world's medical literature. Since these published studies on PHT were not sponsored by a drug company, it follows that they are independent and objective, and the volume of them makes them evidential to the greatest degree.

In our system, a physician is made aware of drugs that are therapeutic by the drug companies, through advertisements and salesmen. If the physician doesn't learn about a drug this way, he's apt to be skeptical.

In recent years, there's been a game called "sue the doctor" in which lawyers sue for valid reasons and for no reason except to make money. It's understandable that physicians and hospital committees try to do things in a conventional way, and the lack of an FDA listing has more influence than intended.

■ ■ ■

As related, in some detail, in the chapter, "A Flaw in the System," Parke-Davis has done little or nothing to get PHT listed for its many uses with the FDA. Since *A Remarkable Medicine* was written there is much more evidence of this. I'll give just one example.

Dr. Stephen Preston, former Head of Research at Parke-Davis, visited our offices, on two occasions, to discuss phenytoin. After he left Parke-Davis he wrote me a heart-warming letter:

> PHT is now a daily part of my life since I have developed a familial type of chorea. After suffering through several experimental drugs I finally demanded that my neurologist put me on PHT and I found that Dr. Dreyfus knew what he was talking about. Except for you...I would not be leading the happy and productive life which I presently am.
>
> In closing I would like to state that neither the Food and Drug Administration nor Parke-Davis could ever have done such a magnificent job of making the medical profession aware of the therapeutic value of PHT as you have.—(excerpt)

A lovely letter, from a former Head of Research at Parke-Davis.

■ ■ ■

Let us go to the FDA. I realize they don't know better. Nothing like this had ever happened. Physicians around the world had published thousands of studies about a remarkable drug, and its parenting drug company had not brought the facts to the FDA. When a Charitable Foundation organized a vast amount of this published information into bibliographies to help the FDA, it didn't occur to the FDA that they should do anything about it. It was not custom. They don't seem to be aware that they were established to help with the health of the American public, custom or no custom.

■ ■ ■

You have read my travail with the U.S. Government in the chapter, "Travels with the Government." There has been much more travail since then. I'll relate just two experiences.

In 1982, Senator Paul Laxalt, a friend from Nevada, introduced me to Secretary of HEW, Richard Schweiker, and Commissioner of the FDA, Dr. Arthur Hull Hayes. It was agreed by all that a committee of ten should be set up to study this matter. Dr. Hayes wiggled on this agreement, and put the matter in the hands of Dr. Marion Finkel, Director of Orphan Products Development. I told Dr. Hayes this was not an orphan drug, this was an orphanage. However...

Dr. Finkel studied the literature conscientiously, even went to Mexico with Dr. Smith and me and saw a variety of uses of PHT, including topical. After three months Dr. Finkel was convinced. At a meeting, at which I was present, Dr. Finkel recommended to the Senator, the Secretary, and the Commissioner, that five or six uses of PHT be published in the May *FDA Bulletin*. This was agreed upon unanimously.

About ten days before the May *Bulletin* was to be published, I was told that the five or six uses of PHT (a vast understatement, but better than nothing) would not be published. "Someone" in the FDA had ruled against it. Imagine. A Senator, a Secretary of HEW, and a Commissioner of the FDA had been overruled by "someone" in the FDA. This was like the Joint Chiefs of Staff being overruled by a sergeant. I was given no explanation.

■ ■ ■

About six years after my book was written, I met with President Reagan. He asked John Svahn, an assistant, to look into the matter. Mr. Svahn did the opposite of what we'd asked and went to the FDA and received the following comment: "The FDA

In the Oval Office again

knows of some anecdotal reports of the success of Dilantin for some few patients but is unaware of scientific studies supporting the claim." The President quoted this in a letter to me.

This statement upset me so much I wrote the following letter—which I didn't send.

My dear Mr. President:
    Thank you for your letter. I have been trying to figure out why it's taken me so long to answer it. I've worked on it every day, including Saturdays and Sundays. But something has had me stumped. Finally I realized what it was. I have run out of hypocrisy—with Government, that is—I have plenty left for civilian life.

For over twenty years, the basis of my approach to Government has been "you can catch more flies with honey" and it's worked—we have barrels of flies. But we're out of honey—or hypocrisy in this case. So, to the truth.

The memo you received was an insult to the office of the President. It was also an insolence, an ignorance, and an arrogance.

The notion that the FDA is an authority on everything medical underlies this matter. It is a bizarre notion. But the author of the memo, note I do not say "the FDA," must believe it. With his twenty minutes of experience on the subject, you would think he would have referred you to this Foundation, which has had twenty years of experience. But no. He gives his considered opinion, "we know of anecdotal reports of some few patients." He could as sensibly have said, "we know of anecdotal reports of some few elephants in Africa."

■ ■ ■

I wrote the President a calmer letter—which I did send. The President called me on the phone, 20 minutes after he'd read the letter, he said, and told me he'd put the matter into the hands of James Miller, Director, Office of Management and Budget.

Mr. Miller arranged for Dr. Frank Young, Commissioner of the FDA, to visit our offices. In three long sessions, we discussed with the Commissioner the tragically misleading listing of PHT. At the end of the third session, Commissioner Young told Dr. Smith, Ms. Raudonat and me, "Jack's been jerked around." I said, "Frank, I haven't been jerked around. The American people have been jerked around."

Well, one couldn't ask for anything better from the Commissioner of the FDA. I was sure something good would happen. Unfortunately, Dr. Young left, or was removed from office a few weeks later. However, I knew the word would be passed along, with emphasis. Would you believe it, Dr. Young wasn't able to get me an appointment with the new Commissioner, Dr. David Kessler. Of course you wouldn't believe it. But it's a fact.

Frank Keating, now Governor of Oklahoma, who'd studied this matter thoroughly, couldn't get me an appointment with Commissioner Kessler either. Governor Keating's letter said embarrassingly nice things about me, but the letter is pertinent:

> For the past 25 years, Jack Dreyfus has selflessly devoted his energies to the health and well-being of our citizenry...Almost single-handedly and with no financial interest, Dreyfus has championed the expanded use of phenytoin...Physicians around the world have made remarkable contributions...Two FDA commissioners (Ley, Edwards) have decried the neglect of phenytoin.
>
> Like Cornwallis at Yorktown, to whom does Jack surrender his sword? Who will take this magnificent man's life treasure and apply it to the needs of suffering people?—(excerpt)

In the Commissioner's response to Governor Keating he said, "Our scientific review staff has reviewed data on Dilantin for various uses and has concluded that effectiveness has not been shown for any of the indications."

If I knew the "scientific" word for rubbish I would use it.

But this statement requires some thought. It's so ridiculous you'd think that Dr. Kessler wasn't telling the truth, but I'm sure he was. In 1970, 1975 and 1988 extensive bibliographies on PHT were sent to all the physicians in the U.S. including those on the scientific review staff of the FDA. The last bibliography contained 3,100 medical references, and hundreds of double-blind, and other controlled studies. Either of two things happened. The "scientific" review staff didn't even glance at these bibliographies, which would be a disgrace. Or, if they read even a tiny amount of the literature, you could say this is not a scientific review staff.

Dr. Kessler's letter continued, "Our Center for Drug Evaluation and Research remains prepared to review formally any fully developed submission of organized data Mr. Dreyfus or his associates is prepared to generate in support of one or more new uses of Dilantin."

Imagine that. The government prates about the private sector helping them. I got out of two highly successful businesses, the Dreyfus Fund and Dreyfus & Co., and have spent $80 million of my own money, and 30 years of my life trying to help the government. The fact that I tried doesn't mean much, but the fact that I've been working in a gold mine of good health means a lot. And the Commissioner of the FDA won't even meet with me.

Millions of people, in this country alone, suffer because of those letters F D A. Another way of spelling FDA is **USA**. The FDA was established by our Congress with approval of our President, yet Congress doesn't even know who's in it.

To become a member of the Supreme Court a candidate is put through many weeks of grueling questioning by Congressmen. Congress knows all the members of the Supreme Court, and almost none of the members of the FDA. We have a strange situation here. If the Supreme Court makes a dumb ruling, and I don't say they do, there would be a public outcry, because we would all know about it. If the FDA does something dumb, and I do say they do, the public says, "It must be so, the FDA said so."

We hear, "The FDA says this," "The FDA says that," "The FDA needs more time to study this," and we get the impression that the FDA is the second edition of *The Gideon Bible*. I assure you it's not. There are many good people in this organization and some of the other kind. But that doesn't matter, they have tenure. The listing of PHT, only as an anticonvulsant, is a sin.*

■ ■ ■

A wise man said, "No man can be a prophet in his own country." Largely due to this Foundation's work, PHT, a drug parented in the United States, is being used widely in many countries.

The Broad Range of Clinical Use of Phenytoin and *A Remarkable Medicine Has Been Overlooked* have been translated into Russian by the Russians, and Chinese by the Chinese.

There follows current uses of this American drug in Russia, China, Ghana, India and Mexico. Additional uses are constantly being reported.

Russia

Anxiety
Concentration
  (uncontrolled thinking)
Alcohol withdrawal
Neurosis
Parkinson's disease
Healing—topical use:
  Burns
  Chronic skin ulcers

Hypertension
Cardiovascular disease
Atherosclerosis
Cushing's disease
Hypothalamic dysfunction
Temperature regulation
Gynecologic dysfunctions
  (infertility, menstrual
  regulation and symptoms)

---

* Sin—commit an offense of any kind. To do wrong.—Webster

China

Attention deficit disorder
Alzheimer's disease
Healing—topical use:
  Burns
  Diabetic ulcers
  Oral ulcers in leukemia
  Varicose ulcers
  Gouty ulcers
  Ulcers of leprosy
  Pressure ulcers
  Traumatic wounds
Scleroderma
Ischemia
Stroke
Cardiac arrhythmias

Enuresis
Depression (including anxiety)
Psychosis, symptoms of
  (violence and agitation)
Heroin abuse
Continuous muscle
  fiber activity
Mountain sickness
Gilles de la Tourette
  syndrome
Atherosclerosis / hyperlipidemia
Pain (stroke, burns, cancer)
Migraine
Trigeminal neuralgia
Restless legs

Ghana

Violent behavior
Anxiety
Asthma
Sickle cell disease:
  Ulcer healing
  Pain
  Crisis

Healing—topical use:
  Burns
  Chronic skin ulcers
  Ulcers of leprosy
  Buruli ulcers
  Dental surgery
Pre-eclampsia (hypertension
  in pregnancy)

India

Healing—topical use:
  Ulcers of leprosy
  Venous stasis ulcers
  Diabetic ulcers
  Abscess cavities
  Burns
Asthma
Migraine headaches
Pain

Neuropathic pain
Cancer pain
Tetanus
Rheumatoid arthritis
Alcohol and heroin withdrawal
Mood disorders
Eclampsia and Pre-eclampsia
  (hypertension in pregnancy)

Mexico

Healing—topical use:
  Burns
  Ulcers
  Surgical wounds
  Dental surgery
Pain
Mood disorders

Excessive fear
Excessive anger
Depression
Pre-anesthesia
Sleep disturbances
Enuresis
Tetanus

PHT is being used in Brazil, Guyana, Iraq, Jordan, Nigeria, Poland, Tanzania, Zambia, and other countries for an increasing number of uses. Dr. Smith has visited many of these countries.

■ ■ ■

The FDA is different people at different times. The FDA has done some excellent things. You will recall the FDA, under Dr. Charles Edwards, in 1972, had Secretary Elliot Richardson write the following letter to Governor Rockefeller:*

June 22, 1972

Dear Governor Rockefeller:

...A review of the literature reveals that phenytoin has been reported to be useful in a wide range of disorders. Among its reported therapeutic actions are its stabilizing effect on the nervous system—its antiarrhythmic effect on certain cardiac disorders—and its therapeutic effect on emotional disorders...

Your interest in encouraging the Department to provide a public clarification of the status of phenytoin is very welcome...(excerpt).

Sincerely,
Elliot L. Richardson, Secretary,
Health, Education and Welfare

* Gov. Rockefeller's and Sec. Richardson's letters are in the Appendix, 425–26.

In their April 1982 *FDA Bulletin*, the FDA made an excellent statement:

Once a product has been approved for marketing, a physician may prescribe it for uses...not included in approved labeling. Such 'unapproved' or, more precisely, 'unlabeled' uses may, reflect approaches to drug therapy that have been extensively reported in medical literature. (excerpt)

■ ■ ■

To the President and to Congress

Although this matter is not your conventional work, please don't think it's not one of the most important matters ever to come before you. Look at it this way. This is not a problem. This is a solution for some of our most serious problems.

The most versatile and benign medicine ever given us is listed with our government agency for only one use. And the reason— it's so cheap. Think of that.

For God's sake, I do not use His name in vain, shouldn't the President and Congress set up a committee of intelligent and conscientious people to study this matter. It would only take a week or ten days. And the rewards for the American people would be inestimable.

In addition to improved health for millions of people, PHT could have a marked beneficial effect on crime and violence, one of our greatest problems.

In our present Bibliography there are twenty-nine studies reporting PHT's beneficial effects on violent behavior, and synonyms for it such as assaultive behavior, destructive behavior, and episodic dyscontrol. Eight of the studies deal with large numbers of patients (over 100 on avg.). Seven other studies are double-blind studies.

An exercise in probabilities will help. If we assess the chance of being correct to the double-blind studies of 10 in 11, the large studies of 5 in 6, and the other studies of 1 in 2, the chance of PHT being useful for violent behavior is slightly more than 275 quadrillion-to-1.

PHT's Use in Prisons

Some of those in prison have committed crimes because of nervous disorders. Being confined gives them time to brood. This exacerbates their tensions. Fear, anger, inability to concentrate, poor mood, sleep problems, pain, and an over-busy brain are symptoms common in prisoners. Phenytoin is therapeutic for all these symptoms. (Careful reading of the chapter Eleven Angry Men will make this clear.)

Allowing prisoners to have phenytoin, a nonhabit-forming medicine, *on a voluntary basis*, would be an act of responsibility on our part. It would also be a great kindness.

There would be tremendous collateral benefits. As prisoners become healthier, tensions in prisons would decrease. Further, when prisoners got out, if they continued to take phenytoin, as they likely would, the physiological need for violence would be reduced. And the terrible cycle of crime and drug abuse would start to be reversed.

Let me stress—it's hard to get this point across—PHT should *not* be given to prisoners to control their anger. It should be given to prisoners to improve their health. Uncontrolled anger would be one of many symptoms that would be improved. And let me stress again, it should be given on a voluntary basis.

■ ■ ■

A Temporary Solution

If the FDA tried to approve PHT, use by use, in their usual fashion, it would take forever, and a century. What they could do (without delay) is allow Secretary Richardson's letter, which he said could be made public (remember the FDA wrote that letter for him), to accompany phenytoin's package inserts.

The FDA could then remind the physicians of the April 1982 *FDA Bulletin*: "Once a product has been approved for marketing, a physician may prescribe it for uses...not included in approved labeling. Such unapproved uses may reflect approaches to drug therapy that have been extensively reported in medical literature."

Having these two simple statements accompanying phenytoin's package inserts would open up the matter for the physicians and hospital committees in this country and be of great benefit to the American public.

Mr. President and Congress and American public, it's in your hands now.

Best wishes,

Jack Dreyfus

Something Personal

This book started with an autobiography, and I'll conclude with something personal.

My life has been incredibly lucky or, as suggested by the Reporting Angel, interfered with from above.

I've had the fortune to have many happy avocations: golf, tennis, bridge, gin rummy, horse handicapping, race horses, and management in the field of racing. In business there has been advertising and marketing, Wall Street research, and making a great amount of money. And then something far more important happened.

I got out of a depression, by finding that great a drug had been overlooked. This gave me a unique privilege—to spend my money, and the last 30 years of my life, trying to get the information to the rest of humanity. I can't imagine a nicer life. I thank God for it.

To The Reader

I'd hoped to include the entire *Broad Range of Clinical Use of Phenytoin* in this book, but our publishers have told me that it would be impractical. However, the most important half—the clinical section is included.

If you would like to have the full Bibliography and Review, please send your address and $6.00, to the Dreyfus Medical Foundation, Lenox Hill Station, P.O. Box 965, New York, N.Y. 10021-0029. If you can't afford the $6.00, and I hope you can, we will send it at no cost.

Dreyfus Medical Foundation

THE
BROAD RANGE
OF CLINICAL USE OF
PHENYTOIN

BIOELECTRICAL MODULATOR

The Dreyfus Medical Foundation is a
charitable foundation and has no
financial interest in phenytoin.

The painting on the cover is by Joan Personette.

For ten years the Dreyfus Medical Foundation had an Advisory Board which met at least three times a year. These were highly qualified persons who understood PHT thoroughly. When the Board was dissolved, the members wrote me such nice letters that excerpts are included here. Their compliments to me were really compliments to PHT.

"There is no one but you that comes to mind who has had the compassion, the common sense, the courage, the patience, the perseverance and the prescience, the greatness of heart, the gentle good humor and the generosity to try to show the entire medical profession *and* the government of the United States of America that a truly remarkable medicine was being not only overlooked, but often consciously avoided by the arrogance of science."
—THEODORE COOPER, M.D.
Former Director, National Heart & Lung Institute;
Assistant Secretary of Health, Education and Welfare

"My admiration and respect for you as an individual, and as a scientist, has grown over the years... But even more than being a scientist, you are also a humanist, and have pursued your goals despite all of the obstacles, wittingly or unwittingly, set in your path by others."
—HERBERT L. LEY, M.D
Former Commissioner FDA;
Associate Prof., Harvard School of Public Health

"You need to know that it has been your unerring insights and guidance which have brought this work to its current state."
—PAUL L. KORNBLITH, M.D.,
Former Chief, Surgical Neurology,
National Institutes of Health;
Chairman, Dept. of Neurosurgery,
Albert Einstein College of Medicine

"As you probably know I was something like 70-80 times abroad attending congresses, conferences, meeting people, attending talks, lectures and and delivering them myself.

Only one of the people I met was a genius—so, please my dearest genius, live as long as possible, be healthy and happy."
—NATASHA P. BECHTEREVA, M.D.,
Former Chariman of the Commission for Healthcare and Welfare of the Supreme Soviet;
Former Director, Institute for Experimental Medicine (formerly the Pavlovian Institute);
Member of Six Academies of Science

"Among this peculiar scenario has risen the strong personality of Mr. Jack Dreyfus, with gentle manners, the mind of a wizard, the quick wit of a bridge champion, but the kind soul of an apostle."
—ANTONIO ALDRETE, M.D.,
Former Professor, Dept. Anesthesiology,
University of Alabama Medical School;
Chairman, Dept. Anesthesiology & Critical Care,
Cook County Hospital, Chicago

"You have demonstrated to the entire world—at no little expense to yourself and considerable effort in going to the far corners of this world—what a valuable medication Dilantin is for many purposes. You have also demonstrated something that Mark Twain once said, 'I have never let my schoolin' interfere with my education.'"
—JOSEPH C. ELIA, M.D.,
Most decorated Flight Surgeon in World War II;
Editor, Medical Page,
New Hampshire Union Leader

"You are a human being that is forever young, forever giving, forever caring, and forever wise. Your works will be forever young."
—EDUARDO RODRIGUEZ-NORIEGA, M.D.,
Professor of Medicine and Chief,
Dept. of Infectious Diseases,
University of Guadalajara

The Broad Range of Clinical Use of Phenytoin

Bioelectrical Modulator

BIBLIOGRAPHY AND REVIEW

Barry H. Smith, M.D., Ph.D.
Samuel Bogoch, M.D., Ph. D.
Jack Dreyfus

THE DREYFUS MEDICAL FOUNDATION

"The greatest crisis facing us is a crisis in the organization and accessibility of human knowledge. We own an enormous 'encyclopedia' which isn't even arranged alphabetically. Our 'file cards' are spilled on the floor. The answers we want may be buried somewhere in the heap."

—*Robert Heinlein*

Photograph of over 10,000 studies from 38 countries,
published in over 250 medical journals,
that form the basis of this Bibliography and Review.

This picture was taken sixteen years ago.
Today it would be twice as large.

Prefatory

If one looks at the Physicians' Desk Reference, one will find that phenytoin's only listing with the FDA is as an anticonvulsant. This is a narrow description of a drug that has been reported by thousands of physicians throughout the world to be useful for over fifty symptoms and disorders.*

The misunderstanding of the broad clinical usefulness of phenytoin amounts to a great catastrophe. Millions of people—in this country alone—suffer because of it. This is not the fault of the FDA. It is not the fault of the FDA. It is not the fault of our physicians. There is a flaw in our system of bringing prescription medicines to the public.

The purpose of this Bibliography and Review is to put together, in one place, for the convenience of the physicians and the government, a comprehensive summary of the world medical literature on phenytoin.**

---

* See Table of Contents, pp. 305–10. This was written in 1988. Today the figure is larger.
** Other than in epilepsy.

A Personal Note

Dear Physician:

In 1963, a great piece of luck led me to ask my physician to allow me to try phenytoin for depressed moods. He had not heard of such a use, but allowed me to try it. It worked promptly. At first, we both attributed my recovery to coincidence. It seemed almost impossible that uses of a drug could have been overlooked for twenty-five years.

In the course of the next year I saw six other people, in succession, have similar benefits. The probabilities had changed. From being almost impossible, it became highly probable that PHT had been overlooked. PHT had taken me out of a miserable condition, and I had an obligation to investigate its potential for others.

I thought it would be easy to sponsor studies on phenytoin, and that the medical profession would then take over. I was mistaken. It became necessary to leave my businesses in Wall Street to spend full time in research on this matter.

The evidence about PHT is no longer at issue. Since its first clinical use, thousands of physicians, in hundreds of medical journals, have reported its usefulness for a broad range of disorders. Only a fraction of this work could be seen by a single physician, unless his or her life were spent reading over 3,000 medical journals.

Accompanying this Bibliography is *A Remarkable Medicine Has Been Overlooked*, a narrative of my experiences with PHT. I think you will enjoy reading it.

With the publication of this Bibliography, and the narrative, I have done what I can to discharge my obligation. The matter is now in the hands of our fine physicians.

I wish you the best of health, and good luck,

Jack Dreyfus

Jack Dreyfus

Brief History

In 1908, a German chemist, Heinrich Biltz, synthesized diphenylhydantoin (phenytoin). He sold PHT, along with other compounds, to Parke-Davis. The company did not patent it, nor did they find a use for it. It sat on their shelves for twenty-nine years.

In 1937, Putnam and Merritt, two doctors outside Parke-Davis, discovered phenytoin's first clinical use, in epilepsy. PHT was more effective than phenobarbital and, unlike that drug, it achieved its therapy without sedation.

That being the day of a single drug for a single disorder, phenytoin was tagged an anticonvulsant. On the basis of clinical experience, it was approved for safety by the FDA.

From its earliest use, there was evidence that phenytoin was more than an anticonvulsant. Reports started to appear in the medical literature of marked improvement in mood, emotional stability, and sense of well-being in the patients who took PHT. Since that time, an ever increasing number of reports and studies, by physicians from at least thirty-eight countries, have demonstrated that PHT is useful for a broad range of symptoms and disorders.

Basic mechanism studies have kept apace of the clinical studies, and make clear how one drug can have so many uses.

Today, fifty years after its first use, phenytoin's only listed indication with the FDA is still "anticonvulsant." There is a flaw in our system of bringing prescription medicines to the public.*

---

* The "flaw" is discussed in *A Remarkable Medicine Has Been Overlooked.*

Evidence

It is customary for a drug company to sponsor new uses for a drug. That hasn't happened in the case of phenytoin. This doesn't make the evidence less evidential.

Physicians around the world, with no interest but the scientific and a desire to help others, have reported PHT useful for a wide range of disorders. Published in more than 250* medical journals, the reports and studies have many forms of control:

1. Double-blind studies with placebo or other drugs as controls.
2. Studies in which PHT has been found effective when other drugs have failed.
3. Trials in which PHT is found effective—withdrawn and symptoms return, reinstituted and symptoms disappear.
4. Promptness of action.
5. Clinical studies in which improvements are confirmed by laboratory means.

The most important control is the fact that the evidence comes from thousands of impartial observers. So many independent reports are like strands in a rope, each adding to its strength.

· · ·

Basic mechanism studies confirm the clinical observations. They demonstrate that phenytoin corrects inappropriate electrical activity at the level of the single cell—with little or no effect on normal cell function. This fundamental property makes understandable how PHT can have so many uses.

* Today (1997) over 350 medical journals.

Use of Approved Drugs for Unlabeled Indications

FDA Drug Bulletin, April 1982

"The appropriateness of prescribing approved drugs for uses not included in their official labeling is sometimes a cause of confusion among practitioners.

"The Federal Food, Drug and Cosmetic Act does not limit the manner in which a physician may use an approved drug. Once a product has been approved for marketing, a physician may prescribe it for uses or in treatment regimens or patient populations that are not included in approved labeling. Such 'unapproved' or, more precisely, 'unlabeled' uses may, in fact, reflect approaches to drug therapy that have been extensively reported in medical literature." (Excerpt) See Appendix p. 424 for full text.

Terminology

The drug that is the subject of this book is known by two generic names, diphenylhydantoin and phenytoin. Phenytoin (PHT) is used in this book.

PHT's best known trade name in the United States is Dilantin. Other trade names, outside the United States, include Aleviaton, Dintoina, Epamin, Epanutin, Epelin, Eptoin, Hidantal, Idantoin, Phenhydan, Solantyl.

Prescription Medicine

PHT is a prescription medicine, which means it should be obtained through a physician.

Table of Contents

Clinical Uses of Phenytoin

*Basic Mechanisms of Action**

* Only the Summary of the Basic Mechanisms of Action section of *The Broad Range of Clinical Use of Phenytoin* is included here. The contents of the remainder of the section, listed in the Table of Contents, is available on request. If you would like to have the full Bibliography and Review, please send your address and $6.00 to the Dreyfus Medical Foundation, Lenox Hill Station, P.O. Box 965, New York, NY 10021-0029. If you can't afford the $6.00, and I hope you can, we will send it at no cost.

Clinical Uses of Phenytoin

NOTE TO THE READER:

Reference numbers for additional published articles accompany many of the articles and summaries in the Clinical Uses of Phenytoin section of *The Broad Range of Clinical Use of Phenytoin* that follows. Because of publishing space limitations, the list of references for all the articles abstracted and those referenced could not be included with this edition, but it is available in the full Bibliography and Review. If you would like to have a copy of the full Bibliography, please send your address and $6.00 to the Dreyfus Medical Foundation, Lenox Hill Station, P.O. Box 965, New York, NY 10021-0029. If you can't afford the $6.00, and I hope you can, we will send it at no cost.

Distinctive Characteristics of Phenytoin

Phenytoin has distinctive characteristics which, when viewed together, set it apart from other substances.

1. PHT regulates bioelectrical activity at the individual cell level. This action, at a level fundamental to all body functions, helps explain how PHT achieves its therapeutic effects in a wide range of disorders.

2. PHT corrects inappropriate electrical activity, but does not affect normal function. It has been found effective in both hyperexcitable and hypoexcitable conditions.

3. PHT has a corrective effect on post-tetanic potentiation and post-tetanic afterdischarge. This action seems to explain how repetitive and uncontrolled thinking is decreased and repetitive messages of pain are modified.

4. PHT has regulatory effects on endocrine and metabolic processes, and on stress. It has been demonstrated to have anti-anoxic effects, and anti-toxic properties, and to promote healing.

5. PHT's action is prompt. Taken orally, it is effective within an hour, intravenously within a few minutes. Used topically, its effect against pain is rapid.

6. In therapeutic doses PHT has a calming effect without being sedative, and an energizing effect without being a stimulant.

7. PHT is effective for a wide range of symptoms and disorders. In addition to being useful for a target symptom, PHT can be therapeutic for many other symptoms—in effect have beneficial "side effects."

8. PHT is not habit-forming.

9. PHT's parameters of safety have been established over a fifty-year period by extensive and intensive use.

THOUGHT, MOOD
AND BEHAVIOR DISORDERS

Summary

Phenytoin has been found useful for so many symptoms and disorders (see Table of Contents) that an overall summary is impractical.

The section on Thought, Mood and Behavior Disorders deserves special attention—not only for the benefits in these disorders themselves, but because of the resultant lessening of tension and stress, associated with many other disorders.

Soon after phenytoin's introduction, in 1938, reports started to appear in the medical literature of patients' improvement in mood, concentration, cooperativeness and sense of well-being. By now, extensive published evidence from widely separated sources has established PHT's usefulness for thought, mood and behavior disorders.

. . .

Phenytoin has been shown to have a calming effect on the overactive brain. Symptoms of this condition are preoccupation, multiple thinking, and flashes and fragments of thoughts coming and going. PHT reduces this uncontrolled activity enabling more normal thinking processes to be restored. This effect is usually achieved within an hour, without sedation.

Anger and fear and related emotions are usually found in combination with the overactive brain. Emotional states related to anger for which PHT is therapeutic are impatience, impulsiveness, irritability, aggression, hostility, rage and violence. Emotional states related to fear for which PHT is therapeutic are worry, anxiety, guilt, pessimism and depression. Although excessive anger and fear states are decreased or

■ 313

eliminated by PHT, realistic reactions of anger and fear are not interfered with.

Sleep disturbances found in combination with the overactive brain
fall into two general categories. The first and most frequent category
is symptomatized by difficulty in falling asleep because of over-think-
ing, light sleep accompanied by unpleasant dreams and frequent
nightmares, and insufficient sleep. A less frequent category is symptomatized by excessive sleep, so-called avoidance sleep. Relief from
both types of sleep disturbances is usually prompt with PHT.

PHT is effective with extremes of mood ranging from depression to
the hyperexcitable state. These apparently disparate effects are observed
in the overactive, impatient individual who is calmed by PHT, and the
tired, energyless individual who has a return to normal energy levels.

Somatic symptoms frequently associated with thought, mood and
behavior disorders are usually relieved by PHT within an hour. Among
them are headaches, pain, stomach discomfort, dizziness, trembling,
excessively cold or warm hands or feet, and shortness of breath.

Stress. When the brain becomes overactive and the emotions of fear
and anger appear, the body goes on alert, and a state of vigilance develops. For short periods this can be normal. But, if this is a chronic condition, there is constant stimulation of the hypothalamic-pituitary-
adrenal (HPA) axis, resulting in the release of the chemicals of fight
and flight. A cycle is created, the chemicals keeping the brain overactive and the overactive brain stimulating release of the chemicals. A
condition of stress develops. By correcting the overactive brain, PHT
seems to break this cycle, causing a more normal state to return—and
stress, commonly associated with a wide range of disorders, is diminished or eliminated.

Basic mechanism studies are consistent with the clinical observations
of the effectiveness of PHT. Of particular relevance are the studies in the
section, Stabilization of Bioelectrical Activity.* They show that PHT,
without affecting normal function, corrects hyperexcitability, as in post-
tetanic potentiation or post-tetanic repetitive discharge. This would seem
to be the mechanism by which PHT corrects the overactive brain.

* See Basic Mechanisms of Action

Thought, Mood and Behavior

From the outset, in its use with epileptics, side benefits of PHT were noted. Improvements in thought, mood and behavior were observed.

"Salutary effects of PHT on personality, memory, mood, cooperativeness, emotional stability, amenability to discipline, etc., are also observed, sometimes independently of seizure control."—GOODMAN AND GILMAN (1955).

BENEFITS IN EPILEPTICS

MERRITT AND PUTNAM, *Journal of the American Medical Association* (1938), in the earliest clinical report on PHT observed: "In addition to a relief or a great reduction in the frequency of attacks, it was frequently noted by the parents of children that they were much better behaved, more amenable to discipline and did better work in school."

McCARTAN AND CARSON, *Journal of Mental Science* (1939), while reporting on the efficacy of PHT in controlling seizures in a group of twenty patients, noted: "Irritability and violent episodes are markedly diminished in frequency and severity. The patients are bright and alert, and there is a subjective feeling of well-being.

"Patients comment on their increased efficiency, and the absence of drowsiness which they experienced on bromide and phenobarbital treatment."

KIMBALL AND HORAN, *Annals of Internal Medicine* (1939), in a study of 220 children treated with PHT, reported that apart from the influence on convulsions, there are other benefits from the use of PHT.

The authors noted that there is a marked change in mental state and personality, evidenced by a definite improvement in memory, concentration, and sense of composure, with a return of social interest.

ROSS AND JACKSON, *Annals of Internal Medicine* (1940), noted that in consonance with the alleviation of seizures almost all reports on PHT remark on the improvement in behavior, well-being, cooperation, alertness, general attitude, irritability, temperament, and personality of many patients. Their findings in a study of seventy-three patients were consistent with these reports.

FRANKEL, *Journal of the American Medical Association* (1940), in a study involving forty-eight patients reported that, besides being an effective anticonvulsant, PHT has the advantage of not producing the sedative effect of the other anticonvulsants.

The author noted that the personality of the epileptic patient treated with PHT is remarkably improved.

FETTERMAN AND SHALLENBERGER, *Diseases of the Nervous System* (1941), observed that an outstanding feature of the benefit of PHT is an amazing improvement in personality.

BAKWIN AND BAKWIN, *Journal of Pediatrics* (1951), found PHT beneficial for irritability, hypermotility and variability of behavior in epileptic children, even when seizures were not the major problem.

. . .

IN NON-EPILEPTICS

LINDSLEY AND HENRY, *Psychosomatic Medicine* (1942), in an early study, observed that problem children given PHT showed behavioral improvement.

BROWN AND SOLOMON, *American Journal of Psychiatry* (1942), reported that delinquent boys committed to a state training school showed important behavioral improvement on PHT therapy.

Improvement was seen in a reduction in extreme hyperactivity, excitability and temper "flare-ups" and in attention span and more efficient work patterns.

SILVERMAN, *Criminal Psychopathology* (1944), in what appears to be the first reported study on the use of PHT in prisoners, found PHT to be superior to all other agents tested. The study was done with sixty-four prisoners at the Medical Center for Federal Prisoners, Springfield, Missouri.

Improvements were noted in sleep, sense of well-being and cooperativeness. These observations were made in a double-blind crossover study with placebo.

BODKIN, *American Journal of Digestive Diseases* (1945), reporting on his ten years of successful treatment of pruritus ani with PHT, noted that all the patients had one thing in common—they were highly nervous. (See p. 386.)

GOODWIN, *Journal of the National Proctologic Association* (1946), reporting the successful treatment of patients with pruritus ani with PHT, agreed with BODKIN that nervousness was a factor common in the vast majority of these patients. (See p. 387.)

WALKER AND KIRKPATRICK, *American Journal of Psychiatry* (1947), treated ten behavior problem children with abnormal EEG findings with PHT. None of the children had clinical evidence of seizures, and physical and neurological examinations were all negative. All of these children showed definite clinical improvement under PHT treatment.

FABRYKANT AND PACELLA, *Annals of Internal Medicine* (1948), in discussing the effects of PHT in labile diabetes, noted that PHT alleviated anxiety, nervous tension and irritability. In addition, the ability to concentrate and to work increased and the patients exhibited a general feeling of well-being.

ZIMMERMAN, *New York State Journal of Medicine* (1956), gave PHT to a group of two hundred children having severe behavior disorders. Improvement was seen in 70% of the cases.

The use of PHT resulted in reduced excitability, less severe and less frequent temper tantrums, reduced hyperactivity and distractibility, fewer fears, and less tendency to go out of contact.

CHAO, SEXTON AND DAVIS, *Journal of Pediatrics* (1964), conducted an extensive study of 535 children classified as having convulsive equivalent syndrome characterized by autonomic disturbances and dysfunction in behavior and communication. A majority of these patients had 14– and 6–EEG patterns. PHT was used alone with 296 of these children and in combination with other drugs in 117 children.

The symptoms benefited included headache, abdominal pain, vasomotor disturbances, nausea, dizziness or syncope, fever and/or chills, shortness of breath, eye pain, photophobia, sweating, weakness, pain in extremities and chest pain.

Behavioral and emotional problems, retardation, school problems in non-retarded, sleep disturbances, speech problems and neurological deficits also responded to treatment. The response was rapid and often striking.

JONAS (1965), in his book *Ictal and Subictal Neurosis,* based on observations of 162 patients over a twelve-year period, found PHT of benefit in a wide range of nonconvulsive disorders.

Among the symptoms which the author noted were helped by PHT were anxiety, depression, agitation, irritability, violence, headache, sleep disturbances, abdominal symptoms, sexual disturbances, hypochondria, visual and auditory phenomena and body image distortion.

LYNK AND AMIDON, *Michigan Medicine* (1965), studied the effect of medication with severely disturbed delinquents under court jurisdiction. The number of patients who received PHT (out of a total of 125) was not given.

They found that some of the children with borderline EEGs but no epilepsy had markedly aggressive behavior. These children responded to PHT when no other drug seemed to help.

DREYFUS (1966) reported on "The Beneficial Effects of PHT on the Nervous System of Nonepileptics— As Experienced and Observed in Others by a Layman."

The author observed that multiple simultaneous thoughts as well as obsessive and preoccupied thinking were relieved by PHT. Coincident with this, marked improvements were noted in symptoms of anger and related conditions of impatience, irritability, agitation and impulsiveness. Also, there was marked improvement in symptoms of fear and the related emotions such as worry, pessimism, anxiety, apprehensiveness and depression.

He noted that the ability to fall asleep more promptly and to sleep more soundly, without nightmares, occurred in the majority of cases. However, with a minority who slept excessively (so-called avoidance sleep) duration of sleep tended to be beneficially reduced.

Based on his observations, the author formed the impression that

excessive bioelectrical activity in the nervous system causes unfavorable emotional responses, anger and fear being chief among them. PHT corrects this excessive bioelectrical activity, causing excessive anger and fear to be eliminated.

ROSSI, *New York State Journal of Medicine* (1967), stated that PHT is clinically effective in impulsivity and behavior in hyperactive children and particularly effective in controlling nightmares.

RESNICK, *International Journal of Neuropsychiatry* (1967), reported a double-blind controlled study with crossover and placebo involving eleven inmates at a prison, selected from a group of forty-two volunteers. The entire study (RESNICK AND DREYFUS, 1966) was recorded on tape. The beneficial effects of PHT were reported in connection with overthinking, anger and fear, tension, irritability and hostility. There was marked improvement in ability to concentrate and in sleep problems. Improvement was also observed in headaches, gastrointestinal disturbances and, in one case, phantom limb pain.

Subsequently similar observations were made at a reformatory in six juvenile delinquents ranging in age from twelve to fifteen. With the administration of 100 mg PHT daily, prompt relief in anger and fear was noted and clearly expressed in marked diminution in fighting by five of the boys. The sixth boy, who was withdrawn and passive, became more outgoing, talkative and had an occasional fight. General improvements in overthinking, tension, impatience, impulsiveness, irritability, anger, fear, sleep difficulties and headaches were also observed.

TURNER, *International Journal of Neuropsychiatry* (1967), studied the effect of PHT on patients seen in psychiatric practice during an eighteen-month period. They suffered from a wide variety of emotional and behavioral disorders. Forty-six of fifty-six neurotic patients improved. Improvement was observed in relation to anger, irritability, tension, sleep disturbances, ruminations, anxiety, depression, feelings of guilt and withdrawal, regardless of diagnostic category or EEG findings.

Because of the lack of sedation or stimulation, the author suggested that PHT might be called a normalizer.

JONAS, *International Journal of Neuropsychiatry* (1967), found that over half of 211 patients seen in general psychiatric practice had a therapeutic response to PHT, ranging from reduction to complete reversal of symptoms in the following conditions: anxiety and tension states, reactive depressions, certain cognitive disturbances, obsessive-compulsive manifestations, hypochondria, psychopathy, obesity, and addiction to alcohol and to cigarette smoking. Many patients

reported favorable reactions within one hour after intake of PHT.

The author suggested that the action of PHT placed it in a category separate from the tranquilizers or stimulants and agreed with TURNER that the term normalizer seemed appropriate.

AYD, *International Drug Therapy Newsletter* (1967), in a summary of the clinical psychopharmacological value of PHT entitled "New Uses for an Old Drug," pointed out the effectiveness of PHT for psychic overactivity, distractibility, short attention span, irritability, impulsiveness, insomnia and behavioral disorders in children.

ITIL, RIZZO AND SHAPIRO, *Diseases of the Nervous System* (1967), studied the effect of PHT, combined with thioridazine, on twenty behaviorally disturbed children and adolescents. Eleven patients had personality disorders; five schizophrenic reactions; and four chronic brain syndrome, two with convulsions.

These patients showed low frustration tolerance, hyperactivity and restlessness, aggressive destructive behavior, impulsiveness, poor school or work performance, antisocial acts, sexual acting out, irritability and stubbornness.

After three months of treatment, fifteen of the twenty patients showed moderate to marked improvement and fourteen of them were discharged.

TEC, *American Journal of Psychiatry* (1968), reviewed his fifteen years' experience with PHT in the treatment of behavior disorders in children.

The author reported that PHT improved disruptive behavior in the large majority of the children seen during that period and emphasized that PHT often helped when the phenothiazines and amphetamines failed.

BOELHOUWER, HENRY AND GLUECK, *American Journal of Psychiatry* (1968) in a double-blind study with crossover features and placebo, reported that PHT alone or in combination with thioridazine (Mellaril) was effective at a statistically significant level in a group of seventy-eight patients, ranging in age from fourteen to thirty. Forty-seven of these patients showed 14– and 6–per second positive spiking, whereas no such abnormality was present in thirty-one.

The thirty-one patients without EEG abnormality responded best to PHT alone. The positive spike group responded better to PHT in combination with thioridazine than to either drug alone.

Significant changes were observed for the following factors with PHT alone: disturbance of affect, lack of social conformity, lack of insight, hostile aggressive behavior, dissociative tendency, thinking disorder, self-destructive tendency, and guilty self-concept. In addition to the above,

significant changes were observed for the following factors with PHT and Mellaril combined: overt anxiety symptoms, dissociative concern, paranoid thinking, and depression.

BALDWIN, *Maryland Medical Journal* (1969), reported on the treatment with PHT of behavior disorders in children (see also BALDWIN AND KENNY, 1966). The most consistent complaint was hyperactivity. Other important problems were temper tantrums or rage reactions, impulsive behavior and social adaptation. Attention span was short and concentration poor. Of 300 cases treated during a six-month period, it was found that 109 had improved so markedly that they were able to return to school. Of the 109 who showed marked improvement, 78 had received PHT—48 of them had behavior problems not associated with seizures.

CASE, RICKELS AND BAZILIAN, *American Journal of Psychiatry* (1969), reported that anxious-neurotic psychiatric clinic outpatients were treated over a four-week period with PHT (100 mg twice daily). While some improvement was observed in this patient group, no statistically significant difference was noted between the PHT and a comparable placebo group.

However, the authors reported an interesting finding, namely, "a paucity of side effects in the PHT-treated group (only one patient reported mild dizziness), while our placebo control group had the usual variety of side effects . . . in twelve of the twenty patients." If the only variable in these two groups was that one took PHT and one took placebo, then the probability that PHT was effective in preventing the placebo "side effects" in these anxious-neurotic patients was at the level of significance of p<0.001.

STEPHENS AND SHAFFER, *Psychopharmacologia* (1970), in a double-blind study with thirty adult outpatients, found PHT to be markedly effective in reducing symptoms relating to anger, irritability, impatience and anxiety.

The therapeutic effectiveness of PHT was demonstrated at statistically high levels by both self-ratings and physician ratings of change. This double-blind study was done on a crossover basis with placebo. The dosage of PHT was 100 mg t.i.d.

When compared to placebo, such standard scale factors as "anger," "furious," and "impatience" improved with PHT at p levels between 0.01 and 0.001. Standard scale factors of "worried," and "angry" improved at levels of p<0.01. Factors of "tension," "grouchy," "ready for a fight," *"nervous,"* "nervousness and shakiness," "trembling," and "quarrelsomeness" improved at levels of p<0.05.

In the crossover analysis, PHT improved "tension," "worried," "uncertain about things," "resentful," "bad tempered," "angry," "impatience," and global change rated by

patient all at the level of p<0.01; PHT improved "bewildered," "nervous," "ready for a fight," "confused," "anxious," "irritability," "quarrelsomeness," "heart pounding," "temper outbursts," "trembling," "nervousness and shakiness," all at levels of p<0.05; and the factors of "furious," "grouchy," and global change rated by physician all were improved by PHT at levels of p<0.001.

The patients' feelings of tranquility, composure, relaxation, optimism and cheerfulness also showed statistically significant improvement with PHT.

No undesirable side effects were encountered.

LOOKER AND CONNERS, *Archives of General Psychiatry* (1970), conducted a double-blind study with PHT on seventeen subjects, ranging in age from five to fourteen years, who had periodic episodes of misbehavior. Although no statistically significant group changes were attributable to drug effect, it was the impression of the authors that among the patients "there were some who responded rather dramatically."

The authors also reported on three children in whom PHT had a marked effect in the treatment of severe temper tantrums. In each case the response to PHT was prompt.

The children were followed-up six months later and the marked improvement had persisted. In two of the cases, when the parents forgot to give

PHT, deterioration was noted within two days. This deterioration was promptly corrected with PHT.

GOLDBERG AND KURLAND, *Journal of Nervous and Mental Diseases* (1970), in a double-blind study, reported the effectiveness of PHT on the emotional, cognitive and social behavior of forty-seven hospitalized retardates, ages nine to fourteen.

Patients treated with PHT showed strong improvement in ability to maintain attention, in self-control, and in improved interpersonal relationships with adults.

There was marked improvement in logical thinking, and decreased temper outbursts, impulsivity and aggression. There were also trends toward increased ability to concentrate and better visual-motor organization.

The effective dose of PHT was 100 mg twice daily. Neither toxicity nor side effects were observed.

DANIEL, *Geriatrics* (1970), states that symptoms of confusion, which are so common in the aged, often are caused by underlying physical illness, frequently cardiac and respiratory disorders resulting in cerebral hypoxia. He states that PHT is therapeutically useful in this group, yet it is often overlooked.*

Among the symptoms of confusion so common in the aged are: disorientation; lack of attention and concentration; fluctuation in state of consciousness; memory loss, particularly of current events; and impairment of conventional judgment.

The author states that although problems of insufficient cerebral blood flow are well known in the aged, direct measurement of cerebral blood flow is difficult. However, the author states that symptoms of insufficient cerebral blood flow are identifiable clinically. Among these symptoms are irritability, restlessness, mental confusion and sometimes severe depression. The author notes that after a cerebrovascular accident the patient often has paresthesias and tingling. He states that PHT not only frequently gives relief from the paresthesias, but that mental symptoms also improve.

* This discussion of PHT by Daniel is part of a larger study of other substances entitled, "Psychiatric drug use and abuse in the aged." For other work on the effect of PHT in cerebral blood flow and hypoxia, see Refs. 790, 1216, 1560, 2142, 2768. See also Anti-Anoxic Effects of PHT, Basic Mechanisms of Action.

BOZZA, in a detailed paper presented at the *Fourth Italian National Congress of Child Neuropsychiatry* (1971), reports on an individual basis on twenty-one slightly brain damaged retarded children who were observed for periods of from twelve to thirty-six months. In most of the cases PHT was tried. The author concludes that PHT and vitamins materially improved the expected intellectual growth rate of these retarded children. (See also Refs. 8, 355, 373, 1626.)

ALVAREZ, in a book titled *"Nerves in Collision"* (1972), reviews his twenty-five years' experience in the use of PHT for a wide variety of disorders.

In his book, Alvarez reports on the successful use of PHT in the treatment of anxiety, nervousness, tension, fear, nightmares, depression, rage, violent outbursts, confusion, fatigue (extreme), abdominal pain, alcoholism, anorexia nervosa, bed wetting, blackouts, dizzy spells, head pain, involuntary movements, migraine-like headaches. (See also Ref. 4.)

STEPHENS AND SHAFFER, *The Journal of Clinical Pharmacology* (1973). In an earlier paper the authors had reported on the successful treatment with PHT of thirty private psychiatric outpatients. This study had been done on a double-blind crossover basis.

About two years later, ten of this group of patients participated in a double-blind study of PHT for four consecutive two-week periods.

Consistent with the previous study, 100 mg t.i.d. of PHT proved significantly more effective than placebo in relieving symptoms of anxiety, anger and irritability as assessed both by self-ratings and physicians' ratings of change.

BRODSKY, ZUNIGA, CASENAS, ERNSTOFF AND SACHDEV, *Psychiatric Journal of the University of Ottawa* (1983),

describe a group of ten patients with recurrent anxiety. Eight responded to PHT alone. The ninth responded to a combination of PHT and clonazepam, and the tenth to carbamazepine. All patients had normal routine EEGs, but abnormal twenty-four-hour sleep-deprived EEGs. (See also Ref. 2356.)

DE LA TORRE, NAVARRO AND ALDRETE, *Current Therapeutic Research* (1985), reported a controlled study of eighty patients with irritable bowel syndrome. Forty patients received PHT (100 mg t.i.d.) and forty received conventional treatment which included either a tranquilizer or an antidepressant.

In addition to greater relief of abdominal pain, diarrhea, constipation, nausea, vomiting and pyrosis, patients receiving PHT had a statistically significant greater number of complete remissions of depression, insomnia and anxiety than patients receiving conventional therapy.

Violent Behavior

Many of the preceding studies have reported PHT useful for anger and related symptoms. Expressions used are aggressive behavior, anger, hostile, temper tantrums, impulsivity, rage, assaultive behavior and violent behavior. The following studies have their main focus on violence.

MALETSKY, *Medical Times* (1972), states that it is currently fashionable to ascribe the roots of violence to social ills. The role of brain dysfunction has been relatively neglected until recently.

The author reports on a study of twenty-two patients with the syndrome referred to as episodic dyscontrol. In describing this syndrome he states that the subjects usually have a history of hyperactivity and poor school performance as children, aggression toward other children and animals and fire-setting. Truancy and petty stealing frequently lead them to grand larceny, assault and battery and even murder. Other typical symptoms are traffic violations and recklessness. The author states that central to this dyscontrol syndrome is the "storm of violence." Upon minimal or even no provocation these patients lose control, wrecking property and directing violence against anyone in their way.

Twenty-two patients with episodic dyscontrol were treated with PHT. Tabulation of the results of this treatment was based on the author's observations and on reports of relatives and friends of the patient. The author pointed out that the patients had all been through futile trials with other drugs.

Nineteen of the patients achieved a result equal to or better than "good response." Fifteen of these achieved an excellent response with virtually complete absence of attacks. This response usually occurred within the first two weeks. Data collected at twelve months showed that all cases responding to PHT remained free of violent outbreaks.

All of the patients said they had not lost the ability to feel anger, but they were better able to conrol its escalation.

MALETSKY AND KLOTTER, *Diseases of the Nervous System* (1974), in a controlled study, found PHT significantly effective (p<.01) in twenty-two patients with episodic dyscontrol syndrome.

The authors state that this study, with placebo, confirms the earlier work of Maletsky in which he found PHT highly effective in the treatment of this syndrome. As a result of these studies, the authors conclude that PHT should be tried in patients with episodic dyscontrol.

DIAMOND AND YARYURA-TOBIAS, *Paper presented at the Fifth World Congress of Psychiatry* (1971), found PHT effective in the treatment of violent and aggressive behavior in schizophrenics. Twenty-two patients were studied.

With PHT, in doses up to 300 mg a day, violent behavior was well controlled in all cases, eleven with excellent results and seven with moderate results.

The authors state that all therapeutic methods used by the patients prior to PHT administration were ineffective.

SOLOMON AND KLEEMAN, *California Medicine* (1971), in reporting seven cases of episodic dyscontrol syndrome, comment separately on the only two in which PHT was given. In both cases the patient's behavior was markedly improved.

In a case detailed, a thirty-nine-year-old woman entered the hospital because of repeated attacks of uncontrolled behavior. Without warning, she would be assailed by intense feelings of either rage or sexual excitement. Tranquilizing medication proved ineffective. PHT caused a remarkable improvement in this patient's behavior.

BACH-Y-RITA, LION, CLIMENT AND ERVIN, *American Journal of Psychiatry* (1971), reported that in the course of two years they had seen 130 patients with assaultive and destructive behavior.

PHT was found useful whether or not EEG abnormalities were found.

Psychoses (excitability, mood)

PHT has been reported useful in decreasing irritability and improving sense of well-being in psychotics. In some cases where the psychosis has occurred in association with metabolic disorders or brain injury, the use of PHT has been reported to correct the psychotic state.

KALINOWSKY AND PUTNAM, *Archives of Neurology and Psychiatry* (1943), reported on the treatment with PHT of sixty psychotic patients. Improvement occurred in over half of the patients during the period of treatment and usually consisted of diminution of excitement and irritability, almost irrespective of the type of psychosis.

Although PHT did not change the basic psychosis, the patients' mood, behavior and emotions were improved.

FREYHAN, *Archives of Neurology and Psychiatry* (1945), reported on a group of forty psychiatric patients. PHT therapy, 300–600 mg/day, resulted in positive behavioral changes in certain excited patients.

KUBANEK AND ROWELL, *Diseases of the Nervous System* (1946), used PHT in the treatment of prolonged chronic disturbed behavior in seventy-three psychotic patients unresponsive to other drugs. They found PHT unquestionably valuable for some of these patients.

HAWARD, *Proceedings of the Symposium on Aggressive Behavior* (1969), reported that PHT was effective in reducing aggressive behavior in a double-blind study involving twenty chronic psychotic patients. Although the basic psychoses were not changed, important benefits in mood were noted.

PINTO, SIMOPOULOS, UHLENHUTH AND DEROSA, *Comprehensive Psychiatry*

(1974), in a study of thirty-two severely regressed chronic schizophrenic patients, found that PHT in doses of 250–350 mg per day, when added to a phenothiazine, improved conditions such as irritability, aggression and negative behavior. (See also Ref. 1551.)

BELLAK, *American Journal of Psychotherapy* (1976), in summarizing thirty years of clinical experience, describes the usefulness of PHT in a subgroup of schizophrenics with minimal brain dysfunction. The author noted that these patients do not do well with phenothiazines, but that PHT, alone or in combination with methylphenidate and imipramine, is frequently effective.

SURMAN AND PARKER, *Psychosomatics* (1981), reported three patients with episodic psychotic disturbances associated with renal disease. All responded to PHT with resolution of the psychotic behavior and/or hallucinations.

Hypoglycemia

STAMBAUGH AND TUCKER, *Diabetes* (1974), describe the successful treatment, with PHT, of five patients with symptomatic hypoglycemia previously unresponsive to dietary management.

Among the symptoms, typical of the hypoglycemic patient, were chronic anxiety, extreme lethargy, chills, frequent nausea, sensory deficits and other neurological complaints. These symptoms disappeared during PHT therapy, and clinical reversal of hypoglycemia was observed in all of the five cases.

Six-hour glucose tolerance and radioimmunoassays of insulin levels, before and after PHT, demonstrated PHT's regulatory effects and confirmed the clinical observations (see facing page).

Cognitive Function

HAWARD, *Portsmouth Journal of Psychology* (1968), found PHT effective in the improvement of concentration. This was demonstrated in a performance test designed to simulate air traffic control tower conditions.

Twelve volunteers, nineteen to twenty-one years of age, were introduced to an air traffic control task requiring a high degree of concentration. The test was done with placebo, on a double-blind basis, and the essential variable was number of errors made. On this basis, improved efficiency was demonstrated by PHT at the significant level of $p<0.01$.

No individual felt a drug effect of any sort. The author stated that this subtlety of action was consistent with what frequently had been observed in the clinical use of PHT.

The author says that because of its high level of safety and its

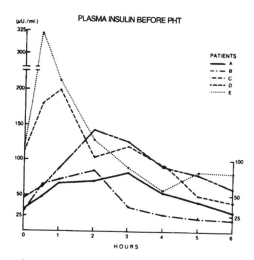

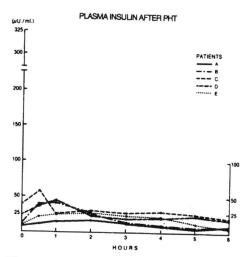

Abnormally large insulin response to a glucose load in hypoglycemic patients.

The same patients, with PHT, have an insulin response in the normal range.

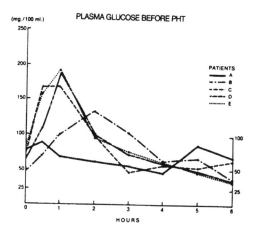

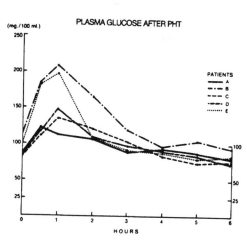

In the hypoglycemic patients, blood sugar falls to abnormally low levels in response to a glucose load.

In the same hypoglycemic patients, with PHT, the blood sugar returned to normal levels.

nonaddictive character, PHT has none of the negative qualities of the amphetamines, which have in the past been used for similar purposes.

HAWARD, *Drugs and Cerebral Function* (1970), studied the effect of PHT upon performance in a complex task, subject to fatigue, in twelve college students who had concentration difficulties. A double-blind crossover procedure was followed.

PHT was found to be significantly effective in delaying the onset of fatigue and accompanying errors.

The author notes that these findings are in accord with the observations of DREYFUS that poor concentration can result from forced ruminative thinking, or the "turned-on mind," and that this can be corrected by PHT. (See also Ref. 527.)

GOLDBERG AND KURLAND, *Journal of Nervous and Mental Disease* (1970), in a double-blind study, reported strong improvement in ability to maintain attention and concentration with PHT. (For more complete summary, see p. 322.)

DANIEL, *Geriatrics* (1970), reported PHT useful for symptoms of confusion in the aged, including lack of attention and concentration. (For more complete summary, see p. 322.)

SMITH AND LOWREY, *Drugs, Development and Cerebral Function* (1972), suggest that improvement in cognitive performance can be due to improved concentration. Using standard IQ tests, the authors compared PHT to placebo on twenty hospital employee volunteers.

The test was done on a double-blind crossover basis. PHT, 100 mg three times daily, improved Verbal Scale and Full Scale scores at highly significant levels and the Performance Scale improvement was also significant.

The authors state that their findings are consistent with those obtained by Haward.

HAWARD, *Revue de Medicine Aeronautique et Spatiale* (1973), found that PHT significantly improved the performance of three separate groups of pilots in simulated flying and radar target-fixing tasks.

Three groups of pilots, twenty-two commercial pilots, eighteen military pilots and nineteen private pilots were studied. Two absorbing tasks were required of the pilots in an attempt to reach their full channel capacity. The first was a standard flight simulation procedure. The second task consisted of monitoring and responding to a new type of radar.

The pilots were scored on their ability to bring the simulated aircraft into position to correctly intercept a moving target. Sixty minutes before each task 150 mg of PHT was given.

With PHT the test results showed significant improvement in performance both in terms of lessened time spent and the increased number of correct responses. In all three groups the improvement was significant.

The author states that he chose PHT because other substances which have been tried for this purpose, such as amphetamine, pemoline and prolintane, can have undesirable side effects.

SMITH AND LOWREY, *Journal of the American Geriatrics Society* (1975), observed the beneficial effect of PHT upon cognitive function in a group of elderly normal subjects.

In the present study ten volunteers, four male and six female, average age sixty-nine years, were studied in a double-blind crossover test with placebo control. This crossover design was used to eliminate possible practice effects on performance.

With PHT significant improvement in scores occurred in information, comprehension, digit symbol and full scale IQ. The authors conclude that these significant improvements illustrate the effectiveness of PHT in improving generalized mental functions.

Speech Disorders

SCHÖNHÄRL, *Medicina Experimentalis* (1960), reported that hydantoin therapy was helpful in a series of one hundred and forty patients treated for speech and voice disorders. The author did not specify which hydantoin was used.

SACK, *University of California, Doctoral Thesis* (1968), conducted a double-blind study with PHT in twenty-four stutterers.

Statistically significant reduction of stuttering intensity was found with PHT (100 mg). The intensity of the stuttering was significantly reduced although the frequency of stuttering was not changed.

RILEY AND MASSEY, *Headache* (1980), report on three patients with aphasia and headache, and left temporal spikes, all of whom were successfully treated with PHT.

The authors note that in one case, when the patient "ran out" of PHT, headaches and slowing of speech returned.

For other reports on a variety of speech disorders, see Refs. 1763, 1821, 1911, 2029, 2154, 2172, 2198, 2206, 2208, 2243, 2568.

Alcoholism and Drug Addiction

PHT has been found useful in alcohol and drug withdrawal, not only for seizure control, but also for mood and behavioral problems.

Problems of the nervous system are frequent causes of drug and alcohol addiction. For this reason PHT's use as a preventive should be considered. In addition to its regulatory effect on the nervous system it has the advantage of being non-addictive.

WILHOIT, *Journal of the Florida Medical Association* (1965), reported that one of the most important steps taken in the treatment of acute alcoholism and delirium tremens is the prophylactic use of PHT. With PHT patients tended to have a much easier and quicker recovery from acute alcoholism.

The author also noted that with PHT treatment, by the fourth to the seventh day, there was a marked improvement in sense of well-being, sleep pattern, appetite and motivation.

Fox, *Modern Treatment* (1966), recommended PHT (100 mg four times a day) for five to ten days for prevention of convulsions due to alcohol withdrawal. The author stated that frequently convulsions due to withdrawal from alcohol are mistaken for epilepsy and the patient is sent home on PHT and phenobarbital. PHT offers no problem, but, in the case of phenobarbital, the danger exists that the patient may gradually increase it to the point of addiction.

Ramirez, *Personal Communication* (1967), described the effective use of PHT during withdrawal of patients with various forms of addiction including heroin.

During a three-year period of clinical study it was found that after physical detoxification most patients went through a stormy period of behavioral difficulties which lasted from seven to ten days on the average. Patients were irritable, intolerant, and frequently showed temper tantrums. In addition, they were insomniac and depressed.

On PHT there was a rapid change in the overall behavior patterns of the patients. Acting out behavior was much less frequent. Sleeplessness, which is a very difficult problem with addicts, was also modified favorably.

After a preliminary study with thirty patients, the author used PHT routinely, 100 mg three times a day.

Chafetz, *Journal of the American Medical Association* (1967), stated that PHT is most effective in the treatment and prevention of convulsions associated with alcoholic withdrawal. He pointed out that PHT is a desirable medication because it lacks the hypotensive effect sometimes found with the phenothiazines.

Thurlow and Gihvin, *Canadian Medical Association Journal* (1971), reported the successful treatment with PHT of two cases of flashbacks (recurrent visual hallucinations after LSD).

In one of the cases the patient had been suffering from flashbacks five months after the discontinuance of all hallucinogenic drugs. She was given chlorpromazine, 25 mg t.i.d., with moderate diminution in the intensity, frequency and affective component of her flashbacks. Hallucinations continued to occur, but were less terrifying. Chlorpromazine was discontinued and the previous level of flashbacks returned within twenty-four hours.

PHT was instituted, 100 mg t.i.d. Within forty-eight hours she noted a very marked reduction in all types of flashbacks.

In the other case, 100 mg of PHT intravenously terminated a flashback while in progress. Before injecting PHT, saline solution was injected, as a control, with no effect. (See also Ref. 1988.)

ADAMS, *Journal of the American Medical Association* (1971), states: "In more than 500 cases of acute alcohol withdrawal, I have yet to see a patient suffer delirium tremens or convulsions when PHT, 100 mg orally four times daily, is given . . ."

FINER, *Journal of the American Medical Association* (1971), reporting on the experience in a 1400-bed hospital, states that it is their belief that the tremors, apprehension and psychomotor excitation experienced in withdrawing alcohol should not be subdued by another depressant drug. The author states that it is their practice to give PHT orally, 100 mg four times a day.

Out of 735 admissions and 565 readmissions over a three-year period, no seizures occurred in alcoholic patients who received PHT.

FISHER AND DIMINO, *British Journal of Addiction* (1975), in discussing their clinical experience, report that they found PHT to be useful in their over-all therapeutic approach to withdrawal from addictive agents, including heroin, amphetamines, and alcohol.

IFABUMUYI AND JEFFRIES, *Canadian Psychiatric Association Journal* (1976), describe the successful use of PHT in treating several cases of drug-induced psychosis and detail three cases which

had previously been unsuccessfully treated with major tranquilizers. All patients had taken hallucinogenic drugs for over five years.

PHT, 100 mg two or three times a day, resulted in prompt improvement in symptoms of psychotic behavior, bizarre visual, auditory and tactile hallucinations, feelings of derealization, fragmented thinking, and lack of concentration.

The authors state that PHT was dramatically effective in treating these refractory cases.

Sleep Disorders

Many of the preceding studies emphasize the benefits of PHT in sleep,* but few studies have been done on sleep disturbances alone. However, reports are consistent that people fall asleep more easily, sleep longer, and are less troubled with unpleasant dreams and nightmares. A less common sleep disturbance, too much sleep (avoidance sleep), is also reported helped by PHT.

* *See Refs. 4, 51, 297, 314, 364, 538, 704, 707, 713, 716, 761, 1841, 2037.*

BJERK AND HORNISHER, *Electroencephalography and Clinical Neurophysiology* (1958), refer to generalities in the literature that anticonvulsants are not effective for narcolepsy.

The authors present a case, which they consider typical narcolepsy, that showed excellent response to treatment with PHT. The patient, a thirty-seven-year-old female, had over-powering attacks of sleep and other typical symptoms of narcolepsy.

On 100 mg of PHT t.i.d. the patient's symptoms left her on the seventh day. The improvement was marked by a complete loss of symptoms, appetite improved and the patient said that she had not felt so well in a long time.

When the patient stopped taking the medication, the symptoms recurred.

ZUNG, *Psychophysiology* (1968), studied the effect of PHT on sleep. Ten adults, between the ages of twenty and forty-six, were studied with all-night EEG and electro-oceulogram recordings. With PHT the time spent in REM sleep was significantly decreased compared to control. Non-REM (deeper) sleep was increased.

BOLLER, WRIGHT, CAVALIERI AND MITSUMOTO, *Neurology* (1975), reported the complete relief with PHT in a sixty-five-year-old man from paroxysmal nightmares, a sequel to a stroke. These nightmare-like episodes gradually increased in frequency (twenty per day) to a point where the patient had to be hospitalized.

During an episode the patient would suddenly bolt upright, pace around with a terrified expression on his face, and shout in a dysarthric voice. At times he related fright visions.

PHT was given, with a loading dose of 300 mg intravenously, followed by 900 mg orally over the next twenty-four hours. Thereafter the patient received daily doses of 300 mg/day. The episodes ceased and the patient remained symptom-free when followed up six months later.

PEDLEY AND GUILLEMINAULT, *Annals of Neurology* (1977), described six patients, between the ages of seventeen and thirty-two years, who had been experiencing unusual sleepwalking episodes characterized by screaming or unintelligible vocalizations, complex and often violent automatisms, and ambulation.

All patients were treated with either phenytoin or carbamazepine, with cessation of the abnormal behavior during follow-up periods ranging from nine to forty-eight months.

FUKUYAMA, OCHIAI, HAYAKAWA AND MIYAGAWA, *Neuropadiatrie* (1979), describe the successful use of PHT in treating an eight-year-old male with choreoathetoid activity. In addition to eliminating the abnormal movements, behavior improvements were noted, and the patient's sleep patterns were improved.

Sleep patterns were evaluated before and after PHT. Increase in sleep time, decrease in number of stages, and disappearance of interrupting awakening were noted.

WOLF, RODER-WANNER AND BREDE, *Epilepsia* (1984), studied polygraphic (EEG, EOG or electrooculogram, ECG and respiration) sleep patterns in forty untreated epileptic patients. They compared phenobarbital and PHT in a randomized crossover design. With both phenobarbital and PHT sleep onset came sooner, but with PHT light sleep was decreased and deep sleep increased. The authors state, "The decrease of light sleep to the benefit of deep sleep, together with the rapid sleep onset, make PHT look like an excellent sleeping medication." In addition, they comment that few patients report sleep "hangovers" with PHT.

See also Refs. 2626, 2858, 2967, 2986.

Enuresis

CAMPBELL AND YOUNG, *Journal of Urology* (1966), reported that twenty-nine patients having enuresis and evidencing EEG abnormalities were treated with PHT, alone or in combination with other anticonvulsant medication.

Only twenty-two of these patients could be followed up. Eleven were reported to be cured or improved and eleven showed no change.

BALDWIN, *Maryland Medical Journal* (1969), in a study of seventy-eight behavior problem children, noted that among the symptoms helped by PHT was enuresis.

Anorexia, Bulimia and Binge Eating

GREEN AND RAU, *American Journal of Psychiatry* (1974), found PHT highly effective in treating ten patients who had three distinct types of symptoms of compulsive eating.

One group was extremely underweight. Sometimes they ate nothing, yet they constantly thought about food. Frequently they would overeat and then would overcorrect this condition by forcing themselves to vomit. Thus they stayed underweight. These patients were considered by the authors to come under the category of primary anorexia nervosa.

The second group consisted of persons of normal weight. They were also preoccupied with food and they had a compulsive wish to eat. Their entire lives were structured to avoid exposure to food through various and complicated maneuvers. They occasionally went on eating binges that lasted for hours or days. They would then diet back to normal, unlike group one, who always dieted back to below normal.

Group three consisted of patients who gave in to their strong compulsion to eat. They became overweight over a period of years, some rapidly, some slowly. They were from 150 to 250 pounds above normal weight.

Of the ten patients, nine had abnormal EEGs but none was epileptic. PHT was highly effective in nine of these patients, including the one with a normal EEG. In two cases PHT was withdrawn and symptoms returned. When PHT was reinstated, the symptoms disappeared.

The authors say that compulsive eating is usually accompanied by other undesirable symptoms, including depression. Improvement in these other symptoms was usually observed.

RAU AND GREEN, *Comprehensive Psychiatry* (1975), report on an additional eight patients with the syndrome of compulsive eating. These patients had abnormal EEGs. They were treated with PHT and five of them responded dramatically. Three had questionably positive responses.

The authors give as an example the case of an emaciated twenty-five-year-old female who weighed seventy-nine pounds. Her compulsive eating episodes were followed by feelings of guilt, vomiting and sleeping difficulties. She was a compulsive stealer.

After two weeks' treatment with PHT, 100 mg t.i.d., she reported a "miracle." She had no further episodes of compulsive eating, was less obsessed with thoughts of food and there were no episodes of stealing. After six months she remained symptom-free and was approaching normal weight.

The authors state that their investigations suggest that compulsive eating has a neurologic etiology.

In a further study, RAU, STRUVE AND GREEN (1979), report that twenty-seven of forty-seven patients (some without abnormal EEGs) responded to PHT therapy. (See also Ref. 2038.)

WERMUTH, DAVIS, HOLLISTER AND STUNKARD, *American Journal of Psychiatry* (1977), based on the findings of GREEN AND RAU conducted a double-blind crossover study, using placebo, to test the efficacy of PHT in treating "binge eating."

After careful screening, medical, psychiatric and EEG evaluations, nineteen female patients, who had suffered for two to twenty-four years with episodes of binge eating, were selected for study.

Six patients markedly improved, two moderately improved, and six slightly improved during PHT treatment. Improvement in six of the patients who had EEG abnormalities was similar to that observed in other patients, and the authors concluded that treatment response did not correlate with EEG abnormalities.

Subjects whose binge eating was markedly reduced during PHT treatment reported better self-control, marked improvement in self-esteem, less preoccupation with eating, and more normal eating habits.

SZYPER AND MANN, *Neurology* (1978), reported a case of classical anorexia nervosa in a sixteen-year-old girl whose weight loss was greater than 16 kg (30% of body weight) over a two-year period. The patient also suffered partial complex seizures uncontrolled by barbiturates.

PHT treatment was begun, resulting in seizure control, EEG improvement and dramatic weight gain.

MOORE AND RAKES, *Journal of Clinical Psychiatry* (1982), describe a twenty-one-year-old student with disabling symptoms of binge eating, difficulty in concentrating and feelings of frustration and guilt.

PHT, 100 mg t.i.d., was started and, by the fourth day, the compulsion to eat had entirely disappeared. Problems with concentration and feelings of guilt and frustration also disappeared. The patient remained symptom-free for a year. PHT was discontinued and another episode of binge eating developed, which again responded to PHT. The patient remained symptom-free on 300 mg of PHT a day.

PARSONS AND SAPSE, *Journal of Orthomolecular Psychiatry* (1985), treated forty-two patients with anorexia nervosa with PHT along with psychotherapy and other medications considered cortisol antagonists. After four to five days the patients exhibited marked improvement in attitudes towards food and they started eating more normally. Feelings of hostility and fear were diminished and feelings of confidence were improved.

For further references see 1869, 2116, 2304, 2556, 2625, 2656, 2800.

STUDIES IN WHICH SIGNIFICANT RESULTS WERE NOT OBSEERVED

PASAMANICK, *Archives of Neurology and Psychiatry* (1951), found that PHT, methylphenylethylhydantoin, trimethadione and phenobarbital caused no significant improvement in behavior in children with EEG abnormalities.

KLEIN AND GREENBERG, *American Journal of Psychiatry* (1967), in a pilot study of the effectiveness of PHT on thirteen severely psychotic patients, found no general beneficial effect of PHT.

KANZLER, MALITZ AND HIGGINS, *Journal of the American Medical Association* (1968), in a double-blind study, evaluated six "commonly prescribed antidepressants," including PHT. They did not find any of the drugs significantly different than placebo.

LEFKOWITZ, *Archives of General Psychiatry* (1969), in a double-blind study with PHT and placebo, found "marked diminution in the disruptive behavior in both groups." Placebo results were better than with PHT.

CARDIOVASCULAR DISORDERS

Summary

Recognition of phenytoin's basic property, stabilization of bioelectrical activity, led to its therapeutic use in cardiology. The first evidence was provided by Harris and Kokernot in 1950 in a basic mechanism study showing that PHT reversed cardiac arrhythmias after coronary occlusion in dogs. The first evidence of its clinical usefulness in cardiac arrhythmias in man was presented, in a detailed paper, by Leonard in 1958.

Subsequent studies have shown that PHT is useful in a wide range of cardiovascular disorders. It is effective in the treatment of a variety of cardiac arrhythmias, including ventricular arrhythmias associated with hypokalemia, digitalis toxicity, ischemia and myocardial infarction, surgical procedures and myopathic processes; paroxysmal atrial tachycardia and atrial extrasystoles; and as prophylaxis against anesthesia- and cardioversion-induced arrhythmias.[1] PHT's ability to offset the toxic effects of digitalis without impairing

---

1. *Cardiac arrhythmias (various):* Refs. 18, 61, 141, 166, 187, 221, 248, 310, 418, 517, 720, 721, 753, 987, 1052, 1121, 1214, 1264, 1339, 1390, 1488, 1847, 2058, 2083, 2251, 2331, 2390, 2528, 2569.
Cardioversion-induced arrhythmias: Refs. 248, 720, 923, 936, 1264, 1289.
Arrhythmias associated with myocardial infarction: Refs. 221, 248, 516, 987, 1120, 1705, 2150, 2151, 2478, 2649, 2650, 2729.

its inotropic benefits allows larger amounts of digitalis to be given before toxic levels are reached.

PHT has been shown to have beneficial effects on the cardiac conduction system. These effects are an example of PHT's biphasic actions since, dependent on the initial state of the tissue, it can either increase or decrease conduction. PHT does not alter normal sinus node function or rate, atrial refractoriness, intra-atrial conduction velocity, or prolong Q-T interval. PHT has been found beneficial in the treatment of the prolonged Q-T interval syndrome, torsade de pointes arrhythmias and tricyclic antidepressant induced arrhythmias.[2]

PHT has been shown to decrease sympathetic nervous system activity with resultant reduction in cardiac contractile force, blood pressure and heart rate. It has been reported to be useful in hypertension.[3]

Both clinical and laboratory studies have shown PHT to be useful in hypoxic-ischemic states. Clinically, PHT has been reported to reduce the frequency and severity of anginal attacks,[4] improving ST depression on the electrocardiogram. It controls ischemia-induced arrhythmias; and improves brain function in ischemic states, including reduction of neurological deficits after cardiac arrest.[5] In the laboratory, PHT has been demonstrated to increase cerebral and cardiac blood flow and to have anti-anoxic and anti-ischemic effects in brain, nerve, heart and lung.

2. *Conduction defects:* Refs. 22, 154, 158, 327, 753, 764, 816, 826, 830, 831, 832, 833, 884, 935, 1114, 1120, 1264, 1390, 1434, 1450, 1488, 1562, 1590, 1645, 1776, 1804, 1822, 2069, 2163, 2223, 2296, 2348, 2361, 2376, 2377, 2478, 2558, 2565, 2664, 2695, 2799, 2883, 2992, 3037, 3052, 3066.

Prolonged Q-T interval: Refs. 764, 1776, 1972, 2069, 2071, 2094, 2223, 2328, 2361, 2370, 2376, 2462, 2558, 2695, 2807, 2837, 2895, 2951, 2957, 3066.

Torsade de pointes: Refs. 158, 764, 816, 935, 2069, 2296, 2478, 2664, 2799, 2883, 2992, 3052.

Tricyclic antidepressant overdose: Refs. 2348, 2377, 2565.

3. *Hypertension:* Refs. 414, 1480, 1717, 1797, 2090, 2316, 2668.

4. *Angina pectoris:* Refs. 18, 1611, 2667.

5. *Cerebrovascular insufficiencies:* Refs. 938, 1216, 1560, 1718, 1719, 2142, 2768. See also Anti-anoxic Effects of PHT.

PHT has been reported to increase high-density lipoprotein-cholesterol (HDL-C) levels. Since there is evidence that there is an inverse relationship between HDL-C levels and atherosclerotic problems such as myocardial infarction and stroke, the use of PHT as a preventive against these disorders is suggested.[6]

In addition to its specific cardiovascular actions, PHT has general properties relevant to the treatment of cardiovascular disorders. These include its usefulness against pain, anxiety, fear, anger and stress, without sedative effect.[7]

6. *High-density lipoproteins (HDL):* Refs. 1893, 1961, 2002, 2162, 2235, 2318, 2319, 2323, 2428, 2542, 2649, 2650, 2652, 2734, 2741, 2813, 2814, 2827, 2897, 2946.

7. See also Thought, Mood and Behavior section—beneficial effects of PHT on fear, anxiety, anger and stress; and Pain section.

Cardiac Arrhythmias

The first use of PHT in cardiac disorders was reported by LEONARD in 1958. Since it was the pioneer paper in this field, it will be summarized in some detail. It brings into focus three important points which develop throughout the literature: 1) PHT is an effective antiarrhythmic, prompt in its action; 2) PHT has a high margin of safety; 3) In the acute stage, substantial amounts of PHT may be required, adjusted to the severity of the condition.

LEONARD, *Archives of Internal Medicine* (1958), demonstrated the beneficial effect of PHT in controlling ventricular hyperirritability complicating myocardial infarction in a patient.

The patient was gravely ill with cardiographic findings of typical ventricular tachycardia. In spite of the previous history of complete heart block, it was felt that intravenous procainamide, if carefully controlled, was the treatment of choice. The patient was receiving Arterenol to maintain his blood pressure at 110/70. Procainamide was given intravenously. During a period of approximately two hours, 2300 mg of procainamide was given, in spite of several episodes of marked hypotension, but finally discontinued because of disturbing widening of the QRS complex without reversion to a normal sinus mechanism.

The patient's condition remained critical, and it was considered advisable to investigate the therapeutic potential of intravenous PHT. PHT was administered slowly intravenously in a dose of 250 mg. A cardiogram recorded approximately two minutes later revealed a normal sinus mechanism coupled with premature auricular contractions. In twenty minutes ventricular tachycardia had recurred. An immediate additional dose of 250 mg of PHT was given and within moments a normal sinus mechanism appeared.

Four hours later ventricular tachycardia returned and was again successfully reverted to a normal sinus rhythm with 250 mg of intravenous PHT. Because the duration of effectiveness of PHT was unknown, a constant, slow intravenous infusion of 250 mg of PHT was started. The normal sinus mechanism was maintained in this fashion for successive periods of six and four hours. At these intervals ventricular tachycardia returned, but was promptly reverted with additional intravenous doses of 250 mg of PHT.

At this time it was considered advisable to supplement the intravenous therapy with 3 grains of PHT and 500 mg of procainamide every four hours orally. Eighteen hours after its initiation the intravenous PHT was discontinued. An electrocardiogram at this time showed posterior myocardial infarction with a normal sinus mechanism.

On the following day procaina-mide was discontinued, and the patient was maintained with 3 grains of PHT orally every six hours. There was no recurrence of signs of ventricular irritability. The patient made an uneventful recovery.

The author suggests that PHT may represent a drug with a wide margin of safety that is effective in controlling serious ventricular hyper-irritability.

BERNSTEIN, GOLD, LANG, PAPPELBAUM, BAZIKA AND CORDAY, *Journal of the American Medical Association* (1965), used oral PHT in the treatment and prevention of recurring cardiac arrhythmias in a group of sixty patients, who had been refractory to or intolerant of conventional medication.

In thirty-seven patients with premature ventricular contractions, twenty-six returned to normal sinus rhythm, and seven had a decrease in the number of ectopic beats. In thirteen patients who had atrial tachycardia, ten had excellent response and two had moderate improvement. Six patients with paroxysmal atrial fibrillation had excellent response. Two patients with premature atrial contractions and one with premature nodal beats had excellent response. One patient with recurrent atrial flutter did not respond. Some side effects were observed. None were serious and all disappeared upon withdrawal of the medicine.

The patients had been evaluated for periods up to nineteen months, the time the study was reported.

CONN, *New England Journal of Medicine* (1965), found that PHT, administered intravenously to twenty-four patients with a variety of cardiac arrhythmias, was particularly effec-tive in supraventricular and ventricu-lar arrhythmias resulting from digi-talis excess. It was also of benefit in controlling paroxysmal atrial and ventricular arrhythmias. In three cases of atrial fibrillation and two with atrial flutter no therapeutic effect was noted. Toxicity consisted of transient bradycardia and hypo-tension in one patient and short-term atrioventricular block with brady-cardia in another.

The author stated that PHT appears to be a significant addition to the drug therapy of cardiac arrhy-thmias.

LUGO AND SANABRIA, *Acta Medica Venezolana* (1966), reported the effectiveness of oral PHT, 100 mg q.i.d., in eleven patients with chronic Chagasic cardiac disease, with multi-focal ventricular extrasystoles.

In eight cases response was excellent with conversion to normal sinus rhythm which continued up to the eight months the patients were followed. In two cases there was excellent response, but the drug had to be discontinued because of skin rash. In one case with ventricular extrasystoles and atrial fibrillation, the extrasystoles were controlled.

KARLINER, *Diseases of the Chest* (1967), described fifty-four patients who received intravenous PHT on fifty-seven occasions for abnormal cardiac rhythm. Nineteen of twenty-three who had digitalis-induced arrhythmias responded with abolition or marked suppression of a ventricular ectopic focus, or with conversion of supraventricular arrhythmias to a regular sinus mechanism. Of twenty-eight patients whose arrhythmias were unrelated to digitalis, seven responded favorably.

As a result of this study the author confirmed the usefulness of PHT in a variety of cardiac arrhythmias, especially those which appear to be related to digitalis excess. Rapidity of action and relative paucity of side effects make PHT an effective antiarrhythmic agent.

MERCER AND OSBORNE, *Annals of Internal Medicine* (1967), reported on their six years' experience in the treatment, with PHT, of 774 cases of cardiac arrhythmias.

The authors state that intravenous PHT is highly efficacious in the treatment of ventricular arrhythmias associated with anesthesia, cardioversion, cardiac catheterization, and cardiac surgery. On the basis of their experience they consider PHT to be superior to quinidine and procainamide in these arrhythmias.

PHT also had a good effect against digitalis-induced ventricular arrhythmias and an even better effect against digitalis-induced atrial tachycardia.

The authors reviewed the literature, including their own series, on the oral use of PHT. There were reported successes in twenty out of twenty-four cases of supraventricular arrhythmias, twenty-six out of thirty-eight cases of ventricular arrhythmias and five out of eight cases of unclassified paroxysmal tachycardia.

BASHOUR, EDMONSON, GUPTA AND PRATI, *Diseases of the Chest* (1968), reported on twelve patients who were treated with PHT, all of whom had clinical evidence of digitalis toxicity. Most patients had more than one type of arrhythmia.

During intravenous administration of PHT, continuous electrocardiographic monitoring was usually performed, and after conversion to sinus rhythm or subsidence of the arrhythmia, monitoring of the cardiac rhythm was continued for a period of ten minutes.

In five of the cases, atrial fibrillation was present with other arrhythmias. Two of these arrhythmias were of recent origin and were restored to normal sinus rhythm by PHT. Three cases of chronic atrial fibrillation did not respond to treatment.

Four of the patients were uremic. The successful termination of their cardiac arrhythmias, especially ventricular tachycardia, with PHT, was of special interest. In uremic patients with arrhythmias the usual therapeutic measures are both less effective and more hazardous.

EDDY AND SINGH, *British Medical Journal* (1969), treated thirty-seven patients with cardiac arrhythmias with intravenous PHT. Twenty-one had acute myocardial infarctions and sixteen had other conditions. There was a favorable response in eighteen of the twenty-one cases of myocardial infarction and in six of the other sixteen cases.

GATTENLOHNER AND SCHNEIDER, *Munchener Medizinische Wochenschrift* (1969), reported fifteen patients in whom they studied cardiac hemodynamics. PHT, in doses of 125 and 250 mg, did not alter or interfere with cardiac output or stroke volume. In the eight patients with digitalis-induced arrhythmias, they noted return to normal sinus rhythm. They conclude that PHT is not only effective but may be lifesaving in digitalis-induced arrhythmias. (See also Ref. 2230.)

HELFANT, SEUFFERT, PATTON, STEIN AND DAMATO, *American Heart Journal (1969),* report on the use of intravenous PHT in a variety of cardiac arrhythmias.

In a controlled study, eight of eleven patients treated with PHT prior to cyclopropane anesthesia did not develop arrhythmias; whereas, in the control group, eight of nine patients did develop arrhythmias. In another phase of the study, PHT restored sinus rhythm in all eight patients who developed arrhythmias during the administration of various anesthetics.

In a second group with ventricular arrhythmias, unresponsive to procainamide, PHT abolished or decreased the ectopia in ten of twelve patients.

In a third group of twelve patients given prophylactic PHT prior to DC counter-shock, none developed arrhythmias.

In patients on digitalis, twenty-one of twenty-four with ventricular arrhythmias, and six of eleven with supraventricular arrhythmias responded to PHT.

The authors confirmed PHT's effectiveness and safety in the prevention and treatment of cardiac arrhythmias.

LESBRE, CATHALA, SALVADOR, FLORID, LESCURE AND MERIEL, *Archives des Maladies du Coeur et des Vaisseaux* (1969), investigated the antiarrhythmic value of PHT in a variety of arrhythmic disturbances with the following results:

	Patients	Successes
Atrial tachysystole	3	2
Atrial extrasystole	3	3
Ventricular extrasystoles	17	16
Bouts of tachycardia	3	3
First-degree block	8	5
Second-degree block	6	5

In another study, they compared forty patients with atrial fibrillation given PHT before cardioversion with a similar group of forty patients given a beta-blocking agent. The results with PHT were better.

GAUTAM, *British Heart Journal (1969)*, reports on the use of intravenous PHT in treating serious cardiac arrhythmias following open heart surgery in fourteen patients. PHT was rapidly and highly effective in abolishing supraventricular and ventricular arrhythmias in thirteen of these patients. Higher doses were required for the more serious arrhythmias.

The author states that the rapidity of its action and the relative paucity of side effects make PHT an effective antiarrhythmic agent.

BIELAK AND POKORA, *Polski Tygodnik Lekarsky* (1970), report their experience in 106 patients with either oral or intravenous PHT for various arrhythmias caused by infarction, digitalis toxicity, valvular heart lesions, chronic cardiopulmonary disease and myocarditis as follows:

	Patients	*Successes*
Ventricular extrasystole	73	63
Ventricular tachycardia	4	2
Supraventricular extrasystole	12	9
Paroxysmal atrial flutter	1	1
Paroxysmal atrial fibrillation	6	4
Paroxysmal supraventricular tachycardia	10	5
TOTAL	106	84

The authors also evaluated the prophylactic use of PHT, 300 mg/day. No arrhythmias were recorded in sixty-three of 125 patients with acute myocardial infarction. Twenty-two patients with ectopic ventricular beats were successfully treated with PHT. In twelve of these patients, ectopic beats returned when PHT was discontinued. In a group of ten patients with recurring atrial arrhythmias, five had no recurrences.

HANSEN, *Medizinische Klinik* (1970), reported the use of PHT in 150 patients who developed arrhythmias during digitalis treatment. One hundred and three of 115 with ventricular arrhythmias responded favorably. Seventy-nine of these converted to normal sinus rhythm. In twenty-four patients who had atrial fibrillation and extrasystoles, the ventricular extrasystoles disappeared, but the fibrillation was not affected.

Seven patients with supraventricular extrasystoles were successfully treated with PHT. Eight of nine patients with paroxysmal atrial fibrillation and five of seven patients with supraventricular tachycardia were also controlled.

In seven of twelve patients with partial second-degree heart block of Wenckebach type, conduction irregularity was reversed by PHT.

CHICHE, BENAIM AND CHESNAIS, *Annales de Cardiologie et D'Angeiolo-*

gie (1971), reported that thirteen of twenty-six patients with atrial arrhythmias, other than atrial fibrillation and flutter, responded to intravenous PHT. In eight patients with atrial flutter or fibrillation, PHT slowed the ventricular response without change in the atrial arrhythmia. Fourteen out of seventeen patients with ventricular arrhythmias responded to PHT. Seven patients undergoing DC cardioversion were pretreated with PHT and there were no arrhythmias.

In the group treated with oral PHT, seven of thirteen patients with atrial arrhythmias and nine of fifteen with ventricular arrhythmias were successfully treated.

HANSEN AND WAGENER, *Deutsche Medizinische Wochenschrift* (1971), in a controlled study of 200 patients with PHT and 300 patients without PHT, evaluated the effect of PHT when added to cardiac glycoside administration.

By combining PHT and glycosides, the incidence of arrhythmias was reduced from 21% in the non-PHT group to 2.5% in the PHT-treated group.

The authors state that this clinical experience indicates that PHT administration reduces the toxic effect of glycosides in man without affecting their inotropic benefits. Thus, the use of PHT improves the chance of effective treatment in heart failure.

KEMP, *Journal of the American Geriatrics Society* (1972), studied the effect of PHT on ventricular ectopic rhythms. These arrhythmias were not caused by digitalis. PHT was given to five patients and five patients were given placebo.

For the first three weeks the dosage of PHT was 100 mg q.i.d. During the rest of the three-month study the dosage was reduced to 100 mg t.i.d. The numbers of premature ventricular contractions during a five-minute continuous ECG monitoring period were recorded before therapy, after three weeks of therapy, and after three months of therapy.

At the end of the three-month period, premature ventricular contractions were abolished in two of the PHT patients and almost eliminated (165 to 1, 100 to 2, and 80 to 3) in three patients. On the other hand, in the control group, contractions increased in two patients, and were moderately decreased in three.

O'REILLY AND MACDONALD, *British Heart Journal* (1973), reported on the successful use of PHT in treating two cases of ventricular arrhythmia induced by hypokalemia.*

---

* *Hypokalemia results in below normal potassium in nerve and muscle cells. Relevant to the above paper is the fact that PHT has been demonstrated to have a regulatory effect on low potassium in cells. (See "downhill movement" of ions, Refs. 157, 387, 728, 731, 1012, 1025, 1225, 1379, 1418, 1642, 1662, 2224, 2374, 2458.)*

The authors emphasize the usefulness of PHT in the management of the notoriously resistant and malignant arrhythmias associated with hypokalemia, where the usual antiarrhythmic agents are at best ineffective and may even be dangerous.

RUMACK, WOLFE AND GILFRICH, *British Heart Journal* (1974), detailed the successful treatment with PHT of a patient who attempted suicide with a massive digoxin overdose.* Serum digoxin levels reached 35 ng/ml. Pronounced hyperkalemia was noted fourteen hours after ingestion.

The patient responded to seven doses of 25 mg intravenous PHT over a period of thirty-six hours. The patient had complete heart block and PHT improved this to a first-degree block.

The authors note that low doses of PHT were effective in this case and they suggest that it should be used early in the treatment of acute digoxin overdose.

* *In addition to the digoxin, seventeen 400 mg tablets of meprobamate had also been ingested.*

ROTMENSCH, GRAFF, AYZENBERG, AMIR AND LANIADO, *Israel Journal of Medical Sciences* (1977), reported on three cases of suicide attempt with massive digoxin overdoses.

Intravenous PHT was dramatically effective in controlling digitalis arrhythmias in these three patients. The authors suggest PHT's early use in the treatment of this type emergency.

CARDIAC ARRHYTHMIAS IN CHILDREN

GARSON, KUGLER, GILLETTE, SIMONELLI AND MCNAMARA, *The American Journal of Cardiology* (1980), reported the use of PHT in treating six young patients with chronic postoperative ventricular arrhythmias and abnormal hemodynamics following surgery for congenital cardiac defects. Arrhythmias varied from ten or more premature ventricular complexes per hour to bigeminy and ventricular tachycardia.

PHT alone controlled the arrhythmias in five patients. In the sixth, a combination of PHT and disopyramide was effective.

GARSON AND GILLETTE, *Pacing and Clinical Electrophysiology* (1981), studied the effects of PHT in fifty-one young patients with chronic arrhythmias consisting of multiform premature ventricular contractions (PVCs), couplets and ventricular tachycardia. The patients were divided into three groups according to hemodynamics. PHT was the initial drug used, followed by the addition or substitution of other drugs if effective response was not obtained. Five patients were not responsive to any treatment.

PHT alone corrected the arrhythmias in thirty-nine patients: twenty-two with severe, and sixteen with moderate hemodynamic abnormalities, and one with normal hemodynamics.

The authors observed that PHT was most effective in patients with the most abnormal hemodynamics, and say that PHT is the drug of choice for children with ventricular dysrhythmias.

ROCCHINI, CHUN AND DICK, *American Journal of Cardiology* (1981), reviewing their records on treatment and follow-up of children with ventricular tachycardias of various etiologies, report that PHT abolished arrhythmias in four patients with ventricular tachycardia following tetralogy of Fallot repair. A combination of PHT and propanolol effectively controlled symptoms and abolished ventricular tachycardias in two patients with prolonged Q-T interval.

KAVEY, BLACKMAN AND SONDHEIMER, *American Heart Journal* (1982), reported the effects of oral PHT in nineteen patients, seen consecutively, who developed ventricular premature complexes (VPCs) late after surgery for congenital heart disease. Arrhythmias included ventricular tachycardia, couplets and frequent multiform or uniform VPCs, documented by twenty-four-hour ambulatory ECG. Sixteen had undergone previous repair of the tetralogy of Fallot and three had had aortic valve surgery. Nine of these children had been unresponsive to previous treatment.

PHT decreased ventricular dysrhythmias in all nineteen patients.

The arrhythmias were completely suppressed in fifteen, and in four they were reduced to uniform VPCs.

The authors state that the high rate of success in treating these patients, who are at particular risk for sudden death, and the relative lack of side effects suggest that PHT is the drug of choice for this patient group.

Conduction

HELFANT, LAU, COHEN AND DAMATO, *Circulation* (1967), studied the effects of intravenous PHT on atrioventricular conduction in fourteen patients at constant heart rates in digitalized and nondigitalized states. In both groups, PHT was found to decrease P-R interval with the changes highly significant ($p < 0.001$). It was suggested that when digitalis excess is manifested by both ectopia and incomplete heart block, PHT would have special utility. In contrast to the commonly used antiarrhythmic agents, PHT enhances A-V conduction in addition to suppressing ectopia.

DAMATO, BERKOWITZ, PATTON AND LAU, *American Heart Journal* (1970), in thirteen patients, showed that PHT enhanced atrioventricular conduction (i.e., shortened the P-H interval) over various paced heart rates. Also PHT did not prolong intraventricular conduction as measured by H-Q interval.

These observations were made while studying His-bundle activity with an electrode catheter technique.

REIMANN, LEMMEL AND THEISEN, *Munchener Medizinische Wochenschrift* (1971), found that, in forty-seven of fifty patients, PHT eliminated extrasystoles and tachycardias of both atrial and ventricular origin. They noted that A-V conduction was not delayed.

Intravenous PHT, 125–375 mg, was usually promptly effective.

BENAIM, CHAPELLE AND CHICHE, *Annales de Cardiologie et d'Angeiologie* (1972), reported fifteen patients with arrhythmias, who were injected with doses of 5 to 10 mg/kg of PHT. Recordings of the His-potential achieved during the therapeutic test showed that PHT does not usually alter the frequency of the sinus node; and it definitely improves atrioventricular conduction. In fact, a shortening of the P-H interval was obtained eight times out of eleven in conducted sinus rhythms. In most cases it did not alter intraventricular conduction: H-V remained constant eleven times out of fifteen. In four cases, a depression in intraventricular conduction was noted with a lengthening of the H-V interval.

In conclusion, the authors emphasize how valuable PHT is in arrhythmias accompanied by atrioventricular conduction defects.

ANDERSON, DAVIS, DOVE AND GRIGGS, *Neurology* (1973), studied the effect of PHT on cardiac conduction in patients who suffered from myotonic dystrophy. They found that PHT was beneficial, not only for the myotonia, but also for cardiac conduction defects common in this disease.

In five of eight patients treated with oral PHT the P-R interval was shortened by 5 to 35 msec. This was in marked contrast to quinine and procainamide. Quinine produced P-R interval prolongation in four of ten patients, and procainamide produced P-R interval prolongation in nine of ten patients.

The authors' studies indicate diffuse involvement of the His-Purkinje system in myotonic dystrophy. They note that studies by others in normal subjects have shown a depression of His-Purkinje conduction with procainamide and quinine, but not with PHT.

BISSETT, DESOYZA, KANE AND MURPHY, *The American Journal of Cardiology* (1974), directly measured conduction in the His-Purkinje system in fourteen patients and found that PHT improved intraventricular conduction.

Utilizing the introduction of premature atrial beats, the relative refractory period of the His-Purkinje system and the functional refractory period of the atrioventricular (A-V) node were measured in the fourteen patients before and after administration of PHT. Before infusion of PHT, His-Purkinje conduction delay occurred with right bundle branch block in nine patients, and with left bundle branch block in five patients. After intravenous PHT (5 mg/kg at a rate of 50 mg/min) the onset or degree of His-Purkinje delay was improved in all patients. In the nine patients, PHT reduced the relative refractory period of the His-Purkinje system to a value of less than that of the functional refractory period of the A-V node, so that His-Purkinje conduction delay no longer occurred after PHT.

In the five patients with left bundle branch block, PHT also reduced the relative refractory period of the His-Purkinje system or altered the degree of aberrant conduction, or both.

The authors note that the present study demonstrates that PHT improves intraventricular conduction in man.

QUIRET, BENS, DuBOISSET, LESBRE AND BERNASCONI, *Archives des Maladies du Coeur et des Vaisseaux* (1974), studied the cardiovascular effects of PHT in 105 patients.

The authors say that PHT appears to have the following properties. It favors, or in any case does not adversely affect, atrioventricular conduction as well as intraventricular conduction. It checks manifestations of atrial and/or ventricular hyperexcitability secondary to organic cardiopathy or an excess of digitalis and has little or no effect on sinoatrial automatism.

DHATT, AKHTAR, REDDY, GOMES, LAU, CARACTA AND DAMATO, *Circulation* (1977), studied effects of PHT on macro-re-entry within the His-Purkinje system in ten patients. In seven patients, PHT modified determinants of re-entry and abolished re-entry in three patients. In all patients PHT significantly shortened functional and effective refractory periods of the His-Purkinje system, without affecting the effective refractory period of the ventricular muscle. PHT either abolished or significantly shortened the retrograde gap zones in the His-Purkinje system.

Q-T Interval Syndrome

LIPP, PITT, ANDERSON AND ZIMMET, *The Medical Journal of Australia* (1970), describe a twenty-year-old male with recurrent syncopal episodes as well as two documented episodes of ventricular fibrillation associated with prolongation of Q-T interval. After the patient was stabilized following a severe episode of fibrillation, he was placed on oral PHT and had no further arrhythmias. He remained free of syncope during the eighteen-month follow-up period.

The authors conclude that PHT is probably the most effective drug for the management of this syndrome since it suppresses myocardial irritability as well as reducing paroxysmal autonomic discharge.

COCHRAN, LINNEBUR, WRIGHT AND MATSUMOTO, *Clinical Research* (1977), did electrophysiologic studies of three patients with hereditary long Q-T interval syndrome. When admitted to the hospital these patients had ventricular tachyarrhythmias unresponsive to maximum doses of intravenous lidocaine. At this point DC counter-shock was used to terminate ventricular tachycardia in two patients. In the third patient, intravenous PHT promptly terminated the tachyarrhythmia.

Intravenous PHT shortened the Q-T interval in all three patients.

SCHNEIDER, BAHLER, PINCUS, STIMMEL, *Chest* (1977), describe a forty-five-year-old patient with congenital prolongation of the Q-T interval and recurrent ventricular arrhythmias. After numerous efforts to stabilize the patient, a transvenous pacemaker was inserted to suppress ectopic activity. Attempts to decrease the pacemaker rate below 150 per minute resulted in recurrence of ventricular arrhythmias and the Q-T interval remained prolonged.

The patient was placed on oral PHT (200 mg t.i.d.), the Q-T interval decreased and her ECG returned to normal. She had no further episodes of premature ventricular systoles or syncope, and was subsequently discharged on 200 mg PHT twice daily.

BROWN, LIBERTHSON, ALI AND LOWENSTEIN, *Anesthesiology* (1981), report a post-operative patient with prolonged Q-T interval and episodes of ventricular ectopic beats progressing to ventricular tachycardia. Oral PHT was started after numerous medications had been unsuccessful over a thirty-hour period. With PHT, no further ectopic beats were observed, even after discontinuation of lidocaine. Maintained on PHT and examined four weeks later, she had normal sinus rhythm and no ectopic activity.

See also Refs. 1972, 2071, 2094, 2223, 2328, 2370, 2376, 2462, 2558, 2695, 2807, 2837, 2895, 2951, 2957, 3066.

Torsade de Pointes

PUCCINELLI, CECCARELLI, MUCCI AND LANDUCCI, *Minerva Cardioangiologica* (1981), described two coronary care unit patients hospitalized for torsade de pointes ventricular tachycardia whose arrhythmias were promptly corrected by intravenous PHT.

The authors point out the electrophysiologic properties and molecular actions of PHT and suggest its utilization as a rapid and safe therapy in this kind of rhythm disturbance.

SUNG, LIANG, WANG, SHIEH AND LU, *Chinese Medical Journal* (1982), report a seventy-nine-year-old patient with complete A-V block, syncope and torsade de pointes ventricular tachycardia. Electric shock and intravenous lidocaine and isoproterenol were given without success. With PHT, the arrhythmia disappeared.

MISSRI AND SHUBROOKS, *Connecticut Medicine* (1982), describe a patient with rheumatic heart disease, cardiomyopathy and torsade de pointes ventricular arrhythmias, including fibrillation. Quinidine and procainamide exacerbated the arrhythmias. PHT (100 mg every six hours) was given with no further episodes of tachycardia. The authors recommend the use of PHT in patients with this type of arrhythmia.

ELDAR, MOTRO, YAHINI AND NEUFELD, *American Heart Journal* (1983), report a patient with acute myocardial infarction complicated by left heart failure, multiple premature ventricular contractions and A-V block requiring a pacemaker. After the pacemaker was discontinued, he developed a run of ventricular tachycardia of torsade de pointes type. Quinidine was stopped. He was placed on PHT (200 mg/day) and the ventricular ectopy immediately subsided. (See also Ref. 2664.)

Tricyclic Antidepressant Overdose

HAGERMAN AND HANASHIRO, *Annals of Emergency Medicine* (1981), demonstrated the effectiveness of intravenous PHT in reversing cardiac conduction abnormalities due to severe tricyclic antidepressant overdose in ten patients. Eight of the patients had combined first degree A-V block and intraventricular conduction delay; one had A-V block alone; and one had intraventricular conduction delay alone.

With PHT (5–7 mg/kg), five patients had complete normalization within forty-six minutes, and the remaining five showed immediate improvement in conduction with complete normalization within fourteen hours.

BOEHNERT AND LOVEJOY, *Veterinary and Human Toxicology* (1985), reported the intravenous use of PHT in the treatment of conduction delay and ventricular arrhythmias in seven patients with tricyclic antidepressant overdose, and compared the results with seven matched controls. All fourteen patients had QRS of at least 0.10 sec.

In the seven patients treated with PHT (average dose 900 mg infused at rates up to 25 mg/min), the QRS duration narrowed by an average of 55% within twenty to ninety-six minutes. Three of these patients had ventricular arrhythmias which resolved during PHT infusion. In the control group there was no change in QRS duration in the first three hours and only slight narrowing by 5.7 hours.

The authors conclude that PHT is rapidly effective and appears safe in the treatment of tricyclic antidepressant overdose.

Cardioversion

MERCER AND OSBORNE, *Annals of Internal Medicine* (1967), in an extensive study of 774 patients with a variety of cardiac arrhythmias, reported the effectiveness of intravenous PHT in the treatment of twenty-one of twenty-three patients with postcardioversion arrhythmias. (For a more full review, see p. 341.)

LESBRE, CATHALA, SALVADOR, FLORIO, LESCURE AND MERIEL, *Archives des Maladies du Coeur et des Vaisseaux* (1969), as part of an extensive study to investigate the antiarrhythmic value of PHT in a variety of cardiac disturbances, gave PHT to forty patients with atrial fibrillation, prior to cardioversion. A beta-blocking agent was given to a similar group of forty patients. Comparison of the two groups showed to the advantage of PHT. (For a more full review, see p. 343.)

DAMATO, *Progress in Cardiovascular Disease* (1969), pretreated ten digitalized patients, undergoing elective cardioversion, with intravenous PHT (5 mg/kg) fifteen minutes prior to procedure. None of the patients developed ventricular arrhythmias following cardioversion.

HELFANT, SEUFFERT, PATTON, STEIN AND DAMATO, *American Heart Journal (1969),* reported that in twelve patients, pretreated with PHT, DC countershock produced regular sinus rhythm with no immediate post-shock arrhythmias.

CUAN-PEREZ AND ORTIZ, *Archivos del Instituto de Cardiologia de Mexico* (1971), found PHT effective in preventing recurrence of fibrillation after cardioversion.

The study included 230 cases. PHT was compared with quinidine and propranolol.

PHT and the other two drugs acted in similar fashion with regard to percentage of recurrence. However, the authors found PHT the drug of choice because no toxic complications were observed with it, and this was not the case with quinidine and propranolol.

LINDE, TURNER AND AWA, *Pediatrics* (1972), in a review, suggest that because of the increased risk in cardioversion following digitalis administration, cardioversion should be preceded by PHT (5 mg/kg) administered intravenously over ten minutes, monitoring the electrocardiogram and blood pressure.

Myocardial Infarction

LEONARD, *Archives of Internal Medicine* (1958), was the first to report the use of PHT for the control of ventricular hyperirritability complicating myocardial infarction. (See p. 339.)

MERCER AND OSBORNE, *Annals of Internal Medicine* (1967), reported the effectiveness of PHT in treating ventricular arrhythmias in 67 of 101 patients with acute myocardial infarction complicated by arteriosclerotic heart disease. (See p. 341.)

BASHOUR, LEHMANN AND PRATI, *Journal of Laboratory and Clinical Medicine* (1967), in a controlled study, report the preventive use of PHT in acute myocardial infarction. In the treated group of thirty patients, PHT reduced both the incidence and severity of ventricular arrhythmias. Twenty did not develop ventricular arrhythmias. In the ten who did have ventricular tachycardia, the episodes were less severe when compared with the control group and only one persisted as long as eight hours.

In the control group of nineteen patients, twelve developed ventricular tachycardia and two ventricular fibrillation. (See also Ref. 2150.)

HANSEN AND WAGENER, *Munchener Medizinische Wochenschrift* (1969), reported the effective use of PHT in the treatment of cardiac arrhythmias following myocardial infarction.

In fifty patients who had a fresh myocardial infarction, PHT was slowly injected intravenously with excellent tolerance.

EDDY AND SINGH, *British Medical Journal* (1969), reported the successful use of intravenous PHT in the treatment of cardiac arrhythmias in eighteen of twenty-one patients who suffered acute myocardial infarction.

LUCKMANN, HOSSMANN, DORNER, ROTHENBERGER AND WICHERT, *Presented at the Third Konigsteiner Symposium in Hamburg* (1973), used intravenous PHT in twenty-six patients with either ventricular or supraventricular extrasystoles resulting from acute myocardial infarction. Of the twenty patients with ventricular extrasystoles, fourteen had elimination of the arrhythmia and three had reduction in extrasystoles.

In six patients, supraventricular extrasystoles were eliminated in two and reduced in three.

YANG, *Journal of the Kansas Medical Society* (1973), states, "When faced with an intractable ventricular tachycardia and bewildered by the failure of treatment, try PHT; it could be life saving."

The author reports on a case of intractable ventricular tachycardia following acute myocardial infarction. Procainamide, large doses of lidocaine, repeated DC counter-shock, and propranolol failed to convert this life-threatening cardiac arrhythmia.

PHT abolished the persistent ventricular tachycardia, and also permitted continuous digitalization when digitalis was so critically needed.

Angina Pectoris

BERNSTEIN, GOLD, LANG, PAPPELBAUM, BAZIKA AND CORDAY, *JAMA* (1965), as part of a larger study (see p. 340), reported the effectiveness of PHT in the treatment of angina pectoris of six years' duration in a sixty-seven-year-old female.

With PHT (100 mg three times a day), there was a marked improvement in the frequency and severity of the attacks, a decrease in the frequency of palpitations, and a dramatic decrease in need for nitroglycerin. Before PHT, she required twelve to sixty nitroglycerin tablets per week; and with PHT, she required none to four tablets per month.

TAYLOR, *Chest* (1974), reports the effectiveness of PHT in angina pectoris, based on a double-blind crossover study with sixteen patients.

The patients had typical symptoms of angina pectoris including chest pain, discomfort and tightness, radiating to arm, neck or jaw, precipitated by exertion, emotion and cold, and accompanied by dyspnea.

No drug therapy, apart from glyceryl trinitrate, was taken in the two-week period prior to the trial. The double-blind study showed that oral PHT used as a prophylactic significantly reduced the frequency of the attacks and the severity of symptoms in patients with angina pectoris.

KOTIA, HALDIA AND GUPTA, *Clinician* (1980), report a controlled study, with PHT and placebo, in thirty patients with ischemic heart disease and angina pectoris. All patients had stable effort-induced angina and all had ST changes at rest and on exertion. Fifteen patients were treated with PHT, 100 mg three times a day, and fifteen patients received placebo.

PHT markedly reduced the incidence of anginal attacks (p<0.01). ST depression was also significantly improved (p<0.05) in the treated group.

Hypertension

STARKOVA, MAROVA, LEMESHEVA, GONCHAROVA, ATAMANOVA AND SEDYKH, *Problemy Endokrinologii* (1972), reported PHT decreased or normalized blood pressure in fifteen hypertensive patients with Cushing's syndrome. (See p. 397.)

DE LA TORRE, MURGIA-SUAREZ AND ALDRETE, *Clinical Therapeutics* ((1980), compared PHT with conventional therapy in two groups of forty mildly hypertensive patients and found PHT useful in the reduction of both systolic and diastolic blood pressure. The authors also found PHT more effective in relieving symptoms such as anxiety, headaches, tinnitus, palpitations, chest pain, and dyspnea than the conventional therapy.

The authors suggest that PHT provides an alternative antihypertensive therapy, simple compared with most conventional therapies, and with fewer side effects.

ALDRETE AND FRANATOVIC, *Archives of Surgery* (1980), studied changes of arterial blood pressure and heart rate occurring during anesthesia and in the immediate post-operative period in three groups (30 patients each) of hypertensive patients. One group was untreated. A second group received 100 mg of PHT, and the third 200 mg of PHT, the evening before and the morning of surgery.

The administration of 200 mg the evening before and on the morning of surgery provided significantly improved hemodynamic stability during surgery.

KOTOVSKAYA AND ERINA, *Biulleten Vsesoiuznogo Kardiologicheskogo Nauchnogo Tsentra AMN SSSR* (1982), studied the effects of PHT, pyrroxan and placebo in preventing hypertensive crises in thirty-five patients. In the PHT group (ten patients) there were no crises in five and in three a reduction of frequency and severity of crises was noted.

BECHTEREVA, NIKITINA, ILIUCHINA, DAMBINOVA AND DENISOVA, *European Journal of Clinical Investigation* (1984), discussed the use of PHT in treating 120 patients with hypothalamic syndrome. With PHT, blood pressure and body temperature were normalized. In addition there was marked improvement in symptoms such as headache, irritability and feelings of fear. Sleep was also improved.

Cerebrovascular Insufficiencies

KENNEDY, ANDERSON AND SOKOLOFF, *Neurology* (1958), studied cerebral blood flow in four epileptic children, before and after PHT for one week, using a modified nitrous oxide test. Although the group was small, the authors found the increase in mean blood flow to be statistically significant (from 85 to 102 cc per 100 gram per minute).

SLOSBERG, *Mount Sinai Medical Journal* (1970), reports on his eight years of experience with medical therapy for cerebrovascular insufficiencies in a series of sixty-one elderly patients. Among these were patients with occlusive disease of the neck arteries; occlusive disease of the intracranial arteries; hypoplastic arteries; vascular anomalies of the circle of Willis; patients with reaction to compression of the common carotid arteries or of the carotid sinus areas; and patients with postural hypotension.

The author found a simple and effective method for treating cerebrovascular insufficiencies of diverse origins. This method consists of the use of PHT in conjunction with carotid sinus therapy and support stockings.

The author found that this method was both applicable and safe in this heterogeneous group of patients with cerebrovascular insufficiency, and has been well tolerated in the acute stages and on long-term follow-up.

DANIEL, *Geriatrics* (1970), says that symptoms of confusion which are so common in the aged often are caused by underlying physical illness, frequently cardiac and respiratory disorders resulting in cerebral hypoxia or ischemia. He states that PHT is therapeutically useful in this group, yet it is often overlooked. (See p. 322.)

ALDRETE, ROMO-SALAS, MAZZIA AND TAN, *Critical Care Medicine* (1981), studied the cerebral protective effects of PHT in ten patients who suffered cardiac arrest during or after anesthesia.

PHT was given after spontaneous heartbeat and systolic blood pressure greater than 100 mm Hg had been restored and the diagnosis of neurological deficit had been established on the basis of unconsciousness, dilated and areflexic pupils and rigid and/or decerebrate posture.

With PHT (7 mg/kg) nine of the ten patients recovered nearly complete neurological function; the other patient had partial recovery but succumbed to other complications.

The authors note that laboratory studies of anti-anoxic protective effects of PHT support their clinical findings that PHT may have a reversing effect on post-ischemic brain injury. (See also Refs. 1718, 1719.)

MASSEI, DE SILVA, GROSSO, ROBBIATI, INFUSO, RAVAGNATI AND ALTAMURA, *Journal of Neurological Science* (1983), report twelve patients treated with intravenous PHT prior to clamping during carotid thromboendarterectomy. During and after surgery no neurological complications or alterations in cardiac function were observed.

Prompt awakening, absence of neurologic deficits, and absence of side effects supported their hypothesis that PHT provides cerebral protection during carotid surgery.

High-Density Lipoproteins—Atherosclerosis

NIKKILA, KASTE, EHNHOLM AND VIIKARI, *Acta Medica Scandinavica* (1978), measured serum high- density lipoprotein-cholesterol (HDL-C) levels in twenty-eight epileptic patients who received PHT. These were compared with ninety healthy controls, forty-four men and forty-nine women. The patients treated with PHT had significantly higher HDL-C levels than the controls.

The authors say that serum HDL-C shows an inverse correlation with the risk of coronary heart disease, and note that some clinicians taking care of epileptic patients have been impressed by the low incidence of myocardial infarction.

HENRY, BELL AND GLITHERO, *New England Journal of Medicine (1979)*, report that nineteen patients on long-term PHT therapy had significantly higher HDL-C levels (p<0.01) as compared to twenty-seven controls.

LUOMA, MYLLYLA, SOTANIEMI, LEHTINEN AND HOKKANEN, *European Neurology* (1980), compared HDL-C levels in ninety-seven epileptics with forty-three controls. Thirty-eight patients on PHT alone, and thirty-nine on PHT in combination with carbamazepine or phenobarbital, had increased levels compared to controls. Patients on PHT alone had significantly higher levels than controls.

MURPHY, REDDY AND MARQUARDT, *Annals of Neurology* (1981), in a study of HDL-C levels in children on various anti-convulsants, report that in eleven children on PHT the HDL-C levels were significantly elevated (p<0.001) compared to controls. The authors suggest that PHT may protect against atherosclerosis.

KASTE, MUURONEN, NIKKILA, AND NEUVONEN, *Stroke* (1982), and (1983), measured serum HDL-C and other lipoproteins before and during PHT therapy (200–300 mg/day) in twenty-seven patients with a history of transient ischemic attacks. Nine of these patients had arterial hypertension; seven, heart disease; and four, diabetes. Three had suffered myocardial infarction and two, brain infarction. Before PHT, HDL-C levels were lower in these patients than in normal healthy controls.

After one month's treatment with PHT, HDL-C concentrations reached normal levels. After nine months of therapy, there was a mean increase in HDL-C of 42% in the males and 68% in females. Low-density lipoproteins (LDL) did not increase, so that HDL/LDL cholesterol ratios improved.

Only seven patients had recurrent transient ischemic attacks. None had brain or myocardial infarction over the two-year period of PHT treatment.

The authors conclude that low serum HDL-C can be increased with PHT and this could retard the development of atherosclerotic disorders such as myocardial infarction or stroke.

O'NEILL, CALLAGHAN, STAPLETON AND MOLLOY, *Acta Neurologica Scandinavica* (1982), measured serum total cholesterol and HDL-C in fifty-two epileptic patients taking either PHT or carbamazepine. Total cholesterol concentrations did not differ significantly from controls, but the percentage of HDL-C and its ratio to total cholesterol increased in both groups. The increase was significant for PHT.

The authors point out that the change in this ratio is of particular significance because HDL facilitates the uptake of cholesterol from peripheral tissues and transports it to the liver for breakdown and excretion.

DANILENKO AND IVANIV, *Vrachebnoe Delo* (1983), reported the effects of PHT (300–450 mg/day for twenty days) on lipid metabolism and microsomal enzyme activity in twelve patients with atherosclerosis, mostly of the pelvis and lower extremities. PHT caused an increase in HDL-C concentrations (average 18% in arterial blood and 15% in venous blood). The ratio of HDL-C to total cholesterol also increased. The arteriovenous differences in concentration for total cholesterol, LDL and very low density lipoproteins decreased significantly.

Based on their data, the authors suggest that the PHT-induced rise in HDL-C results in a decrease in cholesterol and atherogenic lipoproteins in the peripheral vessels and that this may slow the development of the atheroselerotic process.

BELL AND DITTMEIER, *Arteriosclerosis* (1985), in a controlled study, investigated the effects of PHT (200 mg/day for three months) on HDL-C subfractions (HDL_2 and HDL_3) in forty-five patients, forty-one with angiographic confirmation of coronary artery disease. All had HDL-C to total cholesterol ratios of less than 20%.

During PHT treatment, the HDL_2 subfraction increased significantly in twenty-five patients. Total HDL-C also increased in twenty-nine of the forty-five patients, while mean subfraction HDL_3 increased only slightly.

The authors note, that since HDL_2 is associated with reduced coronary heart disease, PHT may be beneficial in preventing the progression of coronary artery disease.

MUURONEN, KASTE, NIKKILA, AND TOLPPANEN, *British Medical Journal* (1985), evaluated all deaths (1399) among epileptic patients in Finland from 1978 to 1980, and compared them with those in a control group, also 1399, matched for age, sex and date of death. Autopsies had been performed on 695 in the epileptic group and 734 in the control group.

There was a 29% (p <0.001) lower mortality rate due to deaths from ischemic heart disease (258) among epileptics who had been treated with PHT, phenobarbital and/or carbamazepine compared with controls (382). Total cardiovascular mortality was also lower in the treated epileptics.

In a discussion of the reasons for the lower cardiovascular mortality seen in the epileptic patients, the authors point out that PHT, carbamazepine, and barbiturates all raise plasma concentrations of high density lipoproteins and induce microsomal liver enzymes. They note that PHT's ability to reduce hyperinsulinemia, an independent positive risk factor in ischemic heart disease, and its antiarrhythmic actions may contribute to its protective effects.

See also Refs. 1961, 2162, 2318, 2323, 2542, 2652, 2741, 2827, 2897, 2946.

NEUROMUSCULAR DISORDERS

Summary

The effectiveness of PHT in a variety of neuromuscular disorders has been observed clinically and, in many cases, demonstrated by quantitative electrophysiology. Some of these disorders cause much suffering and are frequently disabling or incapacitating.

Neuromuscular disorders for which PHT has been reported useful include continuous muscle fiber activity syndromes, such as Isaacs' syndrome and myotonic dystrophy; Sydenham's chorea; paroxysmal choreoathetosis; "restless legs"; muscle spasms; abnormal movements associated with Parkinsonism; intractable hiccups; palatal and respiratory myoclonus; and tetanus.

In muscle, as in nerve, PHT corrects inappropriate electrical activity without interfering with normal function. PHT does not sedate, and does not compromise respiratory function.

Choreas

SYDENHAM'S CHOREA
(CHOREA MINOR)

SHAPERA, *Pittsburgh Medical Bulletin* (1940), discussed the narrowness with which new drugs are frequently viewed and suggested that PHT might have broader uses than that of an anticonvulsant. The efficacy of PHT in conditions of involuntary movements, such as tremors, rigidity and spasticity, was studied. The author found PHT effective in treating involuntary movements in ten of fifteen patients with Sydenham's chorea.

GINABREDA, *Revista Espanola De Pediatria* (1945), reported on the effectiveness of PHT in six cases of chorea minor in children between the ages of five and twelve years. Improvement occurred in all of the cases in an average of fifteen to sixteen days. (See also Ref. 114.)

DE LA VEGA, *Revista Clinica Espanola* (1947), reported on an epidemic of chorea minor or Sydenham's chorea. PHT was used in thirty-four cases with excellent results. In twenty-six cases there was complete elimination of symptoms in three weeks of treatment. There were four relapses when PHT was discontinued. These were corrected with the renewal of treatment.

Not only did PHT shorten the duration of the disease, but there was a marked reduction of complications—even those of cardiac lesions, a frequent and serious sequel to chorea minor.

SCHWARTZMAN, MCDONALD, PERILLO, *Archives of Pediatrics* (1948), in a study of Sydenham's chorea in which many medications were tried, reported that of eight patients given PHT, six were improved and two were cured.

ATHETOSIS

KABAT AND MCLEOD, *Connecticut Medicine* (1959), reported the successful use of PHT in five of six athetosis patients. Treatment with PHT resulted in prompt and striking improvement in neuromuscular performance.

STEVENS, *Archives of Neurology* (1966), reported that PHT treatment was usually promptly effective in the relief of symptoms of paroxysmal choreoathetosis.

HUDGINS AND CORBIN, *Brain* (1966), treated a mother, son and daughter suffering from familial paroxysmal choreoathetosis with PHT and mephobarbital. The relief was prompt and lasting with continued treatment.

KERTESZ, *Neurology* (1967), reported ten patients with paroxysmal kinesigenic choreoathetosis as an entity within the paroxysmal choreoathetosis syndrome. The attacks consisted of athetoid movements or tonic posturing of limbs, trunk and face. Duration was usually fifteen to thirty seconds. Paroxysms were precipitated by sudden movements, associated with surprise or haste.

The author reported that the majority of patients responded well to PHT.

JUNG, CHEN AND BRODY, *Neurology* (1973), reported ten cases of paroxysmal choreoathetosis in two families. The authors state that, to their knowledge, this is the first report of its occurrence among the Chinese. Episodes may occur several times daily with varying degrees of bizarre posturing, which can reach such intensity that the patient is hurled to the floor.

The authors state that the therapeutic effect of PHT is so prompt and so dramatic that there is little doubt as to the effectiveness of the treatment. They state that, except for one early report, PHT has been the drug of choice for this disorder.

ZENTENO VACHERON, CARRASCO ZANINI AND RAMOS RAMIREZ, *Epilepsy Abstracts* (1977), described the successful use of PHT in treating two patients with paroxysmal dystonic choreoathetosis.

WALLER, *American Journal of Psychiatry* (1977), described a case of paroxysmal kinesigenic choreoathetosis in a twenty-two-year old female whose condition was markedly improved by PHT.

GOODENOUGH, FARIELLO, ANNIS AND CHUN, *Archives of Neurology* (1978), reported the complete cessation of symptoms of from two to eight years duration in three cases of familial kinesigenic dyskinesia treated with PHT. The authors state that the response to PHT was prompt.

FUKUYAMA, OCHIAI, HAYAKAWA AND MIYAGAWA, *Neuropadiatrie* (1979), reported the complete elimination of choreoathetoid attacks in an eight-year-old boy with PHT. Marked improvement in sleep was also observed.

HOMAN, VASKO AND BLAW, *Neurology* (1980), report on the use of PHT in the treatment of five patients with paroxysmal kinesigenic choreoathetosis. The patients, two children and three adults, experienced episodes of choreoathetoid posturing without alteration of consciousness.

PHT controlled these symptoms in all cases. Discontinuation of PHT resulted in a return of symptoms.

FRANSSEN, FORTGENS, WATTENDORFF AND VAN WOERKOM, *Archives of Neurology* (1983), report a study of an eighteen-year-old male patient with paroxysmal kinesigenic choreoathetosis of a year's duration. Attacks

were precipitated by anticipated movements, confirmed by enhancement of the slow negative wave component of the contingent negative variation.

With PHT, the attacks of paroxysmal choreoathetosis disappeared and the slow negative wave amplitude became normal.

PLANT, *Journal of Neurology, Neurosurgery and Psychiatry* (1983), presented three cases of unilateral and one case of bilateral paroxysmal kinesigenic choreoathetosis.

In all four patients the attacks were completely abolished by PHT. There were no recurrences during an eighteen-month follow-up.

ZACCHETTI, SOZZI AND ZAMPOLLO, *Italian Journal of Neurological Sciences* (1983), report the treatment of a patient with paroxysmal kinesigenic choreoathetosis. Treatment with PHT, 200 mg/day, led to complete disappearance of the attacks, confirmed in follow-up. It was of interest that symptoms were controlled with PHT blood levels of 3 µg/ml.

WANG AND CHANG, *Therapeutic Drug Monitoring* (1985), reported the effectiveness of PHT at varying therapeutic blood levels in the control of paroxysmal choreoathetosis in eight patients. Successful treatment in all eight patients was defined as complete control of attacks within six months, at which time blood levels were measured. The doses used ranged from 50 to 200 mg per day. Effective blood levels ranged from 1.1 to 10.9 µg/ml. The authors emphasize that, in the treatment of disorders other than epilepsy, lower doses of PHT are often effective.

See also Refs. 718, 1305, 1431, 1610, 2339, 2366, 2721, 2809.

Continuous Muscle Fiber Activity

ISAACS, *Journal of Neurology, Neurosurgery and Psychiatry* (1961), describes the syndrome of continuous muscle fiber activity in two patients, marked by progressive muscle stiffness increased by voluntary muscle contractions and accompanied by fasciculation and weakness. Electromyography recorded a state of constant rapid dysrhythmic discharge of independent muscle fibers. The author defined the state as myotonic afterdischarge and likened it to post-tetanic afterdischarge. Neither patient showed response to numerous medications including quinidine, procainamide, cortisone, and atropine.

Treatment with PHT (100 mg q.i.d.) resulted in dramatic improvement in symptoms and electromyographic changes both at rest and on voluntary effort.

In a five-year follow-up, the author reported that both patients were still well and had lost their abnormal stiffness. He noted that on the occasions when PHT had been stopped, the symptoms returned.

ISAACS, *Journal of Neurology, Neurosurgery and Psychiatry* (1967), reports on another patient with continuous muscle fiber activity, a twenty-year-old Indian male. The rapid effectiveness of PHT was apparent. (See also Ref. 2612.)

MERTENS AND ZSCHOCKE, *Klinische Wochenschrift* (1965), report on three cases of neuromyotonia. Each patient had in common a continuous spastic contraction of the entire skeletal musculature, which did not even diminish while asleep or under anesthesia. Extensive electromyographic, histologic and other laboratory studies confirmed the electrophysiological abnormality. Quinine, quinidine, novocamid, steroids and diuretics had little or no effect.

PHT and mephenytoin were tried. PHT was far more effective. With two injections of PHT, 250 mg, at sixty-minute intervals, it was possible to obtain significant elimination of spastic contractions and inhibition of movement in all muscle groups within two to four hours.

The authors state that with oral PHT they were able to maintain this astonishing effect. A trial of discontinuing the PHT resulted in recurrence or rapid increase of the abnormal contraction.

LEVY, WITTIG AND FERRAZ, *Arquivo de Neuro Psiquiat* (1965), describe a case of continuous muscle fiber activity at rest, diagnosed by electromyography. The condition showed some clinical improvement with corticosteroids, although this improvement was not reflected on the electromyogram.

The authors report that PHT, 300 mg/day, markedly improved both the clinical picture and the abnormal electrical tracing in a few days.

HUGHES AND MATTHEWS, *Journal of Neurology, Neurosurgery and Psychiatry* (1969), described a patient who for thirty-two years had suffered from a form of muscular rigidity clinically resembling myotonia but, in fact, identical with continuous muscle fiber activity.

The patient was treated with 100 mg of PHT q.i.d., which produced immediate and continuing benefits. If he stopped taking PHT, for as short a period as twenty-four hours, the symptoms returned.

BUSCAINO, CARUSO, DE GIACOMO, LABIANCA AND FERRANNINI, *Acta Neurologica* (1970), describe a case of continuous muscle fiber activity syndrome (neuromyotonia).

The man, age forty-five, had suffered for twenty years from stiffness of all muscles, wide-spread fasciculations, myokymia and excessive sweating. The muscular stiffness was present even during sleep.

The nature of the electrical abnormality was documented on the electromyogram.

This condition, present for twenty years, had been treated with a variety of substances without success. The authors state that the condition was dramatically resolved by the use of PHT or carbamazepine.

WALLIS, VAN POZNAK AND PLUM, *Archives of Neurology* (1970), report on two cases involving generalized muscular stiffness, fasciculations and myokymia of peripheral nerve origin. Electomyographic and other laboratory findings were consistent with the clinical diagnosis.

In one case the authors state PHT, 100 mg t.i.d., provided dramatic relief. In the other case it was not found effective. In the successful case, when PHT was discontinued, within three days, all pretreatment symptoms returned. Prompt relief recurred with the reinstitution of PHT.

WELCH, APPENZELLER AND BICKNELL, *Neurology* (1972), report a case of peripheral neuropathy with myokymia, sustained muscular contraction and continuous motor unit activity in a twenty-two-year-old female.

The patient was tried with quinine for one month without success. The patient was then given PHT, 300 mg/day, with almost immediate remission of symptoms. This remission continued with daily PHT.

KOSTOV, TACHEV AND NASTEV, *Zhurnal Nevropatologii i Psikhiatrii imeni S.S. Korsakova* (1973), report on a patient with pseudomyotonia (Isaacs' syndrome) characterized by hypertonia of the distal extremities. Spontaneous electromyographic activity was present at rest, and did not disappear even after novocaine blockade of the peripheral nerve.

PHT and carbamazepine each had favorable therapeutic effect. Withdrawal of the medications resulted in a return of the disorder.

LEVINSON, CANALIS AND KAPLAN, *Archives of Otolaryngology* (1976), reported an unusual case of continuous muscle activity complicated by airway obstruction secondary to laryngeal spasm.

Treatment with PHT, 300 mg/day, resulted in rapid improvement of the peripheral symptoms and the laryngeal spasms.

IRANI, PUROHIT AND WADIA, *Acta Neurologica Scandinavica* (1977), reported prompt and remarkable improvement upon administration of PHT in three of four patients with continuous muscle fiber activity.

LUTSCHG, JERUSALEM, LUDIN, VASSELLA AND MUMENTHALER, *Archives of Neurology* (1978), reported the successful treatment with PHT of a seven-year-old boy who had suffered for two years with the syndrome of continuous muscle fiber activity.

JACKSON, SATYA-MURTI, DAVIS AND DRACHMAN, *Neurology* (1979), report on a case of Isaacs' syndrome with laryngeal involvement, confirmed by clinical, pharmacologic and electrophysiologic findings.

The patient responded well to treatment with a combination of PHT and carbamazepine.

LUBLIN, TSAIRIS, STRELETZ, CHAMBERS, RIKER, VANPOZNAK AND DUCKETT, *Journal of Neurology, Neurosurgery and Psychiatry* (1979), report two cases of continuous motor activity with impaired muscular relaxation. EMG showed continuous motor activity at rest. Treatment with PHT, 500–700 mg/day, resulted in marked diminution in myokymia and continuous motor activity. Clinical improvement persisted in two-year follow-up.

REEBACK, BENTON, SWASH, SCHWARTZ, *British Medical Journal* (1979), report a patient treated for rheumatoid arthritis with penicillamine who developed muscle contractions and weakness suggesting neuromyotonia. EMG showed continuous motor firing at rest. The patient was treated with PHT with marked improvement in three days, which was confirmed by EMG studies six weeks later.

GRASSA, FIGA-TALAMANCA, LORUSSO, GIACANELLI AND PONTESILLI, *Italian Journal of Neurological Science* (1981), report a thirty-four-year-old woman with diffuse muscle contractions and other symptoms of continuous muscle fiber activity syndrome, confirmed by EMG. With oral PHT, 400 mg/day, improvement, which included cessation of the painful muscle spasms and excessive sweating, occurred. EMG, nine months later, showed almost complete disappearance of the abnormal activity.

VASILESCU AND FLORESCU, *Journal of Neurology* (1982), report a case of a male alcoholic who developed continuous muscle fiber activity. Electrophysiologic studies and muscle biopsy confirmed mixed sensorimotor polyneuropathy.

PHT, 400 mg/day, was started and the clinical symptoms and EMG activity at rest disappeared within two days. This result persisted at follow-up six months later.

MARIA AND PISANELLI, *Rivista di Neurologia* (1983), report a fifty-three-year-old male patient with neuromyotonia (Isaacs' syndrome), who had been treated unsuccessfully with dopamine and benzodiazepines. Carbamazepine was tried with partial success. Treatment with PHT, 600 mg/day, resulted in remarkable improvement. When PHT was discontinued, the symptoms reappeared.

ZISFEIN, SIVAK, ARON AND BENDER, *Archives of Neurology* (1983), report a sixteen-year-old boy with severe episodic muscle cramps and gene-

ralized myokymia (Isaacs' syndrome), associated gastrocnemius hypertrophy and ankle areflexia. The patient was treated with PHT, 300 mg/day, with total relief of cramps, marked decrease in myokymia and return of ankle reflexes. There was marked reduction in the muscle hypertrophy after three months.

BROWN, *Archives of Physical Medicine and Rehabilitation* (1984), reports a twenty-year-old male patient with myokymia in all four extremities, hyporeflexia and hypertrophy of thenar musculature, who presented with cramping pain in both thighs and difficulty releasing grip. EMG revealed continuous motor unit activity at rest.

The patient was treated with PHT and showed almost complete resolution of symptoms within twenty-four hours. The author states that rapid response to PHT, in conjunction with clinical and EMG findings, are diagnostic of Isaacs' syndrome.

See also Refs. 836, 1549, 1758, 2016, 2124, 2146, 2147, 2298, 2302, 2312, 2397, 2407, 2409, 2448, 2456, 2572, 2612, 2683, 2692, 2780, 2850, 2920, 3003, 3043, 3057.

Myotonias

DYSTROPHIC AND CONGENITA

MUNSAT, *Neurology* (1967), reported a double-blind crossover study of seven patients with dystrophic myotonia and two with myotonia congenita. The authors found both PHT and procainamide effective in treatment of the myotonic symptoms. PHT was better tolerated and did not increase the preexisting cardiac conductive defects, which were made worse by procainamide.

BHATT, VIJAYAN AND DREYFUS, *California Medicine* (1971), in a review of clinical and laboratory aspects of myotonia, state that of treatments which have been used successfully for myotonia, including PHT, procainamide, quinine, and adrenocorticotropic hormone, PHT appears to be the most effective, the safest and the best tolerated.

THOMPSON, *New England Journal of Medicine* (1972), in a letter to the editor wrote:

"In three members of a family in my practice with myotonia congenita, PHT, 100 mg three times a day, was started. The patients were sixteen, twenty and twenty-three years of age. Their disabilities included inability to dance, difficulty getting up from a sitting position, difficulty relaxing grips, and some falling because of inability to relax the muscles.

On PHT therapy they are all much improved. The sixteen-year-old girl is particularly delighted because she can now dance. No side effects have occurred and the improvement is dramatic."

GRIGGS, DAVIS, ANDERSON AND DOVE, *American Journal of Medicine* (1975), studied the effect of PHT on cardiac conduction in patients who suffered from myotonic dystrophy. They found that PHT was beneficial, not only for the myotonia, but also for cardiac conduction defects common in this disease.

In seven of ten patients treated with oral PHT the P-R interval was shortened by 5 to 50 msec. This was in contrast to quinine and procainamide. Quinine produced P-R interval prolongation in six of thirteen patients, and procainamide produced P-R interval prolongation in eleven of twelve patients.

The authors state that since they and others have found that PHT is an effective antimyotonic agent and since their own findings have shown that it does not have negative effects on cardiac conduction abnormalities as do quinine and procainamide, PHT is the treatment of choice in myotonic dystrophy. (See also Ref. 764.)

BIRYUKOV, *Zh Nevropatol Psikhiatr* (1976), compared the effects of PHT and novocainamid in two groups of myotonic patients.

With PHT, 400–500 mg/day for a period of three to four weeks, there was a significant improvement in nine of the fourteen patients treated. The myotonic contractures disappeared almost completely in six with myotonia congenita, and the myotonic component was signifi-cantly reduced within two weeks in three with myotonic dystrophy.

Sixteen patients were treated with novocainamid, 0.75–1.5 g/day. In two, treatment had to be stopped because significant bradycardia developed. There was some improvement in six of fourteen patients, four with myotonia congenita and two with myotonic dystrophy.

The author notes that PHT was not only more effective, but also better tolerated than novocainamid. Its lack of adverse effects on cardiac function distinguished it from novocainamid.

DURELLI, MUTANI, SECHI, TRACCIS, MONACO AND GLORIOSO, *Electro-encephalography and Clinical Neuro-physiology* (1982), compared PHT, carbamazepine and placebo in a double-blind study of eight patients with dystrophic myotonia (Steinert's disease). Criteria included subjective and objective clinical findings as well as EMG evaluation. Both drugs were found to be effective.

STRIANO, MEO, BILO AND VITOLO, *Encephalography and Clinical Neurophysiology* (1983), report a patient with typical Thomsen's disease (myotonia congenita), who also had evidence of sleep-induced apnea and excessive daytime somno-lence. All-night polysomnography demonstrated obstructive and central apneas with accompanying cardiac arrhythmias.

PHT improved not only the myotonia, but also the breathing patterns, sleep soundness and excessive daytime somnolence.

See also Refs. 1073, 1939, 2446, 2867.

SCHWARTZ-JAMPEL SYNDROME

TAYLOR, LAYZER, DAVIS AND FOWLER, JR, *Electroencephalography and Clinical Neurophysiology* (1972), reported on three patients with Schwartz-Jampel syndrome, a rare autosomal recessive disease consisting of generalized myotonia and bone abnormalities, including dwarfism. PHT improved muscle contractions in two of the patients.

BROWN, GARCIA-MULLEN AND MURAI, *Neurology* (1975), reported two patients with myotonic chondro-dystrophy (Schwartz-Jampel syndrome) which had progressed to marked limitation of joint mobility in adulthood.

PHT resulted in such improvement in ambulation that both patients were able to return to gainful employment.

CRUZ MARTINEZ, ARPA, PEREZ CONDE AND FERRER, *Muscle and Nerve* (1984), reported a seven-year-old girl with Schwartz-Jampel syndrome. EMG showed persistent continuous electrical activity and high frequency discharges. Treatment with PHT, 200 mg/day, resulted in improvement in muscle relaxation and motor ability, including gait.

Stiff-Man Syndrome

NEVSIMAL, SUTA AND TUHACEK, *Cheskoslovenska Neurologie* (1967) describe a case of stiff-man syndrome of fifteen years duration in a fifty-year-old female patient. Treatment with PHT decreased muscular spasms and rigidity.

GOBERNADO, ORTIN, RODRIGUEZ DE CASTRO AND GIMENO, *Prensa Medica Argentina* (1981), describe a patient with severe leg muscle contractions consistent with stiff-man syndrome. The patient had had progressive symptoms for twenty years. Sodium valproate was unsuccessful. Initial treatment with diazepam had to be discontinued due to side effects. A combination of PHT and diazepam produced both clinical and electro-physiological improvement.

Parkinson's Syndrome

SHAPERA, *Pittsburgh Medical Bulletin* (1940), reported on the treatment with PHT of twenty-two patients with Parkinson's syndrome. These patients had received other medication with little or no beneficial effect. With PHT improvement in involuntary move-ments was observed.

The author noted that there was a psychic improvement in some of these patients and that this alone made PHT therapy worthwhile.

KABAT, *Annals of Internal Medicine* (1959), reported the therapeutic effectiveness of PHT in seven cases of Parkinson's syndrome.

Three of these patients, who had been taking the maximal tolerable dose of anti-Parkinson drugs, still showed rigidity, tremor and poor isotonic function. With the addition of PHT isotonic and isometric function improved. Rigidity disappeared in one case and was reduced in the other two cases. Improvement in ambulation and in use of the upper extremities was also noted on addition of PHT.

The other four patients, who had not previously taken any anti-Parkinson drugs, were treated with PHT alone. In each case, prompt improvement in isotonic contraction of the muscles resulted. Rigidity disappeared in one case and was significantly reduced in the others. Tremor was moderately improved. Voluntary motion of the affected extremities was improved significantly in all cases.

DOMZAL, *Neurologia i Neurochirurgia Polska* (1972), reported on the use of PHT in treating fourteen patients with Parkinson's syndrome. Eight of these patients had received synthetic anticholinergic drugs, and six had not received any previous anti-Parkinsonism medication.

With PHT, 300–400 mg/day, over a two-week period, eleven patients reported marked improvement in sense of well-being; ten reported improvement in muscle tone; and six exhibited improvement in general tremor, which disappeared entirely in three. Steadier mobility, better expression and improved gait were observed in three patients.

Other Muscular Disorders

RESTLESS LEGS

HOGG, *Practitioner* (1972), describes the successful treatment of seven cases of "restless legs," or Ekbom's syndrome, with PHT. For this syndrome, of unknown etiology, vasodilators, intravenous iron and Dextran have been tried with only partial success.

The syndrome, he states, derives its name "restless legs" from the fact that the majority of these patients are unable to rest in bed at night and take to moving their legs sometimes vigorously because of the gnawing aches and "crawling pains."

In each of the seven patients, 100 mg of PHT daily resulted in cessation of symptoms. Since the symptoms occurred at night, and interrupted sleep, PHT was given before going to bed.

STEROID MYOPATHY

STERN, GRUENER AND AMUNDSEN, *JAMA* (1973), report on a forty-seven-year-old man suffering with steroid myopathy, who was successfully treated with PHT.

The patient required steroids (prednisolone) for his rheumatoid arthritis. Without changing the regimen of prednisolone, two six-week trial periods of PHT and placebo capsules were instituted with crossover every three weeks. The results of the two trials revealed that while on PHT there was a significant improvement in hip flexor strength, as contrasted to placebo. Muscle strength was measured with a dynamometer.

The authors state that although this was only one case, the results suggest that PHT might be used along with steroids to decrease the risk of steroid myopathy. (See also Ref. 1103.)

INTRACTABLE HICCUPS

PETROSKI AND PATEL, *Lancet* (1974), in a letter to the editor, report on a patient with refractory hiccups and an old right hemiparesis. He was mentally alert, but repetitive attacks of hiccups seriously interfered with his feeding and sleep and left him exhausted. The hiccups did not respond to pharyngeal stimulation by catheter or parenteral prochlorperazine.

On the sixth day, the frequency of hiccups increased to more than thirty per minute. PHT (200 mg), given intravenously over five minutes, completely eliminated hiccuping within an hour. Then 100 mg q.i.d. orally was continued until the eleventh day without any recurrence of hiccups.

RESPIRATORY MYOCLONUS

PHILLIPS AND ELDRIDGE, *New England Journal of Medicine* (1973), describe a case of abnormal repetitive diaphragmatic contractions, which they refer to as respiratory myoclonus.

In the case reported, treatment with quinidine had been ineffective. Because of PHT's membrane stabilizing and synaptic effects, it was tried. A dose of 400 mg of PHT daily was sufficient to inhibit the abnormal muscle activity as demonstrated by diaphragmatic, scalene and intercostal muscle electromyography.

PHT was discontinued on three occasions with a return of symptoms. At the time of the writing the patient had taken PHT daily for a year with no recurrence.

The authors state that in the past the only effective form of therapy for this disorder has been phrenicectomy. They suggest a trial of PHT first.

PALATAL MYOCLONUS

FERRO AND CASTRO-CALDAS, *Annals of Neurology* (1981), report on a case of palatal myoclonus observed in a hypertensive sixty-five-year-old male. Neurological examination, electroencephalogram and CT scan were performed. The lower half of the right side of the face, both eyelids, the tongue, lower jaw, soft palate, and posterior pharyngeal wall showed a rhythmic myoclonus that disturbed speech and swallowing, and persisted during sleep.

Clonazepam improved the myoclonus but caused intolerable drowsiness and confusion. Sodium valproate had no effect, and carbamazepine worsened the condition.

PHT (600 mg/day) improved the myoclonus, reducing its amplitude and the area of the body it affected.

FITZGERALD, *Laryngoscope* (1984), presented a case of palatal myoclonus related to acoustical stimulation and tinnitus. Diazepam was tried with little effect. The patient was switched to carbamazepine without change. He was then placed on a combination of PHT and phenobarbital with remarkable improvement in tinnitus and myoclonus.

SPASMS IN MULTIPLE SCLEROSIS

MATTHEWS, *Brain* (1958), reported the effectiveness of PHT in the treatment of frequent painful spasms in a patient with multiple sclerosis. When PHT, 100 mg t.i.d. was prescribed, the attacks stopped within two days. The author did not claim that PHT had a primary beneficial action on multiple sclerosis itself, but that it was useful in the treatment of the painful spasms.

JOYNT AND GREEN, *Archives of Neurology* (1962), found that PHT had definite suppressing effects on muscle spasms in three patients with multiple sclerosis.

KUROIWA AND SHIBASAKI, *Folia Psychiatrica et Neurologica Japonica* (1968), found that PHT and/or carbamazepine were useful in suppressing the painful tonic spasms in four patients with multiple sclerosis.

The authors noted that, before PHT, a wide variety of drugs had been tried in all four cases, without success. (See also Ref. 1541.)

WEINTRAUB, MEGAHED AND SMITH, *New York State Journal of Medicine* (1970) describe three patients with multiple sclerosis presenting with spasticity affecting the flexor muscles of the forearm.

In two patients, the use of PHT resulted in increased strength and ability to move the extremities. In the third case quinine resulted in slight improvement in strength.

BERGER, SHEREMATA AND MELAMED, *Archives of Neurology* (1984), report the use of PHT in the treatment of four patients in whom paroxysmal dystonia was the initial manifestation of multiple sclerosis. Three of the patients had a good response to PHT.

HYPOCALCEMIA

SCHAAF AND PAYNE, *New England Journal of Medicine* (1966), studied the effect of PHT and phenobarbital in ten patients with overt and latent tetany. Phenobarbital was relatively ineffective alone. PHT eliminated tetany, tetanic equivalents and a strongly positive Trousseau test in six of these patients with hypocalcemia due to hypoparathyroidism or pseudo-hypoparathymidism. PHT was also effective in one patient with hypocalcemia and hypomagnesemia due to malabsorption. Chvostek's sign became negative in five of these patients. Serum calcium, phosphorus and magnesium were unchanged by treatment. PHT was not effective in three patients with idiopathic latent tetany.

The authors cited extensive studies that have confirmed that calcium is a critical stabilizer of neuromuscular membranes. In their study they found that PHT in doses therapeutic in man can counteract the increased nervous excitability in hypocalcemic patients.

TETANUS

RODRIGUEZ, PEREZ, QUINTERO, HERNANDEZ, MACIAS, CHAPA AND ANDRADE, *European Journal of Clinical Investigation* (1984), reported that intravenous PHT was rapidly effective as antispasm therapy in eighteen patients with severe tetanus. Substantial amounts of PHT were used in combination with the usual antibacterial and antitoxin measures.

After the spasms were under control, the patients were watched, carefully, twenty-four hours a day, and additional intravenous PHT was given promptly to keep the spasms under control.

The authors noted that PHT did not sedate the patients or depress respiratory function, as did other drugs they used to control spasms, and the need for respiratory support was decreased. No cardiovascular, sympathetic or autonomic disturbances, frequently seen in these patients, occurred. Compared with the authors' experience, tetanus-related mortality decreased markedly, as did hospitalization time.

Additional unpublished data from Mexico, Brazil and India give further indication of the usefulness of PHT against this disease. It is reported that large amounts of intravenous PHT may be needed in the acute stage (1500 mg a day or more in an adult is not unusual). Dosage depends on patient condition. When contractions recur, more PHT is indicated promptly. Later, when the bacteria and toxin are under control, less PHT should be needed.

It is reported that PHT can be used in combination with other medications commonly used in the treatment of tetanus.

TREATMENT OF PAIN

Summary

Phenytoin has been found effective in the treatment of so many types of pain that it is useful as a general pain medication. PHT's usefulness in pain is enhanced by the fact that it is not sedative and it is not habit-forming. It can be used alone or in combination with narcotics and other pain medications.

PHT's first use in pain, for trigeminal neuralgia, was reported in 1942 by Bergouignan. Since then, PHT has been reported useful for facial and head pain, including trigeminal and glossopharyngeal neuralgia; peripheral nerve neuralgias and neuropathic pain, including that of polyneuritis, late-stage syphillis, diabetic neuropathy, Fabry's disease, and post-herpetic and post-sympathectomy pain states; migraine and other headache; post-operative pain; phantom limb pain; pain of skeletal muscle spasms; post-stroke pain; and pain caused by malignant disease.

In recent years, used topically, in addition to speeding healing, PHT has been shown to rapidly decrease pain of ulcers, burns and wounds.

Initial messages of pain are necessary protective mechanisms. PHT does not interfere with these initial bioelectrical impulses, but it does reduce repetitive neuronal activity, as in post-tetanic (repetitive) afterdischarge.

Trigeminal Neuralgia

BERGOUIGNAN, *Revue de Laryngologie* (1942), reported the complete cure of essential facial neuralgia in three patients treated with PHT, 200–300 mg/day.

BERGOUIGNAN AND D'AULNAY, *Revue d'Oto-Neuro-Ophtalmologie* (1951), reported on the treatment with PHT of seventeen patients with trigeminal neuralgia. On PHT therapy, 300–600 mg/day, sixteen were benefited.

The rapidity of the drug's action was noted. The effects usually were felt within twenty-four hours.

JENSEN, *Arztliche Wochenschrift* (1954), reported on the use of PHT, 300–600 mg/day, in treating forty-five cases of trigeminal neuralgia. Sixteen patients showed complete cessation of pain, which lasted after discontinuance of PHT. Nineteen patients experienced distinct improvement during PHT treatment. Pain recurred when PHT was withdrawn. Four patients showed slight improvement and five patients did not improve.

The author pointed out the desirability of PHT to relieve pain, as opposed to the potent pain relievers and opiates which all too easily lead to addiction.

JENSEN, *Therapiewoche* (1955), in a subsequent study of fifty-nine typical cases of trigeminal neuralgia treated with PHT, reported that fifty-seven were completely freed of pain. Twenty remained so after medication was discontinued; but with thirty-seven, pain returned when PHT was withdrawn. Only two cases showed no improvement.

WINIKER-BLANCK, *Deutsche Stomatologie* (1955), reported that of twenty-seven cases of genuine trigeminal neuralgia treated with PHT, 300–600 mg/day, fifteen remained completely free of pain and seven showed lasting improvement making the condition entirely bearable for the patient. After the pain was under control, the patients were maintained on 100 mg/day.

Because of its safety, PHT therapy was recommended as the treatment of choice.

ENDE, *Virginia Medical Monthly* (1957), reported that over a period of two years he had successfully treated nine consecutive cases of trigeminal neuralgia with PHT.

The author found that not only was PHT effective, but frequently relief began with the first capsule. These patients had been subjected previously to nearly every form of therapy recommended.

BERGOUIGNAN, *Revue Neurologique* (1958), reported that twenty-six of thirty patients who had been treated for trigeminal neuralgia were relieved of their attacks during the first three days of treatment with PHT. Ten of these patients had previously had peripheral or deep alcohol injections with transient or incomplete results and two had neurotomy.

IANNONE, BAKER AND MORRELL, *Neurology* (1958), reported that with PHT definite relief of pain was obtained and paroxysms of pain were controlled in all of four patients with trigeminal neuralgia and one with glossopharyngeal neuralgia.

LAMBERTS, *Journal of the Michigan State Medical Society* (1959), reported on thirty patients with trigeminal neuralgia treated with PHT, 200–400 mg/day. In almost every instance relief from pain was complete within forty-eight hours, but usually not before twenty-four hours after treatment commenced. The dosage had to be increased in two of the patients before the pain disappeared.

KUGELBERG AND LINDBLOM, *Journal of Neurology, Neurosurgery and Psychiatry* (1959), in a study of fifty patients with trigeminal neuralgia, investigated the relationship between stimuli applied to the trigger zone and the pain paroxysm. Intravenous PHT, 3–5 mg/kg, was found to raise the attack threshold as well as to shorten the duration of the attack.

BRAHAM AND SAIA, *Lancet* (1960), used PHT, 300 mg/day, in twenty cases of trigeminal neuralgia. Relief of pain was complete in eight and partial in six.

REEVE, *Lancet* (1961), reported that PHT was effective in nine cases of trigeminal neuralgia and recommended that a trial of PHT precede more radical treatment.

LINDBLOM, *Svensk Lakartidningen* (1961), reported that of thirty cases of trigeminal neuralgia treated with PHT, 300–600 mg/day, complete relief or considerable reduction of the symptoms occurred in seventeen cases. Improvement lasted as long as the drug was administered.

BAXI, *Antiseptic* (1961), reported that eleven of fifteen patients with trigeminal neuralgia, treated with PHT, obtained relief within a week.

The author stated that PHT not only gave lasting relief of pain but also relieved the apprehension of an impending attack.

VON ALBERT, *Munschener Medizinische Wochenschrift* (1978), reported on twelve cases of typical trigeminal neuralgia and two cases of glossopharyngeal neuralgia. Neither oral carbamazepine nor PHT had produced sufficient results. However, intravenous PHT, in some cases up to 750 mg over three to six hours, followed by oral PHT (200–400 mg/day), achieved freedom from pain in the fourteen patients. It was not found effective in four patients with herpetic neuralgia.

VON ALBERT, *Advances in Epileptology* (1983), reviewing eight years experience with PHT, states that intravenous PHT is very effective, not sedative, has only mild side effects, and is the therapy of choice for trigeminal neuralgia in elderly patients.

Glossopharyngeal Neuralgia

KONG, HEYMAN, ENTMAN AND MCINTOSH, *Circulation* (1964), reported the successful use of PHT in treating a patient who had been suffering for ten years with glossopharyngeal neuralgia associated with disturbances of cardiac and cerebral function.

At the time of admission to hospital the patient was experiencing between ten and twenty attacks a day. Treatment with 500 mg PHT a day completely relieved the pain. On 300 mg/day the patient remained symptom-free.

LEE, LEE AND TSAI, *Journal of Formosan Medical Association* (1975), reported the successful use of PHT in treating a case of glossopharyngeal neuralgia. The paroxysms of pain, about thirty a day, were so unbearable that the patient was afraid to swallow or talk. On 400 mg PHT a day the patient became symptom-free.

RUSHTON, STEVENS AND MILLER, *Archives of Neurology* (1981), reported eighteen patients with glossopharyngeal neuralgia, who were treated with PHT. Four patients had good relief for periods up to several months. Five additional patients had good relief, sufficient to avoid surgery.

See also Refs. 2978, 3056.

Migraine and Other Headaches

SHAPERA, *Pittsburgh Medical Bulletin* (1940), reported that two of four cases of migraine were improved with PHT.

MCCULLAGH AND INGRAM, *Diseases of the Nervous System* (1956), in their paper "Headaches and Hot Tempers," reported that their experience showed that PHT was by far the most useful medication in the treatment of a syndrome in which migraine headaches were related to familial cerebral dysrhythmias.

KELLAWAY, CRAWLEY AND KAGAWA, *Epilepsia* (1959–1960), in a report on 459 children, found PHT one of the drugs of choice in the treatment of headache accompanied by 14- and 6-per-second positive spike patterns.

HIRSCHMANN, *Therapeutische Umschau* (1964), reported on a study of forty-four patients with migraine not relieved by ergot preparations alone. Of these, thirty-two remained in treatment. When they were treated with a combination of PHT, caffeine and ergot, nineteen were either completely relieved or had less frequent or milder attacks.

WIEDEMANN, *Medizinische Monatsschrift* (1966), in a series of studies on migraine, found preparations containing PHT and caffeine useful in the treatment of a variety of neuralgias and cephalalgias. This treatment was particularly suitable for patients with true migraine and trigeminal neuralgia.

JONAS, *Headache* (1967), administered PHT to eighteen migraine sufferers. Nine patients afflicted with paroxysmal migraine experienced complete relief. Of six non-paroxysmal patients, four benefited by the use of PHT.

CAPLAN, WEINER, WEINTRAUB, AUSTEN, *Headache (1976),* reported the successful use of PHT in the treatment of a fifty-five-year-old male patient with neurological dysfunction accompanied by classic migraine headaches following cardiac surgery.

The patient was experiencing episodes of neurological dysfunction manifested by tingling, numbness, weakness and pain in the hands, arms, thighs and face, inability at times to find words, slow speech, and dysarthria with repetitive speech.

With PHT, 100 mg t.i.d., no further episodes occurred. On follow-up three years later, the patient continued to do well on PHT.

MILLICHAP, *Child's Brain* (1978), found PHT effective in relieving severe recurrent headaches associated with other symptoms, including nausea, vomiting, dizziness and vertigo, in forty-seven of seventy children.

SWANSON AND VICK, *Neurology* (1978), treated three cases of basilar artery migraine with PHT, 300 mg daily. In two cases the attacks were completely relieved. In the third case the frequency and severity of the attacks were reduced.

Post-Stroke or Brain Injury

FINE, *British Medical Journal* (1967), reported five patients with post-stroke hemiplegia and pain in part or all of the affected side of the body. Three of the patients received PHT alone, one received a combination of PHT and phenobarbital, and one phenobarbital alone. All responded dramatically with complete resolution of pain.

CANTOR, *British Medical Journal* (1972), reports two patients with thalamic pain who experienced good relief with PHT.

The author states that the treatment of the painful, burning dysesthesias, which can occur after thalamic infarction, has been a particularly vexing problem, in that a variety of drugs have been tried with variable but generally ineffective results.

The author reports that in each of the cases, when PHT treatment was stopped, the painful dysesthesia

recurred. Reinstitution of PHT again resulted in alleviation of the pain.

MLADINICH, *JAMA* (1974), reported successful use of PHT for relief of facial pain associated with Wallenberg syndrome.

A forty-year-old man was afflicted with ipsilateral burning facial pain around the eye. Ordinary analgesics did not relieve this pain. PHT, 1000 mg in divided doses the first day and then 300 mg daily, was tried. Symptoms of facial pain were considerably relieved within several days.

AGNEW AND GOLDBERG, *Bulletin of the Los Angeles Neurological Societies* (1976), tried PHT in a group of ten patients with chronic, severe, intractable thalamic pain, unresponsive to previous treatment. Three patients were markedly improved and two were slightly improved.

Other Pain and Neuralgias

DIABETIC NEUROPATHY

ELLENBERG, *New York State Journal of Medicine* (1968), in a study of sixty diabetic patients, reported that PHT was effective in the treatment of pain and paresthesias associated with neuropathy. Good to excellent results were observed in forty-one, fair results in ten, and none were worse.

KANNAN, DASH AND RASTOGI, *Journal of Diabetic Association of India*

(1978), in a double-blind crossover study of sixteen patients with diabetic neuropathy, found that thirteen had significant relief of pain and/or paresthesia on 100 mg PHT t.i.d.

CHADDA AND MATHUR, *Journal of the Association of Phyicians in India* (1978), in a double-blind study with PHT found significant improvement in pain and paresthesia in twenty-eight of thirty-eight patients with diabetic neuropathy.

The authors conclude that PHT is an effective and well-tolerated drug for the relief of pain in diabetic neuropathy, and is preferable to narcotics.

FABRY'S DISEASE

LOCKMAN, HUNNINGHAKE, KRIVIT AND DESNICK, *Neurology* (1973), based on a double-blind study, report the effectiveness of PHT in the relief of the pain of Fabry's disease, a rare lipid storage disorder.

The authors state that the single most debilitating and morbid aspect of Fabry's disease is the pain. Excruciating crises of abdominal, chest and muscle pain, as well as arthralgias and fever, may occur episodically and last several days.

A double-blind crossover study with eight patients was conducted comparing PHT with aspirin and placebo. In the comparison, relief with PHT was statistically significant ($p < 0.001$).

The authors note that the pain in Fabry's disease is only partially relieved by narcotics at soporific doses.

DUPERRAT, PUISSANT, SAURAT, DELANOE, DOYARD AND GRUNFELS, *Annales de Dermatologie et de Syphiligraphie* (1975), described a twenty-three-year-old male patient who from birth had suffered from angiokeratomas and Fabry's disease. Pain progressed in intensity over the years. PHT (200 mg/day) resulted in complete disappearance of pain in less than a week. (See also Ref. 2352.)

DYSESTHESIA (PAINFUL TOUCHING)

GERZ, *Physicians' Drug Manual* (1972), reports an unusual case of "painful touching" (dysesthesia) in which a forty-year-old male patient showed dramatic response to PHT.

The patient reported that a painful, intolerable, cold stream would run all over his body when touched by human hands. Because of the extreme pain on being touched, he frequently became dangerous and violent, and wanted a certificate from the clinic stating that he suffered from a "mental problem."

He was tried on a variety of medications without success. Finally he was given PHT, 100 mg t.i.d. Within two weeks he was completely free of disturbing symptoms.

TABES

DATTNER, in the course of a discussion of a paper by CAVENESS, ADAMS, POPE AND WEGNER, *Transactions of the American Neurological Association* (1949), said that some patients with lightning pains in tabes showed a favorable response to PHT or Tridione.

BRAHAM AND SAIA, *Lancet* (1960), reported PHT effective in treating lightning pains in two cases of tabes.

GREEN, *Neurology* (1961), reported that PHT was administered to two patients with severe lightning pains due to tabes dorsalis. Remarkable relief was obtained in both cases.

POST-HERPETIC NEURALGIA

REEVE, *Lancet* (1961), reported that PHT was effective in four cases of post-herpetic neuralgia, and recommended that a trial of PHT precede more radical treatment.

HALLAQ AND HARRIS, *Journal of American Osteopathic Association* (1969), give a detailed report on the successful use of PHT in a case of post-herpetic neuralgia, with motor paralysis of an extremity, a rare complication. The patient, a seventy-six-year-old woman, had persistent pain in the right upper extremity, causing the entire limb to assume a semiflexed and adducted position. Diagnosis after examination was post-herpetic right brachial neuralgia and monoparesis.

After seven days in the hospital the patient was placed on PHT, 100 mg t.i.d. Within three days she was

free of pain and remained so when narcotic analgesics were withdrawn and an extra 100 mg of PHT was added. The patient continued free of pain as long as she took PHT.

REFRACTORY CHRONIC PAIN

Gabka, Medizinische Monatsschrift (1963), reported PHT (100–300 mg/day), combined with 0.025 g of caffeine, as the most effective treatment for the relief of pain in 115 out of 142 patients. The painful conditions included recurring headaches, migraine, genuine and symptomatic trigeminal neuralgia, postoperative jaw and facial pain, and pain following extensive facial tumor surgery.

The authors state that PHT was by far the best conservative therapy in the treatment of these types of recurring head and facial pain.

RASKIN, LEVINSON, PICKETT, HOFFMAN AND FIELDS, *American Journal of Surgery* (1974), as part of a larger study, reported that two of the patients with post-sympathectomy neuralgia, unresponsive to meperidine, had immediate relief with intravenous PHT.

TAGUCHI, WATANABE AND IOKU, *Neurologia Medico Chirurgica (Tokyo)* (1981), reported a patient with bulbar syringomyelia who developed severe, intractable pain and paresthesias in her legs, abdomen and chest after cervical laminectomy. She also developed muscle spasms of her upper body. PHT, 250 mg/day, stopped both the pain and muscle spasms.

SWERDLOW, *Clinical Neuropharmacology* (1984), reviewed a series of 200 patients with various types of refractory chronic lancinating or paroxysmal pain. The etiologies of the pain included post-laminectomy, post-traumatic, post-herpetic, post-operative, and post-amputation neuralgias, as well as pain secondary to nerve or plexus injury or operation, atypical facial pain, and central pain syndromes. Of fifty-two patients who received PHT as their first drug, twenty-four found it effective. This success rate was higher than that achieved with carbamazepine, clonazepam, and valproate.

PAIN IN MULTIPLE SCLEROSIS

MATTHEWS, *Brain* (1958), reported the effectiveness of PHT in the treatment of painful spasms in a patient with multiple sclerosis. When PHT, 100 mg t.i.d., was prescribed, the attacks stopped within two days.

KUROIWA AND SHIBASAKI, *Folia Psychiatrica et Neurologica Japonica* (1968), found that PHT and/or carbamazepine were useful in suppressing the painful tonic spasms in four patients with multiple sclerosis. In a further study, SHIBASAKI AND KUROIWA, *Archives of Neurology*

(1974), reported the successful treatment of five of seven patients with PHT alone or in combination with carbamazepine.

SKILLRUD AND GOLDSTEIN, *Journal of the American Medical Association* (1983), reported in detail the case of a twenty-seven-year-old male physician with multiple sclerosis and paroxysmal limb hemiataxia and crossed facial paresthesias who became symptom free on 500 mg of PHT per day.

CLIFFORD AND TROTTER, *Archives of Neurology* (1984), reviewing the records of 317 multiple sclerosis patients with a wide variety of painful syndromes and therapies, reported PHT's usefulness in the treatment of limb, facial, head, and thoracic pain.

ABDOMINAL PAIN

KELLAWAY, CRAWLEY AND KAGAWA, *Epilepsia* (1959–1960), in a review of experience with a group of 459 children who had consistent 14- and 6-per-second spike patterns on the EEG and whose primary complaints were headache and abdominal pain, found the most effective treatments were PHT and Diamox, alone or in combination.

PEPPERCORN, HERZOG, DICHTER AND MAYMAN, *JAMA* (1978), found PHT useful in the treatment of three patients with paroxysmal abdominal pain. When two of the patients stopped their medication, the symptoms returned. With the resumption of the medication, symptoms disappeared.

SCHAFFLER AND KARBOWSKI, *Schweizerische Medizinische Wochenschrift* (1981), reported six cases of paroxysmal abdominal pain occurring in association with cerebral dysrhythmias. PHT controlled or reduced the severity of the attacks in the four cases in which it was used alone. In one case, PHT, in combination with carbamazepine, was used successfully and, in another case, carbamazepine was used alone.

WOUNDS, ULCERS, BURNS

The topical use of PHT to promote healing of skin ulcers, burns and other wounds is reviewed in the Clinical Healing section. The important benefit of topical PHT, prompt relief of pain, is discussed here.

CHIKHANI, *Actualites Odonto-Stomatologiques* (1972), in a study of fifty-eight patients, with periodontal disease, reported the beneficial effects of topical PHT on gingival pain as well as bleeding.

LUDWIG AND OTTO, *Russian Pharmacology and Toxicology* (1982), in a controlled study of sixty patients with atrophic gingivitis, found topical

application of PHT (1% gel) controlled gum pain and heat sensitivity. Edema and gum bleeding disappeared. No effects were seen in the control group.

RODRIGUEZ-NORIEGA, ESPARZA-AHU-MADA, ANDRADE-PEREZ, ESPEJO-PLA-SCENCIA AND CHAPA-ALVAREZ, *Investigacion Médica Internacional* (1983), reported a group of twenty patients with venous stasis or diabetic ulcers treated with topical PHT powder. All patients experienced rapid improvement in local pain. In the control group, pain persisted until the lesion was completely healed.

MENDIOLA-GONZALES, ESPEJO-PLASCEN-CIA, CHAPA-ALVAREZ AND RODRIGUEZ-NORIEGA, *Investigacion Médica Internacional* (1983), reported a group of eighty patients with second-degree burns. Twenty patients were treated topically with PHT powder, ten with oral PHT, and ten with both topical and oral PHT. Bilateral burns provided control and treatment sites for the topical applications. Pain improved in five to twenty-five minutes at the treated sites, compared to twelve to fifteen hours at control sites.

Other clinical reviews and studies on the use of PHT in pain: facial pain including trigeminal neuralgia, glossopharyngeal neuralgia, and temporomandibular joint syndrome, Refs. 2470, 2472, 2492, 2523, 2593, 2619, 2801, 2847, 2943; headache including migraine, Refs. 2317, 2492; post-herpetic neuralgia, Refs. 2474, 2657; reflex sympathetic dystrophy and post-sympathectomy pain, Refs. 2492, 3040; pain in multiple sclerosis, Refs. 2601, 2929; central and other chronic pain syndromes, Refs. 2452, 2460, 2492, 2756, 2784, 2997.

HEALING

Summary

Phenytoin, used orally and/or topically, promotes healing. The healing properties of oral PHT were first reported by Bodkin in 1945 in an extensive study of pruritus ani. Subsequently, oral PHT has been reported useful in the treatment of periodontal disease, scleroderma, epidermolysis bullosa, peptic ulcers, and a variety of skin and soft tissue wounds and ulcers.

Topical PHT has been demonstrated to relieve the pain and promote the healing of chronic soft tissue ulcers, including venous stasis, diabetic and decubitus ulcers, and also burns. Recently, PHT has been found effective in healing the chronic trophic ulcers of leprosy.

Relief of pain with topical PHT is prompt, usually occurring in a matter of minutes.

Biopsies of PHT-treated ulcers show increased formation of new blood vessels and increased collagen content. In addition, the scar tissue that forms is more flexible in PHT-treated wounds. Extensive laboratory studies have shown that PHT accelerates the healing and tensile strength of various wounds and fractures, stimulates fibroblast proliferation, increases collagen synthesis, content, and maturation in granulation tissue, and inhibits collagenase and collagen peptidase activity.

Periodontal

SHAPIRO, *Experimental Medicine and Surgery* (1958), conducted a double-blind study of the effects of PHT on healing in patients with various degrees of periodontal disease. Thirty-three patients received oral PHT and nineteen received placebo.

Sections of gingiva were surgically removed and the wounds were covered with protective packs. When the packs were changed at the end of one week, the PHT-treated group exhibited less erythema, less pain and advanced wound healing. On histological section, there was marked acceleration of fibroblastic activity, clot organization, and epithelial proliferation as compared to the control group.

The author stated that PHT may be useful to increase the rate of wound healing in other areas of the body, as in burns.

SAVINI, POITEVIN AND POITEVIN, *Revue Francaise d'Odontostomatologie* (1972), presented a study of the use of PHT locally in the treatment of periodontal disease in 118 cases.

The authors examined the effect of PHT in a gingival paste-type ointment which was applied by the patient with massage to the gingival mucosa inside and outside after normal tooth brushing, morning and evening, and left for about five minutes before rinsing.

The findings were based both on the patient's observations and on physical examination, x-rays and, in forty-six cases, by biopsy.

With PHT, total resolution of pain occurred in most cases. Rapid regression of gingival bleeding and inflammation, increased healing, and decreased dental mobility were also seen. Although lesions were stabilized, there was no periodontal restoration.

The authors conclude that PHT is an effective aid in the treatment of periodontal disease.

PAYEN, *Revue d'Odontostomatologie du Midi de la France* (1972), studied the effect of a topical preparation of PHT for gingival massage in seventy-five patients with periodontal disease. Twenty-nine of the patients were hospitalized and forty-six were outpatients.

With PHT, decreased inflammation and increased production of collagen in the healing process were observed in twenty of the hospitalized patients and in forty-five of the outpatients.

CHIKHANI, *Actualites Odontostomatologiques* (1972), in a study of fifty-eight patients, reported clinical and histological effects of daily PHT gingival massage in periodontopathies. The author states that the study demonstrates the beneficial effect of PHT, particularly on bleeding gums and on pain; and histological findings confirmed the fibroblastic action of PHT and the healing with sclerosis which accompanied the decrease in inflammatory infiltration.

The author states that beneficial effects were clear after forty to sixty days of treatment.

GOEBEL, *Journal of Oral Surgery* (1972), reported a controlled study of the effects of PHT, before and after surgery, on wound healing of extraction sockets. As controls, eighteen patients were given chlorpromazine, and fifteen were untreated.

Compared with controls, significant improvement was observed in wound healing in the nine patients who received PHT.

OTTO, LUDEWIG AND KOTZSCHKE, *Stomatologie der DDR* (1977), in a double-blind study, treated eighty patients with complex periodontal disease with a local application of PHT gel. Compared with the control group, there was marked subjective and objective improvement in the group treated with PHT.

LUDEWIG AND OTTO, *Russian Pharmacology and Toxicology* (1982), studied the effects of topical PHT in the treatment of atrophic gingivitis. Sixty patients were divided into three groups. Two groups were treated with topical PHT in a 1% gel applied twice a day for six and twelve weeks, respectively. A third group was treated with the gel alone and served as control.

The PHT-treated patients ceased to complain of gum pain and heat sensitivity. Edema and gum bleeding disappeared. On biopsy, improvement was evidenced by decrease in inflammatory infiltration and regeneration of connective tissue. No benefits were seen in the control group.

CARIES

APTON, *Dental Hygiene* (1977), conducted a study to determine if there was a difference in the incidence of decayed, missing and filled surfaces of teeth (DMFS) in patients with PHT therapy, versus those without it.

The author compared the incidence of DMFS in forty-five patients taking PHT for at least one year with national statistics from HEW as controls.

Acknowledging that the study was imperfectly controlled, and complicated by the introduction of fluoride, the author says that there was enough evidence that PHT was effective against DMFS to recommend that further work be done in this field.

The author's recommendation is supported by the controlled laboratory study of ROVIN, et al. in which it was found that PHT was useful against caries in mice (see Basic Mechanism studies).

Ulcers

SIMPSON, KUNZ AND SLAFTA, *New York State Journal of Medicine*

(1965), reported that PHT promoted the healing of leg ulcers. The study contained double-blind and crossover controls.

Thirty hospitalized psychiatric patients (age range forty to seventy-seven years) were chosen for the project. The sole criterion for the patient selection was that all had chronic leg ulceration. The ulcers had been present for from two to fifteen years. Occasional healing had taken place but this was minimal and most of the patients had an area of ulceration present at all times despite the fact that they received standard topical treatment and occasional bed rest.

Repeated measurements were carried out under double-blind conditions. Measurements were made by means of a planimeter reading of the ulcer area as well as the actual scaling area around the ulcer. A clinical rating was also given.

All three indices measured showed improvement in the PHT group compared with the placebo group. Statistical analysis of the actual ulcer areas demonstrated a difference at better than the 0.05 level of significance between the two groups.

Small doses such as 200 mg a day were found to be associated with better healing than were larger doses.

STREAN, *Chemical Abstracts* (1966), reported PHT effective in promoting the complete healing of an antecubital ulcer, a diabetic ulcer and two peptic ulcers, all of long duration. It was found that PHT provided for the regeneration of healthy tissue in the denuded zone.

TAYLOR, *Personal Communication* (1969), reported a twenty-four-year-old patient with typical oral and genital ulcerations of Behçet's syndrome. The patient also had involvement of the temporomandibular joints (Costen's syndrome). Clenching the jaw produced pain typical of the syndrome. In addition, she suffered with conjunctivitis, urethritis, vaginitis and arthritis.

By the sixth day, with treatment with PHT, 100 mg/day, the ulcerated areas had healed and all other symptoms disappeared. The patient remained symptom-free when seen five months later.

RODRIGUEZ-NORIEGA, ESPARZA-AHUMADA, ANDRADE-PEREZ, ESPEJO-PLASCENCIA AND CHAPA-ALVAREZ, *Investigacion Médica Internacional* (1983), studied forty patients with venous stasis, diabetic and other soft tissue ulcers. They compared the use of PHT, topically, in twenty patients with conventional treatment in a control group of twenty patients. The average time to healing or grafting in the PHT-treated group was twenty-one days, compared to forty-five days in the control group.

Biopsy of the PHT-treated ulcers showed more rapid infiltration of fibroblasts and greater collagen deposition, as well as increased new blood vessel formation. Bacterial cultures of the ulcer surface improved more rapidly, and more stable scar formation was also seen in the PHT group. (See also Ref. 2690).

BARBA RUBIO, *Presented at the XII Mexican Congress of Dermatology* (1985), presented a report on the use of topical PHT in the treatment of trophic lower extremity ulcers in seven leprosy patients.

The ulcers were chronic and had been refractory to previous forms of treatment for up to fifteen years.

With PHT, three of the patients had complete healing of their ulcers within six weeks. The remaining four patients had good results consisting of diminished exudate, appearance of healthy granulation tissue, reduction in ulcer size, and suitability for skin grafting.

Burns

MENDIOLA-GONZALEZ, ESPEJO-PLAS-CENCIA, CHAPA-ALVAREZ AND ROD-RIGUEZ-NORIEGA, *Investigacion Médica Internacional* (1983), reported the topical use of PHT powder in the treatment of second-degree burns. The study included eighty patients. Forty, given conventional treatment, were used as controls. Twenty were treated with topical PHT, ten with oral PHT, and ten with a combination of topical and oral PHT.

In the control group, the average time to healing or grafting was thirty days. In the oral PHT group, it was twenty-three days. In the topical group and the combined treatment group, the time to healing or grafting was sixteen days.

Topical PHT resulted in rapid elimination of pain at the burn site. Biopsy of the PHT-treated burns showed increased collagen, decreased inflammation, and more capillaries compared to controls. Bacterial burn-surface cultures in the PHT groups became negative after five to ten days of treatment. The bacterial cultures remained positive in the conventional treatment group, until healing or grafting.

Pruritus Ani

BODKIN, *American Journal of Digestive Diseases* (1945), described the successful treatment of forty-one of forty-two cases of pruritus ani upon the addition of PHT to oral therapy.

In this series of forty-two cases, only one showed no improvement and another recovered rather slowly. Almost all of the others responded in a surprisingly short time.

The author stated that, "Pruritus ani has always been a difficult and baffling problem to the proctologist . . . It is notable for its chronicity and resistance to treatment. No one form of therapy has been effective, as is evidenced by the lengthy list of measures employed. It is therefore most interesting to come upon a method of treatment, mainly oral, that gives prompt symptomatic relief and which produces clearly visible results in the skin. It is aimed at the most likely site of origin of the condition—the nervous system . . . The one definite and positive finding that stood out in all the cases that I have carefully studied for the past ten years or more was this: every one of them was highly nervous."

The duration of the symptoms in the group studied was from one to thirty years and included three cases that also had pruritus vulvae. The author had previously used taka-diastase, novatropin and pheno-barbital. When PHT was added, the results were rather striking. Even long standing cases obtained marked symptomatic relief within a few days.

GOODWIN, *Journal of the National Proctologic Association* (1946), described the successful treatment of twenty cases of pruritus ani treated with PHT and a starch digestant. The results obtained were superior to any therapy previously employed. The author stated that this study confirmed the work of BODKIN.

Length of treatment varied. Usually the physical signs of bleeding, maceration, leathery appearance, moist skin, fissures, cracked skin and itching began to disappear from one to three weeks after institution of therapy. The patients usually volunteered before they were examined that they were much better after two or three weeks' treatment.

One severe case of pruritus was observed in which there was ex-tensive maceration and bleeding of the anus, scrotum and groin. So intense was the pruritus that nothing seemed of value in bringing even temporary relief. With PHT and a starch digestant, the patient showed marked improvement to the point that treatment was discontinued at the end of six weeks.

Recurrence was observed in one patient. Reestablishing treatment effected prompt relief.

In the author's experience the rapid relief of symptoms acheived with PHT had not been obtained with the use of any local treatment.

BODKIN, *American Journal of Digestive Diseases* (1947), in an expanded series of 111 cases of pruritus ani, again reported excellent results with PHT. Of the 111 cases treated, only six failed to respond. Five patients discontinued medication and their outcome was unknown.

The author stated that it was a pleasant surprise to find that recurrences were not too numerous and that they were rather easily controlled by reinstitution of PHT.

Scleroderma

MORGAN, *Cutis* (1971), reports that patients with scleroderma, treated with PHT, showed marked improvement when compared with patients treated by conventional therapy.

The study consisted of sixty-five patients with two general types of scleroderma, morphea and systemic. Twenty-nine were treated with PHT and thirty-six were treated by conventional means.

The attention of the author was brought to the use of PHT in scleroderma in an unusual way. A sixty-seven-year-old woman had progressive generalized morphea. For over a year, a wide variety of medications had been tried and failed to halt progression of the disease. Then the patient had a mild stroke and was placed on PHT by her neurologists. Progressive improvement in scleroderma was evident three weeks after she began PHT. Two years later her skin showed no evidence of scleroderma and has remained clear to date.

Because of the unexpected improvement in this case, the author decided to explore the possibility that PHT might be effective in the treatment of scleroderma. In his study the author used PHT in twenty-nine patients and conventional therapy in thirty-six patients. The results follow:

	With PHT	Other Therapy
No. of Patients	29	36
Worse	0	11
No change	2	10
Improved (patient and doctor agree)	12	9
Complete clearing of sclerosis	12	4
Complete clearing of sclerosis, atrophy and pigment	3	2

The author concludes that in this series of patients with scleroderma, the administration of PHT appeared not only to prevent progression of sclerosis but also to aid in its resolution.*

* In a smaller group of patients, the author also investigated the use of PHT in a less serious disorder, lichen sclerosis et atrophicus, and found PHT as effective as conventional therapy.

Localized Linear Scleroderma

NELDNER, Cutis (1978), reported significant reversal of localized linear scleroderma in five patients treated with 100–300 mg PHT daily.

The duration of the disease prior to PHT treatment was one to sixteen years. Morbidity included arthralgia and joint stiffness, decreased range of motion, gait disturbances, inability to grasp or throw, alopecia, headache, neuralgias, and neuroses. The most distressing complication was that of deep atrophy beyond the area of linear sclerosis, which produced facial hemiatrophy or atrophy of an entire limb with varying degrees of permanent joint fixation and deep sclerotic bands underlying cutaneous hyperpigmentation.

The author states that the response to PHT treatment, and the recurrence of the condition when PHT was prematurely discontinued, point towards the true pharmacologic effect of PHT in the treatment of this disorder.

See also Refs. 1729, 2097, 2297, 2360, 2784, 2953, 3030.

Epidermolysis Bullosa

EISENBERG, STEVENS AND SCHOFIELD, *Australian Journal of Dermatology* (1978), studied the effects of PHT on the collagenolytic system in tissue samples from patients with dystrophic epidermolysis bullosa. The collagenolytic system is known to be excessive in this disorder. PHT was found to inhibit the excessive activity.

As a result of these findings, two children with dystrophic epidermolysis bullosa were given PHT. Marked improvement in skin fragility resulted. The authors concluded that the clinical effects of PHT on both blister formation and collagenase activity are consistent with the protective effect observed *in vitro* and suggested that PHT is useful in the management of this disease.

BAUER, COOPER, TUCKER AND ESTERLY, *The New England Journal of Medicine* (1980), citing the work of EISENBERG, STEVENS AND SCHOFIELD, studied the effect of PHT on the collagenolytic system *in vitro,* and clinically in seventeen patients with recessive dystrophic epidermolysis bullosa.

With PHT there was a significant decrease in blistering in all patients. In twelve patients the reduction was from 46% to 90%. The clinical study was controlled in that all patients underwent a period without PHT during which they experienced a notable exacerbation in blistering.

The authors state that the correlation of the clinical responsiveness and *in vitro* inhibition of collagenase indicates that PHT represents a therapeutic option of relatively low risk in a disease for which there has been no rational method of therapy.

BAUER AND COOPER, *Archives of Dermatology* (1981), reported an extended study (76 to 99 weeks) of nine patients with moderate or severe recessive dystrophic epidermolysis bullosa. In seven of the nine patients, the decrease in blisters and erosion with PHT was 70%. In the other two patients, blistering decreased 24% to 40%. (See also Refs. 2176, 2188, 2247.)

BANDMANN AND PERWEIN, *Zeitschrift fur Hautkrankheiten* (1982), in a detailed case report, describe a patient with the rare Gedde-Dahl type of epidermolysis bullosa, with severe blistering, erosions, and dysphagia due to esophageal stenosis.

With PHT, fewer blisters developed, and blisters and erosions already present healed more quickly. (See also Ref. 2863.)

WIRTH, NESCH, OSTAPOWICZ AND ANTON-LAMPRECHT, *Zeitschrift fur Hautkrankheiten* (1983), state that they have used oral PHT in the treatment of eleven patients with recessive dystrophic epidermolysis bullosa (Hallopeau-Siemens and

Inversa type) since 1978. The authors detail six of their cases, ages six weeks to sixty-one years. Treatment with PHT, at blood levels of 8–15 µg/ml, resulted in definite reduction in blistering and lessened skin fragility.

The authors report that four of their patients had esophageal stenosis, one with complete obstruction. With PHT, improvement was such that esophageal dilation could be performed in all four.

COOPER AND BAUER, *Archives of Dermatology* (1984), studied the effects of PHT in twenty-two patients with recessive dystrophic epidermolysis bullosa. Therapeutic response was defined as mean decrease in blistering of more than 40%. The authors stated that, with this strict criterion, fourteen of the twenty-two patients had 46% or more reduction of blistering. PHT, 100–300 mg/day, was adjusted to maintain blood levels of at least 8 µg/ml.

To determine if prolonged treatment altered response, nine of the patients were studied for periods longer than seventy-five weeks. Seven of these patients continued to have a mean decrease in blistering of at least 40%.

The authors noted that with PHT patients had an enhanced sense of well-being.

See Refs. 2247, 2491, 2532, 2546, 2560, 2602, 2617, 2643, 2658, 2793, 2818, 2876, 3009, 3087. Also, regulatory effect of PHT on collagen synthesis and breakdown, Refs. 172, 501, 502, 811, 1867, 1882, 2107, 2571, 2581.

Pachyonychia

BLANK, *British Journal of Dermatology* (1982), reported his experience with PHT in treating a patient with pachyonychia.

The patient had been incapacitated by blisters and erosions of her feet and hands, and painful lesions in her mouth.

She was treated with oral PHT with dramatic results. She became able to walk for many blocks. Although many of the hyperkeratotic lesions persisted, her mouth and hands were greatly improved. After three years of this treatment she felt so well that she planned to marry.

TREATMENT OF OTHER DISORDERS

Asthma

The three papers which follow furnish strong evidence that phenytoin is useful in asthma.

Consistent with these findings are basic mechanism studies which show PHT's ability to relax bronchial smooth muscle, to regulate the autonomic nervous system, and to prevent the effects of hypoxia.

SHULMAN, *New England Journal of Medicine* (1942), selected seven cases of severe bronchial asthma, which were considered intractable because they had not responded to conventional treatment. These cases were treated with PHT. In a detailed study the author reported marked relief of asthma in six of seven cases and partial relief in the seventh.

In this study PHT was used exclusively and was not begun until all other medications were eliminated. With the application of PHT six of the patients were consistently free of attacks of bronchial asthma and the seventh showed some improvement. Two of the patients had stubborn eczema which cleared to a remarkable degree with PHT.

The author notes that the efficacy of PHT was further evidenced by the fact that the patients were able to successfully engage in situations and environments which formerly precipitated attacks of bronchial asthma.

SAYER AND POLVAN, *Lancet* (1968), described sixteen patients with bronchial asthma, with frequent asthmatic crises. Fourteen had abnormal EEGs and two had EEGs within normal limits.

All patients were taken off other medications and given PHT for an average of forty-five days. Ten patients were closely followed up during this period. Seven had neither asthmatic crises nor wheezing. One patient had occasional wheezing and in the other two cases the frequency of crises was greatly diminished.

SHAH, VORA, KARKHANIS AND TALWALKAR, *Indian Journal of Chest Diseases* (1970), conducted a study of the usefulness of PHT in bronchial asthma in twenty-seven patients. Both clinical and laboratory observations were made.

The authors state that the prevention of the spread of electrical discharge is one of the most important, interesting and unexploited pharmacological properties of PHT. Noting that other paroxysmal disorders have responded to PHT, they felt that its use in the paroxysmal spasms of asthma should be explored.

In the study of the twenty-seven patients, careful histories were recorded, including the severity of asthma, graded by age at onset, frequency of attacks during past twelve months, absenteeism from work, number of days absent in the last month, and number of sleepless nights in the last month.

Effort tolerance tests were performed during and between attacks. Appraisal of previous therapy during the last month was noted by the number of adrenaline and/or aminophylline injections and oral drugs (bronchodilators and steroids). Each patient had laboratory investigations, chest x-ray and electrocardiogram to exclude any cardiopulmonary disease simulating bronchial asthma. Venti- lation studies, including maximum breathing capacity, were carried out initially and repeated at weekly follow-up examinations. At the end of the treatment period all examinations were repeated.

Before starting patients on PHT all other medicines were discontinued. Dosage was 100 mg PHT t.i.d. The trial was for one month. Assessment of subjective and objective results was verified by all participating physicians.

While on PHT, twenty-five of the twenty-seven patients experienced impressive relief. Fifteen of these patients showed improved ventilation tests. Although some wheezing persisted in twelve patients, the distress was less evident. As a whole, the patients were more relaxed.

The results of this study led the authors to suggest that PHT would seem to be a useful anti-asthmatic agent.*

* *A number of people with emphysema have reported to the Dreyfus Medical Foundation that since taking PHT for other reasons they had experienced improvement in their breathing. We are not aware of published work on the use of PHT for emphysema. It would seem an area for research. (See Anti-anoxic Effects of PHT—Basic Mechanisms of Action.)*

Gastrointestinal Disorders

IRRITABLE BOWEL SYNDROME

CHADDA, JOSHI AND CHADDA, *Journal of the Association of Physicians in India* (1983), reported a randomized double-blind crossover trial of PHT (100 mg t.i.d.) versus placebo in twenty-five patients with irritable bowel syndrome. Seven had spastic colitis; eight, alternating diarrhea and constipation; and ten, mucous colitis. Twenty-two of the patients also suffered abdominal pain. Trials were for three weeks each, with a ten-day drug-free interval between crossover.

Improvement was observed in twelve of the patients while on PHT. Five improved in the placebo group.

DE LA TORRE, NAVARRO AND ALDRETE, *Current Therapeutic Research* (1985), compared PHT with conventional treatment in a study of eighty patients with irritable bowel syndrome. Forty patients received PHT, 100 mg t.i.d., and forty patients received an anticholinergic, an antacid, and either a tranquilizer or an antidepressant.

With PHT, thirty of the forty patients had an excellent to satisfactory response, compared to eighteen in the group that received conventional treatment.

Abdominal pain, diarrhea, constipation, nausea, vomiting and pyrosis were among the symptoms that responded. In addition, PHT treatment resulted in a statistically significant greater number of complete remissions of depression, insomnia and anxiety.

. . .

ULCERATIVE COLITIS

SCHAERRER, *Personal Communication* (1963), reported observations of forty-six patients with chronic idiopathic ulcerative colitis. Nineteen patients responded to treatment with PHT, 150–300 mg/day. Patients were classified as responding only if they remained symptom-free for a period of at least one year. All patients responding to PHT returned to normal or near-normal bowel habits, had a normal mucosal pattern, and gained weight.

DIABETIC DIARRHEA

THOMAS AND VERGES, *La Presse Medicale* (1985), report the use of PHT (300 mg daily) to treat severe motor diarrhea in five diabetic patients. The patients had been insulin-dependent for two to seventeen years and had advanced neuropathy. With PHT the diarrhea ceased in all five patients within twenty-four to forty-eight hours.

The effectiveness of PHT was further established by the fact that the diarrhea recurred in four patients when PHT was stopped and disappeared when PHT was given again.

With maintenance PHT treatment there were no relapses in the three-month to five-year follow-up.

See also Basic Mechanisms—Smooth Muscle.

Endocrine Disorders

PHT has been shown to influence endocrine function in a number of ways (see Metabolic and Endocrine Regulatory Effects). It modulates the hypothalamic and other neuronal systems that regulate pituitary function. It alters hormone release directly by its effects on calcium-dependent secretion processes, and can alter hormone metabolism and protein binding.

LABILE DIABETES

FABRYKANT AND PACELLA, *Annals of Internal Medicine* (1948), detailed the use of PHT in the treatment of three cases of labile diabetes. In each case, PHT stabilized insulin requirements and reduced negative reactions. In addition, the patients showed re-markable improvement in mood.

As a control, when PHT was discontinued for periods of from five to thirty-three days, the patients reverted to frequent reactions and nervousness.

WILSON, *Canadian Medical Association Journal* (1951), described three cases of labile diabetes whose control was unsatisfactory and not compatible with life outside the hospital. In all instances abnormal electro-encephalograms were found. Prior to PHT treatment, these patients presented extremely labile diabetes, characterized by frequent reactions, uncontrollable glycosuria, and personality changes.

The institution of PHT therapy resulted in a marked improvement in diabetic control and enabled these individuals to lead a relatively normal life, not necessitating a return to the hospital.

FABRYKANT, *Annals of Internal Medicine* (1953), again reported the effectiveness of PHT therapy in the management of labile diabetes associated with electrocerebral dysfunction. In this study of seven patients, five showed an appreciable diminution in the frequency and severity of insulin reactions along with a decrease in insulin requirement. This resulted in better control of diabetes and psychologic improvement. The other two patients did not adhere to therapy, but the author noted that in one case there was a marked improvement while on PHT. (See also Ref. 430.)

ROBERTS, *Journal of the American Geriatrics Society* (1964), reported an extensive study entitled, "The Syndrome of Narcolepsy and Diabetogenic ('Functional') Hyperinsulinism."

Although the use of PHT was not the major focus of his work, the author stated that with regard to the symptoms of labile diabetes his experiences with PHT confirm those of others who have observed clinical and electroencephalographic improvement following its administration.

AV RUSKIN, TIO AND JUAN, *Clinical Research* (1979), demonstrated that

PHT has a modulating effect on basal glucagon in eight type-1 juvenile diabetes mellitus patients. PHT lowered arginine-induced blood glucose and glucagon responses.

The authors suggest that PHT be considered as adjunctive therapy in diabetes mellitus when hyperglucagonemia is present.

See also Basic Mechanisms—Metabolic and Endocrine Regulatory Effects.

DIABETIC NEUROPATHY

ELLENBERG, *New York State Journal of Medicine* (1968), recognized the urgent need for a beneficial therapeutic agent in diabetic neuropathy and stated that this need was underscored by the frequent use of narcotics to control the severe pain, with the ever-present threat of addiction. The author noted that PHT was not addictive, did not sedate and, on the assumption that the symptoms of diabetic neuropathy might have a similar background to tic douloureux in which PHT was used with success, a therapeutic trial was undertaken.

PHT was used to treat painful diabetic peripheral neuropathy in sixty patients. Based on symptomatic relief of pain and paresthesias, excellent results were obtained in forty-one patients and fair response in ten patients. Improvement was noted in from twenty-four to ninety-six hours. As a feature of control, when the drug was discontinued, symptoms frequently recurred. A salutary response was uniformly repeated on reinstitution of PHT.

In two of the sixty cases skin rash occurred, one associated with fever. These reactions disappeared upon withdrawal of the medicine.

Nine years later, in *JAMA*, ELLENBERG repeated his recommendation of the use of PHT in the treatment of painful diabetic neuropathy, eliminating the use of narcotics.

KANNAN, DASH AND RASTOGI, *Journal of Diabetic Association of India* (1978), in a double-blind crossover study of sixteen patients with diabetic neuropathy, found that thirteen had significant relief of pain and/or paresthesias with 100 mg PHT t.i.d.

CHADDA AND MATHUR, *Journal of the Association of Physicians in India* (1978), in a double-blind study with PHT found significant improvement in pain and paresthesias in twenty-eight of thirty-eight patients with diabetic neuropathy.

The authors conclude that PHT is an effective and well-tolerated drug for the relief of pain in diabetic neuropathy, and is preferred to narcotics.

See also Treatment of Pain, p. 48.

·   ·   ·

HYPOGLYCEMIA

KNOPP, SHEININ AND FREINKEL, *Archives of Internal Medicine* (1972), reported that PHT inhibited the stimulated insulin release in a patient with an islet cell tumor. They noted that their observations indicate that PHT may warrant consideration as a safe therapeutic adjunct in inoperable or poorly controlled islet cell tumors.

COHEN, BOWER, FIDLER, JOHNSON-BAUGH AND SODE, *Lancet* (1973), reported the effect of PHT on a patient with a benign insulinoma. PHT was found effective in raising the mean fasting plasma glucose concentration and improved the immunoreactive insulin to glucose ratio.

The authors conclude that PHT appears to be a promising agent in the treatment of certain patients with insulinoma.

STAMBAUGH AND TUCKER, *Diabetes* (1974), describe the successful use of PHT in the treatment of five patients with functional hypoglycemia previously unresponsive to dietary management.

Clinical reversal of hypoglycemia, including marked improvement in mood and emotional stability, was observed in all five cases. Laboratory tests were confirmatory in both six-hour glucose tolerance and insulin level tests, performed before and after PHT therapy.

BRODOWS AND CAMPBELL, *Journal of Clinical Endocrinology and Metabolism* (1974), describe the successful control of refractory hypoglycemia with therapeutic doses of PHT in a patient with a suspected functional islet cell tumor. The authors state that the adequacy of the control of the hypoglycemia by PHT was evidenced by normal overnight fasting glucose levels and the absence of hypoglycemia during total fasting up to twenty-four hours. They note that it is of interest that there was a high degree of correlation between post-absorptive glucose and serum PHT levels and also a significant lowering of basal insulin levels during PHT therapy.

HOFELDT, DIPPE, LEVIN, KARAM, BLUM AND FORSHAM, *Diabetes* (1974), reported on the use of PHT in three patients with surgically proven insulinomas, tested with oral and intravenous glucose.

The authors found that PHT had no significant effect on basal glucose or insulin values, but was useful in reducing insulin secretion after stimuli.

BRICAIRE, LUTON, WECHSLER, MESSING AND HALABY, *Annales de Medecine Interne* (1976), reported the successful use of PHT in a case of organic hypoglycemia due to insulinoma for a period of five months prior to surgical removal of tumor.

AGAPOVA AND MIKHALEV, *Therapeutic Archives* (1977), reported the control with PHT of hypoglycemia attacks in a patient with an adenoma of the pancreas during the preoperative period until the adenoma was surgically removed.

See also Refs. 2533, 2610, 2925, 2932.

CUSHING'S SYNDROME

STARKOVA, MAROVA, LEMESCHEVA, GONCHAROVA, ATAMANOVA AND SEDYKH, *Problemy Endokrinologii* (1972), studied fifteen patients with Cushing's syndrome given PHT, 300 mg per day, for a period of three weeks.

This treatment led to normalization of the urinary excretion of ketosteroids and of aldosterone and pregnanediol, and to a normalization of the content of 17-hydroxyketosteroids in blood. There was also an increase in the potassium content in blood. The rate of secretion of cortisol decreased for all patients.

The authors noted that all the patients displayed a reduction or normalization of blood pressure and body weight, and a decrease in headaches and in weakness. (See also Ref. 427.)

FRENKEL, SAFRONOVA, MAROVA AND LEMESHEVA, *Problemy Endokrinologii* (1976), treated nine Cushing's syndrome patients with PHT, 300 mg/day, for three weeks.

With PHT, reduction or normalization of blood pressure, decrease in headaches, decrease in fatigue, and reduction in excretion of 17-hydroxyketosteroids and ketosteroids were observed. In seven of the patients, there was also normalization of the EEG parameters, especially those indicating diencephalic disturbances.

INAPPROPRIATE ANTIDIURETIC HORMONE SYNDROME

LEE, GRUMER, BRONSKY AND WALDSTEIN, *Journal of Laboratory Clinical Medicine* (1961), using acute water loading as a diagnostic test for the inappropriate antidiuretic hormone (ADH) syndrome in hyponatremia, treated two patients with confirmed inappropriate ADH syndrome with intravenous PHT (250 mg).

Both patients showed an increase in free-water clearance. In one patient with tuberculous meningitis, a normal response to acute water loading was noted after one month of therapy.

FICHMAN, KLEEMAN AND BETHUNE, *Archives of Neurology* (1970), studied the effect of intravenous PHT on antidiuretic hormone (ADH) activity in six patients with inappropriate ADH syndrome. PHT markedly increased the excretion of a 20 ml/kg water load and markedly decreased minimum urine osmolality in four of the patients in three hours. Two of the patients with bronchogenic carcinoma did not respond.

The authors state that their data suggests that, in man, PHT affects water balance by inhibiting ADH release.

LANDOLT, *Acta Endocrinologica* (1974), reported an eight-year-old patient who, following surgery for craniopharyngioma, developed diabetes insipidus followed by inappropriate ADH secretion. Intravenous PHT resulted in an increase in urine output. Serum sodium values returned to normal and the patient became more alert. During a subsequent recurrence of inappropriate ADH secretion, PHT again increased the urine output.

The author concludes that PHT regulates water metabolism during periods of inappropriate ADH secretion, but has no effect in patients with normal water balance.

TANAY, YUST, PERESECENSCHI, ABRAMOV AND AVIRAM, *Annals of Internal Medicine* (1979), reported on the use of PHT in the treatment of a sixty-eight-year-old female who had been admitted to hospital because of precordial pain, headache, nausea, and blurring of vision. In addition, confused behavior and diminished orientation in time and place were observed. A diagnosis of inappropriate antidiuretic hormone secretion was made and confirmed by laboratory findings.

The authors state that treatment with PHT, 100 mg t.i.d., resulted in reversal of the clinical and laboratory findings and demonstrated the effectiveness of PHT in treating this syndrome.

SORDILLO, MATARESE, NOVICH, ZABETAKIS AND MICHELIS, *Clinical Nephrology* (1981), report two patients with inappropriate ADH syndrome who were successfully treated with PHT.

The authors state that PHT can suppress drug-induced, as well as excess endogenous, ADH secretion.

HYPERTHYROIDISM

ROMERO, MARANON AND BOBILLO, *Revista Iberica de Endocrinologia* (1970), describe a variety of treatments for hyperthyroidism including thyroidostatic therapy, surgical resection, and radioisotope therapy, noting these methods have complications and side effects.

The authors state that about twenty years ago they started using PHT, 50 mg t.i.d., in combination with hydrazides. The treatment consisted of alternating PHT one week with hydrazides the next week.

As a result of their long experience with PHT, the authors initiated a detailed study of nineteen patients. Eight patients showed very favorable improvement; four, moderate improvement; one, slight improvement; and two, no improvement. Marked relief of nervousness, characteristic of this disorder, was observed.

The authors state that in some patients treated with PHT there was decrease in size of goiter and exophthalmus. (See also Refs. 1125, 2499, 2846, 2964.)

MENSTRUAL DISTURBANCES

MICK, *JAMA* (1973), reported the case of a girl who had edema of the legs, fingers and puffiness of the face, accompanied by dizzy spells. These symptoms occurred about ten days before each menstrual cycle.

Diuretics had been tried without success. On 100 mg of PHT, twice daily, the patient became completely free of her episodic edema. Improvement in dizziness was also noted.

KRAMER, *American Journal of Diseases of Children* (1977), described a thirteen-year-old girl with a pattern of recurrent psychotic episodes, which seemed to coincide with her menstrual periods. After four to seven days of bizarre, catatonic behavior, the patient would return to a normal state.

The episodes were virtually eliminated by treatment with PHT, 400 mg a day. During a three-and-a-half year follow-up, the patient continued to be symptom-free, as long as she was maintained on adequate PHT.

Fever and Temperature Regulation

RECURRENT FEVER

SNYDER, *Pediatrics* (1958), reported on the use of PHT (100–200 mg/day) in eight children with a variety of paroxysmal symptoms including headache, migraine, vertigo, abdominal pain and nightmares. All experienced prompt relief from these symptoms with PHT.

In two cases, intermittent fevers of unexplained origin were eliminated by PHT.

BERGER, *Postgraduate Medicine* (1966), reported on an unusual case of recurrent fever, successfully treated with PHT.

A sixteen-year-old boy had irregular attacks of fever for eight years. These attacks would last from four to twenty-four hours, and disappear abruptly, regardless of treatment. His temperature would rise to 102°F and stay within a degree of this reading until the attack was terminated. Headache, vertigo, weakness, irritability, and sometimes violent rages accompanied the fever.

Over a four-year period the patient missed 260 days of school because of these attacks of fever. Extensive tests for causes of fever proved negative. Penicillin, tetracycline and sulfadimethoxine were tried without effect.

The patient was treated with 400 mg of PHT per day and the attacks stopped. Subsequently, on a dose of 25 mg q.i.d., he had been free of fever, and the symptoms that accompanied it, for four years.

On four occasions PHT was withdrawn. Each time the fever and other symptoms returned within a few days.

●   ●   ●

FAMILIAL MEDITERRANEAN FEVER

HAMED, ABDEL-AAL, ABDEL-AZIZ, NASSAR, SWEIFY, ATTA, EL-AWADY, EL-AREF AND EL-GARF, *Journal of the Egyptian Medical Association* (1975), stated that since 1966 they have used PHT to treat forty-seven children for a periodic disease of unknown etiology, which has many names and which they refer to as familial Mediterranean fever. Thirty-one of the children were available for follow-up. Twenty-two had improvement in the severity and frequency of attacks, six were unimproved and three became worse.

The authors conclude that PHT significantly reduces the frequency and severity of attacks of familial Mediterranean fever.

TRANSFUSION REACTION

RICEVUTI, MAZZONE, DANESINO, TOSCANO AND RIZZO, *Lancet* (1984), in a study of granulocyte transfusion reactions, noted that six patients pre-treated with PHT did not develop fever; whereas, ten of fifteen non-treated patients did have fever. (see Granulocyte Transfusion Reaction, below.)

HYPOTHALAMIC SYNDROME

BECHTEREVA, NIKITINA, ILIUCHINA, DAMBINOVA AND DENISOVA, *European Journal of Clinical Investigation* (1984), reported on the use of PHT in 120 patients with hypothalamic syndrome of varying etiologies. PHT (50–100 mg b.i.d. or t.i.d.) resulted in stabilization of body temperature as well as cardiovascular function (including blood pressure) and improvements in mood, sleep and headaches.

In the laboratory, PHT was found to inhibit glutaminergic receptor function. The authors suggest that these findings are related to PHT's clinical actions.

• • •

A number of individuals taking PHT have reported to the Dreyfus Medical Foundation that their usual attacks of "flu," "virus," etc., have been accompanied by less fever than they would have expected. Research in this area seems indicated.

Granulocyte Transfusion Reaction

RICEVUTI, MAZZONE, DANESINO, TOSCANO AND RIZZO, *Lancet* (1984), reported twenty-five patients who received granulocyte transfusions. To control common transfusion reactions, including fever, malaise, nausea and vomiting, six were pretreated with PHT (10 mg/kg). Four received hydrocortisone, and fifteen received no pretreatment.

None of the patients who received PHT had any of these reactions. The four who received hydrocortisone had slight fever. Ten of the fifteen nontreated patients had fever. Four of these were subsequently treated with

PHT with gradual, but definite, reduction of fever. In addition, the patients treated with PHT had similar neutrophil function before and after the transfusion; whereas, both the untreated and hydrocortisone groups showed decreased function after transfusion.

Head Injuries and Surgery

HOFF AND HOFF, *Monatsschrift Psychiatrie and Neurologie* (1947), reported a controlled study of the effectiveness of PHT in the prevention of post-traumatic seizures. One hundred World War II veterans with head injuries were randomized into two groups of fifty. One group received 200 mg PHT daily, while the other group, serving as controls, received no treatment unless seizures developed. During the first four years, only two patients (4%) from the PHT-treated group developed seizures, (one after he had become a heavy drinker), while seventeen (38%) developed seizures in the control group.

Four years later, BIRKMAYER, *Wiener Klinische Wochenschrift* (1951), reported additional results of this study. Six percent of the patients in the PHT-treated group had seizures compared to 51% in the control group.

The author concludes that small doses of PHT are sufficient to protect against post-traumatic epilepsy.

THE CZECHOSLOVAKIA HEALTH MINISTRY, *Medical World News* (1968),

issued a directive requiring doctors to give PHT and phenobarbital to every trauma victim who remains unconscious for more than three hours. After six months, if no signs of epilepsy have appeared, the drugs are phased out over the next nine to eighteen months.

This directive was based upon work by DR. KAREL POPEK, chief neurologist at the Neurological Clinic of the University Medical Faculty in Brno, Czechoslovakia. Dr. Popek conducted a controlled clinical study of PHT and phenobarbital in patients with cerebral concussion or other serious head injuries.

He considered the results of the study persuasive enough to warrant routine use of the drugs as preventive therapy. (See also SERVIT AND MUSIL, Ref. 2256.)

WOHNS AND WYLER, *Journal of Neurosurgery* (1979), reported on sixty-two patients whose head injuries were sufficiently severe to cause high probability of post-traumatic seizures. Of fifty patients treated with PHT, 10% developed late onset seizures. Twelve patients not treated with PHT, but who had head injuries of equal magnitude, had a 50% incidence of seizures.

YOUNG, RAPP, BROOKS, MADAUSS AND NORTON, *Epilepsia* (1979), in a study involving eighty-four patients with head injuries, reported the beneficial use of PHT for post-traumatic seizure prophylaxis.

With PHT only five of eighty-four individuals had seizures within a year after severe head injury, and only one of these patients had more than one seizure.

The authors concluded that the greatly reduced incidence of post-traumatic seizures in these patients demonstrates the prophylactic effect of PHT.

SERVIT AND MUSIL, *Epilepsia* (1981), report the results of a long-term study of prophylactic treatment of post-traumatic epilepsy performed in Czechoslovakia during the years 1963 through 1980. The prophylactically treated group of 144 patients with severe brain injuries was compared with a control group of twenty-four equally damaged cases without prophylactic treatment.

Prophylactic treatment consisted of PHT (160–240 mg/day) and phenobarbital (30–60 mg/day) administered for periods of two years in the majority of cases. The incidence of late post-traumatic epilepsy was 25% in the control, compared with 2.1% in the prophylactically treated group.

WHITE, PENRY, BRACKET, LISCO, ART, NEMORE, MANN, MUMAW AND WHITLEY, *NINCDS* (1982), in a double-blind study of forty-nine severely head-injured patients, compared the combination of PHT and phenobarbital to placebo in preventing post-traumatic seizures. Groups were matched for severity of

injury. PHT levels were maintained at 10–20 µg/ml and phenobarbital levels at 20–30 µg/ml.

Patients treated with PHT and phenobarbital had a significantly lower incidence of post-traumatic epilepsy than the placebo group.

NORTH, PENHALL, HANIEH, FREWIN AND TAYLOR, *Journal of Neurosurgery* (1983), reported a double-blind study of PHT versus placebo as prophylaxis against post-craniotomy seizures in 281 patients. One hundred forty patients received PHT and 141, placebo. Patients were followed for one year. PHT significantly reduced the incidence of post-craniotomy seizures in comparison to placebo. For the entire group of PHT-treated patients, this reduction was greatest within the first three months, when the risk of seizures was greatest. In certain high-risk patients (following operations for aneurysm, head injury and meningioma) there was a significantly lower incidence of seizures at both one month and approximately one year.

Glycogen Storage Disease

JUBIZ AND RALLISON, *Archives of Internal Medicine* (1974), report on four patients with glycogen storage disease, two with debranching enzyme system deficiency, one with phosphorylase deficiency and one with glucose-6-phosphatase deficiency.

These patients were treated with PHT for more than two years and there was a good response. This was evidenced by a reduction in liver size and hepatic glycogen content. Hyperlacticacidemia improved.

Ophthalmology

ACCOMMODATIVE ESOTROPIA

GALIN, KWITKO AND RESTREPO, *Proceedings of the International Strabismological Association* (1969), found PHT useful in the treatment of accommodative esotropia.

A study with thirty-five children was completed. Their ages ranged from two-and-a-half to fourteen years. Children less than six years of age were given 30 mg PHT twice daily, then increased to three times daily if after two days it was well tolerated. Standard orthoptic studies were performed before and after PHT.

Of twenty-five patients with abnormal near-point accommodation, twenty improved with a decrease of three diopters and ten of these had a concomitant decrease in esotropia. Because they were too young, the near point of accommodation was not obtained in ten patients.

Nine out of twenty-one patients responded to PHT in the combined accommodative groups (including thirteen accommodative and eight partial accommodative).

Accommodative convergence/ accommodation (AC/A) ratios were most favorably influenced by PHT in those patients having high ratios.

PHT had little effect on normals. Phospholine iodide, which had greater effect on AC/A ratios than PHT, was not selective and had an effect on normals as well as abnormals.

GLAUCOMATOUS FIELD LOSS

BECKER AND PODOS, *Symposium on Ocular Therapy* (1973), in earlier studies had found that PHT partly protected the optic nerve *in vitro* when subjected to anoxia, cyanide or ouabain. They decided to explore the possibility that PHT might reverse some of the effects of ischemia on the optic nerve in humans.

The authors instituted a study to examine the effects of PHT in glaucomatous field loss. This study involved fifty patients who were given 100 mg PHT t.i.d. for two to five months. The effects on visual fields were quantitatively recorded.

When treated with PHT, only one of the fifty patients had a worsening of visual fields, twenty-nine showed no worsening, and twenty patients showed improvement in visual fields. This salutary effect in visual fields occurred despite the fact that intraocular pressures, which previously had been deleterious, persisted.

In seven of the patients that showed improvement, PHT was discontinued and worsening of visual fields occurred. The authors found of considerable interest the fact that when PHT was reinstituted in five of these seven patients, improvement in visual fields again occurred.

The authors conclude that this pilot study suggests that where the blood supply is decreased, PHT may be able to protect optic nerve function.

Arthritis

BABROVE, *Arthritis and Rheumatism* (1983), reported three patients with inflammatory arthritis, two with rheumatoid arthritis and one with psoriatic arthropathy, who developed seizure disorders necessitating treatment with PHT. Within six months of instituting PHT, all three patients had definite sustained improvement in their joint disease. There was a reduction in morning stiffness, intensity and frequency of clinical flare-ups, as well as reduction in the number of painful and swollen joints. Prior to PHT, all had been taking a nonsteroidal anti-inflammatory drug with only modest benefit.

GRINDULIS, NICHOL AND OLDHAM, *The Journal of Rheumatology* (1986), reported a thirty-two week study on the use of PHT in eighteen patients with active rheumatoid arthritis. The patients, thirteen females and five males, ages thirty-five to seventy-two, had arthritis of three-month to ten-year duration. Two of the patients withdrew from the study because of mild side effects, and one because of lack of effect.

The starting dose of PHT was 100 mg/day which was increased to 300 mg/day during the course of the study. Clinical and laboratory measurements were made at frequent intervals throughout the study, and during an eight-week period when PHT was withdrawn. Clinical assessments included articular index, clinical score and visual analog pain score. Laboratory measures included serum C-reactive protein, plasma viscosity and hemoglobin.

With PHT there was significant clinical improvement. Laboratory improvements attained significance occasionally. There was no relapse of the clinical or laboratory measurements during the eight-week period when PHT was withdrawn.

MACFARLANE, CLARK AND PANAYI, *Annals of Rheumatic Diseases* (1986), reported on the use of PHT (100–300 mg daily) in eleven patients with active rheumatoid arthritis (mean duration 12.4 years). Two patients were withdrawn from the study because of other illness and surgery, and two, because of a mild rash.

Seven patients completed a twenty-week course of PHT treatment. All showed continuous clinical improvement. Laboratory improvement (erythrocyte sedimentation rate, C-reactive protein and IgM rheumatoid factor) was also observed at twelve and twenty weeks. When PHT was withdrawn for eight weeks, all patients showed clinical and laboratory deterioration.

The authors note that the usefulness of drugs such as gold, penicillamine, azathioprine and cyclophosphamide in rheumatoid arthritis is seriously limited by side effects. Based on their study, the authors suggest that PHT may be an alternative safe therapy for rheumatoid arthritis.

See also Refs. 2816 and 2979 for laboratory studies.

Rabies

HATTWICK, WEIS, STECHSCHULTE, BAER AND GREGG, *Annals of Internal Medicine* (1972), give an extensive and detailed report on their successful treatment of a six-year-old boy with clinical rabies, with complete recovery. The authors comment that this is extremely rare, and possibly the first documented case of recovery from rabies in humans.

Many conventional and other measures were used to offset this desperate condition. Special attention was given to the prevention of hypoxia, cardiac arrhythmias and seizures.* Approximately forty days after the infection occurred and while the boy had been in a comatose condition for several days, PHT was administered, 150 mg daily. Four days later recovery started and progressed steadily to complete recovery.‡

* *The role, if any, that PHT played in this recovery is not known. However, since no remedy for clinical rabies is known, this case is of interest. It is well established that PHT is effective against seizures and cardiac arrhythmias, and it is also reported to have anti-anoxic effects. Of possible relevance is the evidence that PHT has antitoxic effects against a wide variety of substances.*

‡ *See also Pollen, reporting the use of PHT in the successful treatment in a case of cat-scratch encephalitis.*

Tinnitus

HALMOS, MOLNAR AND KORMOS, *HNO-Praxis* (1982), compared the effects of PHT and carbamazepine (CBZ) in the treatment of 138 patients with tinnitus and sensorineural hearing loss. Seventy-two of the patients received PHT, 100 mg t.i.d., and seventy-five received CBZ, starting with 200 mg b.i.d. and gradually increasing to 400 mg t.i.d.

The severity of tinnitus diminished in thirty-eight of the seventy-two patients treated with PHT. Their hearing loss improved by 5 to 25 decibels. Classified according to etiology, thirty-two of fifty tinnitus patients with eighth-nerve lesions improved, as did two of three cases with otologic defects. Four of fifteen patients with presbycusis improved. There was no improvement in the four patients who developed tinnitus after head injury. No adverse effects were observed in the PHT group.

Improvement was observed in only twelve of the sixty-six carbamazepine-treated patients. It had to be stopped in nine patients because of side effects.

The authors state that they found PHT superior to CBZ for tinnitus. PHT had the additional advantage of being better tolerated. (See also Ref. 2500.)

SURGERY

Summary

Phenytoin has been reported useful prior to, during and after surgery. Among its uses are relief of apprehension and anxiety, prevention and treatment of cardiac arrhythmias, prevention of ischemic brain damage and relief of pain.

PHT, in therapeutic doses, does not depress respiration or cerebral function, thus optimizing preoperative state and post-operative recovery. PHT's ability to relieve pain, without sedation, reduces the need for narcotics.

JAFFE, *Personal Communication* (1966), found PHT useful in the pre-operative and postoperative periods and during the course of cataract surgery.

PHT replaced large doses of barbiturates previously used pre-operatively to combat apprehension. PHT replaced Demerol and opiates preoperatively and was especially useful in cases where unpredictable or aggressive behavior was anticipated.

During the course of surgery where intravenous Demerol had previously been required to control violent outbursts in the operating room, intravenous PHT was successfully substituted.

MERCER AND OSBORNE, *Annals of Internal Medicine* (1967), reported on the use of intravenous PHT in the treatment of 259 patients who developed arrhythmias during and after cardiac surgery. With PHT, complete control of the arrhythmias was achieved in 164 patients and partial response (at least 50% reduction of arrhythmias) was observed in sixty-five patients.

SEUFFERT, HELFANT, DANA AND URBACH, *Anesthesia and Analgesia* (1968), report on the use of PHT, prophylactically and therapeutically, in the treatment of arrhythmias which develop and persist during surgery.

Twenty patients undergoing elective surgery, scheduled to receive cyclopropane anesthesia, were divided into two groups: eleven were pretreated with PHT (5 mg/kg) intravenously, and nine received an equivalent amount of lactated Ringer's solution with or without propylene glycol solvent for PHT, serving as controls.

Eight of the nine patients in the control group developed arrhythmias, whereas only three of the eleven patients pretreated with PHT developed arrhythmias during the entire anesthesia procedure. During "maintenance," eight of the nine in the control group developed arrhythmias, in contrast to only one of eleven pretreated with PHT. The authors pointed out that this difference was statistically significant.

PHT was also given to ten other patients under general anesthesia, who developed arrhythmias which did not respond to standard treatment. PHT promptly restored regular sinus rhythm in eight patients who developed ventricular arrhythmias. It was not effective in two of the patients who developed supraventricular arrhythmias. (See also Ref. 720).

GAUTAM, *British Heart Journal* (1969), reported on the use of intravenous and oral PHT in treating a variety of cardiac arrhythmias following open heart surgery (thirteen Starr-Edwards prosthetic valve replacements and one atrial septal defect closure). The arrhythmias, which included multiple ventricular extrasystoles, recurrent ventricular tachycardia and nodal tachycardia, appeared within two to thirty hours after surgery. PHT was rapidly and highly effective in abolishing the arrhythmias in thirteen patients.

The author states that the rapidity of its action and the relative paucity of side effects make PHT an effective antiarrhythmic agent.

BARASCH, BARAS AND GALIN, *Personal Communication* (1970), found that PHT replaced all preoperative and postoperative medication in cataract surgery other than the local anesthetic. The authors previously had used barbiturates, Demerol, Compazine, codeine and aspirin.

Because PHT does not impair normal function, its use instead of narcotics and sedatives permitted the prompt ambulation of patients. For this reason the use of PHT enabled the discharge of patients within twenty-four hours, in a series of 100 consecutive uncomplicated cases of cataract surgery.

The authors state that since this study, they now use PHT routinely in cataract surgery.

CHAMBERLAIN, *Personal Communication* (1970), reported on the therapeutic value of PHT in a series of 200 surgical cases.

The ages of the patients varied from six months to ninety years.

Dosage of PHT: 25 mg to 600 mg depending on age of patient and severity of symptoms and surgical procedure used.

PHT was successfully employed as follows:

1. As preoperative medication for anxiety.
2. As postoperative medication for anxiety and pain.
3. In the agitated, depressed and alcoholic surgical patient.
4. In long-term treatment of both the operable and inoperable patient with malignant disease.

Certain trends presented themselves with the use of PHT:

(a) In children, PHT (25 mg q.i.d. to 100 mg t.i.d.) reduced or eliminated the use of pre- and postoperative narcotics.

(b) In adults, 200 mg of PHT prior to surgery reduced the need for preoperative narcotics.

(c) In adults, postoperative use of PHT (500–600 mg daily) relieved pain, making it possible to do away with practically all postoperative narcotics. PHT also decreased anxiety and promoted a general feeling of well-being in most cases.

(d) Elderly agitated and difficult patients became much calmer with PHT.

(e) In the inoperable malignant cases, PHT in doses up to 600 mg daily relieved pain, making it possible to greatly cut down on the amount of narcotics used. PHT definitely improved the mental outlook of these forlorn patients.

(f) In postoperative malignant cases undergoing radiation and other forms of treatment, the use of PHT, 400–600 mg daily, relieved pain and allowed for a marked decrease or elimination of the need for narcotics.

The author notes that, in general, there was marked improvement of mental outlook in patients receiving PHT.

WINTER, *International Surgery* (1972), presents a detailed study on surgery in patients with asthma and emphysema.

In this study the author says that severe respiratory problems require careful preoperative and postoperative medical treatment. He states that in patients with severe respiratory problems he does not use narcotics and that, in his opinion, they should never be used in such cases. He further says that barbiturates and tranquilizers should only be used in small doses.

The author states that he has found PHT of considerable value in severe respiratory problems, both preoperatively and postoperatively. He notes that PHT appears to have special value in patients with bronchospastic problems. (See also Refs. 341, 401, 1535, and Anti-anoxic Effects of PHT.)

LANDOLT, *Acta Endocrinologica* (1974), reported a patient who developed the syndrome of inappropriate ADH secretion following surgery for craniopharyngioma.

Intravenous PHT, during two such episodes, promptly increased urine output. Serum sodium values returned to normal and the patient became more alert. (See Inappropriate ADH Syndrome, p. 68).

ALDRETE AND FRANATOVIC, *Archives of Surgery* (1980), studied the effects of PHT on changes of arterial blood pressure and heart rate occurring during anesthesia and in the immediate postoperative period.

In a controlled study, ninety hypertensive patients were separated into three groups. One group was untreated. One group received 100 mg of PHT, and another group received 200 mg, the evening before and the morning of surgery. Both groups receiving PHT had better hemody-namic stability than the non-treated group. The group receiving 200 mg had statistically significant improvement.

ALDRETE, ROMO-SALAS, MAZZIA AND TAN, *Critical Care Medicine* (1981), studied the effect of intravenous PHT in ten patients who suffered cardiac arrest during or after anesthesia.

PHT was given after spontaneous heartbeat and systolic blood pressure greater than 100 mm Hg had been restored and the diagnosis of neurological deficit had been established on the basis of unconsciousness, dilated and areflexic pupils and rigid and/or decerebrate posture.

With PHT (7 mg/kg) nine of the ten patients recovered nearly complete neurological function. The other patient had partial recovery but succumbed to other complications.

GARSON AND GILLETTE, *PACE* (1981), reported the use of oral and intravenous PHT for the treatment of chronic ventricular dysrhythmias in fifty-one young patients, thirty-five of whom had previously undergone corrective surgery for cardiac malformations including ventricular septal defect, tetralogy of Fallot, and valvular insufficiency.

Overall, PHT was the most effective drug, controlling the arrhythmias in thirty-nine of the fifty-one patients.

The authors conclude that PHT is the drug of choice for children with ventricular dysrhythmias, especially those with abnormal hemodynamics. (See also Ref. 1847.)

ROCCHINI, CHUN AND DICK, *American Journal of Cardiology* (1981), reported the elimination of ventricular tachycardia by PHT in four children who had undergone repair of the tetralogy of Fallot.

The authors state that PHT appears to be the antiarrhythmic agent of choice after repair of the tetralogy of Fallot.

KAVEY, BLACKMAN AND SONDHEIMER, *American Heart Journal (1982)*, reported the effects of oral PHT in nineteen patients, seen consecutively, who developed ventricular premature complexes (VPCs) late after surgery for congenital heart disease. Arrhythmias included ventricular tachycardia, couplets and frequent multiform or uniform VPCs, documented by twenty-four hour ambulatory ECG. Sixteen had undergone previous repair of the tetralogy of Fallot and three had had aortic valve surgery. Nine of these children had been unresponsive to previous treatment.

PHT decreased ventricular dysrhythmias in all nineteen patients. The arrhythmias were completely suppressed in fifteen, and in four they were reduced to uniform VPCs.

The authors state that the high rate of success in treating these patients, who are at particular risk for sudden death, and the relative lack of side effects suggests that PHT is the drug of choice for this patient group.

MASSEI, DESILVA, GROSSO, ROBBIATI, INFUSO, RAVAGNATI AND ALTAMURA, *Neurosurgical Science* (1983), reported on the use of PHT for cerebral metabolic protection during carotid thromboendoarterectomy (TEA).

PHT was chosen because of its known therapeutic properties in reducing cerebral metabolic oxygen consumption, preserving energy compounds, increasing cerebral blood flow, and in regulating intra- and extracellular cerebral ion content.

Twelve patients undergoing TEA were given intravenous PHT (15–17 mg/kg), fifteen minutes before clamping. EEG and PHT blood levels were monitored during and after surgery at fixed intervals over a twenty-four-hour period.

The authors stated that patients awakened promptly and did not require intensive care. This was in contrast to their experience with other methods of cerebral protection, including barbiturates. Also, with PHT, no postoperative neurological complications were observed.

PEREZ-RUVALCABA, QUINTERO-PEREZ, CAMPA-URIBE, CHAPA-ALVAREZ, RODRIGUEZ-NORIEGA, *European Journal of Clinical Investigation* (1984), reviewed the multiple uses of PHT in their general hospital. Their review included the use of 100 mg of PHT, as sole preoperative medication the evening before surgery, in fifty patients. Treatment with PHT resulted in excellent control of apprehension and sleep disturbances usually encountered preoperatively.

The authors state that these beneficial effects of PHT were achieved without the undesirable sedative effects experienced with many commonly used sedatives and/or tranquilizers.

PHENYTOIN AS A PREVENTIVE

PHT has been found useful for over fifty symptoms and disorders, and this suggests a broad potential for preventive medicine. There are many reports in the clinical and basic mechanisms literature of PHT's effectiveness as a preventive.[1, 2]

PHT's established ability to calm the overbusy brain and modify or eliminate excessive emotions of fear and anger, and to improve duration and quality of sleep are consistent with the general principle of good health.

PHT's therapeutic effect on blood pressure, its anti-ischemic effects, its ability to stabilize bioelectrical activity, and its ability to increase HDL levels, are indications of protection against cardiac disorders and stroke.

By its regulatory effect on the HPA axis, PHT decreases excessive levels of epinephrine, norepinephrine and cortisol. Since these chemicals are closely associated with stress, this action of PHT could be protective against a wide variety of stress-related disorders.

PHT is not habit-forming. Its long-term safety has withstood the test of millions of people taking it daily for decades. PHT's use in preventive medicine, particularly when people are susceptible to serious disorders, deserves consideration.

1.   *Clinical:* Refs. 91, 92, 105, 161,290, 338, 341,382, 383, 401, 409, 429, 571,697, 701,720, 819, 923, 943, 944, 998, 999, 1033, 1121, 1140, 1253, 1264, 1289, 1328, 1329, 1349, 1359, 1388, 1415, 1510, 1535, 1565, 1583, 1594, 1666, 1717, 1724, 1738, 1817, 1847, 1879, 1893, 1926, 1961, 2002, 2114, 2122, 2134, 2141, 2142, 2149, 2150, 2182, 2223, 2235, 2256, 2306, 2318, 2319, 2340, 2342, 2406, 2428, 2431, 2465, 2528, 2532, 2542, 2599, 2617, 2649, 2652, 2709, 2734, 2741, 2768, 2813, 2814, 2827, 2833, 2868, 2882, 2897, 2907, 3009, 3054, 3060, 3068.

2. *Basic mechanisms:* Refs. 37, 56, 99, 118, 155, 163, 164, 171, 213, 233, 263, 392, 419, 482, 483, 520, 529, 685, 717, 739, 790, 804, 914, 921, 1015, 1027, 1058, 1071, 1092, 1122, 1160, 1208, 1267, 1279, 1354, 1374, 1419, 1485, 1507, 1509, 1525, 1529, 1591, 1668, 1718, 1781, 1791, 1806, 1822, 1828, 1864, 1875, 1878, 1932, 1958, 1969, 2004, 2013, 2024, 2062, 2088, 2144, 2157, 2177, 2185, 2192, 2193, 2195, 2200, 2213, 2229, 2263, 2269, 2272, 2279, 2280, 2281, 2291, 2311, 2349, 2420,2445, 2502, 2516, 2525, 2571, 2583, 2609, 2623, 2627, 2628, 2682, 2698, 2701, 2707, 2708, 2732, 2739, 2740, 2741, 2742, 2743, 2757, 2820, 2844, 2854, 2855, 2900, 2977, 3001, 3005, 3017, 3039, 3063.

SAFETY AND TOXICOLOGY

Background and Perspective

Since its introduction, in 1938, millions of people have taken phenytoin on a daily basis for long periods of time. The world use of PHT is estimated to have been the equivalent of one hundred fifty to two hundred million patient-years. This translates into an estimated one-and-a-half to two trillion 100 mg doses. Thus PHT has been subjected to the important tests of time, volume of use, number of individuals who have used it, and continuous use over long periods.

With this in perspective, reports of serious side effects associated with PHT have been extremely rare. As a point of reference, only six deaths associated with PHT alone have been reported to the FDA's Adverse Drug Experience Monitoring Program in the last eighteen years.

Because it has been in use for such a long time, the literature of PHT's safety and toxicology is extensive. No single reviewer can presume to have all of this information. For this reason, we refer the reader to other reviews.*

* Examples: Refs. 1075, 1586, 1700, 1836, 1884, 1891, 1923, 1940, 2043, 2189, 2244, 2249, 2288, 2423, 2427, 2463, 2467, 2607, 2655, 2845, 2874, 2890, 2903, 2934, 3041, 3048, as well as the Physicians' Desk Reference.

Clinical

PHT's first use was in epilepsy and at that time it was classified as an anticonvulsant. This classification is narrow and misleading. The world medical literature describes PHT more broadly as a bioelectrical stabilizer or normalizer.

Since 1938, PHT has been reported in the world literature to be therapeutic for a wide range of symptoms and disorders. Among them are uncontrolled thinking, occupied with negative feelings of anger and fear and related emotions; bad mood; depression; sleep disturbances; poor concentration; muscle disorders; migraine, trigeminal neuralgia, and other pain; asthma; and cardiac disorders.[1]

1. *See this Bibliography.*

The topical use of PHT is a rapidly expanding field. Used topically, in a variety of conditions including skin ulcers and burns, PHT is effective against pain and promotes healing.

PHT has unusual properties. It calms without sedation. It effects an improvement in energy without being an artificial stimulant. And it is not habit-forming.[2]

The basic mechanism findings explain how PHT can have such broad clinical usefulness.

2. *This is not to be confused with the well-known fact that epileptics should not be suddenly withdrawn from PHT.*

Basic Mechanisms of Action

In the basic mechanism literature PHT has been referred to as a stabilizer of bioelectrical activity or as a membrane stabilizer.

PHT has been shown to have a stabilizing effect on bioelectrical activity in tissues, groups of cells, and in single cells. This ability to regulate bioelectrical activity has been demonstrated in brain, spinal cord, ganglia, peripheral nerve, cardiac, skeletal and smooth muscle.

PHT reduces or eliminates excessive potentiation and repetitive after-discharge. In therapeutic amounts, it has little or no effect on normal cell function. These properties could account for many of PHT's therapeutic applications.

. . .

Dosage

The adult dosage of PHT used in non-epileptic disorders tends to be lower (100–300 mg/day) than that used in epilepsy (300–600 mg/day). Dosage depends on the type and severity of the condition. Acute conditions may temporarily require higher doses.

The usual therapeutic blood level range in epilepsy is 10–20 µg/ml. In other disorders, therapeutic effects are frequently achieved at lower blood levels. Clinical observation is usually the best guide to dosage.

The liver is the chief site of PHT metabolism. Patients with disease-impaired liver function, or patients who metabolize the drug slowly, may require lower doses of PHT. Patients who have lower serum protein binding, such as those with kidney disease, may also require lower doses because the free fraction of PHT in the blood can be higher.

It has been recommended that intravenous PHT be administered slowly—at a rate of 50 mg/min. or less.

Abrupt discontinuance of other medication, on which the patient may have become dependent, is usually not advisable when PHT therapy is instituted.

Possible Interactions

PHT is compatible with most drugs and drug combinations. Interactions with other drugs have been reported. They vary from individual to individual and are difficult to generalize. In some cases, adjustment of the dosage of PHT, the other drug, or both may be necessary. Such adjustments may be guided by clinical observations or, where necessary, by monitoring blood levels.

For information on drugs for which interactions have been reported, we refer the reader to the Physicians' Desk Reference, as well as Refs. 2338, 2422, 2680, 2681, 2824, 2859, 2861, 2862, 2877.

Safety

LIVINGSTON AND WHITEHOUSE, *Modern Treatment,* stated that in their experience with PHT in many thousands of epileptic patients, some of whom have taken it continuously for more than twenty years, "We have not encountered a single instance of a serious untoward reaction to phenytoin which was not reversible on withdrawal of the drug."

GAUTAM, *British Heart Journal,* reporting on the use of intravenous PHT in the treatment of cardiac arrhythmias following open heart surgery, states, "Rapidity of action and the paucity of side effects make the drug an effective antiarrhythmic agent."

CHUNG, *Modern Treatment,* stated "Toxic manifestations of PHT are usually rare and not serious . . . PHT is probably the safest and most effective drug in the treatment of all types of digitalis-induced tachyarrhythmias." (See also Ref. 923.)

BHATT, VIJAYAN, AND DREYFUS, *California Medicine,* in a review of clinical and laboratory aspects of myotonia, state, "Of the various drugs used, PHT appears to be the most effective, the safest and best tolerated."

FISHER AND DIMINO, *British Journal of Addiction,* discussing their clinical experience with PHT in the treatment of drug and alcohol withdrawal, state, "Because PHT is nonaddictive, is not a sedative, and has a wide range of safety, it is particularly well-suited for use in addicted persons."

SCHMIDT, *Adverse Effects of Antiepileptic Drugs,* in an extensive review of forty-four years of world experience with PHT, reports that side effects of PHT are usually mild and transient, and serious adverse effects are very rare.

DELGADO-ESCUETA, WASTERLAIN, TREIMAN AND PORTER, *Advances in Neurology,* report the special usefulness of PHT in the treatment of head trauma and other neurological disorders in which "alteration of the patient's state of consciousness is contraindicated."

TOMAN, *The Pharmacological Basis of Therapeutics,* states, "Doses totaling many grams have occasionally been ingested by accident or taken with suicidal intent . . . deaths have been rare. Fortunately, PHT is a very poor drug with which to commit suicide." (See also Refs. 134, 216, 283, 357, 537, 565, 1870, 2118, 2989.)

Toxicology

Skin Rash/Hypersensitivity: Skin rash, either local or generalized, can occur with PHT. The incidence is estimated to be in the range of 2 to 4%. These reactions, some of which may be dose related, most frequently appear within the first few weeks of therapy, occasionally later. The most common form is the morbilliform (measle-like) rash. If such a rash appears, the medicine should be stopped. The rash usually disappears in a few days. After disappearance of the rash, reintroduction of the medicine may be tried, but only with careful observation and starting with tiny doses.

Serious allergic reactions, extremely rare, are usually symptomatized by severe rash and/or fever. PHT should be stopped promptly and not reintroduced. Failure to do so could lead to serious hypersensitivity reactions such as Stevens-Johnson syndrome, erythema multiforme, hepatitis and blood dyscrasias.

Nervous System: Side effects of PHT therapy referable to the central nervous system are generally dose related and usually disappear on reduction of dosage. These include nystagmus, ataxia, slurred speech and confusion, and, very rarely, dyskinesias. (See Refs. 359, 666, 1075, 1178, 1586, 1700, 2288, 2423, 2463, 2467, 2845, 2890, 2935, 3041, 3048.)

There are reports that at substantial or excessive doses of PHT there may be impairment of some cognitive functions. (See Refs. 2902, 3013, 3025, 3026.) However, extensive evidence has demonstrated that, in therapeutic doses, PHT has a beneficial effect on cognitive function including concentration, memory, and ability to perform in school. (See Refs. 38, 527, 538, 556, 557, 585, 707, 713, 863, 938, 1139, 1140, 1564, 1565, 1808, 2311.)

There have been occasional reports of peripheral neuropathy related to long-term, high-dose use of PHT. (See Refs. 232, 470, 829, 897, 933, 950, 2423, 2534, 2890, 2934, 2935, 3006.)

Connective Tissue: Gingival hyperplasia has been reported during PHT treatment of epileptics. The hyperplasia usually occurs in the presence of gingivitis and can be decreased or eliminated with good oral hygiene. (See Refs. 307, 547, 607, 612, 627, 629, 634, 1074, 1115, 1294, 2463, 2581, 2845, 2890, 2934, 2935.)

The effect of PHT on gum tissue seems to be a stimulation of healing processes. In 1958, SHAPIRO reported accelerated gingival wound healing in non-epileptics treated with PHT. Since then, systemic and topical PHT have been found effective in the treatment of periodontal disease, and in the healing of chronic ulcers and burns. (See Clinical—Healing section, p. 382.)

Skeletal: Lowered levels of vitamin D and calcium and, in rare cases, osteomalacia have been reported in some epileptic patients on PHT. (See Refs. 851, 989, 1296, 1318, 1321, 2423, 2463, 2845, 2890, 2934.) There is laboratory evidence that PHT promotes bone healing and reduces bone resorption. (See Refs. 343, 1104, 1131, 1840, 1878, 2088, 2281, 2571, 2574, 2613, 2623, 2708, 2854, 2855, 2980.)

Hematologic: Low serum folate and macrocytosis, usually not clinically significant, have been reported in patients taking PHT. In rare cases megaloblastic anemia has occurred. It is responsive to folate replacement and usually does not require discontinuance of PHT. (See Refs. 349, 1460, 2043, 2874, 2890, 2903.)

Since 1938, there have been a few reports of pancytopenia, hemolytic anemia, thrombocytopenia and granulocytopenia. These seem to have been related to hypersensitivity reactions. (See Refs. 203, 253, 295, 1460, 2427, 2874, 2903, 2935, 3049.)

Lymphadenopathy, including benign lymphnode hyperplasia and pseudolymphoma have been reported in patients taking PHT. These appear to be related to a hypersensitivity reaction and regress when PHT is discontinued. (See Refs. 217, 294, 322, 615, 620, 632, 736, 874, 1884, 2423, 2467, 2874, 2903, 2935.)

Although lymphoma and Hodgkin's disease, on rare occasions, have been reported in patients taking PHT, a causal link is not established. In an extensive survey, CLEMMESEN states that he did not find a higher incidence of Hodgkin's disease in PHT-treated patients as compared with the general population.

Lowered serum IgA levels have been reported in some patients taking PHT. (See Refs. 1102, 1572, 1940, 2305, 2642, 2812, 2845, 3002.)

Gastrointestinal: Feelings of nausea and stomach discomfort may occasionally occur when PHT is first taken. They usually disappear by themselves, but taking PHT with food may be useful.

There have been rare reports of constipation, but the general experience has been that patients taking PHT have improvement in bowel habits.

Hepatic: Although abnormal liver function tests, such as gamma glutamyltransferase levels, have been reported, these are generally not clinically significant. Hepatotoxicity is rare and usually due to a hypersensitivity reaction. (See Refs. 1884, 2551, 2588, 2607, 2974.)

Endocrinology: In some diabetic patients receiving PHT, moderate increases in blood glucose levels have been reported, but adjustment of the diabetic therapy has not been necessary in most cases.

With toxic levels of PHT, there have been reports of temporary hyperglycemic effects in non-diabetic patients. In normals and non-diabetic patients taking therapeutic doses of PHT, glucose tolerance is normal. (See Refs. 924, 1327, 1330, 1762, 1809, 2646.)

PHT has been reported to increase steroid metabolism in patients on steroid therapy. Adjustment of the steroid dose may be required. (See Refs. 377, 896, 1128, 1627, 1679, 2382, 2485, 2633.) Because PHT may increase the metabolism of androgens and estrogens, oral contraceptive dose may need adjustment. Hypertrichosis has been reported in epileptic patients taking PHT.

Pregnancy: Although there have been reports that children of epileptic women taking PHT have a higher incidence of birth defects than children of normal mothers, the evidence that PHT is the cause of these defects is not clear. The reported defects are frequently associated with developmental abnormalities from other causes. Many variables including use of other drugs, and the reported increase of birth defects in children born to epileptic mothers who took no medication, make the data difficult to interpret. (See Refs. 606, 737, 1298, 1401, 1484, 1575, 1586, 1587, 1836, 1891, 2189, 2432, 2621, 2655, 2803, 2934, 2935, 2987, 2988.) Coagulation defects, which have been reported in neonates born to epileptic mothers taking PHT, can usually be prevented by adequate diet and supplemental vitamin K. (See Refs. 2903, 2935.)

BASIC MECHANISMS OF ACTION
OF PHENYTOIN

Summary

The evidence which has accumulated on phenytoin's basic mechanisms of action, from the earliest studies to the present, is extensive and consistent.

PHT has been shown to have a modulatory effect on bioelectrical activity in single cells, groups of cells and physiological systems. This ability to regulate and/or to correct abnormal membrane function has been demonstrated in brain, spinal cord, autonomic ganglia, peripheral nerve, skeletal muscle, cardiac muscle and conduction systems, and intestinal and vascular smooth muscle.

In the nerve and muscle cell, PHT reduces or eliminates excessive potentiation and hyperexcitability, as in post-tetanic potentiation and afterdischarge. If the cell is depolarized and firing rapidly, PHT normalizes it, reducing the firing. The more rapid the firing, the greater the effect. PHT has little or no effect on normal bioelectrical function at therapeutic levels. In the nerve cell, neither the resting potential nor single impulse transmission is altered.[1]

The basis for PHT's selective effects in neurons and muscle cells is found in its action on the cell membrane—its ability to regulate transmembrane ionic fluxes and also intracellular distribution of sodium, potassium, and calcium.[2] Recent work in neurons suggests that PHT binds to active sodium channels and delays their return from the inactivated, unusable state. This results in a decrease of sodium influx and correlates with PHT's frequency-dependent effects on the sodium-dependent action potential. Similar effects on calcium flux have also been reported. At the synapse PHT influences both calcium-dependent neurotransmitter release and postsynaptic response. Acetylcholine, norepinephrine, dopamine, GABA, and serotonin release, uptake and/or binding may all be regulated, dependent on the state of the neuron or circuit.[3]

The functions of other cell types such as glia, endocrine cells and fibroblasts are also modulated by PHT. Examples of PHT's actions include stimulation of glial cell potassium uptake;[2] modulation of hypothalamic-pituitary adrenal function, including ACTH release and cortisol metabolism;[4] and modulation of thyroid stimulating hormone, thyroxine, insulin, vasopressin, oxytocin, calcitonin and other hormone release and metabolism.[5] PHT stimulates hepatic enzyme metabolizing systems (cytochrome P-450);[6] increases high-density lipoprotein levels;[7] and stimulates healing processes (formation of granulation tissue and neovascularity).[8]

PHT has protective effects on cells. It preserves energy compounds and decreases "downhill movement" of ions, characteristic of energy depletion in neurons, whether such depletion is induced by physiological hyperactivity or chemical, electrical, or anoxic/ischemic injury.[9]

PHT has been reported to diminish or counteract, in animals or in man, the toxic effects of over thirty therapeutic and poisonous substances, as diverse as steroids, cyanide, DDT, digitalis, methaqualone, morphine, ouabain, reserpine and strychnine, and of radiation. [10]

The broad range of clinical use of PHT is best understood in the light of its ability to maintain normal bioelectrical activity. A rational basis for the clinical use of PHT takes into account its basic mechanisms of action, which indicate that it may be useful wherever stabilization or modulation of bioelectrical activity can have a therapeutic effect.

1. See Stabilization of Bioelectrical Activity; and Sodium, Potassium and Calcium Regulation.

2. See Sodium, Potassium and Calcium Regulation.

3. See Neurotransmiter Regulatory Effects of PHT.

4. See Pituitary-Adrenal Hormones.

5. See Pituitary-Thyroid Function and Other Hormones.

6. Enzyme regulation: see Refs. 296, 442, 450, 451, 771, 772, 896, 915, 998, 1003, 1004, 1128, 1130, 1208, 1251, 1573, 1740, 2128, 2129, 2334, 2335, 2336, 2564, 2587, 2732, 2735, 2739, 2740, 2742, 2873, 2891.

7. See Lipid Metabolism—HDL.

8. See Healing.

9. See Anti-Anoxic Effects of PHT.

10. See Anti-Toxic Effects of PHT.

APPENDIX

Lyman and Patuxent Studies

LYMAN

The study at the Lyman Reformatory for Boys was done with six boys aged eleven to thirteen, and the results were similar to those seen at the Worcester Jail. Five of the boys were moody and belligerent. After PHT they became friendly and smiling, and their fights decreased from five or six a day to one or two. The sixth boy was obviously depressed when we first saw him. We had a hard time even getting a *yes* or *no* from him. He never got into fights and stayed apart from the other boys. After he had taken PHT, he became loquacious and started having the "normal" one or two fights a day. The disparate effects of PHT, the calming effect on the boys that needed calming, and the return of energy to the depressed boy, were interesting to observe.

PATUXENT

The Patuxent Institution was different from the Worcester County Jail. Unlike the inmates at Worcester, the prisoners at Patuxent had been convicted of the most serious crimes. But PHT made no distinction and the effects on the nervous systems of the five prisoners studied were similar to those observed at Worcester.

As a result of observations made during this study, Dr. Joseph Stephens conducted two double-blind studies with outpatients at Johns Hopkins and found PHT effective in reducing symptoms relating to fear and anger.*

---

* See Stephens and Shaffer, *Psychopharmacologia* 1970, and Stephens and Shaffer, *J. Clin. Pharmacol.*, 1973, *The Broad Range of Clinical Use of PHT.*

■ 423

FDA Drug Bulletin, April, 1982

Use of Approved Drugs for Unlabeled Indications

"The appropriateness or legality of prescribing approved drugs for uses not included in their official labeling is sometimes a cause of concern and confusion among practitioners.

"Under the Federal Food, Drug, and Cosmetic (FD&C) Act, a drug approved for marketing may be labeled, promoted, and advertised by the manufacturer only for those uses for which the drug's safety and effectiveness have been established and which FDA has approved. These are commonly referred to as 'approved uses.' This means that adequate and well-controlled clinical trials have documented these uses, and the results of the trials have been reviewd and approved by FDA.

"The FD&C Act does not, however, limit the manner in which a physician may use an approved drug. Once a product has been approved for marketing, a physician may prescribe it for uses or in treatment regimens or patient populations that are not included in approved labeling. Such 'unapproved' or, more precisely, 'unlabeled' uses may be appropriate and rational in certain circumstances, and may, in fact, reflect approaches to drug therapy that have been extensively reported in medical literature.

"The term 'unapproved uses' is, to some extent, misleading. It includes a variety of situations ranging from unstudied to thoroughly investigated drug uses. Valid new uses for drugs already on the market are often first discovered through serendipitous observations and therapeutic innovations, subsequently confirmed by well-planned and executed clinical investigations. Before such advances can be added to the approved labeling, however, data substantiating the effectiveness of a new use regimen must be submitted by the manufacturer to FDA evaluation. This may take time and, without the initiative of the drug manufacturer whose product is involved, may never occur. For that reason, accepted medical practice often includes drug use that is not reflected in approved drug labeling.

"With respect to its role in medical practice, the package insert is informational only. FDA tries to assure that prescription drug information in the package insert accurately and fully reflects the data on safety and effectiveness on which that drug approval is based."

Exchange of Letters Between
Governor Nelson Rockefeller and
Secretary of HEW Elliot Richardson

April 19, 1972

Dear Mr. Secretary:

It has come to my attention that a great many published reports, written over a thirty-year period by physicians and other scientists, have indicated that the substance phenytoin has a broad range of beneficial uses. Further, it is my understanding that physicians are prescribing phenytoin for many purposes other than its original indicated use, in 1938, as an anticonvulsant. In spite of the evidence of phenytoin's broad usefulness, I understand that today, in 1972, its only listed indication is that of an anticonvulsant.

I realize that the Food and Drug Administration is set up essentially to rectify errors of commission. This certainly does not fall into that category. However, I believe a public clarification of the status of phenytoin by the FDA would be most valuable, and timely.

I enclose with this letter a publication, *The Broad Range of Use of Phenytoin—Bibliography and Review*, that extensively deals with this subject.

I hope you will give this your consideration.

With warm regard.

Sincerely,

/s/ Nelson A. Rockefeller

June 22, 1972

Dear Governor Rockefeller:

Please forgive the delay of this response to your April 19 letter concerning the current status of the drug, phenytoin.

Conversations with health officials within the Department have revealed that phenytoin (PHT) was introduced in 1938 as the first essentially nonsedating anticonvulsant drug. The dramatic effect of PHT and its widespread acceptance in the treatment of convulsive disorders may have tended to obscure a broader range of therapeutic uses.

A review of the literature reveals that phenytoin has been reported to be useful in a wide range of disorders. Among its reported therapeutic actions are its stabilizing effect on the nervous system, its antiarrhythmic effect on certain cardiac disorders, and its therapeutic effect on emotional disorders.

The fact that such broad therapeutic effects have been reported by many independent scientists and physicians over a long period of time would seem to indicate that the therapeutic effects of phenytoin are more than that of an anticonvulsant.

The FDA encourages the submission of formal applications, which, of course, would include the necessary supporting evidence for the consideration of approval for a wider range of therapeutic uses.

Your interest in encouraging the Department to provide a public clarification of the status of phenytoin is very welcome and I hope that this information is responsive to your concerns.

With warm regard, sincerely,

/s/ Elliot L. Richardson

Survey of Use of Phenytoin

Even though PHT's official listing was for epilepsy, a survey by IMS America in March 1975 showed it was being used by physicians in this country for over twenty symptoms and disorders.

Desired Action	No. of Prescriptions in Thousands
Anticonvulsant	3,057
Prophylaxis	255
Curb Cardiac Arrhythmia	124
Anticoagulant	121
Symptomatic	64
Pain Relief	62
Sedative-Unspecific	46
Control Heart Rate	27
Relieve Headache	24
Withdrawal Symptoms	19
Analgesic	17
Psychotherapeutic	17
Control Dizziness	17
Antineuritic	16
Reduce Tension	15
Relieve Migraine	12
Anticonvulsant and Prophylaxis	12
Sedative Night and Promote Sleep	12
Stimulant	11
Calming Effect and Tranquilizer	11
Antinauseant	10
Uterine Sedative	9
Antidepressant	7
Prophylaxis and Sedative-Unspecific	6
Antispasmodic	5
Mood Elevation	5
Antiallergic and Anticonvulsant	4
Prevent Migraine	4
Control Vertigo	4
GI Antispasmodic	4
Antihemorrhagic	3
Relieve Headache and Anticonvulsant	3
Cardiotonic	3
No Reason Given	1,820
TOTAL	5,826

Thanks for their friendship and help is expressed to:

Dr. J. Antonio Aldrete
Helen Barrow
Dr. Samuel Bogoch
James H. Cavanaugh
Dr. Johnathan O. Cole
Dr. Theodore Cooper
Dr. Stuart W. Cosgriff
Dr. Charles Edwards
Dr. Joel Elkes
Hon. John W. Gardner
Dr. Paul Gordon
Dr. Lionel R. C. Haward
Dr. Richard H. Helfant
Dr. A. D. Jonas
Gov. Frank Keating
Dr. Paul L. Kornblith
Dr. Herbert L. Ley
David B. Loveland

Albert Q. Maisel
Vivian J. McDermott
Prof. Rudolfo Paoletti
Dr. Tracy J. Putnam
Dr. Oscar Resnick
Hon. Elliot L. Richardson
Hon. Nelson A. Rockefeller
Albert Rosenfeld
Dr. Alexander M. Schmidt
Dr. Maximilian Silbermann
Dr. Barry H. Smith
Howard Stein
Dr. Alfred Steiner
Dr. Joseph H. Stephens
Dr. Peter Suckling
Dr. William H. Sweet
Dr. William R. Tkach
Dr. William J. Turner

I would also like to express my deep appeciation to Dr. Natasha Bechtereva and Dr. Sviatoslav Medevdev of Russia; Dr. Liang Derong, Dr. Huang Mingsheng and Dr. Yang Guanghua of China; Lawton Ackah-Yensu of Ghana; Dr. Raul Chapa-Alvarez and Dr. Eduardo Rodriguez-Noriega of Mexico; and Dr. Kanti Jain and Dr. G.N. Menon of India.